INTRODUCTION TO ISLAM

CAROLE HILLENBRAND

INTRODUCTION TO ISLAM

Beliefs and Practices in Historical Perspective

79 color illustrations

To my grandchildren—Samuel, Max, Rebecca, Joseph, and Alexander—in the hope that they will live to see greater understanding between the faiths

ON THE FRONT COVER The mosque of Sidi (Saint) Boumedienne at Tlemcen, Algeria. Photo Werner Forman Archive.

FRONTISPIECE **A fortified garden**. Court of the Myrtles, the Alhambra, Granada, Spain, 14th century. The Qur'an describes Paradise as "a garden flowing with streams." The softly playing fountain in this fragrant courtyard brings that idea to life. So does the huge sunken pool, part cooling device, part reflecting mirror; it also has psychological and spiritual dimensions, for it fosters tranquility and meditation.

Introduction to Islam © 2015 Thames & Hudson Ltd, London

First published in 2015 in paperback in the United States of America by Thames & Hudson Inc., 500 Fifth Avenue, New York, New York 10110

thamesandhudsonusa.com

Library of Congress Catalog Card Number 2014944489

ISBN 978-0-500-29158-0

Printed and bound in China by Toppan Leefung Printing Limited

CONTENTS

ACKNOWLEDGMENTS

It is a pleasure to acknowledge the help that I have received in writing this book. At Thames & Hudson heartfelt thanks go to Ian Jacobs, Lucy Smith, and Jasmine Burville. Ian persuaded me to write it in the first place and his vision and faith in its whole concept have inspired me throughout the writing process. He is the kind of publisher of whom most authors can only dream. Lucy regularly provided most kind and steady guidance. Jasmine worked hard and most skillfully for many months on the book, paying unflagging attention to detail throughout its long editing and production process. I should also like to thank the anonymous copy editor for suggesting many improvements to the text, and Sally Nicholls, the picture researcher, who unearthed many a striking image for the book.

I am most grateful to the anonymous readers who commented on an early draft of this book. They have saved me from a number of errors and have helped me to correct some mistaken emphases. But it has been simply impossible to take up many of their points in the detail that they would ideally have wished, since to do so would have made the book far too long and unwieldy and thus unsuitable as a reference tool for students.

During the long gestation of the book I have benefitted enormously from the library facilities of the Universities of Edinburgh and St. Louis, and of Dartmouth College. I should also like to thank my long-term friends Yasir Suleiman, Thomas Madden, Sheila Blair, Jonathan Bloom, and Kevin Reinhart, who offered very welcome help and support at key moments.

My husband, Robert, has helped me with the illustrations and has been a constant and helpful critic of my work. I will always treasure the discussions, in and out of season, that we have had in the course of writing this book.

PREFACE

This book is intended for the undergraduate student and general reader. I hope that it will be useful for students taking a wide range of courses—in global Islam, comparative religion, Islamic history, the Middle East, and several others. I also hope that many general readers, interested in understanding complex current events happening in the name of Islam, will gain some benefit from exploring the historical and diverse thematic perspectives provided in these pages—perspectives that underlie the way in which Muslims today practice their faith across the world.

I have approached this book with an unwavering emphasis on essentials; it seems sensible to give a good deal of coverage to the majority view to avoid confusing the reader with too much detail. Where appropriate, however, I discuss alternative views. I hope readers will find the discussion both substantive and clear: the chapters are focused, and in order to situate Islam fully in its context, this book considers a range of factors, including historical, social, economic, political, and gender.

I have organized the book into eleven chapters, addressing the most essential aspects of Islamic faith and practice. Of necessity, these topics are closely linked, and chapters frequently refer to related topics (the Qur'an is relevant in every chapter, for example). The reader achieves a greater and deeper knowledge of this huge and complex religion as he or she continues through the book. Each chapter builds on the previous one, and the final chapter provides a carefully considered insight and balance to a discussion of twenty-first-century Islam. Muslims and their faith are of major importance in today's world, and this chapter gives readers an understanding of how the historical background of Islam affects the lives of Muslims and non-Muslims alike, and what this means for the relationship between Islam and the West now and in the future.

The illustrations expand on the text and provide a visual guide to Muslim beliefs and practices over time and in different places and cultures. Explanatory captions enable the reader to achieve a fuller understanding of the Islamic faith, through a wide range of full-color illustrations. The maps in this book are a key visual aid to guiding readers through the development of a faith that began in a single city in Arabia and grew to become a global religion with more than one-and-a-half billion followers.

It is a challenging task to distil a wide array of sources into an accessible work that provides readers new to the subject with a broad understanding. The bibliography for this book includes the most crucial works in English, to help my main audience to read and research the subject further. But in writing this book I have deliberately drawn on a wide range of scholarship in many other languages—using a lifetime's academic research in Arabic, Persian, Turkish, German, French, Italian, and Spanish—including the scholarship of previous generations, wherever its high quality justifies this.

TIMELINE OF ISLAMIC HISTORY

c. 570–632 CE The life of the Prophet Muhammad: see p. 30.

632–61 The period of the first four "Rightly Guided" caliphs.

632 Abu Bakr becomes the first caliph of Islam.

634 Death of Abu Bakr; 'Umar ibn al-Khattab becomes the second caliph.

637 Battle of al-Qadisiyya: the Muslim Arabs defeat a Sasanian Persian army.

638 Muslims conquer Jerusalem and soon begin the construction of the Aqsa mosque. They will hold the Holy City until 1099, allowing Christians and Jews to live and worship freely there.

639 Muslim conquests expand into the Caucasus and Central Asia.

644 Assassination of 'Umar, the second caliph. 'Uthman b. Affan becomes the third caliph; he supervises the task of collecting the Qur'an and finalizing its written format.

656 Assassination of 'Uthman; 'Ali b. Abi Talib becomes the fourth caliph.

656–61 First Muslim civil war, sparked by a succession dispute, leads to the beginning of a Sunni/Shi'ite divide.

657 Battle of Siffin: the Kharijite Muslims secede from 'Ali.

661–750 The Umayyad caliphate: Arab military aristocracy in power.

661 Assassination of 'Ali; Mu'awiya founds the Umayyad dynasty and moves the center of the empire to Damascus, Syria.

680–92 Second Muslim civil war.

680 Failed rebellion of Husayn (son of 'Ali and grandson of Muhammad) against the Umayyad caliph Yazid I.

680 The killing of Husayn at Karbala' on the tenth day of Muharram inaugurates the central martyrdom paradigm of Shi'ism; Husayn's suffering and death are—still today—remembered annually at feast of 'Ashura.

691 The building of the Dome of the Rock is completed in Jerusalem by the caliph 'Abd al-Malik.

711 Arab army crosses the Straits of Gibraltar and expands Muslim power into Europe.

712–13 Conquest of Sindh (in today's Pakistan) inaugurates Muslim presence in India.

714 Death of fourth Shi'ite Imam, 'Ali Zayn al-'Abidin, triggers creation of Zaydi Shi'ite group.

732 Muslim army is defeated at the Battle of Poitiers in central France, halting Muslim expansion into Europe.

733 Death of fifth Shi'ite Imam, Muhammad al-Baqir.

744–50 Third Muslim civil war, ending in defeat of Umayyads by 'Abbasids.

750–1258 The establishment of the 'Abbasid caliphate in Iraq.

754–75 Rule of the caliph al-Mansur.

756 'Abd al-Rahman, fugitive Umayyad prince, establishes the emirate of Cordoba, Spain.

762 Al-Mansur founds the Round City of Baghdad as the 'Abbasid capital.

765 Death of sixth Shi'ite Imam, Ja'far al-Sadiq, founder of Ja'fari school of law; succession to the Imamate is disputed, which leads to the split between Sevener (Isma'ilis) Shi'ites and Twelver Shi'ites.

786 Building of the Great Mosque of Cordoba begins.

786–809 Reign of the caliph Harun al-Rashid; peak of the 'Abbasid empire.

799 Death of Musa al-Kazim, recognized as seventh Imam by Twelver Shi'ites.

813–33 Reign of the caliph al-Ma'mun, who inaugurates a period of intense intellectual activity.

833–48 The Inquisition (*mihna*): the attempt by al-Ma'mun to impose the doctrine of the "created Qur'an" on the 'Abbasid empire.

836 'Abbasid capital moves from Baghdad to Samarra.

864–1126 Zaydi Shi'ite imamate in northern Iran.

874 The eleventh Imam dies; the twelfth Imam, Muhammad al-Mahdi, is believed to be hidden; this marks the end of direct rule on Earth by the Twelver Shi'ite Imams.

893–1962 Zaydi imamate rules Yemen.

899 'Ubaydallah al-Mahdi declares himself Imam of the Seveners (Isma'ilis) in North Africa, thus beginning the Fatimid caliphate.

900–1077 Breakaway Qarmati (Isma'ili) republic in Bahrayn.

c. **900–c.1000** Peak of cultural achievement and political power in Muslim Spain (al-Andalus).

929 Foundation of the Spanish Umayyad caliphate by 'Abd al-Rahman III.

941–present The "Greater" Occultation: chosen deputies transmit to Twelver Shi'ite believers the doctrines of the Hidden Imam until his eventual return.

945–1055 The Buyid dynasty (Twelver Shi'ites) from northern Iran rules Iraq and western Iran; the Buyids keep the Sunni caliph in place as a figurehead.

969 Fatimid Isma'ilis conquer Egypt; foundation of the city of Cairo and of al-Azhar university, the oldest continuously functioning university in the world.

1017 Al-Hakim, the Fatimid caliph, is proclaimed a manifestation of the divine by an Isma'ili breakaway group led by a missionary, al-Darazi. Named after him, the group become known as the Druze.

1055 The Seljuq Turks conquer Baghdad, seat of 'Abbasid caliphate.

1056–1147 Almoravid dynasty rules in North Africa and Spain.

1065–67 The foundation of the Nizamiyya *madrasa* (religious college for teaching Shafi'i law) in Baghdad.

1071 The Battle of Manzikert in what is now Eastern Turkey: the Seljuq sultan, Alp Arslan, defeats the Byzantine army and captures the Byzantine emperor, Romanus IV Diogenes.

1085–1492 The process of Christian reconquest of Muslim Spain.

1094 Death of al-Mustansir, the Fatimid caliph; the Nizari schism then follows. The Fatimids split into two parts: the Musta'lians, who stay in power in Cairo, and the Nizaris, who move to Alamut, northwest Iran.

Eleventh to thirteenth centuries.

1095 Council of Clermont: Pope Urban II calls for a crusade against the Muslim world and the reconquest of Jerusalem.

1099 Crusaders capture Jerusalem and establish the Latin kingdom of Outremer.

1130–1269 The Almohad dynasty rules in North Africa and Spain.

1138 Birth of Saladin, charismatic Muslim general and the founder of the Ayyubid dynasty in Egypt and Syria.

1147–74 Rule of the Turkish military leader Nur al-Din, the major institutor of the twelfth-century Muslim "Counter Crusade" in Syria.

1171 Saladin conquers Egypt on behalf of Nur al-Din, ending Fatimid rule and restoring Sunni Islam there.

1187 Fall of Jerusalem to Saladin following the Battle of Hattin.

1192 Treaty between Saladin and King Richard I of England that permits Christian pilgrimage to the Holy Land.

1206–1370 Mongols rule Central Asia.

1206–1526 Muslim Delhi Sultanate in India.

1212 Battle of Las Navas de Tolosa marks the loss of much of southern Spain to the Christians.

1220–60 Mongol invasions of the eastern Muslim world under Genghis Khan and his successors.

1250–1517 The Mamluk Turkish dynasty rules in Egypt and Syria.

1256 The Nizari (a breakaway Isma'ili Shi'ite group) stronghold of Alamut falls to Mongols.

1258 Mongols sack Baghdad and execute the caliph al-Musta'sim, bringing the 'Abbasid caliphate of Baghdad to an end.

1260 Mamluks defeat Mongols at the Battle of 'Ayn Jalut.

1261–1517 Sultan Baybars re-establishes the 'Abbasid caliphate in Cairo.

1280–1924 Ottoman Turkish dynasty.

1291 Fall of Acre and expulsion of Crusaders from the Holy Land.

Fourteenth to seventeenth centuries: empire-building and Islamic expansion.

1368 *Diwan* of Hafiz, masterpiece of Persian poetry, is completed.

1379–1405 Campaigns of Timur (Tamburlane), a ruler of Mongol–Turkic origin, in Central, West, and South Asia.

c. 1450 Islam spreads over much of East Indies (Southeast Asia).

1453 Ottomans capture Constantinople, capital of the Christian Byzantine empire.

1461 Ottomans capture Trebizond on the Black Sea coast, the last outpost of the Byzantine empire.

1492 The Christian monarchs Ferdinand and Isabella capture Granada, the last Muslim stronghold in Spain.

1500 Ottomans establish control over Greece, Bosnia, Herzegovina, and Albania.

1500–1598 Shaybanid dynasty (of Mongol descent) rules in Central Asia.

1501–1722 The Safavid dynasty, inaugurated by Shah Isma'il, rules the Iranian world and establishes Twelver Shi'ism as the state religion.

1514 Ottomans defeat the Safavids at the Battle of Çaldiran, Turkey.

1517 Ottoman conquest of Egypt, Syria, Hijaz, and Yemen.

1520–66 Reign of Sultan Suleyman the Magnificent: peak of Ottoman power.

1526–1858 Mughal dynasty rules in the Indian sub-continent, spreading Muslim arts and culture, as well as Islamic faith.

1529 Failed first siege of Vienna by Ottomans.

1550–57 The building of the Suleymaniyye mosque in Istanbul, the masterpiece of the architect Sinan.

1566–1605 High point of Mughal power under the emperor Akbar.

1571 Battle of Lepanto: European fleet blocks Ottoman advance into the Mediterranean.

1588–1629 Peak of Safavid power under Shah 'Abbas.

1660–present Alawi dynasty rules in Morocco.

1683 Ottoman–Habsburg war ends with second unsuccessful Ottoman siege of Vienna, which results in curbing Ottoman expansion in Europe.

Eighteenth and nineteenth centuries.

1744–present Rule of Al Bu Sa'id dynasty in Oman.

1794–1864 *Jihad* state in the region of present-day Mali and Senegal, West Africa.

1798–1801 Napoleon and the French campaign in Egypt; basic research is undertaken for *Description de l'Égypte*, a series of publications by scholars and scientists, a landmark in European knowledge of the Middle East.

1801–2 Wahhabis destroy major Shi'ite shrines in Najaf and Karbala' in Iraq.

1804–8 Usman dan Fodio (1754–1817), Hausa religious leader in northern Nigeria, leads a successful *jihad* against the sultan of Gobir and establishes the Sokoto caliphate, one of the largest empires in nineteenth-century Africa.

1805–49 Muhammad 'Ali, a great modernizer, rules Egypt.

1809–1903 Sokoto caliphate in Nigeria.

1857 Indian Mutiny, the failure of which results in the formal British colonization of India and the dissolution of the Mughal empire.

Early 19th century The Dutch impose control of inland Indonesia, prompting resistance.

1830 The French invade and colonize Algeria.

1839–77 *Tanzimat* reforms in the Ottoman empire aim to reorganize the Turkish army, modeled on Prussian lines, and to guarantee security of life and property to all Turkish subjects, regardless of race and religion.

1876–1909 Reign of Ottoman sultan 'Abd al-Hamid; spread of pan-Islamic (the unification of Muslims under one Islamic state) ideology.

1878 Birth of Reza Shah Pahlavi, founder of the Iranian Pahlavi dynasty.

1881 A French protectorate is established in Tunisia.

1885–98 Mahdist state in the Sudan.

Twentieth and twenty-first centuries: reforms and revolutions.

1905 Parliamentary revolution in Iran.

1920–38 Mustafa Kemal Atatürk, father of the Turkish republic, defeats Greeks and introduces secularizing reforms in Turkey.

1924 Atatürk abolishes the caliphate and establishes a secular Turkish republic.

1925–79 Pahlavi dynasty in Iran.

1928 Muslim Brotherhood, one of the largest Muslim political, religious, and social organizations, is founded in Egypt by the scholar Hassan al-Banna' (1906–1949).

1941 *Jama'at-i Islami is* founded in India by Abu'l-'Ala' Mawdudi (1903–1979).

1945–50 Indonesian struggle for independence from Dutch colonial rule.

1947 Partition of India and Pakistan, and independence of both countries from British rule.

1948 Foundation of the state of Israel; Israeli-Arab war.

1950–61 *Dar al-Islam* movements in Indonesia aim to establish it as an Islamic state.

1952 Free Officers' coup in Egypt overthrows the monarchy; Jamal 'Abd al-Nasser takes power as the second president of Egypt.

1952 *Hizb al-tahrir* ("The Liberation Party"), which aims to unify a global Islamic state, is founded by the Palestinian judge Taqi al-Din Nabhani (1909–1977).

1966 Execution of Sayyid Qutb (b. 1906), the radical Egyptian Islamist.

1967 Israelis defeat Arabs in the "Six-Day War"; Israel captures Jerusalem; Israel occupies remaining 20 percent of Arab lands, Sinai Peninsula, and Golan Heights.

1969 Mu'ammar Qaddafi (c. 1942–2011), revolutionary and politician, seizes power in Libya; the *minbar* (pulpit) in the Aqsa Mosque in Jerusalem is burned; Ayatollah Khomeini (1902–1989) introduces the *vilayat-i faqih* (rule of the jurist), on which the Islamic Republic of Iran is later founded.

1971 The secession of Bangladesh from Pakistan; Organization of the Islamic Conference is founded as first official pan-Islamic institution for cooperation among Islamic governments.

1973 Second Arab-Israeli war.

1975–90 Civil war in Lebanon.

1979–89 Afghani *jihad* against Soviet occupation, causing collapse of Afghan society and rise of *mujahidin*; Israel invades Lebanon.

1979 Shah of Iran abdicates; Iranian Revolution; Islamic Republic of Iran is founded and led by Ayatollah Khomeini.

1980 Hizbullah, a Shi'ite Islamist militant group, is established in Lebanon; the Islamic Jihad militant organization is founded in Palestine by Muslim Brotherhood.

1980–88 Iran–Iraq war.

1981 Assassination of President Anwar al-Sadat of Egypt by an Islamist.

1982 President Hafiz al-Asad of Syria destroys much of the town of Hama, killing thousands, to crush opposition from Muslim Brotherhood; Israel invades Lebanon again; massacres at Sabra and Shatilla, Lebanon.

1983 Hizbullah "suicide bombers" cause US and French peacekeepers to leave Lebanon.

1984 Women Living under Muslim Laws (WLML) is founded as a network to promote contacts between women internationally; Hamas (a Palestinian Sunni Islamist movement, linked to Muslim Brotherhood) and Islamic Jihad movements both established as part of the Palestinian uprising (*intifada*).

1988 Usama bin Laden founds al-Qa'ida; Hamas, a Sunni Islamist movement linked to the Muslim Brotherhood, becomes important in Palestine; publication of Salman Rushdie's *The Satanic Verses*.

1988–90 Benazir Bhutto is the first female head of a Muslim state, in Pakistan; she will take power again from 1993 to 1996.

1989 Ayatollah Khomeini issues a death *fatwa* against Salman Rushdie and his publishers for apostasy and blasphemy respectively; death of Khomeini.

1990–91 The First Gulf War follows Iraq's invasion of Kuwait.

1991 Khaleda Zia becomes the first female prime minister of Bangladesh.

1993 Bombing of World Trade Center in New York; Oslo Accords—peace negotiations that began in Oslo, Norway —are agreed upon as a first step toward resolution of Israeli–Palestinian conflict.

1993–96 Tansu Çiller (a woman), becomes prime minister in Turkey.

1994 Taliban appear in Afghanistan, claiming mantle of politico-religious leadership and ending civil war.

1995 Necmettin Erbakan is elected Turkey's first Islamist prime minister.

1997 Muhammad Khatami is elected President of Iran, fostering cultural, scholarly, and economic exchanges with the US.

1999 Abdurrahman Wahid (died 2009), leader of the Nahdlatul 'ulama' (the largest Islamic movement in the Muslim world), is first elected president of Indonesia.

September 11, 2001 Attacks on New York City and Washington, D.C., inspired by al-Qa'ida, kill more than 3,000 people.

2001 War in Afghanistan begins. Allied forces invade in order to dismantle al-Qa'ida and remove the Taliban from power.

2001–4 Megawati Sukarnoputri is the first female head of state in Indonesia.

2002 Terrorist attack on a nightclub in Bali, Indonesia, attributed to Abu Sayyaf movement/Jemaa Islamiyah.

2003 US and UK invade Iraq and overthrow the regime of Saddam Husayn.

2004 Terrorist attack on Madrid, Spain, by al-Qa'ida affiliates; the Amman Message, issued by King 'Abdallah II of Jordan and signed by more than 500 Islamic scholars and leaders, calls for tolerance and unity in the Muslim world.

July 7, 2005 Also known as 7/7: a series of coordinated suicide bomb attacks on London's public transport system during the morning rush hour kills 52 people and injures hundreds more.

2006 Hamas wins power democratically in Palestinian elections. The US and the European Union halt direct payments to the Hamas-led Palestinian government; Palestinians still receive aid through the United Nations and other independent organisations; Keith Ellison is the first Muslim American to be elected to House of Representatives (representing Minnesota).

2007 *A Common Word Between Us and You*, a letter signed by 138 (eventually some 300) prominent academics, politicians, writers, and muftis, broadly representative of the Muslim world, is sent to the heads of the world's major Christian churches, emphasizing foundational principles of both faiths (love of the One God, and love of thy neighbor) as the common ground to bring peace to the world.

November 4–6, 2008 Representatives of the Vatican and of the 138 original signatories of *A Common Word* meet Pope Benedict XVI and hold meetings to establish a Catholic–Muslim forum.

December 2010 Syrian conflict begins: protestors call for the removal of President al-Assad; Arab Spring begins in Tunisia.

January 2011 Fall of President Mubarak in Egypt.

May 2, 2011 Death of Usama bin Laden.

October 20, 2011 Death of Colonel Qaddafi.

January 2013 French intervention in Mali, in aid of troops fighting against rebel Islamist groups in the North.

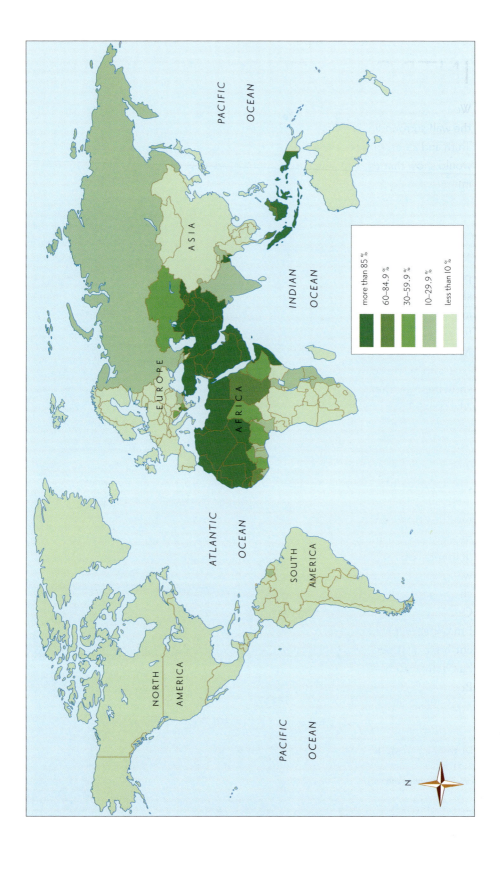

ASIA

INDIAN

OCEAN

more than 85 %
60–84.9 %
30–59.9 %
10–29.9 %
less than 10 %

EUROPE

AFRICA

ATLANTIC

OCEAN

SOUTH
AMERICA

NORTH
AMERICA

PACIFIC

OCEAN

N

▌ INTRODUCTION

We must not, like the frog in the well, who imagines that the universe ends with the wall surrounding his well, think that our religion alone represents the whole Truth and all others are false. A reverent study of the other religions of the world would show that they are equally true as our own, though all are necessarily important. MAHATMA GANDHI[1]

My objective in this book is to describe as accurately and objectively as possible the core beliefs, practices, and doctrines that over the years have shaped and unified the worldwide community of **Muslims**. The book defines and analyzes these basic building blocks, which serve as the indispensable foundation for all studies that aim to explain to non-Muslims how and why Muslims think and act as they do.

I aim to present **Islamic** faith and practice in a historically nuanced way, showing how the past has impacted, and continues to impact, on the present. Modern Islam, as is followed by the vast majority of Muslims throughout the world, rests on a foundation created by a series of historical events, especially in the early centuries of the faith. While most key beliefs and practices were definitively fixed in these years, their details were not set in stone. Accordingly, it is a crucial aim of this book to show that Muslim belief and practice on a multitude of issues developed in the course of the centuries, and saw much modification, adaptation, and refinement during that time. For example, modernist Muslim thinkers have interpreted Islamic law to respond to the demands of modern society (see Chapter 5). The details of how a precept was interpreted and applied in a specific situation were indeed subject to change; but that change was carried out within the familiar context of the **Qur'an** and the sayings and example of the Prophet **Muhammad**. I hope that I may justifiably claim that the particular strength of this book is the consistent historical perspective that it brings to bear on these issues. The emphasis has deliberately been on the formative period, especially the lifetimes of the Prophet Muhammad and his **Companions**, but I have also tried to pay due

Distribution of Muslims worldwide in proportion to the population of each country, 2010. Islam is the second-largest religion in the world (the first is Christianity), with 1.6 billion followers, or 23 percent of the world's population.

attention, notably in Chapter 7, to the eighteenth and nineteenth centuries, since this period was of critical importance in that it saw the revival and reform of Islam, thanks to a succession of towering personalities. Readers will be equipped with the understanding and historical perspective necessary to understand how modern Muslims go about their lives; the book touches on rites of passage, daily rituals, and considers how Muslims respond to contemporary issues, such as the ethics of banking, and political crises.

There are many ways to write a book about Islam, and the perennial demand for such books is an encouraging sign that there are uncounted masses of people, not just in the West but worldwide, and not just non-Muslims but also Muslims themselves, who are hungry to know more about this faith that has become so important globally in the last century or so. So what approaches can one discern among the authors of such books? Happily, many—often written by non-Muslims—offer a description of modern Islam, and that of course is very relevant to a modern audience eager to find out how Muslims live their lives and what they believe, especially given the huge role they play in today's world. The findings of such books are of central importance to this book too. After all, for most people who embark on a study of Islam— no matter whether this is as part of a university course or as a matter of personal curiosity—the driving motive is to understand the post-9/11 world. So books that meet that demand have informed my own work in ways too numerous to calculate. Similarly, it has proved helpful to me in writing this book to take into consideration books written deliberately from within the faith by Muslims who urgently want to lay before a global public what their authors view as eternal religious certainties.

Yet another approach, and this too is one from which this book has drawn constant inspiration, is taken by authors who present the particular version of Islam practiced by a single community, whose customs and interpretation often differ from what can be observed elsewhere in the Muslim world. For it cannot be said too often that Islam is a worldwide faith, practiced not merely from west to east in a line stretching from Morocco to Indonesia, and across every country in between them, but also in a great deal of Africa, in Europe, and in America. There are communities of Lebanese Muslims living in Brazil, and Gaelic-speaking Pakistani Muslims in the Outer Hebrides, an island group off the coast of Scotland.

When one ponders these various approaches, all of which have much to recommend them and all of which have influenced the writing of this book, the inevitable conclusion is that it would be unwise to make dogmatic claims that any one of them describes the only right way to follow in the hope of achieving a deeper understanding of the faith. The present book results from an effort to consider all these approaches carefully, and to learn as much as possible from them. It also tries to present as much material as is practicable from each of them, in an attempt to be as inclusive as possible.

When I was writing the book, I wanted the text to be accessible to that perhaps mythical creature, the general reader. So I have avoided enticing detours into subsidiary topics that are of interest mainly to specialists, and I have also avoided transliteration, which is off-putting for people who know no Arabic and redundant for people who do. In the same spirit I have kept technical terms to a minimum, while also rejecting the temptation to use footnotes to conduct controversies or to pile on extra information. Such a work as this, however well intentioned, could easily be ruined by information overload. The desire to confine the discussion to what most Muslims believe and how they live their lives should also help to explain why I have given relatively less space to certain subjects, such as theology and philosophy, which are of pressing intellectual interest to modern scholars but are often treated with indifference by the Muslim man or woman in the street (see Chapter 7). More generally, I have tried to adopt a sober tone of objective exposition, holding fast to a broad perspective and constantly alert to the dangers of partiality.

Readers have a right to know where I am coming from, since that will color what I say. My background as a university professor of Arabic is that of a historian of Islam as a religion and a civilization. I have devoted most of my adult life to the study of Islam—its doctrines, its history, and its culture—and to studying the principal languages used in the central Muslim lands, passing on the knowledge that I have acquired on these subjects to generations of students. Their responses have often been both stimulating and challenging. In my published writings I make direct use of primary Arabic, Persian, and Turkish sources; and I have taught classical Arabic and Persian religious texts dealing with Islamic law, political thought, and Sufism for many years. I have also taken part in a number of television and radio programs about Islam that have been shown in Britain, the USA, and the Middle East.

I mention all this to justify my taking what may seem to be the bold step of writing this book. I am not a Muslim myself, and indeed I have a deep personal attachment to the Christian religion and culture in which I was raised. So I cannot speak from personal experience about Islam as a faith lived from within. But I would not have lived my professional life in the way I have chosen to do unless I had developed a deep admiration and respect for Islam, both as a religion and as a culture. So this book is shaped by long study of the Muslim world, by almost half a century of visiting its many countries, and by decades of explaining that world to Western students. These experiences have cumulatively had a profound effect on me as a person and as a scholar. They have sharpened and refined my understanding of Islam and my attitudes toward it. I hope that I may claim that they have determined what has gone into this book, and how I have presented the material in it.

In passing, I would add that I regard it as a serious misconception that only a Muslim could write a book like this. Indeed, I would argue that it is easier for a non-Muslim scholar of Islam than for a Muslim to identify which questions about Islam are regularly asked by non-Muslims—be they students or the general public, those of other faiths, or those who have no religious faith at all. The need to explain what is often misunderstood, to present a narrative of the basic facts and concepts that have made the Muslim world what it is, underpins the way this book is constructed. I have thought long and hard in an attempt to identify the key issues, to separate what really matters from what is of merely subsidiary importance. That has involved a difficult and protracted process of selection so as to ensure that nothing of central importance has been omitted. Each of my chapters has a one-word title. That is a deliberate strategy. I adopted it to concentrate my own mind, and I hope that it will correspondingly concentrate the minds of my readers. It means that those of them who want to check out a given topic can find it easily. Hence the lavish use of subheadings within each chapter and on the contents pages.

This is not a book to be read at a single sitting. Instead, it is intended to orientate serious readers and to tell them where to look for more information on a given subject if they wish to pursue it further. It is a curious and perhaps telling fact that, of the many dozens of books published in the last thirty years or so that lay out the essentials of what Muslims believe, and of what governs the way they live, only a few present the requisite information in this way. The interested reader therefore has to look unreasonably hard for discussions that cover the middle ground between a simple summary of two or three paragraphs—a summary that can scarcely avoid being superficial—and an entire book, the level of detail of which proclaims that it is aimed at the specialist rather than at the general reader. Of course it is not rare to find a book that has a discussion of, say, the Qur'an, or the Prophet Muhammad, or of Islamic law, that is of just the right length for that kind of reader. But such a book may have nothing at all to say of other subjects that warrant a full chapter in the present book. So the information is all out there somewhere, but it is so scattered as to be hard for non-specialists to access. The present book aims to solve that problem.

This book, then, examines how the present is shaped by the past, in the belief that to understand the one you need to know about the other. That is particularly true in the case of the Muslim world, where events that happened almost fourteen hundred years ago can have a direct impact on events today. An obvious example is the split between **Sunnis** and **Shi'ites** that is causing such bloodshed in the Middle East at the time of writing (see also Chapter 11). So the material in this book is intended to present the basic information about the Muslim past in such a way as to contextualize the Muslim present as clearly as possible. And it is also worth emphasizing, although it is increasingly obvious in many different parts of the world, that the previous simplistic view held by so many Europeans and Americans, namely that Muslims live only in the Middle East, is no longer tenable. Indeed, it is more untrue than true. Given the ubiquity of the Muslim presence all across the world today, it is more important than ever that this faith should be better understood.

So this book is a modest, one-woman attempt to counter the flood of ignorance that threatens to swamp objectivity and that has created such powerful prejudices against Islam. Its aim is to marshal the facts about Islam and then to interpret them. I hope to do so from the standpoint of religious studies, tempered by a constant awareness of how history molds the development of religion. For no religion exists in a historical vacuum. And no religion is the same in every time and place. The views of certain Islamic scholars have on occasion been taken to represent the faith itself by some believers, without the ever-present necessity to assess those views, as noted earlier, in the context of the Qur'an and the sayings and example of the Prophet Muhammad. And this has influenced the way that many non-Muslims view the faith. For many people in the West, indeed, the word "Islam" has become a convenient, simplifying shorthand for a religion, a society, a culture, and an overarching political entity. In this book, though, I use the term "Islam" in a primarily religious sense, though of course society, culture, and politics are never far away.

One apparently minor issue of usage should be addressed here. The text of this book tries to differentiate clearly between the two words "Islam" and "Muslim," both as nouns and in their adjectival forms. They are often used as synonyms; but they are not. The first denotes a set of beliefs, institutions, and practices that govern human affairs in all their moral, social, and political dimensions. "Islamic" in this sense refers to the religion, the writings, and the culture of Islam. "Muslim," on the other hand, denotes the inhabitants of countries that are largely Muslim, or those individuals who follow the religion of Islam. Examples of these different usages are "the Islamic Republic of Iran" or "the Muslim world" or "the Islamic rules of the **Shari'a**."

It seems appropriate to end with a brief look at how Islam is frequently treated by the modern media. Talented journalists report extensively and often objectively about current affairs in the Muslim world. But these are transient events; to assess them properly requires a degree of distance, which a detailed knowledge of history affords. It is to be hoped that the historical, nuanced discussion in this book will enable the reader to approach with an enquiring, well-informed, but critical mind the superficial and unreliable polemic against Islam and Muslims that unfortunately often passes for news and opinion in segments of the popular press. Of course, Islam is not the only subject to suffer in this way, but it is hard to overestimate the negative impact of that constant drip-drip of disinformation and prejudice. It is a particular tragedy that the good name of a world religion has been besmirched by the murderous, politically motivated deeds of terrorists who call themselves Muslims while acting in ways that the faith roundly condemns. Hence the widespread, kneejerk, but mistaken association of Islam with terrorism in the minds of many non-Muslims across the world. Yet this is the religion of one-and-a-half billion people, of whom the vast majority have no truck with terrorism, and can on the contrary point with pride to a millennial historical tradition of religious tolerance and coexistence with other faiths, from Cordoba to Jerusalem to Delhi—and beyond.

2 MUHAMMAD

Muhammad is the Prophet of **Islam**, the "**Seal of the Prophets**," chosen by God to bring His final message to humanity. This chapter sets Muhammad in his religious, historical, and cultural context, it considers his achievements, and discusses how **Muslims** have understood his life, personality, and significance over the centuries.

ARABIA BEFORE ISLAM

The Prophet Muhammad was born into a particular society at a specific moment in history—Arabia in the sixth century CE—and it is, of course, important to understand the impact this background made on his life and message.

GEOGRAPHY

What was Arabia like at this time? Scholars usually make a clear distinction between South Arabia (especially the southwestern corner, which corresponds to modern Yemen) and the rest of the peninsula. This distinction is based on geographical factors: vast areas of desert, fringed with oases, in the north; and the much more fertile south, called Arabia Felix in the ancient world, which enjoyed plentiful rainfall and highly developed agriculture, supported by extensive and elaborate irrigation systems.

South Arabia was heavily populated; its inhabitants had been largely settled agriculturalists from around the eighth century BCE. Its towns had relatively highly developed political institutions, art, and architecture. The Classical authors of Greece and Rome spoke about the fabled luxury of the Sabaeans (and notably the Queen of Sheba), and archaeological evidence testifies to a mature urban culture in the area. The famous irrigation system at Ma'rib (in modern Yemen), first mentioned in the eighth century BCE, was praised in antiquity as an engineering wonder. Shortly before the advent of Islam, the Ma'rib dam, which had broken several times before, had definitively collapsed, with far-reaching repercussions for the rest of Arabia. This event, as enshrined in later Muslim oral tradition, came to symbolize the decline of the South Arabian kingdom. Significant population shifts northward resulted.

Oasis. Wadi Bani Khalid, Oman. Water, trees, shade, fertility—everything that the desert lacks—loomed large in the imaginations of the nomads of Arabia. No wonder that the visions of Paradise that permeate the Qur'an evoke just these elements, transfigured into metaphors of spirituality.

The rest of the peninsula was very different from the south. Here, human life was unremittingly tough. The inhabitants of the vast deserts, mainly pastoralists, eked out a precarious living, based on the domestication of the camel—"the ship of the desert"—and the cultivation of the date palm. The Arab nomads, known as the Bedouin, were resilient and resourceful; they worked as camel herders deep in the desert or as sheep or goat rearers closer to the agricultural areas around such oasis towns as Yathrib, later to be called **Medina**, and Khaybar. There farmers grew dates and wheat. The balance of power in the desert areas of Arabia lay with the camel herders, whose animals could support more people. They lived symbiotically alongside the inhabitants of the oases, trading the products of nomad life—milk, meat, and hides—in exchange for dates, wheat, and weapons.

The Arabian seaports were connected by trade with the Mediterranean, Africa, and the Indian Ocean. Inland oasis towns, such as **Mecca** and Yathrib, (some 210 miles to the north of Mecca) were stopping places on overland routes for merchants bringing such goods as frankincense, spices, silk, and cotton, and the Bedouin Arabs knew how to guide both regional and long-distance caravans across vast desert stretches using the stars and other natural signs. The **Qur'an** itself (106:1–2) mentions that the Banu Quraysh—the leading tribe of Mecca, to which the Prophet Muhammad belonged—had gained their wealth from the twice-yearly caravan trade; the verses state that God had made "the Quraysh feel secure, secure in their winter and summer journeys."

GOVERNMENT AND SOCIETY

The Arabs in northern, central, and eastern Arabia had no centralized government. Bedouin society refused to be shackled to any overarching political system, remaining in time-honored fashion within a tribal organization that applied equally to pastoralists, farmers, and city merchants. Clans and tribes would vary in size, structure, and prestige. Daily life was probably based around the activities of small tribal groupings that shared camping areas and watering places.

Like other nomadic societies, that of the Bedouin was egalitarian, although each tribal unit had a chief whose own position derived from his personal charisma. His duties included defending the tribe, protecting its sacred symbols, settling disputes and entertaining guests. Justice between tribal groups was maintained by a process of equivalent retribution for injuries received: "An eye for an eye, a tooth for a tooth." Such a system guaranteed an individual member of the tribe safety and protection for himself, his family, and his possessions.

The Bedouin tribesmen lived in a militarized society and they carried arms. Competition for pastures often required them to conduct raids into the territory of other nomadic groups or of those living near or in the towns. The Bedouin had their own codes of honor, which prized courage, endurance, and military skills, and these were probably of greater significance to them than the formal observance of any religious faith.

CULT AND RELIGION

Bedouin cultic practices were **animistic**, involving the worship of idols, stones, and trees, and the Bedouin would run or walk round (circumambulate) these sacred objects a prescribed number of times.[1] Soothsayers (*kahins*) performed a variety of **shamanistic** roles, including foretelling the future, healing, and water divining. The Bedouin venerated holy enclaves (***haram*** or *hawta*), some of which operated without guardians, whilst others were administered by

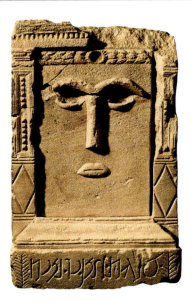

Pre-Islamic idolatry. Stone-carved goddess, Temple of the Winged Lions, Petra, Jordan, Ist century CE. Islam implacably opposed polytheism, including the very idea of depicting divinity—even in the severely abstracted form shown here, which radiates numinous power. Inscribed in Nabataean (an ancient Semitic language) "Goddess of Hayyan son of Nybat," it depicts al-'Uzza, Isis, or Aphrodite. Despite opposition, Muhammad destroyed idols of various deities stationed around the Ka'ba.

a hereditary religious elite. These sanctuaries functioned as places of asylum or as neutral locations in which to settle inter-tribal disputes. The sanctuaries themselves and their surrounding areas were regarded as highly sacred, and no fighting was allowed there. Certain pagan deities became associated with some sanctuaries: the god Hubal was associated with the **Ka'ba**—a cube-shaped building, embedded within which was a meteoric black stone—and three goddesses, Allat, al-'Uzza (both usually identified with Venus), and Manat (the goddess of fate), were especially venerated in the area around Mecca. The three Meccan goddesses were given the title of the 'daughters' of **Allah**, the Creator God, who was widely recognized within the peninsula. Every year markets would be held near their sanctuaries.

Since the fifth century CE the Quraysh tribe that controlled Mecca had looked after the pilgrims who came annually in a sacred month to Mecca to gain the favor of their deities by circumambulating seven times, in a state of ritual purity, the sacred enclosure of the Ka'ba, believed to have been founded by **Abraham** and his son **Ishmael** (Isma'il). The Ka'ba was surrounded by a sacred area (the haram), which served as a place of refuge, and within which a truce prevailed; indeed, when the Arab tribes made their pilgrimage to Mecca, all feuds were suspended. This pilgrimage was a source of wealth and prestige to the Meccans in pre-Islamic times. Nevertheless, any practice of formal religion associated with these pagan deities seems to have sat very lightly on the Bedouin, for whom life just had to be endured with courage

Sacred topography. Pilgrim's guide to the Holy Cities of Mecca and Medina, India, 19th century. These simplified isometric renderings show in graphic form some of the sacred sites incorporated into the standard itinerary for pilgrims. Decorative frames in the costly and celestial colors of gold and blue highlight the sense of holiness.

and endurance before death struck them down at their allotted time. These sentiments resonate in the pre-Islamic oral poetry of Arabia.

Nomads and city dwellers alike shared the crucial bond of the Arabic language, which promoted feelings of pride and solidarity. At times when fighting was prohibited, they would meet to listen to poetry recited by members of the tribe with prodigious memories who declaimed in a high form of Arabic. At such moments the Arabs would feel that they had a common heritage and identity that transcended tribal allegiance. Such a background was to provide Muhammad with a foundation on which to build his supra-tribal community, inspired by Islam, the new **monotheistic** revelation that came from Arabia itself.

JEWS AND CHRISTIANS IN ARABIA

In addition to pre-Islamic **polytheism** it is also important to evaluate what impact external religious traditions had made on the Arabian peninsula. By the late sixth century CE Judaism and Christianity had penetrated into Arabia, especially the southwest and the desert areas that bordered the **Byzantine empire** to the north. The conversion of the ruler of Abyssinia (the Negus) in the early fourth century had created a strong Christian state close to South Arabia. There were also Christian communities in Aden in the fourth century. Adherents of Judaism were found in the oases of central Arabia, notably in Khaybar and Yathrib, where they cultivated the date palm. In South Arabia, prominent figures had been converted to Judaism, such as the sixth-century king of Himyar, Yusuf As'ar, known in Muslim tradition as Dhu Nuwas. **Sasanian** Persia—the last Iranian empire before the rise of Islam—also brought its official state religion, **Zoroastrianism**, to the shores of South Arabia; indeed, in the 570s some Zoroastrian conversions took place there.

While Arabia was not cut off from the monotheistic traditions of the Jews and the Christians, these faiths had not made significant inroads. The Bedouin had their own indigenous religious traditions, with some pockets of Christianity and Judaism; tribes on the borders with Sasanian Iraq and some close to Byzantine Syria had embraced different forms of Christianity. The Arabs also knew about the Samaritans (*Shom'rim*) who are mentioned in both the Old Testament and the New Testament of the Bible. The Qur'an (20:85) mentions a Samaritan (al-Samiri) who tempted the Children of Israel in the desert in the time of **Moses**. It is clear from the allusive way in which the Qur'an mentions the prophets from the Abrahamic tradition—those religions that trace their origin to Abraham—that Muhammad was preaching to people who were already very familiar with stories from the Bible.

Map showing the territories of the Byzantine and Sasanian empires, *c.* 630 CE. Twenty years later Muslim armies had wrenched Egypt and Syria from Byzantine control and conquered the entire Sasanian empire. Islam has remained the dominant religion in these lands for more than a millennium.

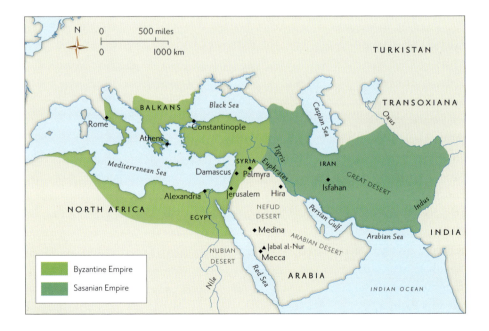

Yet it should be stressed that the Qur'anic message from the One God, which Muhammad preached in Arabic to his fellow Arabs, was also distinct from Judaism and Christianity. Indeed, later Muslim tradition, wishing to distance Islam from the two preceding monotheistic faiths, often mentions the existence of *hanifs*, pre-Islamic monotheists in Arabia, who were not associated with Judaism or Christianity but who practiced the "pure religion of Abraham," the father of the Arabs, who founded the Ka'ba shrine at Mecca. It is questionable whether such an idea truly reflects historical reality, since the complexity of religious practice in pre-Islamic Arabia can never be fully understood.

THE LIFE OF MUHAMMAD: THE TRADITIONAL MUSLIM NARRATIVE

The events of the sacred history of the Prophet's life have been hallowed by centuries of veneration and piety. The narrative that follows is based on traditional Muslim sources only. It is what every Muslim is taught to believe from childhood. Just as the few key events that form the core biography of **Jesus** are seen through the prism of Christian piety extending over more than two millennia, so too everything that is part of Muhammad's canonical life story is perceived through an aura of centuries-old reverence and love of him.

BIRTH AND EARLY YEARS

Muhammad's birth cannot be firmly dated either from Muslim or non-Muslim sources, although it probably occurred around 570 CE. He was born in Mecca in Arabia into the Banu Hashim, a minor clan of the leading Quraysh tribe, which still enjoyed some prestige but whose wealth and power declined after the 570s. Muhammad became an orphan early in his life; his father, 'Abdallah, died two months before his birth and he lost his mother, Amina, when he was only six years old. The Qur'anic verse 93:6 points to this: "Did He not find you an orphan and shelter you?" Muhammad was brought up first by his grandfather 'Abd al-Muttalib, and then by his uncle Abu Talib.

As a young adult, Muhammad became a merchant and he made several successful caravan journeys to Syria, in the service of a rich widow, **Khadija**, whom he subsequently married around 595. The union produced six children: four daughters, and two sons who died in infancy. The most famous of his daughters was **Fatima**, wife of 'Ali and the mother of Muhammad's grandsons **Hasan**

THE LIFE OF THE PROPHET MUHAMMAD *c.* 570–632 CE

c. 570 CE	Muhammad is born in Mecca, Arabia. His father, 'Abdallah, dies two months before his birth.
c. 576	Muhammad is orphaned: his mother, Amina, dies when he is six years old. He is left in the guardianship of his grandfather, 'Abd al-Muttalib, and is later brought up by his uncle, Abu Talib.
c. 595	Muhammad marries Khadija, his first wife. She bears him two sons (both of whom die in infancy) and four daughters, including Fatima.
610	While meditating outside Mecca, Muhammad receives his first revelations from God, transmitted through the archangel Gabriel.
613	Muhammad begins public preaching in Mecca.
615	Meccans begin persecuting Muslims, some of whom—the first Muslim emigrants—leave Mecca to seek temporary refuge in Abyssinia.
619	Death of Muhammad's wife, Khadija, and his uncle, Abu Talib.
620	Muhammad receives a hostile reception while preaching in Ta'if and so he returns to Mecca.
622	Muhammad makes his Emigration (*hijra*) to Medina (called Yathrib at that time). In commemoration of this event, 622 becomes the first year of the Islamic calendar.
624	Muhammad composes the Medina Charter, a foundational document also known as the Constitution of Medina.
624	Muhammad changes the direction of prayer (*qibla*) from Jerusalem to Mecca, and establishes the ninth month of the Muslim calendar (Ramadan) as a whole month of fasting.
624	Battle of Badr: the first major Muslim victory against the Meccans.
624–25	Battle of Uhud: defeat of the Muslims by the Meccans.
626–27	Battle of the Trench: Muslims victorious over Meccans. Muhammad consolidates his leadership in Medina.
628	Truce of al-Hudaybiyyah: Muhammad establishes the terms of peaceful pilgrimage to Mecca for Muslims.
628–29	Muhammad captures the Jewish oasis of Khaybar; he allows the Jews and Christians living there to remain, on the condition that they pay a poll tax (*jizya*).
629	Muhammad takes his army to Mecca after the Meccans break the truce of al-Hudaybiyyah; he agrees new terms with Meccan leaders.
629	Muhammad enters Mecca in triumph and orders the destruction of all pagan idols surrounding the Ka'ba shrine.
630–32	Muhammad spends the next two years consolidating his policy of expanding the Muslim community throughout Arabia.
632	Muhammad makes the first Islamic pilgrimage (*hajj*) to Mecca—also known as the Farewell Pilgrimage—performing the individual ceremonies that become the model for future Islamic practice.
June 8, 632 CE	Muhammad falls ill with a severe fever and dies, leaving no surviving sons. He is buried in his house in Medina.

and **Husayn**. According to Muslim tradition, even as a young man Muhammad was given the title al-Amin (the Trustworthy One) by his contemporaries long before his role as a prophet began, and he was called upon to settle disputes.

REVELATION AND PERSECUTION

In middle age (this point is traditionally fixed at around the age of forty, an important symbolic number in **Semitic** tradition), Muhammad, deeply dissatisfied with the pagan environment of Mecca and its shrine and by the greed of his fellow Meccans, began to go outside Mecca to meditate and concentrate on religious devotions for lengthy periods in a cave called Hira on the Jabal al-Nur (Mountain of Light). There he received his first revelations from God through the angel **Gabriel**, who instructed him to recite the following words: "Recite in the name of your Lord who created: Created man from a blood-clot" (Qur'an 96:1). These are believed to be the first verses of the Qur'anic revelation, the revelation sent to Muhammad by God. Muhammad was overwhelmed by this and by similar experiences that followed, and he was beset by self-doubt. But bolstered by the loving comfort and encouragement of Khadija, he became more and more confident that he was truly being called by God as His messenger.

Around 613 Muhammad felt a strong impulse to begin preaching in public to his fellow Meccans. The first prophetic messages, which form the earliest Meccan chapters (*suras*) of the Qur'an, emphasize the imminence of the **Last Day** and the urgent need for human beings to repent and turn to the One God before it is too late. This call went unheeded. But gradually Muhammad assembled around himself a small group of enthusiastic followers, who "surrendered themselves to God" (this is the meaning of the word **Muslim**). At this stage he seems to have seen himself as a messenger sent to the Arabs to warn them of the terrible consequences of their wrongdoing.

The gulf between Muhammad and the polytheistic Meccans widened as the revelations continued and the doctrine of the One God central to his preaching became more pronounced; this threatened the economic wealth of the Meccans, who derived great profit from the pagan ceremonies, fairs, and pilgrimage activity conducted around the Ka'ba shrine in the city. So the Meccans began persecuting the Muslims, some of whom, according to Islamic tradition, left around 615 to take refuge in Abyssinia,[2] where they were protected by the Christian ruler, the Negus. Muhammad, however, did not go with them, since at this point he still had the support of his clan and its leader, his uncle Abu Talib.

A harsh and unforgiving landscape. The mountains behind Mecca. The Prophet Muhammad regularly retreated to these mountains to pray and meditate. The Muslim tradition recounts how the angel Gabriel came to Muhammad here and gave him the first of the revelations that constitute the Qur'an.

The year 619 proved to be one of great personal suffering for Muhammad. Khadija and Abu Talib both died, and another uncle of his, Abu Lahab—his name means the "father of flames" (of Hell)—took over the leadership of the clan and proved irrevocably hostile to Muhammad's preaching. Now without tribal protection, Muhammad had to find somewhere else to live where he could spread the message of Islam without persecution or threat to his life. He went first in 620 to Ta'if, some sixty miles southeast of Mecca, where he preached for several days. He was mocked and pelted with stones and fled the town. A year or so later a much more fortunate opportunity came when people who had come from Yathrib to perform religious rites in Mecca listened to his message, accepted Islam, and invited him to come back with them and to use his skills as a wise arbitrator to settle some difficult internal disputes. He accepted their invitation and all those in Mecca who had become Muslims gradually left the city in small groups. This exodus from Mecca was well organized. They all arrived safely in Yathrib and were given lodging by the Muslims there. Only Muhammad, his devoted friend **Abu Bakr**, and his faithful cousin and son-in-law 'Ali remained in Mecca. Finally, 'Ali slept in Muhammad's bed, to deceive the Prophet's enemies, whilst Muhammad and Abu Bakr left Mecca and hid in a cave south of the town (Qur'an 9:40).

Muhammad and Abu Bakr finally arrived in Yathrib on September 24, 622. (Yathrib was soon renamed *Madinat al-nabi*—the city of the Prophet—and known thereafter as Medina.) Later, when the Muslim calendar was introduced, this day marked the beginning of the new Islamic era, commemorating Muhammad's *hijra* ("emigration") from Mecca to Medina. His achievement in Mecca had been to found a new religion, Islam. In Medina he would establish the Muslim community (the *umma*).

EARLY YEARS IN MEDINA, 622–26

In Medina the Arabs already residing there were divided into two principal and mutually hostile tribal groups, the Aws and the Khazraj. Also living there were three important Jewish clans, the Banu Nadir, Banu Qaynuqa, and Banu Qurayza, which played an important part in the economic life of Medina. It soon became clear that the Jews of Medina firmly rejected the message preached by Muhammad, with serious consequences to themselves and to the subsequent evolution of Islam.

The next ten years in Medina (622–32) provided the Prophet with an opportunity to preach freely, to worship openly, and to create the umma, a **theocratic** Islamic community. Here the social aspects of Islam assumed great importance, for the Muslims had to learn to live together according to the new faith. The newcomers, the Meccan Muslims (the so-called **Emigrants**, *Muhajirun*), who had arrived in Medina without resources or support, needed to be integrated into Medinan society. This problem was solved initially by the system of "brotherhood" established by Muhammad between the Meccan Emigrants and the Medinan Muslims (the so-called Helpers, *Ansar*). A foundational document known as the **Constitution**, or **Charter**, **of Medina**, which seems to be authentic, is preserved in the writings of **Ibn Ishaq** (*c.* 704–767), the early Muslim biographer of Muhammad. Dating from the second or third year of the Medinan period, this document reveals Muhammad's great skills as an arbitrator and his attempts to weld the widely different elements of Medinan society into a unified community. He needed to establish a social order to give him and his followers vital protection in a new environment and to prevent civic unrest in Medina. The text that he drew up shows that even at this early stage the ethos of the umma was clearly Islamic—the highest authority was supra-tribal and belonged to God and His prophet Muhammad. The document speaks of a community of believers—the umma—from Mecca and Medina, but it also allowed for the inclusion of Jews, Christians, and pagans. Indeed, some of the Medinan Jews fought alongside Muslims in the later struggle again the Meccans. The pragmatic outlook of this document was soon changed, however, as the Prophet's position became stronger and the need for an exclusively Muslim community became ever more pressing.

While Muhammad was laying the foundations of the umma, the Qur'anic revelations continued. The Medinan chapters differ from the Meccan chapters in that they pronounce at some length on the conduct of Muslims in every aspect of their personal and communal lives. It is difficult to chart a precise chronology of the Medinan period. The Qur'an speaks of hypocrites (*munafiqun*)—subversive, disloyal elements within the umma. It is clear that Muhammad's early attempt to gain acceptance of the Islamic revelation from the Medinan Jews whom he wished to include within the community met with rejection, and many of the Qur'anic verses revealed in the Medinan period are in the form of refutations for Muhammad to use against the false statements of his enemies. The Qur'anic message reveals an increasing disenchantment with the Jews and a heightened emphasis on the exclusivity and originality of the new faith, Islam. Muhammad believed that his was the true faith of Abraham who through his son Isma'il, the ancestor of the Arabs, had established the Ka'ba at Mecca. He changed the Muslim direction of prayer (*qibla*), which had originally been toward Jerusalem, pointing it toward the Ka'ba at Mecca. He also established the ninth month of the Muslim calendar as a whole month of fasting.

As well as building a harmonious community from within, Muhammad had to fend off external attacks from the Meccans, who threatened the very existence of the umma. Islamic tradition records his struggle against the Meccans in a series of battles, which have become the prototype of *jihad*, defined by Muslims as a defensive struggle against external aggression (see Chapter 9). The Muslims' first major victory against the Meccans, the Battle of Badr in 624, damaged Meccan prestige and provided a vital boost to Muslim morale, a potent proof that the new faith enjoyed God's favor. His successful struggle against the enemy from without was accompanied by a sharpening of his resolve to remove elements that threatened the umma from within Medina, above all the Jews. Muhammad besieged the Jewish clan of Banu Qaynuqa in their forts in Medina and they were soon forced to move to other Jewish settlements in Arabia, such as Khaybar just to the north of Medina; their possessions became the property of the umma.

A year later, in 624–25,[3] the Meccans, wishing to avenge their defeat at Badr, sent an army to Medina said to have comprised three thousand men, under the leadership of Abu Sufyan. Muhammad and his followers went outside the city to a hill called Uhud. This name is infamous in Islamic history, since it came to denote the ensuing battle that saw the defeat of the Muslims by the Meccans. The Meccan leader, Abu Sufyan, carried the goddesses Allat and al-'Uzza into battle. At one point during the battle many Muslims fled when a rumor spread that the Prophet himself had fallen. This incident is thought to be linked to the revelation of the Qur'anic verse 3:144 in which the Muslims are reproached: "Muhammad is only a messenger before whom many messengers have been and gone. If he died or was killed, would you revert to your old ways?" But Muhammad was only wounded and he managed to escape. The Meccans' prestige was temporarily restored and they left without pressing home their advantage. Although Muhammad had lost face, this defeat became a lesson to him as well as to his followers when the following Qur'anic verse (3:154) was revealed: "God did this in order to test everything within you and in order to prove what is in your hearts. God knows your innermost thoughts very well." The Jews in Medina who had not fought against the Meccans exulted in Muhammad's misfortune and soon afterward a second Jewish group, the Banu Nadir, were forced to leave Medina and migrate to Khaybar and other Jewish settlements in the north.

STRENGTHENING THE UMMA, 626–30

A new threat from Mecca soon appeared. Realizing that Muhammad was not weakened, the Meccans together with the Jews of Khaybar raised a large army, around ten thousand men, and moved on Medina in 626–27, intending to occupy it. The Jews within Medina were also suspected of being involved in this initiative. Muhammad dug a trench in front of the unprotected parts of Medina. A siege began but the trench deterred the enemy and the siege was finally lifted. The so-called Battle of the Trench then followed, with Muhammad emerging victorious. Muhammad then declared war on the remaining Jewish group in Medina, the Banu Qurayza, and he besieged them in their forts. This time no mercy was shown; according to Ibn Ishaq, all the men of Qurayza—numbering between six and nine hundred—were executed following a judgment by a man from their own tribe called Sa'd bin Mu'adh, to whom Muhammad had delegated the decision on what their fate should be; the women and children were enslaved.

This event was a major turning point in the development of the new Muslim community. With the removal of the three Jewish groups from Medina, Muhammad was now closer to organizing the umma within the city on an exclusively Muslim basis. He was also in contact with some Arab tribes on the edge of the Syrian desert, with the aim of persuading them to embrace Islam and to submit to the authority of the umma under the rule of God and His prophet. In 628 he felt strong enough to make a new move, and learning that Mecca was gradually becoming better disposed toward him he decided to try to incorporate that key city into the umma. At this point he used his exceptional powers of negotiation and was able to win over the Meccans by forming alliances with them rather than engaging in any more armed conflict. Within two years he had laid the foundations for a peaceful entry into the city. In 628 he had announced his intention to perform the pilgrimage to Mecca. In the event, when he encamped at a place called al-Hudaybiyya on the outskirts of the Meccan sacred area, he made an agreement with the Meccans that he could return to Mecca the following year to perform the Lesser Pilgrimage (the *'umra*), and he signed a ten-year truce with them. What happened at al-Hudaybiyya was a diplomatic triumph for the Prophet. Instead of trying to destroy him, as well as the new faith and the new community, the Meccans—who had turned a deaf ear to his preaching and expelled him from their city only six years earlier—had actually negotiated with him on equal terms.

In 628–29 Muhammad captured the Jewish oasis of Khaybar. This was his first conquest outside Medina. The way in which this city was treated was to serve as a model for subsequent Muslim conquests, both in the remaining years of the Prophet's life and thereafter. He did not expel or kill the Jews of Khaybar; instead he allowed them, as "People of the Book"—communities, such as Christian and Jews, that had established scriptures—to remain there and to practice their faith, on payment of a poll tax (*jizya*). According to Muslim tradition, it was around this time that Muhammad had letters sent out to the most powerful rulers in the area, including the Byzantine emperor, the Sasanian Persian king, and the Negus of Abyssinia, inviting them to embrace Islam. Whether these letters were genuine remains a subject of scholarly debate, but they do show at the very least how later generations of Muslims looked back and saw the far-reaching aims of the Prophet to spread Islam beyond the confines of Arabia. At the same time Muhammad was keen to bring into the Muslim fold all the Arab tribes, including those who lived on the borders with the two great empires of the time, Christian Byzantium and Zoroastrian Persia.

In 629, in accordance with the truce of al-Hudaybiyya, the Meccans left their city for three days while the Muslims performed the 'umra. At this stage a number of key figures in Mecca, who had earlier been his bitter opponents, converted to Islam. But the hard core of the Meccans still refused Muhammad's offers of reconciliation and they broke the truce of al-Hudaybiyya. So in 629 Muhammad set out with an army to Mecca. Meccan leaders came out to parley with him and an amnesty was agreed for all Meccans who laid down their arms.

In January 630 Muhammad entered Mecca in triumph without a struggle and destroyed all the pagan idols that were strewn around the Ka'ba, although he is reported to have covered with his hands the picture of **Mary** and Jesus that was painted on a pillar, to protect it from destruction.[4] The message was unequivocally clear—polytheism was dead and monotheism now reigned supreme. Some weeks later he defeated a large army of central Arabian tribes at Hunayn.

MUHAMMAD'S FINAL YEARS, 630–32

What remained of Muhammad's life—only two more years—was spent in Medina, consolidating his policy of securing the northern routes to Syria in order to expand the umma, as well to protect the caravan trade. Muhammad himself took part in a Syrian campaign to Tabuk in 630. In that year many tribal embassies came to visit him in Medina and he drew up agreements with them. Ten years after his momentous hijra to Medina from his home town of Mecca, in 632 the Prophet performed the first Islamic pilgrimage (*hajj*)—known ever afterward as the Farewell Pilgrimage. All the individual ceremonies of the pilgrimage that he performed on that occasion became the model for future Islamic practice (see Chapter 4, pp. 109–11). He thus transformed the pagan rituals of the Ka'ba, reconsecrating the shrine, founded by Abraham, in the name of Islam. God's favour was bestowed on Muhammad in the words of the Qur'anic verse 5:3, believed to have been revealed to him on this momentous occasion: "Today I have perfected your religion for you, completed My blessing upon you, and chosen as your religion Islam."

On his return to Medina Muhammad began planning a new major expedition across the Jordan, which he intended to lead himself. But just before the campaign's scheduled departure, he fell ill with a severe fever. He died on June 8, 632 and was buried in his house in Medina in a simple ceremony. He left no surviving sons. The issue of who should lead the Muslim community after him became ever more critical (see Chapter 6).

SOURCES FOR THE LIFE OF MUHAMMAD

It is impossible to reconstruct an objective historical account of the life of the Prophet of Islam. But it was not long before Muhammad's biography had become a fixed narrative and the focus of Muslim sacred history: the important stages of his career on earth assumed symbolic and normative significance.

In other words, not just the sayings and opinions of Muhammad but also his actions, including the military campaigns, as observed and recorded by his closest associates, the **Companions**, and their successors, became paradigms for the entire Muslim community. And sacred history to those who are believers is not easily subject to analysis, change or refutation, either in detail or in an overarching way.

TRADITIONAL MUSLIM SOURCES

There are three major traditional Muslim sources which together have provided the building blocks for constructing the sacred history of the life of Muhammad—the Qur'an, the canonical sayings of the Prophet Muhammad (the *hadith* reports) and his standard biography (the *sira*) written by Ibn Ishaq. These will now be considered in turn, although they are, of course, closely interconnected.

First, then, the Qur'an. It is not easy to use this work of revelation as a historical source, although attempts have been made to extract from it the evolution of the Prophet's life. To be sure, by its condemnation of certain aspects of Arabian life it sheds light on some of the prevailing social conditions and practices that the Prophet sought to reform, but trying to trace the successive stages of his career through Qur'anic allusions is apt to result in crude and simplistic conclusions. There is even ongoing debate amongst non-Muslim and Muslim scholars about the chronology of its chapters and individual verses.[5]

Holy writ. Qur'an, possibly Arabian, parchment, 7th–8th century. Written in unvowelled and unpointed Kufic *ma'il* script—the oldest Qur'anic script—in a backward-sloping hand, with twenty-four closely packed lines per page, primitive letter forms, occasionally erratic spacing, a ragged left margin, and almost no verse markings, this text was certainly difficult to read. A script and page layout more appropriate for Scripture lay in the future (see the Qur'an of Ibn al-Bawwab, dating from c. 1000–1, on page 58).

So the Qur'an cannot be said to provide a biography of the Prophet. When it is read in conjunction with the two other key Islamic sources—the hadith reports and the sira—however, the Qur'an does reveal deep insights into the stages of Muhammad's development, recording the trials he underwent and the triumphs that he experienced. Where the Qur'anic statements are difficult to understand, the hadiths can often clarify and amplify them. The hadith reports and the sira are discrete genres in Muslim religious literature but what they say about the Prophet is often to be found in both. Together they form the *Sunna* (the Prophet's "customary or normative behavior").

The hadith reports comprise a vast corpus of recorded sayings and deeds of the Prophet, believed to be transmitted by the Companions, and thereafter hallowed by subsequent generations of early Muslims. They give a remarkably detailed picture of Muhammad's preaching and activities, especially in the Medinan period (622–32). The hadith reports are, however, impossible to rely on as a historical source: there is still controversy amongst non-Muslim hadith scholars about whether they really date back as far as the early 600s, and their often fragmentary, parable-like nature makes it impossible to piece them together coherently. Sometimes they contradict each other, and some certainly contain later interpolations. They do, however, faithfully reflect the fluidity, diversity, and evolutionary aspects of early Islamic ritual and law, and the efforts of the pious scholars in the first two or three centuries of the Muslim era to establish the path of 'true Islam'. Indeed, in the course of time the hadith reports came to provide the foundations for the development of Islamic law, which instructs Muslims in every aspect of their daily life (see Chapter 5). Four hadith collections put into standard form in the ninth and tenth centuries are regarded by Sunni Muslims as authoritative (*sahih*); vast additional hadith material which was collected by other scholars has also survived. **Shi'ites** too have their hadith collections which in some ways give alternative accounts of what the Prophet said and did.

What is important to stress about the hadith reports, whether Sunni or Shi'ite, is their legislative function. In them the Prophet is shown giving pronouncements, whether succinct or detailed, on what Muslims should believe and how they should conduct themselves. The Qur'an and the hadith reports thus complement each other; the allusive nature of the former is amplified by the rich fullness of the latter. Indeed, the hadith reports quote the Prophet's views on an enormous range of topics, including clothing, jewelry, food, gossip, swearing, and even toothpicks, as well as matters of the greatest spiritual moment such as jihad, prayer, pilgrimage, heaven, and hell, and the judgment and mercy of God. In the hadith reports he is shown to be deeply human, with individual likes and dislikes, with concern for metaphysical matters on the one hand and the finer points of ritual on the other. His voice in the hadith reports is confident and strong. He is presented there as the authoritative legislator and the ideal model for all Muslims to try to emulate in their daily lives.

The third important source that helped to construct the sacred history of the life of the Prophet is the formal biographical literary genre known as the sira, beginning with the work of that name written in the eighth century by Ibn Ishaq and then compiled by **Ibn Hisham** (d. 833). This is a very long work of fascinating complexity, based to a large extent on the hadith reports. It is full of personal details about Muhammad's life and personality, juxtaposed with miraculous, mystical, and legendary elements. Later biographies throughout the centuries are deeply indebted to the sira of Ibn Ishaq, which remains a most revered work of faith and piety.

Unlike the hadith reports, which are arranged according to theme, the sira tells a story, with a beginning, middle, and end. This is an epic narrative. In it the events of Muhammad's life are presented in the precise and unchanging order that most Muslims know. Although the sira is recognized as being overlaid with miraculous and legendary elements, it has also formed the basis of modern biographies of the Prophet, including those written by Western non-Muslim scholars. Aware of the historiographical problems associated with the sira, problems that they analyze fully, they nevertheless rely on it, given the virtual absence of any other sources.

Supplementing the sira, with its broad approach to the Prophet's life, other works with a narrower focus were written, such as the literature that is specifically devoted to Muhammad's military expeditions (the *maghazi* books), as well as the biographical dictionaries containing details about Muhammad's Companions and their successors. Other important sources of information are the works of the great Muslim historians of the 'Abbasid period, above all al-Baladhuri and al-Tabari. Their chronicles spring from the double inspiration of several generations of oral tradition (carefully memorized by the faithful, anxious not to forget the contours of the Prophet's career and the glorious victories of the Muslim conquests) and the corpus of material inherited from the first written Islamic historical sources, now no longer extant. Some of the great 'Abbasid historians were "compilers": they were mostly religious scholars meticulously collecting and sifting nuggets of information, both full and fragmentary, left by their predecessors. Such snippets and anecdotes were furnished with an apparatus (the so-called *isnads*, which traced the chain of narrators of a particular event right back to the Prophet's time, if possible) intended to demonstrate the authenticity of the data mentioned.

NON-MUSLIM SOURCES FOR THE LIFE OF MUHAMMAD

In the last fifty years or so non-Muslim Western scholars have conducted a lot of research on Muhammad and the origins of Islam. Their work distinguishes clearly between the sacred history of Muhammad's life, outlined above, which was compiled in canonical form by ninth-century Muslim scholars, and the material found in non-Muslim written sources of the seventh to the tenth centuries—Jewish, Christian, and Zoroastrian—which speak about Muhammad and the rise of Islam. Such sources, taken as a whole, cannot provide a continuous, coherent narrative of the life of Muhammad in the requisite detail. Nor are these few sources devoid of bias; many of them have a distinct agenda of their own. But what they say should be examined because of the alternative perspectives they give from outside the Muslim tradition on the phenomenon of the career of the Prophet and the rise of Islam.

It is clear from non-Muslim historical and religious writings that Muhammad was a real person. The earliest account of Muhammad's career comes from an anonymous untitled historical chronicle of Armenia written in the 660s.[6] Its author mentions that Muhammad was a merchant and that he preached a message to his people about "the living God who had revealed Himself to their father Abraham." His history also speaks of conquering lands, and records Muhammad saying: "Only love the God of Abraham, and go and take possession of your country which God gave to your father Abraham."[7] Non-Muslim sources do not mention Mecca or that Muhammad was in Arabia. Instead, they emphasize the importance of Palestine. Christian writers focus primarily on the damage done to their self-image by the conquering Arabs whom they describe in apocalyptic tones as "the sword of God." The late eighth-century northern Mesopotamian author of a work known as the *Zuqnin Chronicle* writes about Muhammad as follows: "The first king was a man from among them (the Arabs) by the name of Muhammad. This man they also called a prophet, because he had turned them away from cults of all kinds and taught them that there was one God, the Maker of Creation.... They called him prophet and messenger of God."[8]

A much more famous writer, **John of Damascus** (676–749), writing a polemical work about heresies in the 730s,[9] calls the Muslims "Ishmaelites,"

"Hagarenes," and "Saracens." In his diatribes against Islam he reveals that he has had access to the Qur'an.

In addition to these and a few other non-Muslim sources between 700 and 1000 CE that specifically refer to Muhammad, it is interesting to mention that a papyrus document of the year 643 is dated "year twenty-two"; this suggests that something important happened in 622 (the year that Muslim accounts give for the *hijra*, and the beginning of the Muslim calendar).[10] Moreover, a gravestone in Cairo is dated to the Muslim month called Jumada II of the year 31, which corresponds to January–February of the Christian year 652.[11] These two random pieces of evidence, insignificant in themselves, nevertheless corroborate the historical framework of much later Muslim chronicles.

So what may be concluded from the external non-Muslim evidence about the life and message of Muhammad, and how does it mesh with the received Muslim version of the rise of Islam? This is an ongoing debate amongst non-Muslim scholars. But this much can be said. Christian, Jewish, and other non-Muslim sources are important since they reflect the context in which these communities were responding to the coming of Islam. At the same time, too much credibility should not be placed on them since they undoubtedly view the rise of Islam through a lens of prejudice and misunderstanding and they are as full of ideological elements as the Muslim writings themselves.

For Muslims the "sacred history" of Muhammad's life cannot be subject to alteration, whether in detail or in its grand sweep. As is the case for Christians with the "sacred history" of the life of Jesus, the canonical version of Muhammad's life and message does not obey the rules of "ordinary" history. Although there is a strong probability that this accepted version does enshrine an actual histori-cal kernel, even the most committed scholars cannot identify it beyond dispute. There is, in short, no way of reconciling history and sacred history. This book presents the view of Muhammad that is generally accepted by Muslims. The patchy references to aspects of that view in the early non-Muslim sources are quite simply not enough to paint a coherent alternative picture.

REFLECTIONS ON MUHAMMAD'S LIFE AND MISSION
AS PRESENTED IN THE MUSLIM TRADITION

During his short but momentous career—it occupied only the last third of his life—Muhammad displayed great courage, dynamism, and foresight. As well as fulfilling his role as a divinely appointed prophet, Muhammad was also a statesman, lawgiver, and military leader whose exceptional personal charisma made an impact on the Muslim community from his own times right up to the present day.

MUHAMMAD AS PROPHET

Muhammad had to fulfill a number of roles all at the same time, and this he did consummately well. But first and foremost he was the Prophet of God, and in this he was simply a vehicle for God's revelations which came to him regularly throughout his mission. The Judaeo-Christian tradition has a long line of prophets who undergo suffering, mockery, and rejection from the peoples to whom they preach God's message. Muhammad stands in that line. The earliest Qur'anic verses revealed at Mecca show clearly that the revelations that came to Muhammad closely resembled the messages preached by earlier monotheistic prophets in the Middle East, both those recorded in the Bible as well as earlier Arab monotheistic prophets. But it is important to remember that Muhammad did not see himself initially as the founder of a new faith. This awareness grew only gradually as he began, in the face of taunts from the pagan Meccans, to seek to restore the pristine monotheism that had once existed in Arabia. Although he became the leader of the umma at Medina, his role as prophet never ceased. He continued to experience mockery, hostility, and rejection after the hijra.

As was the case with some of the prophets before him, on a significant number of occasions Muhammad's life is shown in Muslim tradition, and especially in the sira, as being miraculous. The sira relates that before Muhammad's birth, Jewish and Christian seers foretold his coming in the same way that the Christian Gospels interpret the advent of Jesus as the fulfillment of the prophecies of Isaiah and other Jewish prophets who have preceded him. Such ratifying of the prophethood of Muhammad is very important to the credibility of the revelation he brought to mankind. Moreover, just as the coming and the birth of Jesus are heralded by heavenly portents such as the Star of Bethlehem, the Annunciation to Mary, and the Virgin Birth, so too with Muhammad. His birth is announced to his mother, Amina, by a voice that has sometimes been thought to be Gabriel's. When Muhammad is born, Amina says that she saw a light coming out from her that illuminated the space between east and west.

An even more famous miraculous episode is recorded in the sira when in his early childhood Muhammad's breast is opened up by two angels who cleanse his heart. Later on, in the same way as the young Jesus is described in the Bible as being taken by Mary and Joseph to the Temple in Jerusalem where an aged devout man named Simeon sets eyes on him and says that he may now die in peace having seen "the consolation of Israel," so too the sira relates that when Muhammad is a young boy, he meets a Christian holy man called al-Bahira in Busra in Syria. This man recognizes in him the signs that he is the prophet foretold in the Christian tradition: "He looked at his back and saw the seal of prophethood between his shoulders."

The account of the first revelation from God to Muhammad through His intermediary the angel Gabriel is recorded by Ibn Ishaq in a dramatic and miraculous way. While asleep Muhammad is visited by an angel who commands him to recite words that are written on a piece of brocade (the very first words of the Qur'an). This he struggles to do. Later on, while Muhammad is meditating in the cave of Hira, he receives another visit from Gabriel "in the shape of a man with extended wings, standing in the firmament with his feet touching the ground."

According to Muslim tradition, it was at some point toward the end of his preaching in Mecca, in the last year before his hijra, when Muhammad was experiencing fierce opposition and persecution from his fellow Quraysh tribesmen, that he received the crowning reassurance of God's support through his Night Journey and Ascent into Heaven (the *mi'raj*). Several versions of this event—which have their parallels in the ascension stories of Elijah and Jesus in the Bible—can be found in the sira but there is general agreement that Muhammad was awakened one night by Gabriel who led him to a winged animal called Buraq. Muhammad mounted Buraq and he and Gabriel travelled to Jerusalem "to see the wonders between heaven and earth." The associations of Jerusalem with famous prophets and the **Day of Judgment** make this a significant destination. One version of why Muslims pray five times a day recounts that Muhammad negotiated this number with God at this time. According to one version of the story, their journey went from the mosque at Mecca to a location, called the Furthest Mosque (*al-masjid al-aqsa*), where Muhammad met Abraham, Moses, and Jesus. Other versions of the account mention that, like Jacob before him, Muhammad then saw a ladder (this is the prime meaning of the word mi'raj) reaching up to the heavens, which he ascended with Gabriel. There he beheld thousands of angels and was taken in turn to each of the seven levels of heaven. On each level he met different prophets, beginning on the second level with Jesus and his cousin John, and going backward in time to Abraham in the seventh heaven where Muhammad stood before God's throne and spoke with Him. Muhammad then returned to earth. It is important to note that this inspiring testimony of God's confidence in Muhammad in showing him the glories of the heavens and allowing him to meet the prophets of old is placed in the sira toward the very end of his time in Mecca when he was at his lowest ebb, vulnerable and persecuted.

Thus the biography of Muhammad that has come down over the centuries has a miraculous aura, as befits the founder of a new faith. It was originally revealed to his own people, the Arabs, in Arabic but, as soon became apparent, was meant for all humanity. Almost all of the incidents in his life that contain miraculous elements occur in the early period at Mecca as he struggles with the experiences of adopting his momentous role as a prophet. However, the miraculous still does appear from time to time in the last ten years of his life, as Ibn Ishaq records that angels assist Muhammad and the Muslims in their military victories. Not surprisingly, the miraculous events related about Muhammad's life have proved to be extremely important in the lives of the **Sufis**, the mystics of Islam (see Chapter 8). They see him as the first Sufi and model their conduct as closely as they can on his. In particular, Muhammad's Night Journey forms an important focus for the meditations of Sufis seeking a closer proximity with God.

MUHAMMAD AS LEADER AND WARRIOR

This miraculous element in the Prophet's life and career, an outward mark of God's approval, is complemented by his many-sided qualities of leadership. He saw himself charged with the responsibility for establishing a community that would safeguard the faith and spread it after his death. He was a brilliant leader of men. He is portrayed as showing his skills of statesmanship and diplomacy from early on in his career, for example in the way he chose where to live. According to Muslim tradition, rather than show partiality to any one faction in the strife-ridden city of Medina, he allowed his camel to wander around and he made his residence at the place where the camel eventually came to a halt.

Muhammad also served as a lawgiver and judge. During the ten years he spent in Medina he had to deal on a daily basis with a multiplicity of problems, both great and small. He had to make decisions and pass judgments and solve problems. Revelations would come to support and guide him, and they form the notably specific subject matter of the longer Medinan chapters of the Qur'an, which speak with authority on all kinds of matters of faith and practice. Like the books of Mosaic law (the law derived from Moses) in the Old Testament, the injunctions of Chapter 2 in the Qur'an, for example, are remarkably detailed over a wide range of aspects of ritual and law. The corpus of hadith contains a mass of statements and decisions made by Muhammad and written down by his devoted followers. Much of the sira too reveals the Prophet's need to devote his time to legal matters.

Muhammad is also sometimes shown in Islamic sacred history as a warrior. In Mecca his peaceful attempts to win over his fellow Quraysh tribesmen by preaching the message of the One God, and to persuade them to embrace the new faith of Islam, had met with only limited success. By 622 he was left without tribal protection. After he had moved to Medina it became clear that the only way to ensure the triumph of his prophetic mission and the establishment of his Islam-based community was by fighting the Meccans. Qur'anic verses make it clear that Muhammad was initially reluctant to take up arms against his fellow Meccans, because of ties of blood and kinship, but that—once reassured by God that this was the only way forward—he was prepared to attack them. As the Qur'an puts it: (2:216): "Fighting is ordained for you, though you dislike it." It was difficult for him to persuade his fellow Muslims that it was acceptable to fight the Meccans, but he managed to do so. He was capable of making tough decisions and seeing them through. A further difficulty was the necessity to make an attack on the Meccans in the traditional sacred month when fighting was banned in Arabia; but again he was reassured that he could proceed with this course of action: "They ask you [Prophet] about fighting in the prohibited month. Say, 'Fighting in that month is a great offence, but to bar others from God's path, to disbelieve in Him, prevent access to the Sacred Mosque, and expel its people, are still greater offences in God's eyes: persecution is worse than killing'" (Qur'an 2:217).

Muhammad undertook only three major military engagements—the battles of Badr, Uhud, and the Trench. Victories at Badr and the Trench were a sign of God's continuing favor and they were an enormous boost to the morale of the umma. And even the defeat at Uhud was turned by Muhammad into a lesson to the Muslims that they must have stronger faith.

What is clear is that in the milieu of seventh-century Arabia, just as had been the case for Moses (another warrior prophet associated with many miracles) many centuries earlier, the only way to protect the beleaguered community of Muslims and to safeguard the continued existence of the new faith of Islam was to take up arms. The Meccans would fight to the end to defend their economic livelihood and their long-cherished pagan cults, so they had to be resisted, on some occasions by force. Thus, as with the fighting conducted by Moses and Joshua in the Old Testament, Muhammad's military expeditions have been viewed by Muslims throughout the ages as being sanctioned by God in the name of religion. But they were also about sheer survival.

According to the traditional sources, and especially the maghazi books, which describe his military activities in Medina as striving (jihad) in the path of God, Muhammad was present in the heat of battle to lead and inspire the Muslim warriors. On one occasion, at the Battle of Uhud, he was injured, losing two teeth. He proved to be a resourceful military leader, taking advice when required on how best to combat enemy forces and learning, for example at the Battle of the Trench, how to defend Medina when it was besieged by the Meccans. The victory at Badr was won not only through heightened religious fervor but also because of Muhammad's astute choice of terrain for the fighting. But where possible, fighting was to be avoided. Fighting would be allowed only when all other means of persuasion had failed, and it was due to Muhammad's exceptional negotiating skills that he made a peaceful entry into Mecca in 630.

MUSLIM AND NON-MUSLIM VIEWS OF MUHAMMAD

The image of Muhammad that emerges from the Qur'an, as well as from pious biographies of him, is of a man who is fully human. As the Qur'an puts it, addressing Muhammad directly: "Say, 'I am only a human being, like you'" (18:111). Muhammad is absolutely not depicted as God's son, or as part of a Trinitarian God, as Jesus is in Christianity. Nor is he shown as the "suffering servant," as Jesus is in the Gospels. Muhammad is not presented as being without sin. He is a man with human feelings and failings, reliant on God to help him on the path of prophethood that God has assigned to him, and asking God for guidance at every step of the way. His defeats, setbacks, and failures are as faithfully recorded in the Muslim sources as are his victories. Muhammad was the vehicle for one supreme miracle—the Qur'an—and to emphasize the miraculous nature of the Islamic revelation, Muslim scholars came to believe that he was *al-nabi al-ummi* ("the unlettered prophet"), unable to read and write. All his knowledge of the prophets who had preceded him was thus the result of divine inspiration alone.

Yet, despite the essentially human nature of Muhammad, over the centuries and into the present he has been revered amongst Muslims above all other human beings. He is the model for them to follow. In many parts of the world Muslims celebrate the Prophet's birthday (*mawlid*) on the twelfth day of the third Muslim month (Rabi' I). The Isma'ili Shi'ites (see Chapter 6, p. 151) made much of this festival in Cairo in the eleventh century and it became more widespread from the thirteenth century in areas where Sunni Islam predominated. Sermons and poems in praise of the Prophet form the centerpiece of the celebrations. A famous British scholar of Islam, Edward Lane, gives a lively detailed eye-witness description of a mawlid celebration in Cairo in 1834. Lane pays particular attention to the role of the Sufis in the celebrations, but the ordinary people are fully involved too and they are delighted with all kinds of other street festivities, including conjurers, sweetmeat stalls, coffee shops, and lamp-lit processions. Despite some dissenting voices through the ages, the *mawlid* is a holiday celebrated enthusiastically to this day throughout much of the Muslim world.

Poetry praising Muhammad is recited in Turkish, Persian, Urdu, Swahili, and many other languages, but pride of place goes to perhaps the most famous poem ever written in Arabic, known simply as the *Qasidat al-burda* (*The Ode of the Cloak*). Written by **al-Busiri** (1212–c. 1294), the ode has had more than ninety commentaries devoted to it. In it the poet thanks Muhammad for coming to him in a dream and curing him from paralysis by throwing his cloak over him. The poem, which praises the birth, mi'raj, and jihad of the Prophet, is regarded as having special powers and is read at funerals and other religious ceremonies. If, for example, it is recited 1001 times, some Muslims believe that it will produce lifelong blessings; recited once a day on a journey, it will guarantee safety for the traveller. The central importance of Muhammad is underlined in the following verses: "Muhammad (peace and blessings be upon him) is the leader of both worlds and both creations, and of both groups, Arabs and non-Arabs. Our Prophet, the one who commands (good) and forbids (evil)....He is (God's) most beloved, whose intercession is hoped for..." These verses end by mentioning a key role assigned to the Prophet Muhammad in popular belief—that of intercessor on the Day of Judgment, when he will intercede before God on behalf of his community. The most famous medieval Muslim scholar, **al-Ghazali**, attributes the following saying to Muhammad: "I am the right one (to intercede) insofar as God allows it for whomever He wills and chooses." God then says to him, "O Muhammad, lift your head and speak, for you will be heard; seek intercession and it will be granted."[12]

Hall of mirrors. Great Mosque of Cordoba, Spain, interior, 8th–10th century. Continually shifting lines of sight and perspectives create a dizzying sense of constant movement. It was the largest mosque in the Islamic West; its stone forest of re-used columns (taken from older Roman and Christian buildings) supported a unique system of striped, superposed arches that made the roof much higher.

MUSLIM REACTIONS TO CRITICISM OF MUHAMMAD

The special respect and reverence that Muslims hold for Muhammad have led—and still do lead—to very strong reactions when he is criticized, satirized, or vilified by non-Muslims. Three examples, one from the medieval period and two from our own time, illustrate this very persuasively. Passionate feelings of love for the Prophet go back a long way in history. Long before the Crusades exacerbated rivalries between the two monotheistic religions that had emerged after Judaism—Christianity and Islam—there were episodes that highlighted the unassailably sacred status of Muhammad in Islam. Already in the ninth century in Muslim Spain, the "land of the three religions," known for its relative tolerance in matters of faith and peaceful coexistence, a group of Spanish Christians denigrated the name of Muhammad publicly in the city of Cordoba. The incident, involving a group who came to be known as the Martyrs of Cordoba, is recorded in both Muslim and Christian sources. Their accounts suggest that those who vilified the name of the Prophet were actively seeking martyrdom and that they knew exactly how to be sure of achieving their aim. Indeed, they deliberately left the reluctant Muslim authorities no option other than to execute them.

THE SATANIC VERSES

Coming to our own time, **Salman Rushdie's** novel *The Satanic Verses*, published in 1988, aroused great controversy and heightened emotions around the world; its publication led to widespread violence and the killings of thirty-eight people. The book was burned publicly by Muslims in the UK and banned in India. The religious, political, and social issues surrounding these events have been aired in literally thousands of books and articles. (It is doubtful, however, if many Muslims have actually read the book.) The author's first name, Salman, is that of the revered first Persian convert to Islam, and Rushdie derives from *Rashidun*, the name given to the esteemed first four Rightly Guided **caliphs**, so it was peculiarly insulting to Muslims that a writer bearing these hallowed names should choose a provocative title for the book, and that he adopted in it the pejorative name Mahound, used for Muhammad by hostile European Christians in the Middle Ages. Global Muslim indignation, especially in Iran, Pakistan, and India, and the *fatwa* delivered by **Ayatollah Khomeini** of Iran, soon followed. Since then, the spectrum of Muslim opinions on the book has ranged from disapproval of the fatwa and support for Rushdie's right to say what he thinks to downright horror at his insulting attitudes toward the Prophet.[13] Rushdie himself claimed that his novel was not about Islam but "about migration, metamorphosis, divided selves, love, death, London and Bombay."[14] If so, one might conclude that *The Satanic Verses* is not an obvious title for a book with those seven themes.

The title of the novel is a reference to a little-known episode in which Muhammad allegedly pronounced a revelation, saying that the three Meccan goddesses, al-'Uzza, Allat, and Manat—worshiped at the Ka'ba by the polytheistic Arabs and known as "the daughters of Allah"—could intercede with God on behalf of Muslim worshipers. Such an intercession would, of course, have destroyed the uncompromising message of Islam—the belief in the One God and Him alone. Later, Muhammad allegedly then realized that this was a false revelation that had come to him from Satan. A true revelation followed from God, which definitively abolished the credibility of any possible intercession on the part of the three goddesses: "[Disbelievers], consider al-Lat and al-Uzza, and the third one, Manat...these are nothing but names you have invented yourselves, you and your forefathers. God has sent no authority for them" (Qur'an 53:19–20, 23).

Some scholars, both Muslim and non-Muslim, and both medieval and contemporary, have argued that the whole episode of the Satanic Verses is a fabrication and that there is no mention of this story in the hadith collections.

Others say that the Prophet did once receive a false revelation from Satan (Shaytan), before returning to the true path of the One God. Indeed, many early Muslim commentators in the first two centuries after Muhammad's death, including Ibn Ishaq and al-Tabari, faithfully record this incident, in accordance with the clear statement in the Qur'an, and elsewhere in the record of Muhammad's life, that he was only a fallible human being who was subject to human frailties and feelings. However, all Shi'ite commentators rejected the truth of this incident, basing their position on the principle that God's prophets have immunity from error, and, as Shahab Ahmad has written, "the historicity of this incident is strenuously denied by modern Islamic orthodoxy."[15] Western scholars, by contrast, have tended to accept that this event happened, arguing that it is unlikely that Muslims would have invented such a story.

Whatever the truth may be, the controversy over Rushdie's book highlights a major and ongoing problem, namely how to maintain the balance between the democratic right to speak and publish freely and the need for those of other faiths, or indeed of no faith at all, to respect the beliefs that the world's Muslims hold sacred.

THE DANISH CARTOONS

In 2006 cartoons were published in a Danish newspaper, and later in a French one, depicting the Prophet in a way that was extremely offensive to Muslims. The reactions from certain groups of Muslims round the world were violent, since the publication of such material hit at the very heart of Muslim piety and veneration of Muhammad. Scenes of public outrage took place in many countries and some protesters even threatened death by execution to those who had published the cartoons.

Many Western commentators viewed the cartoons as tasteless and childish. One such cartoon, however, could not be dismissed as mere mischief; this depicted the Prophet as a suicide bomber, wearing a ticking bomb in the form of a turban on which was inscribed the Muslim profession of faith: "There is no god but God." This caused profound offence to Muslims everywhere, to the normally silent majority as well as to the minority of politically radicalized Muslims in the world (who, according to a recent worldwide poll, constitute only 7 percent of Muslims).[16]

Why the offence? Apart from linking Muhammad with a suicide bomber, a transgression was involved here that escapes the eyes of most non-Muslims. There has long been a reluctance on the part of Muslims to create visual representations of the Prophet. Islam, like Judaism, is a religion of the word, not the image. This was a natural move away from the worship of visible pagan idols. By contrast, there is no such absence of human images in Christianity; many churches show images of the crucified Jesus, of episodes in his life, and of holy people as part of a long tradition that goes back at least to the third century. For a brief window of time in the late Middle Ages there were a large number of pictures of Muhammad, produced by Muslims in the eastern Islamic world, following the Mongol invasions; on some of these his face is shown, sometimes it is veiled, and sometimes it has been whitened over or rubbed out by a later hand. Although this custom of painting pictures of Muhammad did not become deep-rooted in the Muslim world, it has not totally disappeared. Today, iconic pictures of Muhammad are sold openly on the street in Iran. The creation, sale, or owning of such images is, however, illegal in some Muslim countries. In general, Muslims nowadays believe that visual representations of the Prophet are forbidden. Even in the classic film of Muhammad's life, *The Message*, his face is never shown on the screen. His presence is only felt. So the Danish cartoons, regardless of their content, already broke a strong Muslim taboo by drawing pictures of the Prophet at all.

But the cartoons went further than that. They set out not just to depict Muhammad visually but also at best to ridicule him, and at worst to vilify him. And this took place in a heightened climate of Western Islamophobia. As one British newspaper, *The Independent*, wrote in February 2006: "The affair is an example of western ignorance and arrogance combined. We have lit a fire and the wind could take it a long way." Similar concerns were expressed in newspapers across the world. *The Times* of London even widened the discussion by pointing out that "many in Europe today think nothing of mocking the most revered aspects of Christianity—often in a crass, tasteless fashion."[17] Whilst many Muslims were justifiably appalled and shocked by what had happened, they did not, however, condone the responses from some radicalized Muslim circles threatening to kill those responsible for the cartoons. Instead, Muslim countries chose a peaceful but powerful means of protest by initiating a short-lived economic boycott of Danish exports, such as butter.

PREJUDICES AND STEREOTYPES

The material presented in this chapter so far makes it clear that Muslims accept without question that Muhammad was the Prophet of God, the "Seal of the Prophets," the bringer of the final and perfect monotheistic revelation.

But this present book is addressed primarily to those who, while they are not Muslim, nevertheless wish to see more clearly what Islam is about. They have probably been exposed to many of the deeply ingrained negative prejudices about Muhammad that have come down over the centuries in the West. Some of these perceptions of and judgments on the Prophet will now be examined here.

One of the fundamental issues in this connection is the need to take a hard look at how Muhammad has been viewed by non-Muslims, and especially Christians, at times when people were defined more strongly than today by their religious faith. Such a discussion also needs to take into account how believing Christians and Jews, as well as those who reject religious faith of any kind, speak about Muhammad today.

Muslim and non-Muslim extremists alike have severely criticized one another's beliefs from medieval right up to modern times. From the early medieval period onward, in Christian polemical writings, Islam was attacked on a number of counts, just as Muslim polemical works criticized certain Christian doctrines. Such dogmatic differences, rather than their shared Abrahamic beliefs, formed the subject matter of numerous Muslim–Christian interfaith encounters, public debates, and polemical writings in front of the caliphs from **Umayyad** times (661–750) onward. In the early eighth century, for example, John of Damascus called Muhammad "a false prophet" and challenged Muslims to prove Muhammad's claims to having received "divine revelations."[18] Competition, not a desire for fruitful dialogue, was what drove these debates.

The debates between Christianity and Islam, the second and third of the Abrahamic revelations, were more intense than the debates that both these faiths had with Judaism, which was broadly speaking not an evangelizing religion. War sharpened the intensity. By the end of the Crusading period in the Middle East—that is, from the beginning of the fourteenth century— anti-Muslim polemic, directed especially at the Prophet, had become quite virulent. The vehemently hostile representation of Muhammad given by Italy's most famous poet, Dante, in his poem *The Divine Comedy*, in the part called *Inferno* (Hell), which places Muhammad in the depths of Hell, is well known. Muhammad is depicted as the chief of those souls damned for eternity for having brought schism (division) to religion.[19]

The stereotypes formed in medieval times continued to prevail in the nineteenth century when Christian Europe began to colonize the Muslim world. And these negative images of Muhammad are still with us today. They cause understandable distress to all Muslims, not just to the few who make their feelings known more vociferously and violently in public to the world at large. The fundamental problem lies in the fact that whilst Christians can accept wholeheartedly the first half of the Muslim profession of faith—the part that pronounces that there is only one God—they utterly reject the second half and deny the prophethood of Muhammad. This is in direct contrast to Muslims, who have no difficulty in accepting Jesus as a prophet; indeed, they venerate him deeply and regard him as the immediate predecessor of Muhammad in a prophetic line that stretches back as far as Abraham. So, although Islam rejects aspects of Christian doctrine about Jesus—his crucifixion, his atonement, and his status as part of the Trinity—Muslims do not vilify Jesus either as a person or as a prophet. In his book *The Muslim Jesus*, Tarif Khalidi has shown very eloquently the deep love that generations of Muslims have had for Jesus. Many Christians, on the other hand, who believe in a faith that predates Islam, cannot bring themselves to recognize the mission of Muhammad who came *after* Jesus. So they denigrate Muhammad *as a person*. This they did throughout the Middle Ages, and they continue to do so, especially in today's highly charged political atmosphere.

An underlying problem for Christians in understanding the life of Muhammad is that his career does not resemble that of Jesus, whose self-confessed role as the "prince of peace" does not fit the exemplary model conduct embodied by Muhammad. Christians find it difficult to accept the concept of a "warrior prophet," such as Muhammad became in the final decade of his life. Yet both Jews and Christians are very familiar with the lifestyles of the Old Testament figures of Moses, Joshua, David, and others who had to engage in warfare against hostile, pagan enemies who threatened to destroy the religion of the One God. It is clear, moreover, that if Muhammad had not taken up arms against his pagan kinsmen, the Quraysh of Mecca, and against those who opposed him within Medina, both pagan Arabs and monotheistic Jews, these enemies would have destroyed him, his community, and the new religion of Islam.

Another issue that causes difficulties for Christians when viewing Muhammad arises from the fact that, unlike Jesus, who said firmly that his kingdom was not of this world, Muhammad engaged fully in worldly matters, and indeed he became the leader of a small theocratic state in Medina, the umma. One of the best-known and most respected books on the Prophet by a Western scholar is that by Montgomery Watt, who tackles this issue directly by giving his book the title *Muhammad, Prophet and Statesman*.

Such an explicit division of the Prophet's career into two halves, Mecca and Medina, reveals the difficulties that some non-Muslim scholars have experienced in understanding Muhammad's career. They find it hard to reconcile the Meccan chapters of the Qur'an, which speak in apocalyptic terms about the imminence of the Day of Judgment and the need to repent and turn to God, with the Medinan chapters, which contain detailed instructions about how to behave as Muslims in their daily life. The hadith reports of the Prophet reinforce the point that Muhammad was a brilliant administrator and legislator. So the transition from persecuted prophet to resourceful leader has proved hard to accept for some non-Muslims. How, they say, can a prophet in the grip of such powerful encounters with the Divine also possess the necessary acumen and practical wisdom to deal with legal problems and defend the community against external and internal threats? Muslims would respond by saying that just because Muhammad was faced with the day-to-day running of a new community in the most demanding circumstances, this did not mean that he or his followers ever forgot the potent message of the revelations that he had received in Mecca. Indeed, even as they heard the Prophet transmitting to them the continuing revelations which came from God in the Medinan period, the members of the umma would constantly remember and recite the Meccan chapters, for reassurance and encouragement on the path of God.

It should also be noted that in the Christian tradition Jesus is portrayed as celibate. Contrasts have therefore been made between him and Muhammad, who is presented in the hadith collections and the sira as enjoying human pleasures, including sensual ones. More specifically, non-Muslims have ridiculed Muhammad over the centuries for the number of wives he had. However, Solomon had seven hundred wives, as well as three hundred concubines (I Kings 11:3). Just as monogamy was not the practice in ancient Israel, so too in pre-Islamic Arabia: the historical context must always be taken into consideration. Muhammad is reported to have had many wives. He married his first wife, Khadija, when he was quite young and she was fifteen years older than he was. While she was alive he took no other wife. Thereafter, he married a number of women (the estimate varies from ten to twelve); five of them were the widows of Muslims who had been killed in the fighting against the Meccans. They could not have survived without tribal support; and it should not be forgotten that the Muslims who had come from Mecca with the Prophet at the time of the hijra (the Emigrants, or Muhajirun) had left everything they had behind and had broken off their links with their clans there. So the widows of such men had no protection or means of support without the marriage ties. Just as in medieval times, rulers and chieftains in late antiquity in the Middle East used marriage alliances for socio-political purposes. Four of Muhammad's marriages were part of political alliances made to consolidate the authority of Medina in Arabia. His favorite wife seems to have been 'A'isha, the spirited daughter of Muhammad's faithful companion, Abu Bakr, who became the first caliph of Islam after 632.

EVALUATING MUHAMMAD

It is exceptionally difficult for non-Muslims and Muslims alike to evaluate Muhammad. But nobody can deny his central importance for the faith and the community of Islam over the last fourteen centuries.

Non-Muslims have prejudices against him, pre-conceived notions of which they may not even be aware. Christians make comparisons between Jesus and Muhammad, preferring Jesus who opted for a path of peace and a clear division between this world and the next. Christians find it hard to accept the fact that Muhammad was not only bringing a new religion to the world but also establishing a community of Muslims so that the new faith, Islam, would survive and expand in a land deeply committed to idol-worship. Although a brilliant statesman and arbitrator, Muhammad, like Moses before him, sometimes had to fight battles and take hard decisions to protect his fledgling community. Like Moses again, he was obliged to lay down detailed and specific regulations about many facets of daily life and to solve practical problems as they arose.

Muslims too do not see Muhammad objectively. They have no criticisms of their Prophet. They love him. Their feelings toward him are molded by the deepest reverence for him. Many pious Muslims, whenever they mention Muhammad's name, follow it with the formula "Peace be upon him" and when they write about him they place the abbreviated form PBUH after his name. Just as is the case with the founders of other world religions, it is impossible to separate historical "truth" about Muhammad from pious legend. The biographical literature about him bears the stamp of very different approaches, from historicized memory and myth to doctrine and law. Muhammad's life has always been the focus of sacred history and pious Muslim tradition, but it is natural that all generations of Muslims have also interpreted the model of his conduct according to their own contemporary religious, cultural, and political situations. What Muhammad said and did forms part of the daily life of every Muslim in every age. Despite their great diversity of ethnicity and custom, Muslims across the globe believe that Muhammad was the last in a long line of monotheist prophets and that he brought to the world the final, complete, and perfected revelation from the One God.

There is no doubt that Muhammad was a charismatic leader in a multiplicity of ways. Had he not been so, his grief-stricken community could not have had the strength and will to carry on the work that he had begun, for he had shown the way forward. The achievements of the Prophet had been phenomenal. He had become a leader of men, a legislator, a judge, and a military commander. By the end of his life most of Arabia acknowledged the authority of Medina. He had been the vehicle for the revelation of a new monotheistic religion—Islam. He had made the revelations the basis of a small but dynamic theocratic community of believers, united in the new faith, which would shortly burgeon into a vast Muslim world empire. He had left behind the Qur'an, which remained embedded in the memory and the hearts of his devoted followers, and which, in oral and written form, was passed on to subsequent generations of Muslims. And, perhaps above all, through his powerful personality, he had inspired his followers to continue in the new path of God (*fi sabil Allah*) on which he had set them. In the complex religious environment of late antiquity in which new religions, sects, and cults came and went, it was the revelation of Islam that would endure and develop in due course into a world faith, the third of the religions of Abraham.

SELECTED READING

Brown, Jonathan A. C., *Muhammad. A Very Short Introduction*, Oxford: Oxford University Press, 2011

Cook, Michael, *Muhammad*, Oxford and New York: Oxford University Press, 1983

Hoyland, Robert G., *Arabia and the Arabs: From the Bronze Age to the Coming of Islam*, London and New York: Routledge, 2001

Lings, Martin, *Muhammad: His Life Based on the Earliest Sources*, New York: Inner Traditions International, 1983

Schimmel, Annemarie, *And Muhammad is His Messenger: The Veneration of the Prophet in Islamic Piety*, Chapel Hill, NC: University of North Carolina Press, 1985

3 THE QUR'AN

If We had sent this Qur'an down upon a mountain, you would have seen it humbled and split apart in its awe of God. QUR'AN 59:21[1]

On the first reading, the overwhelming feeling is of awe. SAHAR EL-NADI[2]

God has purposely strewn difficulties throughout the Holy Books He has Himself inspired in order that we may be stimulated to read and study them with greater attention and in order to exercise us in humility by the salutary recognition of the limited capacity of our intelligence. POPE PIUS XII[3]

This chapter investigates the central religious text of **Islam** in order to discover why it is that more than a billion and a half **Muslims**[4] cherish a profound love and respect for the **Qur'an** and see it as the principal guide to how they live their lives and how they can come closer to God. For Muslims the Qur'an is a perfect entity revealed by God to humanity in an unchanging

Understated splendor.
The richly illuminated *Fatiha*, the opening chapter from a pocket-sized Qur'an, copied on paper in highly legible cursive script by the celebrated calligrapher Ibn al-Bawwab, Baghdad, *c.* 1000–1. The comforting words of the *Fatiha* are as well known to Muslims as the Lord's Prayer is to Christians. Such books foster private devotion.

and unchangeable form. In the Qur'an God tells human beings how they come to be on earth, how to look after His creation, and how they should behave toward each other. Such messages apply to all ages and to all conditions of men and women. And indeed the Qur'an has been the foundation for all aspects of Islam as it developed into a world religion—faith, ritual, law, theology, and mysticism. Given the supreme importance of the Qur'an in every discussion of Islam, it will be referred to in all the chapters of this book; the present discussion will concentrate on matters to do with the text itself.

The very first chapter of the Qur'an, appropriately called the *Fatiha* (the Opening), goes some way to encapsulate the essence of the Qur'an and its significance for Muslims in their daily life. Here, in measured simple language, Muslims are invited to praise God for His mercy and His greatness. They are warned to avoid occasions of sin and to cling to the right path. The *Fatiha* is the Qur'an in miniature, the essence of Islamic belief. It is a necessary part of all Muslim worship, and pious Muslims recite it before they begin on a journey. It is breathed into the ear of a baby at birth and into the ear of anyone at the point of death:

> Praise belongs to God, Lord of the Worlds,
> the Lord of Mercy, the Giver of Mercy,
> Master of the Day of Judgement.
> It is You we worship; it is You we ask for help.
> Guide us to the straight path:
> The path of those You have blessed, those who incur no anger and who
> have not gone astray.

THE NATURE AND STRUCTURE OF THE QUR'AN

The word Qur'an means "recitation" or "reading." Muslims refer to it as the Noble Qur'an (*al-Qur'an al-karim*) and they regard it as unique and miraculous. There has been nothing like it before or since. Anyone who tries to imitate it finds that task impossible; as God says: "If you have doubts about the revelation We have sent down to Our servant, then produce a single sura like it" (2:23). There is no surviving written Arabic, apart from graffiti and a few inscriptions, before the Qur'an was written down in its canonical form, which according to Muslim tradition was a couple of decades or so after the death of **Muhammad** in 632 CE. In particular, no document containing an extended passage of written poetry or prose predating Islam has yet been found. Linguistically, therefore, the Qur'an is nothing short of phenomenal. It is not a book of logic, nor is it a rational treatise. It is a spiritual work containing the revelations sent down from God to Muhammad over a period of about twenty-three years, from around 610 until just before his death. Sometimes it takes the form of an evolving revelation, inconsistent, ambiguous, or mysterious. On other occasions it is unequivocally clear in its message.

Unlike the Bible, which is long and contains books by many different authors, the Qur'an is short and is believed by pious Muslims to have been composed by a single author—God Himself. That marks a very significant difference. Muslims also believe that the Qur'anic text was revealed orally to Muhammad from God through the Angel **Gabriel**. The Qur'an claims that it confirms and completes the Jewish Torah and the Christian Gospel. Moreover, it is the final revelation that subsumes and supersedes these two earlier monotheistic revelations.

The Qur'an is divided into thirty sections, which make it easier to recite during **Ramadan**, the month of fasting, when the whole book is read out aloud. It is further divided into 114 chapters (*suras*). These—apart from the first chapter, the Fatiha, which is a short prayer—are ordered roughly according to descending order of size. In fact, the suras are sometimes of strikingly different length; some consist of only a few lines, whilst Chapter 2, the longest chapter of all, contains 286 verses. As Islamic scholar Carl Ernst rightly says, "Nobody really knows how or why the fixed arrangement of suras took place in this way."[5] Within the sura, the individual verses (*ayas*) are organized by rhyme schemes more than by the topics about which they speak. Sometimes, the rhyme uses formulaic phrases such as "God is all-knowing, all-wise." Each chapter has a name, such as "The Bee," "The Cow," "The Spider," "The Resurrection," and "The Victory." The names were not part of the original chapters but they are often based on an important reference in the text. It is common practice amongst Muslims to call each chapter by its name rather than its number.

Muslims believe that the present arrangement of the Qur'an is exactly the order that God wishes it to be. The order of the chapters is not precisely chronological, although they are arranged in two main groups—those chapters that are believed to have been revealed to Muhammad in **Mecca**, when he was beginning to receive divine revelations from around 610, and those that came to him later in **Medina** after his *hijra* (emigration) there in 622. Although it would be simplistic to classify the suras of the Qur'an and the individual

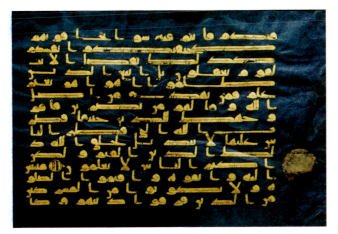

A religion of the book.
Leaf from the "Blue Qur'an," parchment dyed with indigo, 9th–10th century. Letters expand or contract dramatically, following mysterious rhythms and slowing the reading process: a fitting reflection of the awesome enigmas of the sacred text. Qur'ans dyed salmon pink, saffron, and lemon yellow are also known, a colorful tradition possibly deriving from Byzantine royal-purple codices.

groups of verses within them too firmly into the two broad categories of a Meccan or a Medinan origin, certain generalizations can be made. Modern scholars have identified four periods in the revelation to Muhammad: the first three are Meccan, during the years 610–22. In the first Meccan period, the chapters preach the message of the One God and the pressing need to turn to Him before the coming of the **Day of Judgment**. In the second Meccan period the themes are those of God's creation, Heaven and Hell, and the dire punishments that await those who do not heed God's prophets. The third Meccan period contains what might be classified as longer "transitional" chapters or verses, which correspond roughly to the time when the Prophet started preaching publicly until the moment of his hijra to Medina. These sections take the form of sermons, and reflect the teachings given by the prophets in the stories of old. As for the fourth period of revelation— the chapters revealed in Medina from 622 to 632—they focus a great deal on social conduct and legislation, as the Prophet needed guidance in his new responsibilities as the leader of the infant Muslim community. The Medinan chapters also highlight a gradual deterioration in the relationship between the Muslims and Christians, and above all the Jews of Medina. The Medinan chapters are the longest, and come first in the book; the Meccan chapters, which are shorter, are found toward the end.

The first revelation in the Qur'an is believed to be the beginning of Chapter 96. This recounts how in middle age the Prophet Muhammad began to seclude himself for periods of meditation in the cave called Hira outside Mecca (see Chapter 2, p. 31). On one such occasion, the Angel Gabriel appeared to him with the first revelation from God:

> Recite! In the name of your Lord who created:
> He created man from a clot.[6]
> Read! Your Lord is the Most Bountiful One
> who taught by the pen,
> who taught man what he did not know. (96:1–5)

The chapter then warns of the dangers of Hell if man does not repent, prostrate himself, and draw near to God.

The very last revelation of the Qur'an (5:3) is generally thought to be God's triumphant affirmation of Muhammad's prophethood, shortly before his death in June 632: "Today I have perfected your religion for you, completed My blessing upon you, and chosen as your religion Islam." It was in this way that the religion that the Prophet had established received its name.[7]

THE LANGUAGE OF THE QUR'AN

The Qur'an contains many different kinds of language. One of its most famous translators, the British scholar Arthur Arberry, writes that the Qur'an is "neither prose nor poetry, but a unique fusion of both."[8] Some of the Qur'an is written in beautiful rhyming prose in which the lines reveal patterns of internal alliteration and assonance. The sounds of the first two verses of Chapter 96—the very beginning of the revelation that came to Muhammad— are rendered all the more solemn in Arabic by the way in which the final words contain similar sounds:

> Recite! In the name of your Lord who created (*khalaqa*):
> He created man from a clot (*'alaqin*).
> Read! Your Lord is the Most Bountiful One (*alakramu*)
> who taught by the pen (*bi'l-qalami*)…

The impact of reading aloud lines like the first two verses of both Chapter 99 (The Earthquake) and Chapter 81 (The Shrouding in Darkness), which portray the dreadful, cataclysmic coming of the Day of Judgment, is very powerful indeed:

> When the earth is shaken violently (*zulzilat*) in its quaking (*zilzālahā*)
> When the earth throws out its burdens (*athqālahā*)…(99:1–2)

> When the sun is shrouded in darkness (*kuwirrat*)
> When the stars lose their light (*inkadarat*)…(81:1–2)

Antiquity transfigured. Great Mosque, Damascus, Syria, mosaic, before 715. Drawing on Roman rather than Byzantine models depicting architecture and landscape, the Umayyad caliph's craftsmen imparted paradisal meanings to these themes, in tune with Qur'anic descriptions of the mighty trees, gorgeous palaces, and purling streams awaiting the blessed in the hereafter.

The chapters are divided into groups of verses of varying lengths and different rhythms to suit the subject matter, for example explosive ecstatic statements about the **Last Day**; a narrative style, such as that used in the story of Joseph; and legal injunctions couched in the more formal language of treaties and other official documents.

The earliest chapters of the Qur'an read almost like oracles, with striking opening verses and short, sharp warnings issued both to Muhammad and to his listeners. These chapters are poetic and dynamic, grabbing the listener by the throat with their intensity. They focus on the beauty of creation, which is a sign of God's benevolence. However, mankind has sinned and there is an urgent need for repentance, for the Day of Judgment is imminent. Hell and Heaven are powerfully described; there is a stark contrast between the fire of Hell, to which the wicked will be dragged by the forelock, and the delights of Paradise, which is a garden where rivers flow. The Meccan chapters toward the end of the Qur'an likewise contain extraordinary resonances and imagery that linger in the memory, especially when they are recited. Take the example of Chapter 82, verses 1–5, which describe the cataclysmic prelude to the Day of Judgment, evoking the image of an apocalyptic tsunami:

> When the sky is torn apart,
> when the stars are scattered,
> when the seas burst forth,
> when graves turn inside out:
> each soul will know what it has done and what it has left undone.

These lines carry an even more powerful charge in the resonant rhyming prose of the original Arabic. None of the Meccan chapters is long, and some comprise only a few verses. Reading them aloud, even in translation, it is not difficult to understand why they had such an explosive effect on their hearers.[9]

The Medinan chapters are like the calm after the storm. They are usually longer and are written in a more straightforward style than those revealed in Mecca. They tell Muslims how to conduct themselves in every aspect of their daily lives—how to worship God, how to behave toward other Muslims as well as to non-Muslims—and they give detailed instructions on countless other aspects of Islam, whether to do with worship, such as ritual purity, prayer, or pilgrimage, or with daily life. The legal flavor of these chapters gives them many points of contact with the law of **Moses** enshrined in the Old Testament books from Exodus to Deuteronomy, and especially Leviticus, for example the emphasis on ritual purity. Like Judaism, Islam has rightly been called a religion of the law; thanks to the law, the Muslim can lead a righteous life.

Other verses of the Qur'an bear a much more complex message; they invite further contemplation, couched as they are in richly symbolic words. A famous example is the lengthy, mysterious, so-called "Light Verse" (24:35) so beloved of the **Sufis** (see Chapter 8, p. 193):

> God is the Light of the heavens and earth.
> His Light is like this: there is a niche, and in it a lamp,
> the lamp inside a glass, a glass like a glittering star,
> fuelled from a blessed olive tree from neither east
>   nor west,
> whose oil almost gives light even when no fire touches it—
> light upon light—God guides whosoever He will to
>   his Light.

A metaphor of divine light. Glass mosque lamp, Syria, c. 1330. Made for a Mamluk court cup-bearer; note his heraldic cup at the top left and right. Qur'anic inscriptions on the lamp shine in the gloom and underline the religious significance of such objects.

Another verse (31:27) is deeply suggestive of the never-ending power and pro-fusion of God's wisdom; it can also be taken as a symbol of the multiplicity of possible interpretations that the Qur'anic text offers to those who meditate upon it:

> If all the trees on earth were pens and all the seas,
> with seven more seas besides, were ink,
> still God's words would not run out:
> God is almighty and all-wise.

MAJOR THEMES OF THE QUR'AN

The Qur'an contains many themes familiar to the other two **Abrahamic** religions, Judaism and Christianity. It stands firmly within that tradition. But there are differences, as well as clear similarities. Three key themes stand out: the One God, God the creator, and the Day of Judgment.

THE ONE GOD

The Qur'an constantly declares that God is One. He cannot have partners. He is not one of a pantheon of gods nor is He one of three gods. This uncompromising emphasis on God's oneness (**tawhid**) is the central message of the Qur'an. That is why it contains such strong attacks on the **polytheism** of seventh-century Arabia, and especially Mecca, and also on the Christian doctrine of the Trinity.

Sometimes God is referred to by the pronouns "I," "We," or "He." He also has ninety-nine "Beautiful Names" (20:7–8) that allude to His attributes. His compassion toward humanity is shown in the two names—*al-Rahman* (the Merciful) and *al-Rahim* (the Compassionate)—that occur in the pronounce-ment "In the name of God the Merciful, the Compassionate," which comes at the beginning of every chapter of the Qur'an, except Chapter 9.

GOD THE CREATOR

The Qur'an extols in matchless language the wonders of God's creation, embracing the heavens and the earth, the planets, the stars, the vast seas, and the creatures that crawl. Chapter 55, entitled "Al-Rahman" (The Merciful), is a symphony of praise to God for the wonders of His creation, composed with a recurring refrain, addressed both to human beings and to the spiritual beings created by God and known as the jinn: "Which, then, of your Lord's blessings do you both deny?"[10] Perhaps the most memorable part of this remarkable chapter are verses 26–27:

> Everyone on earth perishes;
> all that remains is the Face of your Lord,
> full of majesty, bestowing honour.

All created beings worship their Creator (16:49); indeed, God created the angels, the jinn, and human beings. The Qur'an states that He made the jinn from "the fire of scorching wind" (15:27) and human beings from "dried clay formed from dark mud" (15:28).

God's culminating achievement in creation is humanity. Human beings are superior to all spirits and angels because God breathed into man from His own breath (38:73). He ordered even the angels to prostrate themselves before Adam, whom he placed as custodian over the earth. Satan refused to prostrate himself before "a mortal," so he was cast out from God's presence and cursed until the Day of Judgment (33:35). Satan (called *Iblis* or *shaytan* in Arabic) roams the earth as a tempter of human beings, whispering to them to disobey God. God gives human beings responsibility for looking after the earth because they have the capacity to think. Human beings are good by nature and are changed in a negative way by their environment. Unlike in the Christian New Testament, there is in the Qur'an no concept of original sin nor of redemption from it; as John Esposito puts it: "There is no theological need for the all-atoning sacrifice of Jesus through his crucifixion and resurrection."[11] Each human being on the Day of Judgment is responsible before God for his or her own actions. Salvation lies simply and totally in the act of surrendering oneself to God (which is the meaning of "Muslim").

God is omniscient and omnipresent. He knows not only where a person lives and what he or she has done, but also what is in the inmost heart of each individual person: "God knows whenever any of you move, and whenever any of you stay still" (47:19). His wrath against those who disbelieve is fierce and devastating: "God will not forgive those who disbelieve, who turn (others) away from God's path, and who then die as disbelievers" (47:34). And there is ample testimony in the Qur'an for the dreadful punishment that God has meted out to those communities in the past who have disobeyed His command to turn and submit to Him. The Qur'an reminds its listeners of the fate that befell the disobedient Arab tribe of Thamud, who did not heed the words of God's prophet Salih whom He sent to warn them (91:14-15):

> Their Lord destroyed them for their crime and levelled them.
> He did not hesitate to punish them.

God is thus implacable in visiting His dreadful punishment on those who disbelieve.

THE DAY OF JUDGMENT

The Qur'an uses a number of different terms for the Day of Judgment: these include the Hour, the Day of Reckoning, the Last Day, the Day of Decision, the Day of Resurrection, and the Day of Assembling. On the Day of Judgment the dead will be removed from their graves: "When graves turn inside out, each soul will know what it has done and what it has left undone" (82:1–5). All humanity will be gathered together on that day: "Our Lord, You will gather all people on the Day of which there is no doubt" (3:8–9). The deeds of each human being will be weighed in the balance. Those whose good deeds outweigh their bad ones will be placed on God's right side, and will then be rewarded by entering Paradise with all its delights. Those whose bad deeds prevail will be on God's left side and then be dragged into the fire of Hell.

When will this Day come? Qur'anic time is not chronological or linear. Its message is constantly focused on the end time, and the imminence of God's judgment is always looming. It may strike at any time He wills:

> All that is hidden from view in the heavens and earth belongs to God.
> The coming of the Hour of Judgement is like the blink of an eye, or even quicker:
> God has power over everything. (16:77)

This powerful message evokes awe and dread in the human heart and warns of the need to repent and turn to God, not at some comfortable time in the distant future, but right now—this very minute. Salvation for Muslims on the Last Day will come to those who seek God's forgiveness, keep to the Straight Path (42:53), and obey God's law, adhering to what is lawful and avoiding what is forbidden.

What will the Day of Judgment be like? The many verses that speak of this awesome event are terrifying in their rhetorical impact and apocalyptic imagery. Chapter 75, aptly given the title "The Resurrection" (*Al-qiyama*), speaks of the awesome inevitability of God's judgment:

> So, when will this Day of Resurrection be?
> When eyes are dazzled and the moon eclipsed,
> when the sun and the moon are brought together,
> on that Day man will say, "Where can I escape?" (75:6–11)

The concepts of Heaven and Hell are drawn in sharply contrasting imagery in the Qur'an. This is well illustrated in Chapter 47. In this chapter, God promises that He will look after those who believe and perform righteous acts. He will surely let them enter Paradise. For those who disbelieve, perdition awaits (47:4–6). But those who believe will be allowed to enter gardens beneath which rivers flow (47:12). The believers in Paradise will drink from rivers of pure-tasting water, milk, wine, and purest honey. As for those condemned for ever to the Fire, they will be given boiling water to drink that will rip their bowels to pieces (47:15). Chapter 56, ominously called "The Coming (Calamitous) Event" (*Al-wāqi'a*), is devoted to an unforgettable description of the Last Day; the final verses (88–94) speak of a dying person who "will have rest, ease, and a Garden of Bliss; if he is one of those on the Right, [he will hear], 'Peace be on you,' from his companions on the Right; but if he is one of those who denied the truth and went astray, he will be welcomed with scalding water. He will burn in Hell."

PROPHETS AND PROPHECY

Non-Muslim scholars of Islam, who are often influenced by the Judaeo-Christian tradition, see the Qur'an within a chronological framework. The Qur'an is the third in the line of monotheistic revelations, coming as it does after the Old and New Testaments. This viewpoint inevitably gives rise to comparisons being made between Islam and its two monotheistic predecessors, especially in the sphere of the Qur'anic stories of those prophets[12] who are also mentioned in the Bible. Indeed, Jews and Christians have often criticized the Islamic versions of familiar Biblical stories, alleging that the Qur'an has "got them wrong." Such an approach is clearly inappropriate in the light of the rich and diverse heritage of stories and legends common to all three Abrahamic faiths, a heritage that is much fuller than the Biblical accounts. Such material is called *Isra'iliyyat*—narratives that came from Jewish and Christian traditions as well as ancient Middle Eastern folklore known right across the area. It is worth remembering that the history of

Judaism and Christianity is much less linear than the Bible, as it is now consti-
tuted, would have us believe.

The Qur'an is a rich repository of material about the prophets who are
mentioned in the Old Testament, but their "stories" are sometimes presented
differently in the Qur'an from the way in which they are told in the Bible.
Many of the details in the Qur'anic narratives, however, are found in the Jewish
tradition; indeed, the Midrash (especially the Haggada) and the Talmud—
written teachings and commentaries sacred to the Jews—are treasuries of
such information. In comparable fashion, the Qur'anic perspectives on key
Christian figures, such as John the Baptist, **Mary**, and **Jesus**, trace their origins
back not only to the Gospels of Matthew, Mark, and Luke, but also to the
Apocryphal Gospels—the ones that did not make it into the New Testament—
as well as to the dogmas of mystical **Gnostic** sects of the Near East.

All prophets bring the same message of the need to repent and turn to
the One God; if not, his terrible punishment will be visited on them in the
afterlife. Having listed the names of **Abraham**, **Ishmael**, Isaac, Jacob, Moses,
and Jesus, God states in the Qur'an: "We make no distinction between any of
them" (2:136; 4:150). In addition to Muhammad, the Qur'an mentions twenty-
eight prophets by name. Many of them are known to Jews and Christians,
as their stories are told in the Bible. They include Abraham, Ishmael, Isaac,
Jacob, Moses, Job, Jonah, Aaron, Solomon, David, and others. Apart from

A Biblical story in Chinese dress. Rashid al-Din, *World History*, Tabriz, Iran, 1314. Following
the Judaeo-Christian tradition, some images in this manuscript highlight God's miraculous
intervention to rescue His chosen ones. Here, Far Eastern elements appear; for example the great
fish has become a languid Chinese carp, and the conventions for water recall Chinese painting.

the extended narratives given to Joseph, Moses, and Jesus, the prophets are mentioned in passing, in a way that implies an easy familiarity with these personages. Allusions to them often begin with phrases such as "Do you remember the story of Moses?" or "Do you recall what happened to Noah?" These tales are so familiar that they do not need retelling. Instead, they are used to point a moral and to serve as a warning. One sees here how firmly the Qur'an is the heir to earlier monotheistic, and especially Judaic, traditions. The Qur'an also mentions the stories of other religious figures largely unknown outside the Middle East—monotheistic Arab prophets, such as Luqman, Salih, and Hud, who lived and preached in Arabia before Islam; they spoke about God to wicked tribes who had strayed from the path of true monotheism. All these peoples rejected God's message brought by the prophets sent by God, and so He punished them. The Qur'an depicts prophets as warners whose words go unheeded and ignored; Chapter 43 declares: "We have sent many a prophet to earlier people and they mocked every one of them" (43:6–7).

Abraham is alluded to in many Qur'anic passages and is singled out as being especially significant. He is the founder of the **Ka'ba** shrine in Mecca, the place where he used to pray with his son Ishmael (2:125–7). It is "the religion of Abraham, the upright" that Muhammad has embraced (2:136). Islam restores pristine Abrahamic monotheism. Indeed, Abraham is the model example of a figure known in the Qur'an as a *hanif*—someone who has attained true monotheism: he says to his people: "I have turned my face as a true believer (hanif) towards Him who created the heavens and the earth. I am not one of the polytheists" (6:79). A hanif is neither a Jew, nor a Christian, nor a polytheist. And it is in the nature of all human beings at birth to embrace this pure monotheism, undistorted by Jewish, Christian, or polytheistic interpretations of the true faith.[13]

JOSEPH

A whole chapter of the Qur'an—Chapter 12—is devoted to the story of Joseph, and it is named after him. It is the only chapter in the Qur'an that is exclusively about one topic, and where a proper, continuous story is told, although much of Chapter 19 is devoted to the Virgin Mary (see p. 73). The story of Joseph as narrated in Chapter 12 is different from the Old Testament story in the Bible (Genesis 42) in some respects—for example, it is not a continuous narrative full of circumstantial detail—but it is very similar in others. Its technique is to highlight certain aspects of the story. Joseph is put into a pit by his jealous brothers and taken away by a passing caravan. Joseph is

Temptation overcome.
*Yusuf (Joseph) escapes
Zulaykha (Potiphar's
wife),* painting signed by
Bihzad, illustrating the
Bustan of the poet Sa'di,
Herat, 1488. This reworks
the Genesis account in
mystical terms, evoking
a ladder (*mi'raj*) to
heaven. Zulaykha builds
a palace and leads Yusuf
through seven successive
rooms adorned with erotic
paintings, vainly trying to
seduce him. Green and
red symbolize holiness
and passion respectively.

bought in an unnamed country by an unnamed ruler (named in the Bible as
Potiphar) who tells his wife (Zulaykha) to look after Joseph honorably. She
lusts after him and attempts to seduce him. Joseph tries to escape her advances
and while they both race to the door, she tears his shirt from behind. Standing
at the door is her husband. His wife tries to blame Joseph but because his shirt
is torn from behind it is clear that she is lying. Her husband tells her to ask
forgiveness for her sin, saying, "Lo! This is the guile of you women."[14] Later,
the ladies of the city gossip about the ruler's wife, so she invites them to
a feast. She sits them on a couch and gives them each a knife (presumably to
cut their fruit with)—tradition identifies the fruit as oranges. She then calls on
Joseph to show himself; at this point the Qur'anic text says (12:31):

> When the women saw him, they were stunned by his beauty,
> and they cut their hands, exclaiming,
> "Great God! He cannot be mortal! He must be a precious angel!"

Still later, in prison, Joseph interprets dreams, as in the Biblical account. He is
portrayed as a virtuous person following the religion of his fathers, Abraham,
Isaac, and Jacob. His story provides a lesson of faith and piety rewarded. In
many ways Joseph is pictured as the perfect example of a God-fearing man.

MOSES

Moses receives more attention in the Qur'an than any other pre-Islamic religious figure.[15] He does not have a chapter devoted to him, nor is there a single continuous narrative about him, but he is mentioned 136 times in different places, often in great detail. Most of the references to Moses are found in the Medinan chapters, when Muhammad is in contact with the Jews there. The allusions to Moses in the Qur'an refer to familiar stories in the Biblical Old Testament, though they sometimes have different details. In the Qur'an the tribulations endured by Moses and the way in which he is helped by God in his prophetic mission foreshadow the setbacks in Muhammad's own career.

As a baby, Moses is thrown into the sea in a box (instead of being put in a basket in the bulrushes, as the Bible story goes). He is found by Pharaoh's wife, (not by his daughter, as in the Bible story), who then brings him up (26:18). Moses' sister keeps a watchful eye on the baby and arranges for her mother to feed him herself (26:18). Later, Moses goes to Pharaoh with his prophetic message but he is accused of "blatant sorcery" (10:76), as Muhammad was to be later; when asked by Pharaoh to give him "signs," Moses turns his rod into a serpent and he makes his hand become white. God liberates Moses and the Children of Israel from Pharaoh and brings them safely across the Red Sea, drowning Pharaoh and his army (7:136–37 and 10:90). Whilst wandering in the wilderness, Moses spends forty days alone. During his absence his people start to worship a golden calf and God reproaches them for this idolatry: "We appointed forty nights for Moses [on Mount Sinai] and then, while he was away, you took to worshipping the calf—a terrible wrong. Even then We forgave you" (2:51–52 and 7:148). More miracles are revealed by God to Moses in the desert: God sends down manna and quails to eat (2:57; see also Exodus, Chapter 16)[16] and, when Moses asks for water and God tells him to strike the rock with his rod, twelve springs of water spurt forth (2:60).

Such stories as these are presented to Muhammad as reassurance to him; just as God looked after His prophet Moses and His people, He will surely do likewise for Muhammad. Above all, Moses is presented as a monotheist. Like Muhammad, God has given Moses "the Scripture, and the means to distinguish [right and wrong]" (2:53).

MARY, THE MOTHER OF JESUS

Mary[17] is mentioned in the Qur'an whenever Jesus is mentioned, since he is always called "Isa b. Maryam" (Jesus son of Mary).[18] Amongst the epithets given to Mary is the title *Al-'adhrā* (the Virgin). She is also called the one obedient to God, an honoured servant of God, and a strict upholder of the truth. She is the most important female exemplar in the Qur'an and the only woman mentioned in it by name (see Chapter 10, p. 255).

Three key episodes in the life of Mary are narrated in detail in the Qur'an— her own birth and upbringing, the Annunciation, and the Nativity of Jesus. Whilst Mary is still unborn, her mother dedicates her to God, saying: "Lord, I have dedicated what is growing in my womb entirely to You; so accept this from me" (3:35). Later, when the child is born, her mother says to God: "My Lord! I have given birth to a girl...I name her Mary" (3:36). Chapter 3 then relates that God received the child with gracious favor and caused her to grow up in a good manner. She is put in the care of Zachariah in the Temple at Jerusalem. He is amazed that while she is in the Temple she is always supplied directly with food from God (3:37).

Chapter 19 of the Qur'an is called "Sūrat Maryam" (the Chapter of Mary). It contains an account of the Annunciation that is quite familiar to Christians. Mary withdraws from her people to "an eastern place" where she is visited by "God's spirit" in the guise of a well-proportioned man.[19] He tells her that he is only a messenger come from God to give her "a boy most pure." Mary asks: "How can I have a son when no man has touched me? I have not been unchaste" (19:20). The messenger, never named as Gabriel, reassures Mary, saying that such a matter is easy for God. This is the Qur'an's version of the doctrine of the Virgin Birth.

The story of Jesus' nativity in the Qur'an, however, is different from the one in the New Testament Gospels. Mary conceives a son, and when her time of confinement approaches, she withdraws to a remote place where the pangs of childbirth drive her to the trunk of the palm tree.[20] Overwhelmed by her pain she cries out, "I wish I had died and been forgotten long before all this!" (19:23). Then the baby Jesus speaks to her, saying that she should not be sad; he points to a stream that God has placed below her, and tells her to shake the palm tree, and dates will fall upon her. Thus she is miraculously provided by God with food and water. Mary then returns to her people carrying the child. They reproach her for having committed "a monstrous thing." Mary then points to the child, who begins to speak, saying: "I am a servant of God. He has granted me the Scripture and made me a prophet;...Peace was on me the day I was born, and will be on me the day I die and the day I am raised to life again" (19:30, 33).

This is the sum total of what the Qur'an says about Mary. It is clear, moreover, from the allusive way in which Mary's story is told, that those listening

An Oriental Annunciation. Al-Biruni, *Chronology of Ancient Nations*, Tabriz, Iran (?), 1307. The apocryphal Gospel of James describes Mary receiving the angel's message while spinning purple wool for the Temple curtain—a reference to Jesus' death. Here she sits under an Islamic arch with a pseudo-Kufic inscription. Buddhist elements include the facial types, her cross-legged pose, and Gabriel's flame halo and fluttering sash.

to Muhammad reciting the Qur'an to them knew the story already. There is no lengthy narrative about Mary; just the essentials are told to present her as a wondrous person, and thus fit to be the mother of Jesus. Clearly there are some similarities with the accounts of the Annunciation and the Nativity found in the Gospels of the New Testament; above all, the Qur'an confirms the Virgin Birth. Mary is portrayed as an exceptional woman, virtuous and pure; she is the chosen one of God. But there is nothing here about the stable in Bethlehem, the coming of the shepherds, nor the adoration of the Magi; and Joseph the carpenter is never mentioned.

JESUS

Like Adam, Jesus is given no human father in the Qur'an; he is named as Jesus son of Mary. He is seen as the last prophet before Muhammad and he is given the honorary title of Messiah (al-Masih).[21] He comes "with clear proofs" (43:63) from God but people laugh at him. In the Qur'an Jesus confirms what was revealed before him, namely the Torah (the Book of Moses), and he brought the Gospel: "We gave him the Gospel with guidance, light, and confirmation of the Torah already revealed" (5:46). Jesus also looks forward to another messenger who will come after him:

"Jesus, son of Mary, said, 'Children of Israel, I am sent to you by God, confirming the Torah that came before me and bringing good news of a messenger to follow me whose name will be Ahmad'" (61:6). Since the name Ahmad means "the One who is praised" and comes from the same Arabic root as Muhammad, this allusion is seen by Muslims as referring to the Prophet Muhammad.

As already discussed, Jesus is closely linked to Mary in the Qur'an. Together they are seen as a miraculous sign from God, a model for all to follow, a portent (23:50) and a token for all peoples (21:91). Jesus performs miracles: the angel tells Mary that Jesus will shape a bird from clay and blow life into it;[22] he will heal the blind and the leper, and raise the dead to life again (3:49 and 5:110).

Jesus is also called "a Word from God (*kalima min Allah*)": "The angels said, 'Mary, God gives you news of a Word from Him, whose name will be the Messiah, Jesus, son of Mary'" (3:45). One Muslim interpretation of this verse argues that Jesus is called "a Word from God" "because it was God's command that brought him into being, rather than the intervention of a human father."[23] Given the echo here, however, of the New Testament's use of the phrase "the Word of God" (*logos*) in the first chapter of St John's Gospel, it may be possible to detect a Christian influence here.[24]

Despite the deep reverence in which Jesus is held in the Qur'an, certain core doctrines that are applied to him by Christians are explicitly denied. Jesus is emphatically not the Son of God, nor is he a part of the Holy Trinity:

> The Messiah, Jesus, son of Mary, was nothing more than a messenger
> of God, His word, directed to Mary, a spirit from Him.
> So believe in God and His messengers and do not say "Three"
> God is only one God...God is only one God, He is far above having
> a son. (4:171)

The Qur'an goes even further than this, as Jesus is described as refuting the doctrine of the Trinity: "When God says, 'Jesus, son of Mary, did you say to people, "Take me and my mother as two gods alongside God"?' he will say, 'May You be exalted! I would never say what I had no right to say—if I had said such a thing You would have known it'" (5:116).

The meaning of one Qur'anic verse (4:157), which denies the crucifixion of Jesus, has created considerable debate amongst non-Muslim scholars and some Muslim ones. The verse is as follows:

> They [the Jews] did not kill him, nor did they crucify him,
> though it was made to appear like that to them.

According to the generally accepted Muslim interpretation of this verse, Jesus was not killed. As he was a prophet, someone other than Jesus was crucified,[25] but the Qur'an goes on to say that Jesus was taken into heaven by God, as the following verse emphasizes: "God raised him up to Himself" (4:158).[26] In subsequent Muslim religious tradition there were a number of differing versions about Jesus' crucifixion in what are known as "substitution legends." In one version Judas (Iscariot) was crucified in Jesus' place.

To sum up, it is clear that the Qur'an, despite its many similarities with the Gospels, depicts an alternative Jesus in a number of crucial doctrinal ways.

MUHAMMAD

The Qur'an is intimately related to the sequence of events in Muhammad's life, but it is not possible to chart a biography of him based on the evidence from that source alone (see Chapter 2). Muhammad is seen as not just one in a long line of prophets but also "the **Seal of the Prophets**" (33:40), in other words, the last one. He is especially addressed and praised by God: as a witness, a bringer of good tidings, a warner, and "as a light-giving lamp" (33:45–46).

The Qur'an comforts Muhammad and reassures him in his moments of self-doubt and persecution that God is with him and that he is indeed a noble messenger (81:19–22). He is presented as a mere mortal, although certain miraculous events are associated with him in the Qur'an, such as his experience outside time—his Night Journey from Mecca to Jerusalem and thence to the seven heavens into God's presence, an occasion that is mentioned in the first verse of Chapter 17. The Qur'an also refers to a number of people close to the Prophet, such as his adopted son Zayd (33:37) and his wives (33:50), and to events that occurred in his lifetime, such as the victory of the Persian army over the **Byzantine** army in 615 or 616 (33:2–3).

RECITING AND READING THE QUR'AN

The society into which Muhammad was born had long-established oral traditions of poetry and storytelling based on remembering the glorious deeds of the ancestors and declaiming these exploits to an appreciative and critical audience. It was natural, therefore, that the chapters of the Qur'an were recited aloud before they were written down. Indeed, it is not surprising that the Qur'an is believed to have been declaimed aloud during the Prophet's lifetime. There is internal evidence of this within the Qur'an itself, since God commands Muhammad to say and recite His revelation on frequent occasions, for example at the beginning of Chapter 112: "Say: He is God, the One," and in the opening verses of Chapter 96, the earliest chapter believed to have been revealed to the Prophet: "Recite! In the name of your Lord who created: He created man from a clot." The nature of the very first revelation, transmitted to him through the angel Gabriel, is alluded to in Chapter 53:4–10:

> He [Gabriel] stood on the highest horizon
> and then approached—coming down
> until he was two bow-lengths away or even closer—
> and revealed to God's servant what He revealed.

On this occasion Muhammad's experience with God was both aural and visual.

RECITATION

Muslim sources often speak with great emotion about the impact on faithful believers of listening to the reciting of the Qur'an. The Qur'an itself records the powerful effect that recitation creates: "When they listen to what has been sent down to the Messenger, you will see their eyes overflowing with tears" (5:83). A number of traditions (*hadith*) record the beauty of the sound of the holy text being recited by Muhammad himself; when one listener heard the Prophet reciting Chapter 95 of the Qur'an, he said, "I have never heard anyone reciting it in a more beautiful voice than his."[27]

The recitation of the Qur'an is a skill highly valued in Muslim societies, and one said to bring both spiritual and material rewards. It has always been regarded as the most authoritative method of transmitting holy writ. It can move listeners to shiver, tremble, and weep, and it has an indisputably melodic dimension, deriving in part from the strong musical pulse. Accomplished reciters, male or female, child or adult, are trained to follow formal guidelines (*tajwid*), which cover such elements as speed, emphases, pauses, stops, rhythm, sound, pronunciation, and the need for ritual purity and utter concentration. Recitation of the Qur'an is part and parcel of Islamic worship, practice, and education—and, of course, piety, for example during Ramadan and the pilgrimage. Egypt and Indonesia are especially renowned for their reciters. Not surprisingly, Qur'anic recitation has proved a powerful instrument in revitalizing the faith.

Twenty-nine chapters of the Qur'an begin with individual letters of the Arabic alphabet, and whenever the Qur'an is recited aloud they are always included as an integral part of the text. Some chapters begin with a single letter; for example, Chapter 68 has the letter "n" (*nun*). Chapters 19 and 42 have a row of five such letters. There are many interpretations and theories about these letters. Some say they are just the scribe's initials; others believe that they possess mystical significance. But the meanings and purpose of these mysterious letters remain unknown to both Muslim and non-Muslim scholars.

Ordinary Muslims through the ages have been accustomed to learning the Qur'an by heart and reading it aloud. A person who has memorized the whole of the Qur'an, known as a *hafiz*, is much respected, and their number may well run into the hundreds of thousands. Teaching the Qur'an in prison in Saudi Arabia is an old tradition; after the passing of two decrees (1987 and 1990), prisoners who have learned the entire Qur'an, or parts of it, by heart can receive a remission in their sentences.[28] Dubai has the same practice; there is a section of the annual Qur'an recitation competition there allocated to those who are learning the Qur'an in prison.[29]

READING THE QUR'AN

Although the Qur'an is a short book, it is not easy to read, as the nineteenth-century writer Thomas Carlyle famously commented in his tirade against it: "It is as toilsome reading as I ever undertook....Nothing but a sense of duty could carry any European through the Koran."[30] Of course, Carlyle's approach to reading the Qur'an was blinkered and ignorant. The Qur'an is not a book to read from cover to cover, fifty pages at a time. It should be read slowly, ideally in Arabic, and section by section or chapter by chapter. The reader should study its verses slowly and with respect, allowing time for the words to sink in and have an effect. Negative remarks have been made and are still being made by people who do not allow this process to occur. Given the fact that whole books have been written by Muslim commentators about separate chapters—or even individual verses—of the Qur'an, it is rash to make generalized statements about its nature on the basis of speed-reading and preconceived opinions.

HISTORY OF THE TEXT

There are many different theories and traditions surrounding the way the Qur'an has been assembled as a written text.

THE TRADITIONAL MUSLIM VIEW

God did not send down His revelation to Muhammad all at once. Its appearance was oral and intermittent. Some parts of the Qur'an were written down as and when Muhammad transmitted them to his **Companions**, so that they were preserved by various families and tribes. The Qur'anic message was also probably memorized—the Arabs, as already noted, had a long tradition of reciting poetry orally and some of them had phenomenal memories. The first **caliph, Abu Bakr** (d. 634) is said to have asked Zayd ibn Thabit, one of the Companions of the Prophet, to collect the Qur'anic revelations "from pieces of papyrus, flat stones, palm leaves, shoulder blades and ribs of animals, pieces of leather and wooden boards, as well as from the hearts of men."[31]

Muslim doctrine has it that Muhammad himself was unable to read and write and that he "recited" what he heard during the moments of revelation. Certainly, given the prevalence of an oral tradition in Arabia for the passing on of knowledge and culture, it is quite easy to see why Muslims believe that such a tradition could preserve the Qur'anic text from the time of the revelation itself.

According to some Muslim traditions, the canonical Qur'anic text in written form was collected as early as the time of Abu Bakr. But a more widely accepted version states that during the reign of the third caliph, 'Uthman (644–56), he called in all the variant versions of the Qur'an (small differences in reciting the text had developed in different parts of the new Muslim empire) and Muhammad's scribe, Zayd ibn Thabit, and a group of others who had been close to the Prophet, produced a final canonical Qur'anic text, copies of which were sent out to the major provincial cities. Having a canonical version of the Qur'an reinforced a feeling of unity amongst the new Muslim community, and earlier versions of the Holy Book, which probably contained only very minor textual variants, fell into disuse.

Whether the Qur'an was "created" or "uncreated" (i.e. co-eternal with God) was hotly debated by medieval Muslim scholars, especially in the ninth century when the caliph himself, **al-Ma'mun** (786–833), entered the fray on the side of those who supported the doctrine that the Qur'an had been "created" (see Chapter 7, p. 172). Other groups and prominent spokesmen vigorously denied this, stating that the Qur'an was "uncreated." The latter viewpoint became the one embraced by **Sunni** Muslims, and the belief became current that the primordial Qur'an exists in heaven on the "Well-Preserved Tablet."

MODERN SCHOLARSHIP

There is certainly much more to learn about the early history of the written text of the Qur'an. The most outstanding monument for the early Islamic period is the Dome of the Rock in Jerusalem, with a foundation inscription of AH 72 (692 CE) [32], which has 790 feet (240 metres) of Qur'anic inscriptions. Although this evidence was published by the Swiss scholar Max van Berchem as early as 1927, few Qur'anic scholars even mention it, let alone draw any conclusions from it, and many Orientalist Qur'anic scholars have resolutely turned their faces away from it. It is an urgent task for future research.

A cache of many thousands of Qur'anic fragments, some of them datable to the eighth or even the seventh century, tucked away in a sack in the attic of the Great Mosque in Sana'a' in Yemen, caused great excitement when they were discovered in 1972. But so far they have yielded few insights in published form. There seems to be tangible evidence, however—in the form of isolated pages of the Qur'an written on papyri, coins, and even building inscriptions—of the existence of a Qur'anic text within less than a century of the Prophet's death, and these fragments corroborate the canonical text used today; a carbon-14 test carried out on a leaf of Qur'anic text has yielded, with 95 percent accuracy, the momentous date of 645–90 CE.

Since the great period of German Orientalist scholarship in the nineteenth century many Western scholars across the world have been studying the history of the collection of the Qur'an, using the language- and text-based methods familiar in Biblical scholarship. It has rightly been called a "minefield of chronological problems,"[33] according to one eminent professor of Islamic studies, Gerhard Böwering from Yale. Since the 1970s a number of non-Muslim scholars, such as John Wansborough, Patricia Crone, and Michael Cook, have produced radical theories using non-Muslim sources about the rise of Islam, the origins of the Qur'an, and where and when it was written down. These have not received approval in Muslim academic circles. Wansborough, in particular, established a controversial "school" of text-critical scholarship about the Qur'an, arguing that its text was probably not firmly canonized until the end of the eighth century.[34] Probing though these questions posed by non-Muslim Western scholars are, especially as to the mechanics of Qur'anic transmission, such research has had no significant impact on the text itself or on the love and respect for it that Muslims show across the globe.

Some reformist Muslim scholars, approaching the Qur'an cautiously and reverentially, have also been looking for new ways of interpreting the text and studying its history. The Egyptian scholar Nasr Hamid Abu Zayd, for example, has researched time-bound aspects of the Qur'an and emphasized that certain parts of the text should be analyzed within the historical context in which Muhammad lived. He was called an apostate (a person who has renounced his religious faith) in 1992, his marriage was declared void, and he was eventually forced to flee to Europe; he settled in Holland.[35]

Many of the issues raised about the Qur'an by Western scholars, therefore, especially in recent decades, do not trouble the respect of Muslims for their Holy Book. But the Western scholarly tradition of dissecting the Qur'anic text in a hunt for historical understanding is regarded as an insult by many Muslims. That project focuses on tiny details while avoiding coming to terms with what the book is all about. The British scholar Arberry eloquently described such critics of the Qur'anic text as being "ambitious to measure the ocean of prophetic eloquence with the thimble of pedestrian analysis."[36] And even that "pedestrian analysis" has not resulted in a single accepted change to the text of the Qur'an itself.

TRANSLATIONS OF THE QUR'AN

The Bible traveled a long way from its original Hebrew, Aramaic, or Greek, being translated into Latin (the Vulgate Bible) and thereafter into European languages and, for English-speaking people, eventually into the King James Version of 1611, which became the standard Bible for Protestants. Translations of the Qur'an have been slower in coming. The earliest translation in the West was made into Latin by an English scholar, Robert of Ketton, in 1142–43, though since then there have been many translations of the Qur'an into English, French, German, and other Western languages.

However, there is a general belief among Muslims that the Qur'an is untranslatable. It is a miracle. It was revealed to the world as an Arabic Qur'an: "So We have sent down the Qur'an to give judgement in the Arabic language" (13:37). Muslims have argued that no translation can be anything other than an interpretation or explanation of the meaning of the Qur'an, as Marmaduke Pickthall admits in the foreword to his translation of the Qur'an published in 1930 (the first such attempt by a British convert to Islam). He describes his work as "only an attempt to present the meaning of the Koran— and peradventure something of the charm—in English."[37] Pickthall goes even further, stating in a spirit of piety that "no Holy Scripture can be fairly presented by one who disbelieves its inspiration and its message."[38]

Certainly such a statement may well have been valid in connection with the early translations of the Qur'an into Latin, since these had an undoubted polemical purpose in that the translators were aiming to prove that the Qur'anic message was a falsehood. But Pickthall's statement is probably going too far in respect of a number of fine translations of the Qur'an in recent times which have been undertaken by Muslim and non-Muslim scholars from a wide spectrum of linguistic, religious, and cultural backgrounds.[39] All of these in their different ways contribute to the ongoing task of understanding the complexities and mysteries of the Qur'anic text. The *Koran Interpreted* of Arberry, for example, completed in 1962, though criticized by some for straying too far from a literal translation of the sacred text, manages to convey much of the power and grandeur of the original Arabic and is still justifiably held in high regard by Muslims. Though not a Muslim himself, Arberry could write with great passion at the end of his foreword: "I pray that this interpretation, poor echo though it is of the glorious original, may instruct, please, and in some degree inspire those who read it."[40]

It is difficult to translate the Qur'an into the languages of today. Most people in the West have lost much of the sense of the "sacred," and concepts that underlie the Qur'anic world view, such as "forbidden" (*haram*) and "permitted" (*halal*), have lost much of their resonance in the twenty-first century.

There has long been strong resistance in many Muslim religious circles to the idea of translation of the Qur'an at all. Many Muslims believe that translations are unusable in ritual or liturgy. For them, the sounds of the Arabic Qur'an are sacramental, numinous, and inimitable; only an Arabic recitation of the Qu'ran is valid. But word-for-word Persian "translations" of the Qur'an written between the lines of the Arabic are known as early as the tenth or the eleventh century and the first printed translation of the Qur'an—into Ottoman Turkish—was produced by an Armenian (not Muslim) printer in Istanbul in 1726. It took a while before translations appeared in other Muslim languages, such as Urdu, Malay, and Chinese. A landmark decision was made in 1933 by the reformist Muslim scholar Mahmud Shaltut, who was later given the prestigious post of Shaykh al-Azhar in Cairo by President Nasser. Shaltut said that a translation of the Qur'an would be useful for non-Arabs and that such a translation still contained God's word.

The many Muslims in the West today who do not know Arabic have now created an unprecedented and urgent need for translations of the Qur'an into numerous modern languages. For example, there have been many translations into English, and several produced in the twenty-first century. Those that have been produced by Muslims tend to be very literal, and retain certain key words in their original Arabic form; this results in a text that is difficult for non-Muslims to understand. The general situation has, however, moved on a long way from the days of the first reputable English translation in the Qur'an, published in 1734 by George Sale, who despite revealing great learning and interest in Islam, reassured his readers in his preface that no good Christian "can apprehend any danger from so manifest a forgery."[41]

In European countries, such as Sweden, where significant numbers of converts to Islam are a relatively new phenomenon, more translations will be needed. The first-ever translation of the Qur'an into Romanian, for example, was published as recently as 2006. The present book uses the translation by the eminent Muslim scholar M. A. S. Abdel Haleem, published in 2004. It is written in an English style fitting for contemporary readers who do not know Arabic.

THE QUR'AN TODAY

The Qur'an is the first port of call for Muslims seeking guidance on every aspect of their lives. It is a source of inspiration, "guidance and mercy to those who believe" (16:64), to be recited often, and especially in times of trouble. Muslims sometimes open it at random when seeking God's guidance on their affairs. Certain chapters are believed to possess special beneficent powers (*baraka*); for example, Chapter 36 is usually recited over dying or dead persons and it is also recited daily by individual Muslims who wish to gain favor with God.

The Qur'an instructs Muslim believers to show kindness to parents, children, and orphans. Its many rules and regulations about daily life, about what to do and what not to do, have a consistently spiritual dimension. A Muslim's belief in God and the Last Day must also be translated into piety on a daily basis. So the Qur'anic prohibitions of pork and alcohol and its rules on ritual purity, marriage, divorce, inheritance, and other important facets of social living must be obeyed.

THE SACRED STATUS OF THE QUR'AN
Nowadays reverence for the Qur'an is much greater in the Muslim world than is reverence for the Bible in the West. The Qur'an is still regarded as a miracle. No amendments may be made to it and there is only one canonical version.

Children are taught the Qur'an in traditional schools in traditional ways, practicing an orality that the West has long lost. The teacher recites a Qur'anic phrase, the children repeat it in unison, and then he corrects the errors. It is not uncommon for children of seven to have learned the whole Qur'an by heart. And a great deal follows from these and lesser feats of memory; by adulthood, the Qur'an resonates in the mind of Muslims in the way that the Bible no longer does in most traditionally Christian-majority countries. One may question how many Christians can quote even one percent of their scriptures.

The Qur'an's sacred status is respected in everyday life. A copy of the Qur'an can be used for administering oaths and certain verses are recited to those who are sick. A copy of it must not be put on the floor. It is usually placed, wrapped in a clean cloth, in a high place in the room above head height. It should be touched only when a Muslim is in a state of ritual purity (see pp. 92–94). Not surprisingly, therefore, stories of the abuse given to copies of the Qur'an at Guantanamo Bay in May 2005 caused Muslims to protest worldwide.

As a work of spiritual revelation, the Qur'an is not organized on a thematic basis. It has been, and still is, interpreted in multiple ways. Nor does it contain definitive answers to every problem faced by Muslims. So there is ample room for controversy in the matter of what the Qur'an-based

Starting early. A Qur'an teacher at work, Sunehri ("golden") mosque, Peshawar, Pakistan, 2010. Muslim children often learn the Qur'an by chanting it, a practice perhaps ultimately derived from the sonorous recitation of Christian texts by Syriac monks. It is not rare for children seven years old to have learned the Qur'an by heart.

response should be to a host of modern problems, for example genetically enhanced crops or stem-cell research. But there are more traditional and long-standing problems too. In particular, Muslims have argued for centuries about the issue of who should legitimately rule the Islamic community. Sunnis and Shi'ites disagree about this (see Chapter 5, pp. 138–39); the Qur'an does not pronounce clearly on this all-important point.

Since early times pious Muslims in every generation have produced many learned commentaries on the Qur'an. These discuss the meaning of obscure words and phrases and they describe the context in which particular verses were revealed. However, some aspects of the Qur'an still remain mysterious, as is to be expected in a work of spiritual revelation. It remains to be seen whether Muslim scholars will eventually allow the kind of textual criticism that the Bible has undergone since the nineteenth century.

LANGUAGE, SCIENCE, AND ART

The language of the Qur'an has become the basis of formal high Arabic, both literary and spoken, over the centuries. Quotations and echoes of it occur very frequently in literature, everyday language, and political speeches. Indeed, the Qur'an may be regarded as an unseen force, which brings together Muslims of all countries and all walks of life and bonds them into a single community. In the early twentieth century, when the Arabs were seeking to liberate them-selves from the centuries-old yoke of Ottoman rule, both Arab Muslims and Christians recognized the unifying power of the Qur'an amongst all Arabs.

For most Muslims, the Qur'an is compatible with modern science since it deals with a different sphere of knowledge and human experience. Some groups, on the other hand, try to argue that modern scientific theories are to be found or are foreshadowed in the Qur'an. By contrast, the Qur'an is always the prime foundation of Islamic law, and there have been attempts to make it the basis of government constitutions, for example in Malaysia.

Quotations from the Qur'an are used as a major type of decoration in Islamic architecture. Specially selected and appropriate verses of the Qur'an are found in monumental inscriptions, placed on the doorways, walls, pulpits, and other parts of **mosques**, *madrasa*s (religious colleges), and mausolea. In the mosque the Qur'an is set on a special stand next to the **mihrab** (the niche in the wall that points in the direction of Mecca). The so-called Throne Verse (2:255; see p. 88) is often found on walls, swords, textiles, and tiles. Some tombs in India have the entire Qur'an written on their walls, and it is common to see buildings bear very lengthy Qur'anic quotations. In this way

Sacred text in stone. Quwwat al-Islam mosque, Delhi, 1192. Muslim buildings in India often inscribe lengthy Qur'anic passages on their walls. This mosque, erected immediately after the Muslim conquest of Delhi, proclaims in Persian that it was "built from the ruins of twenty-five idol temples." Thus the mosque becomes an instrument of conversion, triumphalism, and appropriation of sacred space.

the building itself becomes a symbolic copy of the holy book. Qur'anic quotations are found on medieval armor and on talismanic shirts, with the purpose of warding off evil. Exquisitely written Qur'anic manuscripts have been produced from the early Islamic period onward in a variety of fine scripts, starting with the beautiful angular Kufic and moving on to more flowing cursive calligraphy.

No other culture deploys holy writ so lavishly as does Islam. The Word is, as it were, iconic, and sanctifies even everyday objects, from ceramic dishes to metal incense burners, from textiles to carpets, bringing blessing to the home. Conversely, it is hard to think of a single church anywhere in the world with even one chapter of a Gospel inscribed on its walls.

"AN INIMITABLE SYMPHONY"

It is customary for non-Muslims to view the Qur'an alongside the Bible in a comparative way. And certainly there is much to be discovered through this approach. The three so-called "religions of Abraham" share very similar beliefs about the end of time and the Last Day, many stories of the prophets, and numerous ethical and legal tenets. However, the comparative approach can go only so far.

Although the Qur'an draws on a rich heritage of monotheism, which it shares with Judaism and Christianity, there are marked differences between the Jewish scriptures, the New Testament, and the Qur'an. It reveals clear similarities with Judaism in its uncompromising monotheism and its strict emphasis on ritual purity but, in its firm confirmation of Muhammad's prophethood, it departs sharply from the Jewish faith; the Jews of Medina roundly rejected such claims. Likewise the Qur'anic message shares much with Christianity, including the doctrines of the Virgin Birth and Jesus' resurrection; however, it totally rejects the Christian belief in the divinity of Jesus and the doctrine of the Holy Trinity:

> The Christians said, "The Messiah is the son of God":...How far astray they have been led! (9:31)
> The Creator of the heavens and earth!
> How could He have children when He has no spouse,
> when He created all things, and has full knowledge of all things? (6:101)

The Qur'an emerged at a particular historical moment in a particular place. And not surprisingly, therefore, it reflects a certain milieu, that of seventh-century Arabia, a society on which the preaching of the Prophet was to have such an extraordinary reforming and transforming influence, one example being the Qur'an's eloquent condemnation of the practice of female infanticide. The whole context of Arabian polytheism in which Islam developed adds important dimensions to the Qur'anic message of uncompromising monotheism, and the tribal milieu in which the Prophet lived needs to be understood in order to appreciate the ways in which the social injunctions of the Qur'an made such an impact.

Many more insights into the Qur'anic revelation can be gleaned by reading the text with an open mind. It can be understood in countless ways and on numerous levels. It contains time-bound comments, which shed light on seventh-century Arabian society; but it also conveys messages of universal validity to all people in all ages. Anyone who reads the Qur'an slowly and carefully cannot fail to be impressed by its nature as a work of profound religious inspiration. The Qur'an serves as an indispensable guide to Muslims. It provides them with constant spiritual comfort, reassurance, and advice.

It allows them to reflect on this life and the next. It presents Muslims with a clear set of doctrinal, ethical, and social instructions. Although many non-Muslims have found some aspects of the Qur'an's message fierce and angry, Muslims would respond by saying that God's mercy and compassion are mentioned at the beginning of all but one of its chapters.

Whether or not Muslims can understand Arabic, they wish to hear the Qur'an in the sacred language of Islam. Otherwise its message is heard only in muffled tones. Despite the fact that the vast majority of the world's Muslims cannot understand all the Qur'an in Arabic, they feel its power and they marvel at its sounds; as the Sufi scholar Frithhof Schuon puts it, "they live in the effect, without knowing the cause."[42] For Marmaduke Pickthall, the Holy Book is "an inimitable symphony, the very sounds of which move men to tears and ecstasy."[43]

It seems, then, appropriate to end this chapter with the Throne Verse (2:255), which embodies the spirit of the Qur'an, the omnipresence and omnipotence of the One God:

> God: there is no god but Him,
> The Ever Living, the Ever Watchful.
> Neither slumber nor sleep overtakes Him.
> All that is in the heavens and in the earth belongs to Him.
> Who is there that can intercede with Him except by His leave?
> He knows what is before them and what is behind them,
> But they do not comprehend any of His knowledge except what He wills.
> His throne extends over the heavens and the earth; it does not weary Him
>   to preserve them both.
> He is the Most High, the Tremendous.

SELECTED READING

Abdel Haleem, M. A. S., *The Qur'an: A new translation*, Oxford: Oxford University Press, 2004

Cook, Michael, *The Koran: A Very Short Introduction*, Oxford: Oxford University Press, 2000

Ernst, Carl W., *How to Read the Qur'an: A New Guide, with Select Translations*, Edinburgh: Edinburgh University Press, 2011

Esack, Farid, *The Qur'an: A Short Introduction*, Oxford: Oneworld, 2002

Sells, Michael, *Approaching the Qur'an: The Early Revelations*, Ashland, OR: White Cloud Press, 1999

4 FAITH

It's pure monotheism. It has a clear moral system and an intact tradition of religious scholarship. No scripture expresses its message of the oneness of God as clearly as the Qur'an. YAHYA, A YOUNG BRITISH STUDENT CONVERT TO ISLAM[1]

This chapter gives a brief survey of what **Muslims** believe and how their faith and practice shapes their lives. Later chapters will examine in much greater detail the various aspects of that faith and that practice. This chapter, then, deals with the heart of **Islam** as experienced by its followers—what constitutes their faith and how they worship the One God.

According to Muslim tradition, soon after the death of the Prophet **Muhammad**, certain deeply significant aspects of the religious life of the early Muslims were highlighted to serve as symbols of the faith—defining practices that helped to enhance their worship of God and foster their communal identity. These devotional duties (*'ibadat*) are known as the five **pillars** (*arkan*) of **Islam**—the profession of faith, prayer, almsgiving, fasting, and pilgrimage.[2] The observance of these five pillars is an absolute requirement for Muslims, whatever the group or sect to which they belong. This observance, however, does not just involve outward actions to be performed in a legalistic way: adhering to the pillars of the faith is a joy and a blessing to the faithful and it gives deep spiritual meaning to their lives. As the medieval Muslim scholar Abu Hamid **al-Ghazali** (d. 1111) so succinctly expresses it: "Every act of worship has both an outer and an inner aspect, a husk and a kernel."[3]

The details of how these pillars are to be observed, and what they signify, are explained in detail in the books of Islamic law that were written down from the ninth century onward. Whether practiced on a daily basis or occasionally, when taken together they form the framework within which Muslims live their lives.

THE FIRST PILLAR OF ISLAM
THE PROFESSION OF FAITH (*SHAHADA*)

A creed or confession of faith is a canonical formulation of the beliefs of a religious community. The first and most important pillar of Islam is the profession of faith: "I testify that there is no god but God. I testify that Muhammad is the Messenger of God" (*rasul Allah*). This concise statement is said aloud three times before witnesses when a person wishes to become a Muslim, to submit himself or herself to God. All Muslims start each of their daily prayers by pronouncing the *shahada*.

The shahada is short and uncomplicated. It is in two distinct parts. The first statement, "I testify that there is no god but God," is one of pure and uncompromising **monotheism**.[4] This message was directed by Muhammad both at his fellow countrymen in Arabia, many of whom were still **polytheists**, and also at the Christians. It is an abominable sin, called *shirk* in Arabic, to claim that God has any entity or persons that can share in his unique Oneness. That claim was made by the pagan Arabs in connection with the three **Meccan** goddesses (known as "the daughters of Allah") who were worshiped at the **Ka'ba** shrine at the time of Muhammad's mission (see Chapter 2, p. 26). Moreover, the statement that "There is no god but God" is also a powerful challenge to the Christian doctrines of the Trinity and the divinity of **Jesus**.

The second part of the shahada is an affirmation and validation of Muhammad's prophethood: he is indeed the Messenger of God. In his homeland of Arabia, Muhammad's claim to be a true prophet bringing a revelation from God was disputed and ridiculed by his pagan countrymen. And only a few of the Jews of Arabia would accept the message that he preached. After his death some Christians also doubted Muhammad's claim to be a prophet. Whilst some Christians do support the monotheism of the first part of the shahada, the general Christian view of Muhammad, as expressed in the second part of the shahada, is hostile. Nevertheless, more than a billion and a half Muslims around the world today confirm their belief every time they pray that Muhammad is the Messenger of God.

The oneness of God (*tawhid*) is all-important in Islam. The Qur'an argues that it is a grave sin to attribute divinity to Jesus:

> People of the Book, do not go to excess in your religion, and do not say anything about God except the truth: the Messiah, Jesus, son of Mary, was nothing more than a messenger of God, His word, directed to Mary, a spirit from Him. So believe in God and His messengers and do not speak of a "Trinity"—stop [this], that is better for you—God is only one God, He is far above having a son, everything in the heavens and earth belongs to Him and He is the best one to trust. (4.171)

Islam shares with Judaism this central tenet of faith, the oneness of God. It was a message revealed, according to tradition, to **Moses** on Mount Sinai in the form of the first commandment: "Thou shalt have no other gods before

Me" (Exodus 20:3). The key Qur'anic chapter on the oneness of God in Islam is Chapter 112: "Say, 'He is God the One, God the eternal. He begat no one nor was He begotten. No one is comparable to Him'" (112:1–4).

The core of the shahada—"There is no god but God"—is the most frequently encountered phrase in Arabic inscriptions. It is found repeatedly in the prayer niches of **mosques**, and for many centuries it was stamped on the coins issued by Muslim dynasties. By such means it spread throughout the Muslim community, a constant reminder of God's role in human life.

Over the centuries, Muslim scholars wrote more extended creedal texts, elaborating the fundamental message of the shahada and explaining its deeper significance to the Muslim community. According to al-Ghazali, for example, "In his essence God is one, without partner, alone and without any like, enduring and without opposite, unique and without equal ... He is the first and the last."[5] Al-Ghazali also emphasizes that both parts of the shahada must be said together. The shahada is incomplete and invalid if "it is not accompanied by the witness to the Messenger in the phrase 'Muhammad is the Messenger of God.'"[6]

The quintessential importance of the shahada is summed up eloquently and with obvious passion by the fifteenth-century Muslim scholar Muhammad ibn Yusuf al-Sanusi, who lived in Algeria, far from al-Ghazali's Iran:

> Revelation has made the shahada an expression of the Islam there is in the heart, and no-one's belief is acceptable except in it. The reasonable person, then, should remember it frequently, while bringing to mind the articles of belief it contains, so that these and their meaning are mingled with his flesh and his blood, for, if God wills, he (the believer) will see in them an infinity of secrets and wonders.[7]

Al-Sanusi also makes it clear that when Muslims pronounce the second half of the shahada, those words also encapsulate belief in earlier prophets and what they preached, "since Muhammad came confirming the truth of all that."[8]

How is the shahada performed? It must be recited by every Muslim at least once in a lifetime. It must be memorized exactly and recited aloud, with sincere intention and proper understanding of its meaning. Ideally, Muslims should affirm and deepen their experience of the significance of the shahada, pronouncing it on a daily basis, all through their lives. It has permanent force and validity in any time and place; it urges humankind not to bow down to any false gods, but to focus exclusively on the One God. As the Qur'an declares: "God: there is no god but Him, the Ever Living, the Ever Watchful" (2:255).

There is no issue about which Islam is so resolute as that of monotheism. The shahada expresses and encapsulates this overarching framework of belief, on which a Muslim's daily life is based. This tenet of faith penetrates all the other pillars of Islam.

THE SECOND PILLAR OF ISLAM—PRAYER (*SALAT*)

Prayer (*salat*) is the second most important of the pillars of Islam. The prescribed movements made during ritual prayer epitomize the submission of Muslims to God, and the words that they recite in prayer remind them of their obligations to Him. The frequency and regularity of these ritual prayers ensure that Muslims do not forget the deeper significance of their lives despite the worldly worries and preoccupations that beset them. The act of performing the prayer together reinforces the bond shared by Muslims across the planet, and it follows the same pattern throughout the Muslim world, so that Muslims far from home can find comfort in participating in a deeply familiar ritual.

According to a Muslim proverb, "To pray and to be a Muslim are synonymous," and indeed the sheer number of times that Muslims are required to pray every single day of the year make prayer the core ritual in their worship of God. They are regularly reminded of Him even in the hurly-burly of their daily lives; in the act of prayer they stop and reflect upon spiritual truths and their own commitment to God. Many recent converts to Islam comment on the way in which performing the ritual prayer five times a day gives structure and meaning to their lives.

Muslims are considered ready to perform prayer on reaching puberty, but they are encouraged to pray from the age of seven. Two kinds of prayer are identified. Private prayer (*du'a'*) on the part of individual Muslims can happen at any time and is not subject to specific rules; in principle, it can be of any content—for example, praise, supplication, or repentance. Such prayer is not associated with specific body movements. Ritual prayer (salat), on the other hand, which is performed five times a day and must be in Arabic, is subject to strict rules both in content and in the requisite movements of the body.

RITUAL PURITY IN *SALAT*
It is essential for Muslims to be in a state of ritual purity (*tahara*) before they pray, otherwise their prayers are not valid. Fountains and ablution basins are

to be found at every mosque, so that Muslims may prepare themselves for prayer. According to the rules laid down in Islam, they must wash before they pray. Two kinds of ablution are specified: the minor and the major. The minor ablution (*wudu'*) involves washing in running water the face, hands, arms as far as the elbow, and feet, including ankles, and wiping part of the hair with water. If the person has had sexual intercourse, or performed what are viewed in Islamic law as unclean bodily functions, then the major ablution (*ghusl*) must be performed.[9] This necessitates a washing of the whole body, including the mouth and inside the nose. Menstruating women are regarded as being in a state of impurity and must carry out the major ablution;[10] the same rule applies to new mothers until forty days after the birth of their child.[11]

In order to perform salat, other conditions must be met: as well as having clean bodies, both men and women should wear clean clothes. A man must have no bare flesh showing between his navel and his knees and a woman must have her whole body covered, except for her face and hands. The ground on which they stand for prayer must also be clean, hence the frequent use of regularly swept carpets in mosques, and of individual prayer rugs for use

Preparation for prayer. A man washes his feet, New Mosque, Istanbul, Turkey. As so often in Islam, an outward physical practice has an inner spiritual dimension. Pools, basins, and fountains all serve for ritual ablution; some modern mosques have more elaborate facilities. The Hanafi legal school, to which most Turks belong, stipulates the use of running water.

Stark simplicity. A nomad prays in the desert, Douz, Tunisia. "All the world is your mosque," said the Prophet; "wherever the hour of prayer overtakes you, there pray." When he prayed in the desert, a spear stuck in the sand sufficing to indicate the *qibla*, he performed his ablutions with sand. As this picture shows, such austerity lives on.

elsewhere. If a Muslim is traveling and water is not available for ablutions, sand may be used instead,[12] a reminder of the desert environment in which the early Muslims lived.

The specific detail of the ablution procedure serves to emphasize the inner spiritual dimension of salat. It allows Muslims to reflect on the cleansing of their minds and to remove impure thoughts in preparation for the worship of God. Al-Ghazali stresses this greater meaning and spirituality of the ritual ablutions so that the actions of the faithful in this important preparation process should not be perfunctory and superficial. After specifying that they should recite particular prayers at different moments in the washing of their bodies, al-Ghazali sums up his advice by saying: "If a man says all his prayers during his ablution, his sins will have departed from all parts of his body, a seal has been set upon his ablution."[13]

PERFORMING *SALAT*

Salat must be performed facing the direction of the Ka'ba in Mecca. This direction, the ***qibla***, is commonly marked in mosques by the niche known as the ***mihrab***. If Muslims are not in a mosque at the time for prayer and make a mistake in the direction they are facing to pray, their prayer will still be pleasing to God because their intention is good.

The five times of day specified for the ritual prayer, called to the community by the *muezzin* (or nowadays by loudspeaker) from the **minaret**, are dawn, midday, mid-afternoon, sunset, and nightfall. The words of the invitation to prayer (*adhan*) are heard recited in Arabic five times a day across the world wherever Muslims live:

> God is most great. [four times]
> I testify that there is no god but God.
> I testify that Muhammad is the Messenger of God.
> Hasten to prayer (*salat*) [twice]
> Hasten to salvation [twice]
> God is most great [twice]
> There is no god but God.

The phrase "Prayer is better than sleep" is added after the fifth line in the dawn prayer. In a **Shi'ite** neighborhood the words "I testify that 'Ali is the Friend of God" are recited twice after the third line. After the sixth line the Shi'ites add the phrase "Hasten to the best of works."

It is preferable, but not obligatory, for the prayers to be performed in the company of other Muslims in a mosque. However, as the Prophet said, the whole world is a mosque and a Muslim may therefore pray anywhere, and alone if need be. Muslim women may pray in a mosque, either in a special gallery set aside for their worship or in a section of the mosque roped off or otherwise dedicated to their use. Otherwise, they may pray at home (see also Chapter 10, pp. 270–71).

The requirement to perform five daily prayers is a strict one. If Muslims happen to miss prayers, they should make up for this later, but if they are on a journey, they are permitted to combine into one the midday and afternoon prayers and the two prayers that take place in the evening—at sunset (*maghrib*) and nightfall (*'isha'*). Muslims who live in such regions as Scandinavia or northern Russia, where the hours of daylight vary dramatically from season to season, are permitted to make certain adjustments to the times of prayer.

When praying, each Muslim is in direct contact with God; Islam does not have priests to serve as intermediaries with God. The noon prayer on Friday in the mosque, which men, unlike women,[14] are required to attend, is led by the prayer leader (*imam*), who positions himself prominently in front of the assembled Muslims, who stand in rows behind him. The imam faces

LEFT **Portal to Paradise.** *Mihrab,* Great Mosque, Cordoba, Spain, 961–5. The mosaic, executed with Byzantine help, recalls the otherworldly biomorphic vegetal forms of the Dome of the Rock, Jerusalem. The rayed design would have haloed the caliph at prayer; the Qur'anic inscription features the celestial colors of blue and gold. Behind is a small room of uncertain function.

BELOW **Togetherness.** Rows of men at Friday prayer, Tunahun mosque, Istanbul. In large mosques a prayer leader (imam)—here, clad in white—standing in the *mihrab,* and supplementary prayer leaders, stationed on platforms at regular intervals further back, ensure that the entire congregation performs the many ritual movements of prayer at exactly the same time.

the mihrab, which points toward Mecca, and thus the congregation sees only his back. He then makes a series of movements in strict sequence, which are followed by all the Muslims behind him in sweeping synchronization. When there are very large congregations, supplementary imams placed on raised platforms are visible to those worshipers set much further back, and this avoids the danger of a staggered and therefore discordant and disordered sequence of movements. The sight of thousands of believers performing the same ritual movements in perfect time is deeply impressive and moving— a powerful metaphor of unity and brotherhood.

THE PRAYER CYCLE

Each sequence of movements in the prayer cycle is called a *rak'a*; within it, Muslims perform several basic movements or stances—raising and extending the hands, standing, bowing, reclining back on their haunches, prostrating themselves and touching the forehead to the ground, and reverting to a seated position before repeating the prostration. This completes the cycle of a rak'a. The specified external movements symbolize aspects of the Muslims' faith in God. The standing position, for example, is a solemn reminder of the standing before God on the **Last Day** that all humanity must do when they hear His judgment. The bowing down they will then make is to seek His forgiveness. Prostration on the ground is an act of adoration given only to God. As the Qur'an says: "Believers, bow down, prostrate yourselves, worship your Lord, and do good so that you may succeed" (22:77).

The number of rak'as varies according to the time of day: two at dawn; four at midday, mid-afternoon, and nightfall; and three at sunset. There are obligatory rak'as that must be performed and other rak'as that one can miss if one is travelling, sick, or simply does not wish to perform them. Each rak'a begins with the formula "God is great" (*'Allahu akbar*'), followed by the recitation of the first chapter of the Qur'an, known as the *Fatiha*:

> In the name of God, the Lord of Mercy, the Giver of Mercy! Praise belongs to God, Lord of the Worlds, the Lord of Mercy, the Giver of Mercy, Master of the Day of Judgement. It is You we worship; it is You we ask for help. Guide us to the straight path: the path of those You have blessed, those who incur no anger and who have not gone astray.
> (1:1–7)

Worshipers stand while reciting this *sura*, and at this point in the first two rak'as some Qur'anic verses are recited, followed by the formula "God is most great," which is known as the *takbir*. When they bow they silently repeat three times the phrase "Glory be to God the Mighty." Next, in a standing position, worshipers say, "God listens to him who praises Him," followed by the response, "Our Lord, and to Thee belongs praise." Then, saying the takbir, they prostrate themselves, and in that position repeat three times, "Glory to my Lord Most High." They pronounce the takbir both before and after the next prostration.

This is a necessarily abbreviated account of the prayer cycle, which has variations prescribed by each of the four major **Sunni** schools of Islamic law (let alone the Shi'ite practices). Its main intention is to show that ritual prayer is a complex combination of movements and religious invocations and statements, in which repetition is an essential element.

SPECIAL DAYS OF WORSHIP

The Prophet Muhammad chose Friday as the special day of worship for Muslims. To mark this day each week, adult Muslim men who are sound in body and mind are required to attend the Friday congregational prayer at noon in the mosque.[15] As the Qur'an says:

> "Believers! When the call to prayer is made on the day of congregation, hurry towards the reminder of God and leave off your trading—that is better for you, if only you knew" (62:9).

Before the Friday prayer begins, the imam, who traditionally stands on the second highest step of the pulpit, gives a sermon (*khutba*), which can contain political or social themes in addition to spiritual counsels.

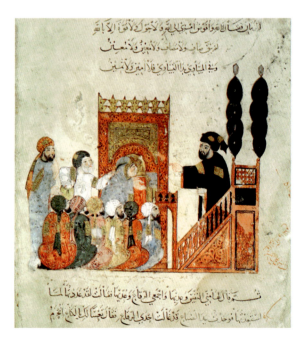

The sacred meets the secular. Preacher in a mosque, al-Hariri, *Assemblies*, Baghdad, 1237. Standing on the *minbar* or pulpit, he delivers the *khutba*, part sermon, part statement of political allegiance, though heckled vigorously. His black robe and turban, the black wooden panel, and the furled flags attest his loyalty to the then-ruling 'Abbasid dynasty, the identifying color of which was black.

In the Muslim religious year prayers are also said on certain special occasions, such as the two great annual festivals, one at the end of the fasting month of **Ramadan** for the *'id al-fitr* (see p. 104) and the other on 10 Dhu'l-Hijja, the month in which the pilgrimage takes place (see p. 110). There are also prayers for funeral ceremonies and even ceremonies in which God is asked to send rain; the latter typically involve the entire community. Additional night prayers may be performed voluntarily, and are especially recommended for the later part of the night.

THE THIRD PILLAR OF ISLAM—ALMSGIVING (*ZAKAT*)

Islamic doctrine identifies two kinds of charitable giving—donations that are voluntary (*sadaqa*) and those that are obligatory (*zakat*); the latter is the third pillar of faith. It would seem that almsgiving in Islam began as a voluntary act of piety but that it gradually developed into an obligatory duty.

Payment of zakat reminds Muslims that what they possess in this life is on loan from God: they are only stewards of their wealth. At the personal level, giving away part of one's wealth is a way of thanking God for His beneficence—it is an act of worship—and it is also a means of purifying oneself of greed and avarice (the literal meaning of the term zakat is "something that purifies"). At a community level, the donations given as zakat by those Muslims who are able to do so enhance social solidarity, harmony, and wellbeing.

The Qur'an requires that the faithful be generous with their wealth: "You who believe, give charitably from the good things you have acquired and that We have produced for you from the earth" (2:267). It is especially recommended to behave charitably in secret rather than in an open and boastful manner: "If you give charity openly, it is good, but if you keep it secret and give to the needy in private, that is better for you, and it will atone for some of your bad deeds" (2:271). There is a dire warning in the collected sayings of the Prophet (the *hadith*) directed at those who fail to give zakat when they are legally obliged to do so: their punishment on the **Day of Judgment** will be terrible.[16]

TRADITIONAL PRACTICE

The Qur'an provides some clues as to how zakat was put into practice in the early days of Islam. It briefly mentions three times in Chapter 2 the requirement for Muslims to pay zakat; 2:43, for example, states: "Establish worship, pay the poor-due (zakat) and bow your heads with those who bow." Much more detailed information about zakat is given in the hadith, however, and Muslim law books, drawing on the hadith, provide precise and comprehensive guidelines and rules on many aspects of the practice.

As for the question of who should receive zakat, Muslim scholars relied very closely on Qur'an 9:60: "Alms are meant only for the poor, the needy, those who administer them, those whose hearts need winning over, to free slaves and help those in debt, for God's cause, and for travellers in need. This is ordained by God."

Muslims on whom there is an obligation to pay the zakat to help the poor should be sane adults, who are in possession of the *nisab* (the minimum amount of wealth that one must have before zakat is payable). So every Muslim whose income is above that prescribed level must make a contribution of a fixed portion of his or her wealth each year to help the poor. In other words, Muslims who are not well off are excused from this payment. A sense of fairness, therefore, underlies this regulation.

Zakat is payable on certain possessions after they have been owned for a whole lunar year. In the early days of Islam, the emphasis on the giving of wealth related to the social and economic conditions of particular historical societies at different times and in different places in the Muslim world. So the precise regulations in classical Islamic law books about zakat referred to income gained from such agricultural products as grains, fruits, and livestock, as well as to gold, silver, and precious objects.

MODERN PRACTICE

Of course, many of the regulations given in the Muslim law books are no longer directly applicable or relevant to modern urban life, much as devout Jews no longer follow the detailed prescriptions for burnt sacrifices laid out in some books of the Pentateuch (the first five books of the Hebrew Bible). In the early days of Islam it was important, for example, to know how much zakat a Muslim should pay on his camels, but the majority of Muslims today are not involved in agriculture; living in cities, as they do, they no longer need to know the exact amount of zakat payable on wheat, barley, rice, and other food products.[17]

The official rate fixed for zakat payable by Sunni Muslims today is 2.5 percent of one's wealth every (lunar) year. Twelver Shi'ite Muslims pay a tax called *khums* ("a fifth") of their income. This duty is based on Qur'an 8:41: "Know that one-fifth of your battle gains belongs to God and the Messenger, to close relatives and orphans, to the needy and travelers." Wealth is now regarded as including a wide variety of components, ranging from the yield on livestock and crops to the income earned from commerce, bonds, and stocks and shares.

Modern Muslims differentiate between paying their taxes, which is a requirement of secular law, and zakat, which is used exclusively to help the poor and needy. Many Muslims choose Ramadan, the holy month of fasting, as the time to pay their zakat, believing that the reward for their good deeds in this special month will be greater. Nowadays zakat is often voluntary and is a matter of individual conscience.

Zakat is usually collected by special committees, which then distribute it as they deem appropriate to the poor and needy. In some Muslim-majority countries today, such as Saudi Arabia and Pakistan, almsgiving is obligatory and zakat is collected in a centralized manner by the state. In other predominantly Muslim countries, such as Kuwait, Jordan, Bahrain, and Lebanon, zakat contributions are voluntary, but they are regulated by the state. There is thus a wide range of practice. Muslim charities today use zakat funds to provide emergency relief for the millions of people afflicted by disasters— both natural ones, such as earthquakes and tsunamis, and those caused by human greed and wickedness, such as the collapse of poorly constructed skyscraper housing and the use of chemical weapons.

THE FOURTH PILLAR OF ISLAM—FASTING (*SAWM*)

Each year, for the whole of the month of Ramadan, the ninth month of the Muslim lunar calendar, Muslims all across the world observe the fourth pillar of Islam, fasting (*sawm*). This is a duty prescribed for all believers. But it is not just a ritual obligation; it is an act of profound religious significance. Ramadan is a very special month for Muslims; in it they feel that God's blessings are closer to them than at other times. Indeed, despite the physical hardships of a month of fasting throughout the day, Muslims in general agree that they gain enormous benefits from this experience. There is a happy atmosphere, even excitement and exultation, amongst them as the month progresses. They feel that they are learning spiritual lessons and that they are renewing their faith in Islam and their commitment to it. They are convinced that their bodies have been purified. They have suffered from hunger and thirst during the day for a whole month and can now empathize with the millions of people in the world who go to bed hungry every day. By performing this pillar of their faith, both privately and publicly in the workplace, today's Muslims proclaim the strength of their faith on a global canvas, and millions of non-Muslims take note of this.

THE ORIGINS OF *SAWM*

The Ramadan fast goes back to the time of the Prophet. The custom of fasting was well known to his polytheistic contemporaries within Arabia. The Qur'an hints at this when addressing Muhammad's fellow countrymen: "You who believe, fasting is prescribed for you, as it was prescribed for those before you, so that you may be mindful of God" (2:183). On his journeys north from Mecca on behalf of his wife **Khadija**, Muhammad must have heard of, or even seen, Christian hermits performing spiritual exercises, including fasting, in the deserts of Arabia and Syria. He knew too about the stories of the Jewish prophet Moses, who went without food or drink on Mount Sinai for forty days, and about Jesus, who withdrew into the desert for the same length of time to fast (in **Semitic** tradition the number "forty" is used to mean "many").

Muslim tradition records that once Muhammad had emigrated to **Medina**, he initially established the Jewish Day of Atonement (Yom Kippur) as the day for the Muslim fast. Later, however, he announced that henceforth the whole of the ninth Muslim lunar month of Ramadan should be set aside as a period of fasting for Muslims. This momentous decision came after the revelation of this Qur'anic verse: "It was in the month of Ramadan that the Qur'an was revealed as guidance for mankind, clear messages giving guidance and distinguishing between right and wrong. So any one of you who is present that month should fast" (2:185).

At a purely practical level, when he was setting up his community of Muslims in Medina, Muhammad's choice of Ramadan for the month of fasting was astute and far-sighted; this month was one of the pre-Islamic months of truce, when warring tribesmen would lay down their arms. However, the choice of Ramadan has always had a profound and exclusively Islamic significance. It was in the year 610 during one of the last ten nights of Ramadan, known as the **Night of Power** (*laylat al-qadr*), that, according to Islamic belief, the Qur'an descended in full into the soul of Muhammad: "We sent it down on the Night of Power. What will explain to you what that Night of Power is? The Night of Power is better than a thousand months" (97:1). This night, celebrated on 26–27 Ramadan, is viewed as the holiest night of the Muslim calendar.

THE PRACTICE OF *SAWM*

There are strict and precise rules laid down for fasting in Ramadan. Every able-bodied adult Muslim, male or female, must fast during daylight hours for the entire month. Certain categories of Muslim society are exempted with good reason from this obligation: old people, those who are sick, children under the age of puberty, travelers, those engaged in heavy labor, and women who are pregnant or breastfeeding. In the case of old people, no precise age is given for when a person becomes old. This is a far-sighted provision, for it leaves ample room for maneuver within the spirit of the law. Fasting is forbidden when an individual's life is in danger or when a woman is menstruating. Those adults who are unable to fast on some days of Ramadan should compensate by fasting an equal number of days at a later time, or by feeding a person in need, as the Qur'an declares: "Fast for a specific number of days, but if one of you is ill, or on a journey, on other days later. For those who can fast only with extreme difficulty, there is a way to compensate—feed a needy person" (2:184).

Fasting in Ramadan involves total abstinence from all sensual pleasures—such as food, drink, smoking, sexual intercourse, and listening to music—from dawn until sunset for the whole month. It is recommended that Muslims should break the fast soon after nightfall, and following the example of the Prophet they should eat dates and water, before having a bigger meal later on. They should then eat the last meal of the night shortly before the beginning of the new day of fasting. The alternation of fasting in the day and shared meals taken with family and friends after nightfall strongly enhances Muslims' sense of community and social solidarity.

As Ramadan is a sacred month, it is recommended that Muslims should refrain from evil thoughts and actions and perform additional pious deeds, such as reciting the special prayer (*salat al-tawarih*) earmarked for Ramadan every night. This extraordinarily long prayer, recited only in Ramadan, is accompanied by twenty or thirty-two rak'as, and is performed at regular intervals through the night until the the dawn prayer, and in the evening after the nightfall prayer. After every four rak'as, time is allowed for individual Muslims to perform a private prayer. The salat al-tawarih is a real test of endurance for the imams who are leading the prayer. As well as directing the unusually large numbers of rak'as, they choose long Qur'anic passages to recite aloud to accompany the prayer. So they often have to take turns in leading the prayer.

In addition, the Qur'an should be read in full by the end of Ramadan; according to Islamic tradition, that is why it has been divided into thirty equal

The joy of fasting. Hafiz, *Divan*, Herat (?), 1527 (?). Everyone at court enjoys music, food, and wine as Ramadan begins. Traditionally, a judge validated the sighting of the crescent moon—celebrated here by the fashionable courtiers thronging the palace roof—signalling the start of Ramadan. The text accompanying this illustration refers to roses in blossom, fixing the season as early summer.

sections and seven subsections. Ramadan ends joyfully with the festival known as 'id al-fitr (the feast of breaking the fast). At this time, Muslims wear their best clothes, they exchange gifts, as Christians do at Christmas, they visit the mosque, and they celebrate, eating special meals with their family and friends.

The requirement to fast begins when the new moon of Ramadan is sighted or when thirty days of the previous month of Sha'ban have passed. The day's fasting begins when a thread of light may be seen on the horizon at dawn; it ends at dusk. Since the Muslim year is lunar, the fasting month of Ramadan occurs eleven days earlier each year, and so in different seasons over the decades. There are severe problems of thirst for Muslims who live in the hot climates of the Middle East, Africa, and Asia, when Ramadan falls in the summer. Moreover, now that Muslims also live in the lands of the north, in countries not even known to the Prophet, nor to those who compiled the Islamic legal books after his death, they also experience acute difficulties when Ramadan falls in summer, when the days are very long.

In modern times, Islamic scholars have shown concern about this issue, and they display flexibility and humanity in finding a solution, as the following *fatwa* shows: "We believe that Muslims living near the North and South poles and what is close to them, in which the days are long and nights short, have two choices when it comes to fasting in Ramadan."[18] The first is to fast the same number of hours as in Mecca and Medina, "where day and night are in moderation." As for the second option, Muslims in these remote places should choose the hours of fasting that are followed in the country nearest to them where the hours are manageable. Not surprisingly, for both religious and practical reasons, the fatwa recommends the first option. The London Olympics in 2012 posed a significant challenge to Muslim competitors, since the games overlapped with Ramadan. The reaction was mixed: some of the competitors observed Ramadan even to their own cost, while others took advantage of the exemptions.

In practical terms, the law on this matter is essentially humane. It is the spirit of the law, not its letter, that matters, and this leaves Muslims free to follow their conscience in how to observe Ramadan in situations not foreseen in earlier times.

THE FIFTH PILLAR OF ISLAM—PILGRIMAGE (*HAJJ*)

The Muslim pilgrimage is inseparable from Mecca. Mecca is the birthplace of the Prophet Muhammad. It is the capital city of Islam. The organizing principle of Islamic ritual and imagination, Mecca has become the defining node for a worldwide community of believers who are linked to the Prophet Muhammad, to Mecca, and to one another through networks of faith and family. To be Muslim is to be connected to co-religionists who turn toward Mecca five times each day. Each year, Mecca attracts millions of Muslims from all over the world who perform the great pilgrimage, or *hajj*, the fifth and final pillar of Islam.

The hajj takes place in the month of Dhu'l-Hijja at the Grand Mosque in Mecca (*al-masjid al-haram*), as well as in Mina, Muzdalifa, and 'Arafat; these are all places adjacent to Mecca. The requirement to perform the pilgrimage is clearly stated in the Qur'an: "Pilgrimage to the House (of God) is a duty owed to God by people who are able to undertake it" (3:97).

HISTORICAL BACKGROUND

To understand the underlying background and significance of the rites of the pilgrimage, it is important to recognize the role played by **Abraham** in Islamic tradition. This differs from the way he is seen in the Judaeo-Christian tradition, as narrated in the Book of Genesis. Muhammad saw himself as a true heir to Abraham, and there is much underlying the pilgrimage rites that has to do with the story of the life of Abraham as it had come down to Muhammad and his contemporaries.

Two key aspects of Abrahamic legend stand out in the Muslim tradition. Firstly, and above all, Abraham worshiped God as a pure monotheist (*hanif*). It was Abraham who came to Arabia to carry out God's command to build the stone structure known as the Ka'ba. It was Abraham who founded the hajj: as the Qur'an mentions: "We showed Abraham the site of the House, saying, 'Do not assign partners to Me. Purify My House for those who circle around it, those who stand to pray, and those who bow and prostrate themselves. Proclaim the Pilgrimage to all people'" (22:26–28).

The story of **Hagar** and **Ishmael** (Isma'il) is also important in the Muslim tradition. The Muslim narrative goes as follows. God told Abraham to take his wife Hagar and their son Ishmael to Arabia to escape the jealousy of Sarah, Abraham's first wife. God then instructed Abraham to leave Hagar and Ishmael alone in Arabia for a while. Ishmael began to thirst and, desperately looking for water, Hagar ran seven times between the two small hills of Safa and Marwa outside Mecca. Finally, in response to Hagar's prayer, the miraculous water of **Zamzam** was revealed when the angel **Gabriel** struck the ground with his wing.[19]

In the days before Islam, the Arabs had performed a pilgrimage to the Ka'ba shrine in Mecca. They had made it a place of pagan worship, setting up idols all around it. Their rituals are strongly criticized in the Qur'an as hollow, meaningless, and displeasing to God: "Their prayers before the House are nothing but whistling and clapping. Therefore (it is said to them) 'Taste the punishment for your disbelief'" (8:35). When Muhammad performed his two pilgrimages to Mecca—in AH 7 (March 629) and then in AH 10 (March 632)—however, he reshaped and sanctified the pilgrimage; what he did there on those occasions became the model conduct for all Muslims in every age.

RITUAL REQUIREMENTS

Muslims, both men and women, should perform the pilgrimage to Mecca once in a lifetime, if they are able to do so. There, and in certain areas nearby, they

Embarking on the experience of a lifetime. Al-Hariri, *Assemblies*, Baghdad, 1237. Fluttering standards, beating drums, and sounding trumpets accompany the beautifully dressed pilgrims as they depart for Mecca with palpable joy and excitement. Note the silken canopied camel seat, perhaps an early *mahmal* (a textile litter carrying a Qur'an).

must perform several days of elaborate prescribed rituals. They may go on the pilgrimage more than once in the course of their lives; this is regarded as praiseworthy but it is certainly not obligatory. Not all Muslims are permitted to go on pilgrimage to Mecca. Would-be pilgrims must be able-bodied adults, with sufficient funds to make the journey and to support their families while they are away. Specific categories of Muslims are exempted from performing the pilgrimage: those who are insane, prisoners, minors, and women who do not have male family members to accompany them.

In the Middle Ages, the journey to Mecca was both arduous and long for most Muslims. Moreover, if by some accident they missed the prescribed days in the month of Dhu'l-Hijja, they would have to wait a full year before they could perform their hajj. Careful planning was therefore essential, and their plans would need to incorporate a margin of safety. Given the complexity of the different rituals of the pilgrimage, many Muslims spent, and still do spend, a long time studying the way in which these rituals should be performed and trying to understand their inner significance before they embark on the most important journey of their lives.

On arrival in Mecca the pilgrims are full of joy; for them, seeing the Ka'ba in this life is a promise that they will see God's face in the next world. All pilgrims must be in a state of ritual purity of a special kind (*ihram*) to perform the rites of the pilgrimage. The hajj begins with the pilgrim making

Rapturous prayer. Majnun at the Ka'ba, Nizami, *Khamsa*, Herat, c. 1490. Most pilgrims wear the *ihram*, two lengths of white cloth; thus distinctions of race, wealth, and social status disappear. In this painting, the Ka'ba's silk covering, formerly technicolor, termed a bridal veil by medieval poets, is black, with Qur'anic inscriptions and chevrons highlighted in gold thread. It is still made annually in Egypt.

a statement of pious intent. The men then put on special garments—two seamless, unsewn pieces of cloth, one of which is a waist-wrapper from the navel to the knee and the other is a shawl covering the left shoulder and tied under the right. Women do not wear the same garments as those worn by men. They should leave their faces uncovered, but their hair should not be visible; their bodies should be covered to the wrist and the ankle. Wearing special clothing to perform the pilgrimage adds a spiritual dimension to the ritual. Once again al-Ghazali identifies some of the religious significance for the believer: "The pilgrim should recall the shroud in which he will be wrapped for burial.... While he may never finish his journey to the House of God (the Ka'ba), what is certain is that he must go to meet God...wrapped in the cloth of the shroud."[20] Some Muslim legal schools allow women to perform the pilgrimage when they are menstruating, while others do not.

From the moment that the pilgrims are in a state of ihram, they must refrain from certain activities: sexual relations, the cutting of hair and nails, shaving, and using perfume. They should not get into arguments or resort to fighting. Every Muslim wishing to enter the state of ritual purity performs a prayer consisting of two rak'as and recites the special words: "At your service, O God, at your service." These words, believed to have been uttered by Abraham, are repeated by Muslims hundreds of times throughout the pilgrimage.

It is possible for a pilgrim to enter into the state of ritual purity necessary for performing the pilgrimage while still at home, or on first entering Saudi Arabia. Pilgrims must also complete all the rites and stages of the pilgrimage unless there are really pressing reasons for terminating it early. From the moment when pilgrims enter the sacred precinct surrounding the Ka'ba, the pilgrimage rites must be strictly observed. Individual Muslim legal schools differ on certain minute details of how these rites should be carried out. These differences cover many pages of the law books.

THE DAILY STAGES OF THE *HAJJ*

A special service takes place on the day before the pilgrimage, on 7 Dhu'l-Hijja, in the Sacred Mosque in Mecca. The daily stages of the hajj proper begin on 8 Dhu'l-Hijja. This is a day of reflection, when pilgrims in a state of ihram perform the first rite, the circumambulation (walking around) of the Ka'ba. This must be done seven times in an anticlockwise direction. It is

Epicenter of the universe. The Ka'ba, Masjid al-Haram, Mecca, frequently restored since it was first built in 608 CE. For Muslims, this mosque marks the prescribed direction of prayer, the *qibla*. Sevenfold circumambulation of the Ka'ba is an obligatory part of the pilgrimage. A million Muslims converge on Mecca to pray throughout the Night of Power (*laylat al-qadr*).

an echo of the angels encircling the Throne of God. Then follow the kissing and touching of the Black Stone, an ancient stone fitted into the eastern wall of the Ka'ba; this symbolizes submission to God. Given the vast crowds of people involved, it is simply not possible for all of them to kiss or touch the Black Stone, but the pilgrims make a gesture toward it. They then proceed to the "place of running." Here the pilgrims run seven times the stretch outside Mecca between the two small hills of Safa and Marwa. According to one legend, it was between these hills that Hagar ran to and fro seven times in search of water for her son Ishmael. After the running, the pilgrims drink some Zamzam water and they then leave for Mina. According to Muslim tradition, the running performed by pilgrims between Safa and Marwa may be seen as symbolizing their running between their bad deeds and their good ones, between punishment and forgiveness.

On 9 Dhu'l-Hijja—this day is called the Day of Standing (*yawm al-wuquf*)—the pilgrims visit 'Arafat where they stay (not necessarily standing) from noon until after the sun has set. This is a solemn day, during which the words "At your service, O God, at your service" (known as the **talbiyya**) are recited often. At the end of this day the pilgrims depart for Muzdalifa, another valley between 'Arafat and Mina, where they spend the night. Muslims believe that the enormous multitudes of people assembled at 'Arafat are a reminder of the gathering of all human souls gathered on the Last Day on the plain outside Jerusalem waiting to receive God's judgment.

10 Dhu'l–Hijja—the Day of Sacrifice (*'id al-adha*)—is a great day of celebration throughout the Muslim world. The pilgrims collect pebbles and they then move to the so-called lapidation rite at Mina, where they must throw stones at three granite pillars that mark the place commemorating where Abraham threw stones at Satan. Pilgrims take a prescribed number of pebbles, the size of chickpeas, and they throw them at each pillar in turn.

The pilgrims remain one night at Muzdalifa, and on the last day animals are sacrificed—camels, oxen, or rams. The length of the pilgrimage rites is a minimum of five days and a maximum of six. The state of ihram is terminated by men shaving their heads and women cutting off a small lock of hair. The pilgrims have now finished the official part of the hajj ; they have gained great favor in the sight of God.

The hajj is not the only form of pilgrimage in Islam. A shortened version of it, called the *'umra*, "the lesser pilgrimage," exists, and this is often performed before the full pilgrimage, although it can also be undertaken on its own at other times of the year. The 'umra is not classified as a pillar of

Islam, and therefore it cannot replace the obligation of performing the hajj. It can be completed in one and a half hours, and involves seven circumambulations of the Ka'ba and seven crossings—part running and part walking—between Safa and Marwa. It can be done by proxy on behalf of another person, if they are unwell or deceased.

In the recent past, and even more so in the Middle Ages, when Muslims from Spain, for example, would be away from home for around two years, the reality of the journey to perform the pilgrimage to Mecca was simply extraordinary. It is amazing that so many Muslims actually managed to go, given the enormous distances that faced them—for they came from as far afield as Spain in the west and China, Malaysia, and Indonesia in the east. And the distance itself was only one of many challenges, given the hardships endured, the dangers encountered, the expense involved, and the possible economic privation inflicted on the pilgrim's family—for there was no telling when, or even if, the pilgrim would return. Yet people did go, "swayed," as the great fourteenth-century Muslim traveler **Ibn Battuta** so eloquently put it, "by an overmastering impulse within me."[21]

The logistics of the pilgrimage in today's world are extremely intricate, but the government of Saudi Arabia has invested much money and effort in a bid to accommodate the vast numbers of pilgrims taking advantage of cheaper and faster travel to perform the hajj. In 2012, according to Saudi Arabian statistics, the number of Muslims performing the pilgrimage reached 3,161,573. Since there is a stipulated sequence of events for the first three days—8, 9, and 10 Dhu'l-Hijja—this means that, for example, millions of people have to be able to throw stones and sacrifice animals on the Day of Sacrifice ('id al-adha), and that well over three million people each day for that period must be accommodated at the pilgrimage sites. This is a formidable challenge in terms of administration and people management.

SIGNIFICANCE OF THE *HAJJ*

The fifth pillar of Islam involves the most important earthly journey of a Muslim's life. The custom of performing pilgrimage to a holy city or to a sacred place, such as the tomb of a saint, is an ancient one in both Christianity and Judaism. Throughout the Middle Ages, thousands of Christian pilgrims traveled, often on foot, to visit and worship at Canterbury, Assisi, Santiago de Compostela, Rome, and—above all—Jerusalem, the city where Jesus suffered and died. And Christians still go on pilgrimage to this day. But unlike Muslims, they do not go in such huge numbers in a prescribed month to the

A pilgrim's pride. The Pilgrim House, Luxor, Egypt. A typical Egyptian village house facade adorned with paintings in a humble folk style. The one nearest the door depicts a man—probably the householder himself—in pilgrim dress praying "O Lord" at the Ka'ba, with the mountains of Mecca behind. Above left is the ship that took him there.

same holy place, nor are they under any doctrinal obligation to do so. Since the very beginning of Islam, however, Muslims have always performed the rite of pilgrimage.

At a human level, performing the shared rites of the pilgrimage is an act of reinforcement—a visual demonstration of the unity of all believers and their equality in the sight of God, be they rich or poor, man or woman, no matter where they come from or to what ethnic group they belong. Visually speaking, it is a stupendous and inspiring spectacle, the emotional impact of which can be overwhelming. On their return home pilgrims are still treated with great respect by their fellow Muslims. They receive the title of *hajji*. At a more profound level, their journey to Mecca and their experiences there have changed them, enabling them to transmit the blessings of Mecca to those who have stayed at home. Many Muslims whose faith was lukewarm before they went on the hajj return in a state of heightened spirituality.

It is small wonder that on medieval Muslim circular maps Mecca is situated at the very center of the whole world. Many Muslims have striven to express the spiritual dimensions of the sacred journey to Mecca, the place toward which they pray every day. It has been described as that point on the horizon that speaks so eloquently of things unseen. For many, the experience of visiting Mecca is described as "returning home," a foretaste of what awaits the soul in the afterlife.

Muslim commentaries and interpretations over the centuries have assigned symbolic significance or spiritual meaning to many of the detailed rituals of the pilgrimage. Many pilgrims do not enquire into, or are not aware of, these rich associations. For them the communal nature of the hajj rituals and the experience of walking on the ground on which the Prophet also once walked, and the intense emotions that all this generates, fills their hearts and souls with joy and makes the hajj the unforgettable high point of their lives. As a young Muslim woman expressed it in 2011: "Hajj is more than just a ritual—it is a revolution. Every aspect of Hajj involves a struggle to reform oneself—to deconstruct our self-made ego and embrace humility as slaves to God."[22]

The performance of the pillars adds multiple layers of meaning for believers. But equally, there are clear rules given in the Qur'an and the law books on how to discharge these core religious requirements. Such a framework provides Muslims with immense reassurance and comfort. And for those who wish to probe the mysteries of the five pillars there are endless opportunities for individual reflection and contemplation. The inevitable differences of interpretation and tradition within the global Muslim community cannot undermine the cohesion and sense of unity created by the faithful shared observance of the five pillars.

SELECTED READING

Cornell, Vincent J., "Fruit of the Tree of Knowledge. The Relationship Between Faith and Practice in Islam," in Esposito, John L. (ed.), *The Oxford History of Islam*, Oxford and New York: Oxford University Press, 1999, pp. 63–105

al-Ghazali, Abu Hamid, *Inner Dimensions of Islamic Worship*, trans. Muhtar Holland, Leicester: Islamic Foundation, 1983

Rippin, Andrew, *Muslims: Their Religious Beliefs and Practices*, Abingdon: Routledge, 2005, pp. 103–117

Watt, W. Montgomery, *Islamic Creeds*, Edinburgh: Edinburgh University Press, 1994

Wolfe, Michael, ed., *One Thousand Roads to Mecca: Ten Centuries of Travelers Writing About the Muslim Pilgrimage*, New York: Grove Press, 1999

5 LAW

Now We have set you [Muhammad] on a clear religious path (shari'a), so follow it.
QUR'AN 45:18

They stone women to death in countries that have Sharia law.
KANSAS STATE SENATOR SUSAN WAGLE[1]

The Shari'ah is the ideal pattern for the individual's life and the Law which binds the Muslim people into a single community. It is the embodiment of the Divine Will in terms of specific teachings whose acceptance and application guarantees man a harmonious life in this world and felicity in the hereafter.
SEYYED HOSSEIN NASR, IRANIAN SCHOLAR[2]

The origin of the word *Shari'a* gives a good indication of its significance. It means a watering place, or path to water, a God-given, life-providing way. Just as within Judaism the term *halakha*, a "way," is used to denote Jewish law, and just as the early Christians spoke about their entire religion as the "way,"[3] so too individual pious **Muslims** follow a way called the Shari'a. This is not seen as an externally imposed obligation; it comes from within the person, who embraces the way joyfully.

The Shari'a gives meaning and structure to all aspects of the religious and social lives of Muslims, in their personal relationship with God and in their dealings with their fellow humans. It tells Muslims what they may and may not do. Ideally every step in daily life is determined by the directives of the Shari'a: it covers all things, human and divine. Christians often distinguish between the obligations of this world and those due to God, as **Jesus** did in response to a difficult question posed to him by the Jewish doctors of the law.[4] In contrast, the Shari'a concerns the duties of Muslims both in their daily lives and in their religious obligations.

This chapter will examine the development of **Sunni Islamic** law within its historical context and show how complex and multi-faceted this subject really is. It will also try to analyze the diverse ways in which the ideal of the Shari'a has been interpreted by Sunni Muslims over the centuries—and how it is today. (For aspects of the Shari'a concerning *jihad*, see Chapter 9; for those concerning women, see Chapter 10; **Shi'ite** law is discussed in detail in Chapter 6.)

THE EVOLUTION OF LAW IN THE EARLY ISLAMIC WORLD

From the beginning of his time in **Medina**, the Prophet **Muhammad** was a law-giver. While he was alive his decisions were definitive. After his death, however, the need for more detailed guidance arose in the rapidly expanding Muslim community, when the early **caliphs** (Muslim rulers) and their provincial governors constantly had to face new problems—social and economic as well as spiritual—and pass difficult judgments. So, from the very outset, Islamic law had to respond to unexpected challenges. These early Muslim rulers tried to act in the way that the Prophet had done, and stories of what he had said were cherished. But pragmatic solutions to problems had to be replaced in due course by firm new legal foundations, based on what were held to be true Islamic principles.

THE *HADITH*

Early scholars of the Islamic religious sciences (called *'ulama'*) wished in a true spirit of piety to follow faithfully the new religion of Islam. So their first port of call in dealing with all aspects of their daily lives was, of course, the *Qur'an*. But the Qur'an is a book of revelation, not a legal treatise. In fact, out of its 6,346 verses, the Qur'an contains only around five hundred verses that have to do with law, and despite the central importance of the holy book in the daily lives of Muslims, only a few core rulings are explicitly mentioned in it or explicitly derived from it.[5] So early religious scholars also sought to shape what they regarded as true Islamic guiding principles by drawing upon another sacred source, the *hadith*—the carefully remembered reports that related what the Prophet had said to his **Companions**, and the actions that he had performed or silently approved in their presence (see also Chapter 2, pp. 39–40). Doing this helped them to amplify Qur'anic statements on particular issues, such as prayer or pilgrimage, and enabled them to begin to formulate precise rules of conduct in all aspects of their religious life, both as individuals and as a new community.

In the first two generations immediately following Muhammad's death (632 CE), the memory of what he had said and done remained fresh, especially in Medina where he had spent the last ten years of his life. With the expansion of the Muslim community, however, this memory bank needed to be recorded more formally, in case it was forgotten, or not even known by those who converted to Islam in more distant places. So the early 'ulama' collected hadith, and a science of hadith criticism developed in which criteria were formulated to establish the authenticity or otherwise of statements that related to Muhammad. Chains of reliable transmitters whose testimony could be traced right back to the Prophet or his Companions were required before a given hadith could be classified as true. The early Muslim scholar **Ahmad ibn Hanbal** (750–855), speaking of the status of Muhammad's Companions, said: "The least of these in companionhood is better than the generation that did not see him."[6] The most respected of all the hadith collections were those of **al-Bukhari** (810–870) and **Muslim** (c. 815–875), whose thousands of hadith provided a firm foundation for a comprehensive system of jurisprudence (legal theory).[7]

During the period from 632 until the fall of the **Umayyad** dynasty in 750, the caliphs, with the help of a growing class of religious scholars who immersed themselves deeply in the Qur'an and the hadith, gradually developed the foundations of what was to become the Shari'a. But there were obvious difficulties. By the beginning of the eighth century, Muslim territories already covered vast tracts of the world, from Spain to India, and because such distances presented difficulties of communication, it was inevitable that uniformity of interpretation in legal matters across the whole empire was impossible. Thus local schools of law, called *madhhabs*, "ways (of interpreting the law)," developed, based at important cities, such as Damascus, Kufa, Basra, and Medina (see pp. 119–21).

THE INFLUENCE OF NON-MUSLIM PRACTICE

The various ways in which Islamic law was practiced were greatly influenced by the earlier legal systems that had been in place in a given region before the coming of Islam. Indeed, much of Islamic law reflects a Jewish background, or the particular bedrock of laws and practices in existence in the conquered lands, and especially Roman law.[8]

Just as Christian canon law owed much to Roman legal codes, so too did Islamic law in the pre-modern era draw on non-Muslim elements as it evolved. Indeed, until the arrival of the European colonial powers in the Muslim-majority countries of the Middle East, Islamic law developed alongside a diverse blend of pre-Islamic practices, local custom, and administrative edicts by the rulers. *Qanuns* (secular laws) were passed alongside Muslim law in many areas. It is also clear that other kinds of courts existed from an early stage in the Muslim world. The best known of these were the *mazalim* (grievances) courts, a pre-Islamic Persian tradition, in which justice was dispensed by the secular rulers themselves. In the *Siyasatnama*, a treatise on government written by the great Persian **vizier** of the Turkish **Seljuq** dynasty, **Nizam al-Mulk** (d. 1092), he advises **Sultan** Malikshah as follows: "It is absolutely necessary that on two days in the week the king should sit for the redress of wrongs, to extract recompense from the oppressor, to give justice and to listen to the words of his subjects without any intermediary."[9]

CLASSICAL SUNNI JURISPRUDENCE (*FIQH*) 8TH TO 18TH CENTURY

The pragmatic legal rulings of the Umayyad period (661–750) gradually gave way to the firm centralizing authority of the 'Abbasids (750–1258), who from their new capital of Baghdad imposed greater order and systematization on Islamic law. It was in the 'Abbasid period that the classical principles of Islamic jurisprudence were formulated.

FIQH **AND** *SUNNA*

The original meaning of *fiqh* as found in the Qur'an and the early Islamic period is "understanding" or "discerning,"[10] but it came to bear the specialized meaning of "jurisprudence." Amongst all the branches of Islamic religious knowledge, most Muslims would agree that it is jurisprudence that determines for them what right action is.[11] The process of fiqh culminates in a *hukm* (judgment), one that, however, could be modified or reversed.

As a practical source of jurisprudence, Qur'anic injunctions were consulted first; these cover such topics as marriage, divorce, illicit sexual intercourse, alcohol, inheritance, property, theft, and homicide. Although Qur'anic rules do not fully encompass the multitude of legal cases that arose in different periods and geographical locations, the Qur'an validates the Prophet's right to legislate on God's behalf: "Obey God and His Prophet so that you may be given mercy" (3:132). So legal scholars, accustomed to the ancient Arab tribal concept of *sunna* (a way of acting according to the established custom of previous generations),[12] gradually reinterpreted the word sunna to mean the exemplary conduct of the Prophet—the actions and behavior of Muhammad

The study group. Al-Hariri, *Assemblies*, Baghdad, 1237. The main figures vividly evoke the cut and thrust of scholarly debate, closely followed by a rapt audience. Academic stars commanded hefty salaries in the *madrasa* system inaugurated by the Seljuq vizier Nizam al-Mulk. Note too the discreet luxury of the furnishings, and the figure to the right operating the fan to provide a cool breeze.

as a template for how to lead their own lives. It was thus that the *Sunna* of the Prophet, incorporating as it did his attested sayings (the hadith), became an authoritative guide to clarify or amplify a particular piece of legislation found in the Qur'an. The great Muslim thinker **Ibn Khaldun** (1332–1406) sums up the status of the Qur'an and the Sunna as follows: "The basis of all the traditional sciences is the legal material of the Qur'an and the customary behaviour (Sunna) of the Prophet, which is the law given to us by God and His Messenger."[13]

PRINCIPLES OF JURISPRUDENCE

Al-Shafi'i (767–820), who is generally regarded as the principal early systematizer of jurisprudence, relied on four core elements—the Qur'an, the Sunna, consensus (*ijma'*), and analogical reasoning (*qiyas*). The first two are sources of law, whilst the other two are more methodological foundations, or principles of applying the law.[14] Consensus came to mean agreement amongst scholars at a particular time, for, according to a famous hadith, "My community shall never agree on an error."[15] A given judge would make public a judgment on a legal matter, and if no religious scholar made convincing counter-arguments, and all others agreed with it, then a consensus had been reached. The principle of analogy involved applying an established law to a new situation. A well-known example of analogy concerns the drinking of alcohol. The Qur'an calls the drinking of intoxicants "Satan's doing,"[16] and drinking date wine is forbidden in the hadith. Although other alcoholic drinks, such as grape wine, beer, and whisky, are not mentioned in these canonical sources, the 'ulama' have prohibited the drinking of them, since just as date wine is intoxicating, by analogy so too are other alcoholic drinks.

Human actions, personal and in society, are classified in the Shari'a into five categories—obligatory (*fard*), recommended (*mandub*), allowed (*mubah*), reprehensible (*makruh*), and forbidden (*haram*).[17] There are two kinds of obligatory actions: those that are individual obligations, such as ablution before prayer (see Chapter 4, pp. 92–94), and those that are performed if a sufficient number of Muslims are involved in the action, such as the corporate ritual prayer in the mosque on Fridays (see Chapter 4, p. 98), or carrying out the lesser jihad (see Chapter 9, p. 219). There is no crude simplification here of dividing these five categories of action into "good" or bad" deeds; instead, the Shari'a presents a nuanced sliding scale.

Other principles of jurisprudence were allowed within the remit of the Shari'a: *ijtihad* (the exercise of a legal scholar's independent reasoning in coming to a decision)[18] and *maslaha* (making a decision in the public interest). The role of custom (*'urf*) was also important, and scholars allowed a certain degree of flexibility in preserving local customs and retaining time-honored traditions in different areas of the Muslim world, always provided that they did not contradict the Shari'a. But the use of a different word ('urf) to describe such customs and traditions decisively distinguished them from the tenets of the Shari'a.

SCHOOLS OF LAW

In the early centuries of Islam, students of law congregated around particular figures in the major cities of the Muslim empire and would often travel far in search of knowledge of the legal sciences. Some schools of law (madhhabs) appeared and disappeared, but by the eleventh century, the four major schools of Sunni Islamic law—**Hanafi, Maliki, Hanbali,** and **Shafi'i**—had become firmly established; they continue today. Each is named after an early religious scholar who helped to formulate the specific characteristics of each particular legal school—**Abu Hanifa** (d. 767), **Malik ibn Anas** (d. 801), Ahmad ibn Hanbal, and al-Shafi'i (both mentioned above). The disciples of these legal schools were loyal not to a particular specialist in the law but to a carefully constructed methodology, based on recorded historical legal decisions. This was a methodology that had been elaborated over generations by many pious men, who had immersed themselves in studying the Qur'an and the Sunna. The consolidation of distinct groupings of 'ulama' (also called *fuqaha'*—those who interpret fiqh) with shared methods and opinions into named legal schools was thus the final stage of a long development.[19]

Islamic law was dynamic, not static, and flexible, not rigid. Muslim legal scholars were generally tolerant of one another's positions, although they often disagreed, sometimes when there were significant differences of opinion and at other times about what may appear to be tiny details. In the important area of the drawing up of a marriage contract, for example, there were often widely diverging views between the different legal schools: as one contemporary scholar observes in this context, "the language of offer and acceptance generated detailed juristic discussion" and "although it was normative for the marriage offer to be made by the man, some scholars permitted the woman's guardian to do so."[20] On the other hand, legal opinions could concern trifles. As Imber points out in his book on the **Ottoman** legal scholar **Ebu's-Su'ud** (*c.* 1490–1574), there was great intellectual enjoyment in dealing with such obscure problems as the share of an inheritance due to a hermaphrodite (as men and women had different rights under the law). Knowledge of the law was a sign of piety and a prestige indicator, and Ottoman legal scholars would hold debates in front of the sultan, alongside firework displays, mock battles, and feasts, at such court festivities as the circumcision ceremony for the sons of Sultan Süleyman in 1530.[21]

The Hanafi legal school was particularly important; it was favored by the 'Abbasids (750–1258) and then by the various Turkish dynasties, such as the Seljuqs (1040–1194), who conquered Iran, Iraq, and Syria. The **Mamluk** Turkish dynasty (1250–1517), which ruled a vast empire with its centre in Cairo, allowed all four Sunni legal schools to flourish. The Ottoman Turks (1300–1922) terminated the Mamluk dynasty in 1517 and came to rule all central Muslim lands. Their official legal school was that of the Hanafis. By the sixteenth century the Hanafi legal school had spread to Turkey, the Balkans, Central Asia, and the Indian subcontinent. The Maliki legal school moved westward and became dominant in Spain until the Christian reconquest in 1492, and in North and West Africa, where it remains the major

"'Seek ye knowledge, even unto China,' advised the Prophet." The *Assemblies* by al-Hariri, Baghdad, 1237. Scholars debate eagerly; behind them, books are stacked horizontally (often they were chained down, for security). The practice of dictating texts to large groups, instead of having one person at a time copying the original, improved the accuracy of transmission and fostered the growth of huge libraries.

legal school today. The Shafi'i legal school became popular in parts of the Arabian peninsula and East Africa, and later on in Malaysia and Indonesia. The Hanbali legal school is now principally concentrated in the Arabian Gulf area. This madhhab played an important role in the religious history of the Muslim world, despite its comparatively small numbers of adherents. It came to prominence particularly in the fourteenth century at the time of the Hanbali scholar **Ibn Taymiyya** (1263–1328), and again in the eighteenth century with the rise of the **Wahhabi** movement in Arabia (see Chapter 7, p. 184).

It would be true to say that, despite its political divisions, what the Muslims called the "House of Islam" (the vast area of the world inhabited by Muslims, which at its height stretched from Spain to India) applied some form of Islamic law until the end of the eighteenth century and the coming of European colonialism. The great fourteenth-century Muslim traveler **Ibn Battuta**, for example, who recorded his twenty-eight years of journeying throughout the Muslim world, was equally able to practice as a religious scholar and a judge (*qadi*) in his native Morocco and in the distant Maldives, in the Indian Ocean, where he stayed for a while.

APPLYING THE SHARI'A

In the Sunni tradition the caliph served as the symbol of the supremacy of the Shari'a (see Chapter 7, pp. 180–82). The responsibility to apply and defend the Shari'a was his. It was incumbent on his fellow Muslims to obey him—but only because he was the representative of the Shari'a, to which he too was subordinate. Even when secular power in the House of Islam was in the hands of military usurpers—as was increasingly the case from the eighth century onward—Sunni Muslims everywhere looked to the caliph as a figurehead, a symbol of the universality of their faith. And the military overlords felt the need to seek him out in order to legitimize their credentials to govern the territories they had seized.

Sunni law was in the hands of legal scholars (*fuqaha'*), who defined it and issued *fatwa*s (legal opinions) on specific cases when asked, and also of judges who sat in religious courts to try cases that were brought to them. Shari'a courts were firmly established across the 'Abbasid empire under the jurisdiction of such judges. They had existed already under the Umayyads, but did not operate in such a systematic and thorough manner as in the 'Abbasid period. Three of the four main Sunni legal schools tended to prohibit the appointment of women as judges, following their interpretation of a Qur'anic verse (4:34), which states: "Men are in charge of women." The Hanafi legal school, on the hand, did permit the appointment of women judges.

Dispensing justice.
Al-Hariri, *Assemblies*, Egypt or Syria, *c.* 1335. A barefoot, crafty rogue grovels before a suspicious judge, who wears the *taylasan*, a hooded mantle, over his turban. The hands and eyes of the two principal figures spell out in dumb show their complex interaction.

College life. Ben Yusuf *madrasa*, Marrakesh, Morocco, 1325. The origins of many *madrasas* in the teacher's own house are reflected here in the domestic flavor and small scale. The imposing and glamorous public face, prinked out with carved wood and stucco and glazed tilework, contrasts with the austerity of the students' quarters, safely out of sight.

The legal elite did not enjoy total independence in medieval Muslim societies and they needed the support of the ruling class. In turn, those who usurped power needed the legal scholars to legitimize their position, and the legal scholars often reminded the rulers of their obligation to govern according to the Shari'a. The scholars also often acted as a bridge between the ruler and the ordinary people.

From the eleventh century onward, would-be legal scholars would study in **madrasas**, institutions devoted above all to the teaching of the jurisprudence of a particular legal school. The curriculum at madrasas was not restricted to jurisprudence but probably covered in its program the whole range of the religious sciences, including the Qur'an, theology, hadith, as well as Arabic grammar. (For further discussion of Islamic theology and philosophy, see Chapter 7.) Under the enlightened rule of the caliph **al-Mustansir** (ruled 1226–42), the famous Mustansiriyya madrasa was built in Baghdad in 1232 to house all four Sunni madhhabs. This was the first madrasa to have been

The first universal *madrasa*. Courtyard of al-Mustansiriyya *madrasa*, Baghdad, 1227–34. Built by the penultimate 'Abbasid caliph as a measured political statement of his authority over the entire Muslim world, it gives equal space to each of the principal four legal schools, a bold ecumenical gesture. It boasts an unprecedented range of accommodation and facilities, including a kitchen and library.

built by a caliph, and although there had been earlier madrasas that were designed for more than one madhhab, this was the first really universal Sunni madrasa, symbolizing al-Mustansir's aim as the figurehead of the Shari'a to create under his auspices an all-encompassing Muslim unity, an urgent task given the devastating impact of the Mongol invasions from 1220 onward.[22] The same practice of housing all four Sunni legal schools in one madrasa was also adopted in the fourteenth century in Cairo by the Turkish Mamluks.

Modern books about Islamic jurisprudence tend to describe its development rather simplistically, as if it suddenly appeared in its final form. But in the early centuries of the Muslim era, as noted above, Islamic law was a constantly evolving entity, operating from Spain to India. When later generations of religious scholars looked back on the legal issues that had confronted their predecessors, their work was often simply to refine what must have been a very lively and complex set of intellectual debates in earlier times.

BOOKS OF JURISPRUDENCE

There are thousands of medieval Arabic books of jurisprudence in the libraries of the Muslim world, many of them still only in manuscript form. These books follow a very similar format, whenever and wherever they were written. Within a given legal school a work of jurisprudence written in the seventeenth century differs very little from one written in the tenth.

The format of books of jurisprudence is firmly fixed under two major groupings; first, actions associated with the worship of God (*'ibadat*), and second, those that deal with Muslims' relationships with their fellow human beings (*mu'amalat*). These books often provide extremely detailed information about how the Muslim faithful should perform the duties prescribed by the Shari'a—duties connected with the five pillars of the faith (see Chapter 4), as well as how to eat, how to behave in the bathhouse, how to trade, how to achieve happiness in marriage, how to conduct jihad, how to treat non-Muslims living in Muslim lands, and a multitude of other precisely described rules. Nothing is deemed too trivial to be explained. The differences between the legal schools concern such matters as whether certain prayers should be said in a loud or a soft voice and how high the hands should be stretched out when saying "Allahu akbar." A given chapter usually begins with relevant quotations from the Qur'an; appropriate hadith are then cited. The scholar next moves on to mention the views of early scholars on the particular theme of the chapter before adding comments of his own, often in copious detail.

FATWAS

As well as consulting and memorizing the books of jurisprudence, Muslim legal scholars were regularly asked to pronounce their opinions on matters of public or private concern. A ruler or any individual Muslim within the community would consult a ***mufti***—a person qualified to give a legal opinion (fatwa)—about a specific issue. Such an opinion could concern a family problem, such as inheritance or divorce, or a matter of grave political importance, such as whether it was legitimate for a Sunni sultan to wage the lesser jihad against Shi'ite Muslims. Having consulted the Qur'an and the Sunna, and having followed the guiding principles of analogy and consensus, the scholar then used his independent reasoning to deliver a fatwa to the person or persons who have sought his views. Fatwas can be expressed in a single word such as "yes" or "no," or they can cover many pages of text. If necessary, the matter would be followed up in the Shari'a court, where the judge would pronounce a judgment and on occasion decree that a penalty should be imposed.

Fatwas were not, however, a requirement in court. Judges could take them into consideration, but they were not obliged to do so.

The many fatwas of the Hanbalite Sunni scholar Ibn Taymiyya are forceful. In one famous fatwa he records with great vehemence the horrors of two Mongol invasions of Syria from 1299 to 1301.[23] At no point does he accept that the Mongols are Muslims, even though the Mongol ruler Ghazan publicly converted to Islam in 1295. Ibn Taymiyya argues that the Mongols did not apply the Shari'a, continuing instead to follow their own legal code, the *yasa*. So he calls them the "enemy" and pronounces that jihad must be waged against them by the Muslims. Within the confines of Muslim Syria, Ibn Taymiyya was also irrevocably hostile to the Shi'ite minorities living there, accusing them of collaborating with the Mongols. Indeed, in 1300 he personally took part in a jihad campaign against local Shi'ites, against whom he also issued a fatwa, authorizing such an attack.

Fatwas were needed when new issues arose in Muslim societies. Inevitably, in the course of time, legal scholars were faced with the task of adjudicating on matters that had not been problematic, nor even been in existence, in the era of the Prophet. An interesting example was the legal status of coffee-drinking and coffee-houses in the sixteenth century.[24] Questions were raised as to whether coffee was an intoxicating drink and should be prohibited for that reason (the Arabic word *qahwa* originally meant "wine" but the same word was also used to denote "coffee"), and also whether it was permissible

Social hub. Fishawi's coffee house, Khan al-Khalili, Cairo. The introduction of coffee, like that of tobacco, caused consternation among Islamic lawyers at first, but before long both were universally accepted. Tea-houses and coffee-houses have long been favored locations for male social interaction (including idle chatter), for storytelling, for puffing away, and for playing backgammon.

to allow the existence of coffee-houses where, it was suggested, undesirable elements of society met to discuss the dangerous subject of politics. Heated discussions about the legal status of coffee raged, but by the mid-sixteenth century the anti-coffee lobby had lost the fight. Before long, coffee and coffee-houses spread to all corners of the Ottoman Empire and beyond.

PENALTIES

The Shari'a contains a specific group of fixed penalties known as the *hudud* (literally "limits"); these can be broadly defined as "bounds set by God on human freedom."[25] As is made clear in the Qur'an, these penalties are intended to be carried out in public as an example to others. Certain crimes have particular penalties stipulated in the Qur'an or the Sunna. For example, the Qur'an specifies one hundred lashes for illicit sexual relations (Qur'an 24:2), if that act is satisfactorily proven. Theft is punishable by the amputation of a hand; the Qur'an states (5:38): "As for the thief, both male and female, cut off their hands." The Shari'a requires detailed evidence for these and other hudud penalties; in practice they were not often carried out.

Stoning used to take place in Jewish society, as the Bible shows.[26] Muslims also adopted this practice. The Qur'an refers to the practice of stoning only as the way in which preceding generations of unbelievers had killed the prophets sent by God to teach them true religion. A connection is frequently made nowadays, by Muslims and non-Muslims alike, between sexual misconduct and stoning as viewed in Islamic law. The Qur'anic word *zina'* means sexual intercourse outside the institution of marriage,[27] and this practice is strongly condemned both in the Qur'an and in the hadith. The Qur'an states: "And do not go anywhere near unlawful sexual intercourse: it is an outrage, and an evil path" (17:32). The prescribed Qur'anic punishment for proven illicit sexual intercourse (one hundred lashes) nevertheless requires—and this is a very important qualification—that four male eye-witnesses of good character have seen the act of penetration, a condition that makes this rule almost impossible to apply. The same Qur'anic chapter (24:4) prescribes eighty lashes for those who accuse honorable women but do not bring with them four men who have witnessed the deed. A woman who has been raped cannot be punished by any such penalty. There is no mention in the Qur'an of stoning as a penalty for committing illicit sexual intercourse.

A cluster of around ten hadith, however, mentions stoning as a punishment ordered by Muhammad for men and women caught in illicit sexual intercourse.[28] Despite this very flimsy basis in hadith,[29] stoning became enshrined as a penalty in jurisprudence for an act of illicit sexual intercourse, although the requirement of four male witnesses to the act of penetration has been considered to be a safeguard against its being used very often.[30]

The issue of stoning in today's world is hotly debated by Muslim feminist scholars and activists as well as by human rights organizations. The 2003 Nobel Peace Prize winner, **Shirin Ebadi**, has called for the abolition of stoning in the Muslim world, basing her arguments both within a human rights framework as well as on the fact that there is no mention of stoning as a punishment for illicit sexual intercourse in the Qur'an. She argues that according to the Quran, the offense of illicit sexual intercourse must be proven through voluntary confession or by testimony of four witnesses of good moral character who state under oath that they have seen the crime itself take place. It is near impossible to have four people of good morals testify that in the same place, at the same time, they saw the act of penetration. It is important to note, however, that pregnancy is often used as the basis for accusing a woman of this crime, although Islamic law does not mention pregnancy as evidence of illicit sexual intercourse.[31]

There is no doubt that the field of jurisprudence was the most prestigious branch of the Islamic religious sciences until the period of European colonialism and the impact of Western ideas in the eighteenth century. It was valued more highly than theology, and much more highly than philosophy. Of course, there was overlap at times with these other spheres of knowledge, given that many of the most famous medieval Muslim scholars, such as **Ibn Sina** (980–1037), **al-Ghazali** (1058–1111), and Ibn Taymiyya, were well versed in more than one branch of the religious sciences. But the law was at the heart of their endeavors. Until the eighteenth century the Muslim legal scholar saw it as his duty to pass on the faithfully preserved tradition of his own madhhab to his successors, and to do his best to apply the rules at his disposal as creatively as possible in order to solve the legal problems that faced him.[32]

THE IMPACT OF EUROPEAN COLONIALISM: MODERNIZING ISLAMIC LAW, 18TH TO 20TH CENTURY

The story of the relationship between the legal systems of European colonial powers and the Shari'a in Muslim-majority countries is almost invariably told from one perspective only—that of the colonizers. According to that story the colonizers came and occupied Muslim countries. They then removed indigenous laws and put European ones, such as the Napoleonic Code or British common law, in their place. This version of events is not entirely wrong, but it is undeniably one-sided and simplistic.[33] In fact, colonial governors, administrators, and judges found the existence of the Shari'a and the presence of the Muslim legal scholars a major problem. They may have tried to impose European laws on the colonized lands and may have succeeded in doing so, but there were limits to this imposition. Indeed, they were obliged to accommodate into their own legal processes certain elements of the Shari'a as practiced in those lands. Furthermore, the legal changes that occurred in this period were not always connected with colonial rule.

EIGHTEENTH TO NINETEENTH CENTURY

The first countries in which changes introduced from outside took place were eighteenth-century India and Ottoman Turkey. In these countries commercial and penal legal codes, based on European models, were established and secular courts were set up to deal with civil and criminal cases. The first governor-general of India, Warren Hastings (in power 1773–84), provided an

The peak of Ottoman power. Süleymaniye mosque complex, Istanbul, 1550–57. Dominating the city's skyline, this imperial monument glorifies Süleyman the Magnificent, caliph, sultan, and upholder of Sunni Islam, feared and respected in Europe. Ingeniously landscaped, it is a multi-purpose foundation of fourteen buildings serving worship, welfare, educational, and funerary purposes.

example of reform imposed by the colonizer. The British colonial government did not like the way in which Muslim law allowed for a range of possible penalties for murder; such penalties might on occasion include the perpetrator being permitted to provide compensation to the victim's family, instead of being given the death penalty. Hastings saw to it that this law was replaced, and henceforth it was the state that would prosecute and pronounce judgment in cases of homicide brought against one of its legal subjects.[34] The family of the victim could no longer avenge the murder of their family member.

Muslim religious scholars were willing at times to cooperate with the colonial power to reform their own legal traditions. Drawing on the well-established principle of *maslaha* (public interest), colonized and postcolonial lawyers were able to harmonize the precepts of the Shari'a with those of a modern secular state in the sphere of family law. Muslim reformist thinkers, such as **Sayyid Ahmad Khan** (1817–1898) in India and **Muhammad 'Abduh** (1849–1905) in Egypt, viewed European legal systems more favorably than their more traditional co-religionists. The views of 'Abduh have been very influential. In his last years, from 1899 onward, he became grand mufti of Egypt and set in place important reforms in the Shari'a using his informed personal judgment (ijtihad) to interpret the spheres of family and individual law in a less rigid way than had previously been the case. According to one scholar, 'Abduh has been "widely revered as the chief architect of the modern reformation of Islam."[35]

TWENTIETH CENTURY

From the end of the nineteenth century Islamic law in much of the Muslim world was relegated to the sphere of family law only. More developments took place in the early twentieth century. In 1917, just shortly before the demise of the Ottoman empire, a Law of Family Rights was passed, based principally on Hanafi jurisprudence but also on that of the three other Sunni legal schools. This law had an impact on other Muslim countries, such as Egypt, Syria, Iraq, Tunisia, Morocco, and Pakistan, where legal scholars used the principle of personal judgment to reform their marriage and divorce laws, which had previously been dominated by the Shari'a. The new Republic of Turkey (established 1923) was unique in the Muslim world in the early twentieth century, with its new entirely secularized state and legal system (based on the Swiss civil code), which had been inaugurated by **Kemal Atatürk** (1881–1938) in 1925. In 1949, **'Abd al-Razzaq al-Sanhuri**, a key figure in the Arab world, introduced a new Egyptian civil code, which drew on French models and existing legislation in Egypt as well as on elements of the Shari'a. Al-Sanhuri was later invited to draw up new legal codes in Kuwait and Iraq. By the 1930s the legal systems operating in the Arab world followed a similar pattern. As the scholar Albert Hourani describes it: "Criminal, civil and commercial cases were decided according to European codes and procedures and the authority of the Shari'a and of the judges who dispensed it was confined to matters of personal status."[36]

The Lebanese scholar **Sobhi Mahmassani** (1909–1986) was another important advocate of change, arguing that Islamic law should be adapted to the conditions of modern society: "The door of ijtihad should be thrown wide open for anyone juristically qualified. The error, all the error, lies in blind imitation and restraint of thought. What is right is to allow freedom of interpretation of Islamic jurisprudence, and to liberate thought and make it capable of true scientific creativeness."[37] Whilst remaining devoted to his faith, Mahmassani encouraged his fellow Muslims to be guided also by "true science" and "keen thinking."[38] He went even further, adopting an attitude similar to that of post-Enlightenment Europe, arguing that religion is for the private sphere and that law belongs to the secular state: Muslims should give "what belongs to religion to religion and what belongs to the world to the world;"[39] only in this way, he argued, would Muslim ignorance and backwardness be overcome. The impulse toward liberating Islamic law from the shackles of the past is also forcefully encouraged by the Indian Muslim scholar **Asaf Fyzee** (1899–1981), who speaks of the spirit of Islam in his own time as being "throttled by fanaticism"; he sees the need for modern Islam to separate religious matters from legal ones.[40]

MUSLIM LAW TODAY

Given the global spread of Islam today, it is very difficult to generalize about how and to what extent, or if at all, the Shari'a is applied in greatly diverse Muslim-majority and Muslim-minority countries across the world. Indeed, the vast majority of citizens in these countries today are subject to legal codes that are not so very different from those operating in the West. In almost every country with a Muslim majority the Shari'a view of matrimonial and inheritance law is enshrined in the legal code. In Muslim-minority areas different countries are working out their own particular reactions to the issues of integration in relation to retaining strands of Muslim law.

FOOD REGULATIONS

From the very beginning of Islam, Muslims were permitted to eat the food of Jews, Christians, and other religious communities with an established scripture; as the Qur'an states: "The food of the People of the Book is lawful for you as your food is lawful for them" (68:5). Whilst animals should be slaughtered in the Muslim or Jewish kosher way, Muslim butchers must also observe the laws of health and hygiene of a non-Muslim state. Most Muslims do not drink alcohol and virtually none eats pork.

BANKING

Muslims have always been forbidden to practice usury (money lending). The Qur'anic statement (2:275) on charging interest on debts is unambiguous: "God has allowed trade and forbidden usury." The emphasis in the Qur'an is on giving charitable donations, not acquiring private wealth through usury. The Qur'an (2:274) is severe on usurers but very supportive of those who give of their wealth to other people: "Those who give, out of their own possessions, by night and day, in private and in public, will have their reward with their Lord: no fear for them, neither will they grieve. But those who take usury will rise up on the Day of Resurrection like someone tormented by Satan's touch." In their financial dealings Muslims are urged to be honest. They are allowed to work with non-Muslim partners.

The opinions of modern Muslim scholars about contemporary Islamic banking vary considerably. Khan and Ramadan, in their book of 2011 on Islamic legal practices, paint the following picture.[41] According to Islamic law, bank loans on which interest is charged are forbidden. This runs contrary to the credit-based economy ubiquitous in the West, where interest is charged. Khan and Ramadan mention that in such Gulf countries as Qatar and Bahrain, and in Malaysia, Muslim capital markets have been set up to offer their clients borrowing mechanisms, investments, and securities that comply with the Shari'a. Such centers attract both Muslim and non-Muslim customers (the latter disenchanted with the perceived malpractice and greed shown by the world's bankers). Moreover, as another Muslim legal scholar, Maleiha Malik, mentions in her report of 2012, HSBC Amanah—the global Muslim financial services section of the HSBC banking group—has used Muslim legal principles to develop Islamic mortgages, which do not attract interest.[42]

On the other hand, Timur Kuran, a well-respected Turkish economist working in the USA, voices strong objections to this idealized picture of Muslim banking, arguing that the giving and taking of interest in Muslim contexts has long existed. He mentions that interest is disguised in a variety of financial strategies, following the time-honored way in which classical Muslim legal scholars on occasion used "ruses" (**hiyal**) to deal with difficult problems. Not surprisingly, he argues, many Muslims in the West, exercising their own judgment, are pragmatic in such matters and they no longer observe these financial prohibitions.[43]

CONTROVERSIAL ISSUES OF SHARI'A AND STATE LAW
IN THE USA AND BRITAIN

The Shari'a is the core issue about Islam that causes the most disquiet and hostility amongst non-Muslims worldwide. It is a matter of crucial importance to the world at large—in the new Egypt and other transformed political entities that the extraordinary events of the **Arab Spring** (see Chapter 11, p. 279) are creating, as well as in Europe and in the USA, where storm clouds of controversy about the Shari'a hover over such states as Tennessee, Kansas, and Alaska. Heads of state pronounce on this topic; speaking in December 2006, the then prime minister of Britain, Tony Blair, cited "forced marriages, the importation of Shari'a law and the ban on women entering certain mosques" as being "on the wrong side of the line."[44] Sweeping statements of this kind are misleading, for it is not the whole of the Shari'a that actually troubles non-Muslims, but their perception of only two aspects of it—the treatment of women and severe penalties, such as capital punishment and the amputation of hands. They know little about the rest of its contents.

A study of 2011, which aims to encourage "more debate and engagement" about Shari'a issues in the USA, analyzes a number of published legal cases that relate to "conflict of law" between Shari'a and American state law.[45] After examining fifty cases from twenty-three different states, the report concludes that there are a significant number of legal decisions "at odds with the state's public policy." Some of the cases analyzed involved what are described as Shari'a-motivated honor killings, assault against a person who was "an alleged blasphemer against Islam," and "jihadist violence against institutions or persons." In all these cases the accused declared that their motivation was "driven by Shariah or Islamic law."[46] The report goes on to say that it has no difficulty with Muslims in the USA practicing "personal, pietistic religious observances"[47] that do not conflict with American laws. It is, however, concerned with what it calls those who advocate an "institutionalized, authoritative Shariah."[48] The report remarks that the cases chosen in the sample represent only "the tip of the iceberg."

In Britain the most senior cleric in the Church of England, the then Archbishop of Canterbury, Dr Rowan Williams, was widely criticized in February 2008 for saying publicly that adopting certain aspects of the Shari'a into the English legal system seemed unavoidable. To quote his exact words, he said that there would be a place for "a constructive accommodation with some aspects of Muslim law," as is already the case with some other aspects of religious law.[49] These remarks sparked a widespread and in the main extremely hostile discussion in the media. There was much criticism of the archbishop, whose views were often taken out of context or just misunderstood. And yet he was right when he referred to the existence of other religious courts in the UK, since it has long been the case that British Jews have been able to turn to the Beth Din, their own religious courts, for the settlement of a range of civil disputes, ranging from divorce to commerce.[50]

It is clearly a little-known fact that Christians, Jews, and Muslims all have religious institutions in Britain that are allowed to apply some aspects of religious law, and that such systems work well generally. Nevertheless, the atmosphere of hostility to Muslims since 9/11, and since the so-called 7/7 attack in London, has been inflamed by the dominant discourse of extremist Muslim groups, such as Islam4UK and Al-Muhajiroun, which speak about the "Islamization of Britain" and reinforce stereotypical and hostile images of the Shari'a in the minds of the British public.[51]

VIEWS OF MUSLIMS ON THE SHARI'A

In the 1960s the Pakistani scholar Fazlur Rahman, who taught for many years in the USA, argued that law in Muslim societies should be worked out from the ethical teachings of the Qur'an and the Sunna of Muhammad but also bearing in mind the contemporary context: "Thus, law will adjust to changed social situations, but ethical values…will remain constant."[52] A Malaysian scholar of Islamic law, Mohammad Kamali, shares this view: "Only a small portion of the legal contents of the Qur'an and Sunnah is conveyed in specific and unalterable terms." He goes on to explain that by far the greater part of the Qur'an and Sunna can be interpreted and developed in different ways.[53]

When extremist Muslim groups in certain parts of the world, such as Nigeria or Afghanistan, seize power and announce the establishment of Shari'a law, the fixed penalties (hudud) are applied unusually often and with great fanfare to excite awe and terror amongst the population. It is as if doing so gives their regime credibility as an authentic Muslim state. In such a situation the hands of thieves are amputated, those found guilty of adultery are stoned to death, those who have committed fornication are lashed, and a strict dress code is imposed on women. In such situations, the vast number and range of carefully phrased and nuanced rulings found in the books of Islamic jurisprudence compiled over many centuries are brushed aside or ignored in favor of a violent and disgracefully simplistic ideology that has no place in the twenty-first century and that most Muslims reject.

As already mentioned, non-Muslims today often equate the Shari'a with its fixed penalties (hudud). And this ill-informed view is reinforced by the pronouncements and actions of such groups as the **Taliban**. The novels of Khaled Hosseini,[54] an Afghan writer in exile in the USA, are an eloquent condemnation of barbaric deeds perpetrated by Muslim men on Muslim women in his homeland. Naghib Mahfouz, the Nobel prize winner in literature in 1988, had perceptive words to say about the hudud in his homeland of Egypt, criticizing the double standards that existed in a society in which, for example, wine is sold and gambling centers are set up for tourists, whilst hudud are also carried out in that same society.[55] In most Muslim-majority countries these penalties are not imposed, nor are they even included in the government legal codes. In those few countries, such as Saudi Arabia, Pakistan, and Iran, that have adopted the Shari'a as state law, these penalties are formally instituted. Whilst it is undoubtedly true that there have been occasions when the hudud have been enforced even in recent times, Kamali argues that such penalties are not implemented with great speed or enthusiasm.[56]

The report written in 2012 by Maleiha Malik mentioned above argues that it is reasonable for minorities in the UK, such as Jews, Christians, and Muslims, to ask for some of the practices that form part of their community-based law to be accommodated in the state legal system. This can be done through minority legal orders.[57] The report also stresses that Jews, Christians, and Muslims already have religious councils that deal with civil disputes within their faith communities, that there is ongoing constructive dialogue between their representatives and state legal bodies, and that there is "a dynamic relationship between religious courts and the civil law."[58]

Today's ethical issues steadily occupy the minds of Muslim specialists in law, who reinterpret the Qur'an and Sunna for their co-religionists. The Islamic attitude to dogs is a case in point. Traditionally, Muslims have regarded dogs as unclean, basing this view on the Shari'a. However, the American Muslim scholar **Khaled M. Abou El Fadl**[59] has judged the hadith that is hostile to dogs to be unreliable; indeed, he has found what he argues is a more trustworthy hadith in which the Prophet is shown praying in the presence of dogs.

In Britain, Muslim attitudes to dogs were recently modified when Muslim restaurant owners and taxi drivers, who had previously refused access to blind people with guide dogs, were permitted to allow them in, after discussion had taken place between Muslim religious leaders and the Disability Rights Commission. Guide dogs may now even enter some mosques.[60]

THE FUTURE

Islamic law is an organic, living entity, not a fixed, dead, and immovable one; it is not a system set in stone. History shows us its evolution. Modern dogmatic ideology only distorts this truth and obscures the key fact that, like so many other legal systems around the world, it is a work in progress.

Over the centuries those who have specialized in studying what Shari'a means have practiced varying degrees of pragmatism in interpreting it to fit different societies in diverse parts of the world. Religious specialists in both Muslim-majority and Muslim-minority countries have a range of views on the relationship between Muslim religious law and secular state systems in the contemporary world. The solutions adopted in each country have and will continue to have a crucial impact on the lives of more than a billion and a half Muslims in both East and West, and especially the one half of that number who are women.

Will modern Muslim legal scholars exercise ijtihad and erase altogether from the legal books some long-outdated aspects of Islamic law that arose in a particular historical period and place—and, above all, the hudud for adultery and theft? How will Muslim scholars deal with new problems, such as bioethics, organ transplants, abortion, contraception, and Internet issues? In the Middle East, the events of the Arab Spring are producing and will no doubt continue to produce varying types of government and legal systems, ranging from the secular, through a mixed form of legislative structures, to the establishment of what individual countries may perceive as a government with a constitution based on the Shari'a. The Jordanian constitution, for example, is based on the Shari'a but there is no role for the application of hudud in it.

One scenario seems unlikely, however; although some jihadist groups today still speak about the caliphate, there is little probability that there will be a strong move toward the revival of that institution. But whilst modern territorial states have put down deep roots and nationalist loyalties are sometimes stronger than universalist Muslim aspirations, the concept of the ***umma***, the global community of Muslims, still evokes resonances with many believers. What seems certain is that in the daily spiritual life of Muslims, following the Shari'a will continue to guide them in their worship of the One God and in their conduct toward their fellow human beings. The Shari'a is what binds that community together.

SELECTED READING

Dien, Mawil Izzi, *Islamic Law: From Historical Foundation to Contemporary Practice*, Notre Dame, IN: University of Notre Dame Press, 2004

Gleave, R., *Scripturalist Islam: The History and Doctrines of the Akhbari Shi'i School*, Leiden and Boston, MA: Brill, 2007

Hallaq, Wael B., *A History of Islamic Legal Theories: An Introduction to Sunni Usul al-Fiqh*, Cambridge: Cambridge University Press, 1997

Kamali, Mohammad Hashim, "Law and Society. The Interplay of Revelation and Reason in the Shariah," in John L. Esposito (ed.), *The Oxford History of Islam*, Oxford and New York: Oxford University Press, 1999, pp. 107–54

Khadduri, Majid, *Al-Imam Muhammad Ibn Idris al-Shafi'i's al-Risala fi usul al-fiqh. Treatise on the Foundations of Islamic Jurisprudence*, trans. Majid Khadduri, Cambridge: The Islamic Texts Society, 1997

6 DIVERSITY

God willed us to be different and learn to live with each other.
HTTP://ISLAMTOGETHERFOUNDATION.BLOGSPOT.COM

God is just and has given us the freewill to be righteous in our own ways.
MUHAMMAD ASAD, COMMENTARY ON QUR'AN 6:159

Given that **Muslims** now reside in every part of the globe, in the Middle and Far East, Europe, and the Americas, it is scarcely surprising that there are many variations in Muslim doctrines and rituals that have evolved over the centuries since the death of **Muhammad** in 632. We are accustomed to hearing in the media about **Islam**, what Islam is, what Muslims do, and other sweeping generalizations of this kind. The idea of there being one monolithic, single, united body of Muslims is also nurtured by some Islamists who wish to convey this impression to the world at large for their own political and religious reasons. It is therefore essential to take a long look back into Islamic history in order to begin to understand some of the complexities of the Muslim world today. This is the aim of the present chapter. The past is very familiar to contemporary Muslims, who regularly invoke famous episodes or movements from their history as parallels or solutions for modern issues or crises.

The chapter also explores in detail the beliefs and practices of **Shi'ism**. It is hard to estimate how many of the world's Muslims are Shi'ites. But assuming that they constitute some 10–15 percent of the Muslim population globally, even a conservative calculation would indicate that there are at least one hundred and fifty million Shi'ites in the world,[1] both in Muslim-majority countries such as Iran, Iraq, Bahrain, and Syria,[2] as well as in communities in Europe, America, Australia, South Asia, and Africa. Clearly it is important that their beliefs are known by non-Muslims and distinguished from those of the **Sunnis**.

Sunnis and Shi'ites share the core beliefs of Islam—about the **Qur'an**, the Prophet and the five **pillars of Islam**. There are differences between these two groupings, however. Put simply, the core doctrine that separates the Shi'ites from the Sunnis is the Shi'ite doctrine of *imama*—charismatic authority vested only in the family of the Prophet in a continuous line of Muhammad's descendants, known as **Imams**. For the Shi'ites, only the Imam has absolute authority in the community; he alone is the authoritative source of Muslim doctrine and law. Sunnis saw the **caliph** as the guardian of Islamic law (*Shari'a*), whereas the Shi'ites viewed the Imam as more than that. As this chapter will show, the Shi'ites also developed their own special ceremonies, not performed by the Sunnis; these ceremonies commemorate significant events in their history, and especially the martyrdom of the Prophet Muhammad's grandson, **Husayn**, in 680.

DIVERSITY IN CONTEXT

Around 90 percent of Muslims are Sunnis. So one should expect a good deal of diversity among the Sunnis, and avoid the media cliché that diversity resolves itself smoothly into a Sunni–Shi'ite division. Morocco is solidly Sunni and so, at the other end of the Muslim world, is Indonesia; but there is a world of difference in religious attitudes and practice between these two countries. Sunnis living in Muslim-minority countries can sometimes develop a siege mentality, which separates them from their co-religionists in predominantly Muslim countries; and the Shari'a, which so often reflects local customs, can be very differently interpreted from one Muslim country to the next (see Chapter 5). These differences fuel internal debates over what it means to be a Sunni Muslim and exactly how far tolerance of difference, of pluralism, should go. As the quotations at the head of this chapter make clear, there is plenty of room for difference in modern as in medieval Sunni thought. For example, a prominent Muslim legal scholar in the United States, **Khaled M. Abou El Fadl**, is a stern critic of puritanical Islam; he specializes in the field of human rights and is celebrated for his clear engagement with interpreting Sunni Islam for today's world. This approach can be contrasted with that of the Algerian scholar **Mohammed Arkoun**, who lived in France until his death in 2010 and discussed Islam within a context of French philosophy, intellectual theory, and cultural debate; he too advocated modernist approaches to Islam. And prominent female Sunni Muslim scholars, too, such as **Amina Wadud** and Mona Siddiqui, can be heard on different sides of the Atlantic discussing gender issues and Qur'anic interpretations. But all these variations can be accommodated comfortably within the rubric of Sunni Islam.

It would, therefore, be as serious a mistake to treat "Sunnism" as a single entity as it would be to regard Christianity as a single consistent global phenomenon. In popular usage the word "Sunni," just like the term "Christian," embraces a full range of belief and practice from the purely nominal to the devout. Since most of this book concerns Sunnism in all its complexity, it would be a very artificial exercise to attempt in this chapter alone a digest of either core Sunni or minority Sunni beliefs and attitudes. Readers who wish to discover what Sunnis feel and think about given issues should therefore consult both the chapter headings and the index of this book.

Before launching into the issue of diversity and difference in Islam, it is essential to remember what all Muslims share. This crucial common ground is often forgotten, both by non-Muslims and—in turbulent times, especially since the so-called **Arab Spring**—by some Muslims themselves. There are hallowed beliefs, concepts, and rituals shared by almost all Muslims, however disparate their backgrounds, societies, and languages, and this reinforces a strong sense of unity amongst them. At the heart of Islam is the belief in the One God (*tawhid*; see Chapter 4). Moreover, the binding power of the Arabic Qur'an for the world's Muslims is indisputable (see Chapter 3). It serves as an indispensable guide to them. It provides them with constant spiritual comfort, reassurance, and advice. It allows them to reflect on this world and the next. It presents Muslims with a clear set of doctrinal, ethical, and social instructions, and it does so in language of unique power. Then there is the universal reverence for the Prophet Muhammad (see Chapter 2). Almost from the very beginning of Islam, despite the clear statement in the Qur'an that he was only a man, Muhammad became the focus of Muslim veneration—and he has remained so. He is not a prophet for the Arabs alone, nor just for the peoples of the Middle East; he is a "Bringer of good news and a Warner to all mankind" (Qur'an 33:45). Now that Islam is a global religion, these words take on an even greater significance for believers.

Moreover, in the performance of all the pillars of Islam the faithful are like the teeth of one comb. The five pillars—the *shahada* (the profession of faith), prayer, almsgiving, fasting, and pilgrimage to **Mecca**—are shared by Sunnis and Shi'ites alike. The communal nature of prayer, for example, performed in a strictly timed sequence of movements, strengthens feelings of solidarity. And the pilgrimage is a life-changing experience, the **Ka'ba** standing as a sign of universal Muslim brotherhood. Thus the amount of common ground shared by all Muslims is huge, and it far outweighs the differences between them.

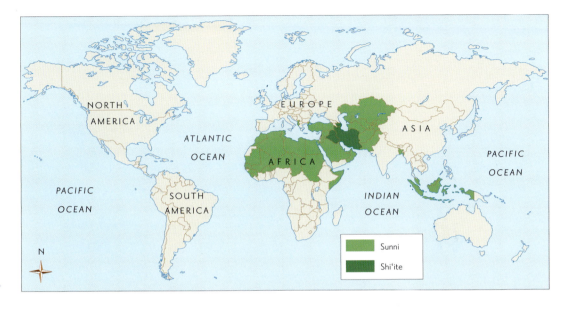

ABOVE **Map showing the distribution of Sunnis and Shi'ites**, highlighting countries with a population of more than 50 percent Sunni or Shi'ite Muslims in 2009.

BELOW **Branches of Islam.** Most Muslims are Sunnis, a definition that ranges from Wahhabi to modernist approaches. Shi'ites divided along doctrinal lines into many sub-groups. The Kharijites' moderate descendants, the Ibadis, are neither Sunni nor Shi'ite.

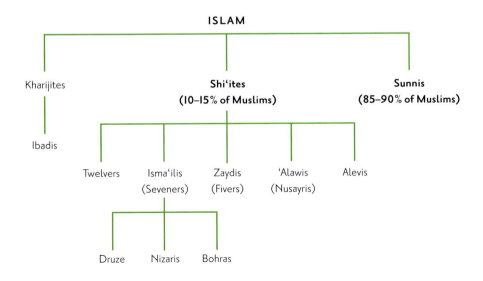

THE EMERGENCE OF SUNNI ISLAM

Diversity amongst Muslims in their beliefs and practices can be attributed to the fact that, from the death of the Prophet Muhammad in 632 onward, there have been differing interpretations amongst them as to which is the right way to practice Islam. In addition, religious groups, be they Muslim or those of any other world faith, have always had political aims and ideals. Thus almost from the outset the Muslim community, composed as it was of diverse persons, families, and groups, had different opinions about issues to do with the faith and the way in which the community should be governed. In this way divisions developed amongst the believers, which crystallized after a while not only into the Sunni/Shi'ite divide—the major division within the Muslim community— but also into other smaller sectarian groupings. Further differences amongst Muslims in their beliefs and rituals emerged as a result of the other religions that were being practiced in their countries before Islam came. This factor has a continuing impact. For example, there is a wide gulf between the Muslims in Indonesia, in Bosnia, in the Caribbean, in India, in Nigeria, in Saudi Arabia, and in America. Proximity to Christians, Jews, Buddhists, Hindus, atheists, those who engage in **animist** rituals, to mention but a few instances, has influenced the way in which Islam is practiced in certain regions of the world.

After Muhammad's death the earliest Muslim groupings were often fleeting and their importance was only short-lived; they were centered on one key person and when he died his followers disappeared, formed a new group, or joined another one. Our knowledge of these developments is vague and probably over-simplified, since it comes to a large extent from later Sunni books on what their writers view as heresy, books that consider the early groups within Islam retrospectively and in too simplistic a manner. For example, within thirty years of Muhammad's death in 632, the young Muslim community saw the appearance of a marginal breakaway group known as the **Kharijites** (see also Chapter 9, pp. 229–30). They believed that the most virtuous person in the community should lead it, and that person would not necessarily be from the Prophet's family or someone elected by the whole community. Anyone who did not agree with them was, in their view, not a Muslim at all and should be killed. This uncompromising sectarian group of early Muslims was persecuted by the early caliphs for around two centuries. They fled to distant regions, such as Oman and Algeria, where they still exist even today under the name of **Ibadis**, although they have long since ceased to wage war against other Muslims.

In a sense there was never a movement which promoted Sunni Islam from the beginning. The Sunnis gradually evolved as the mainstream body of the Muslim community. The historical importance of these early groups is that they allowed the majority Sunni position in Islam to form itself in response to personal, political, and doctrinal differences and what were seen as heterodox (highly unorthodox) views, and also in response to oral and written debates with followers of other faiths in the Middle East, such as Christians, Jews, and **Zoroastrians**. Sunni Islam defined and sharpened itself in the face of the challenges of sectarianism, and in particular the very different model of Islamic government propagated by the groups that came to be called Shi'ites.

The differences between Sunnis and Shi'ites centered originally on the question of the kind of person who should lead the Muslim community— what qualifications he should possess and what duties he should perform. The first community founded by Muhammad in 622 in **Medina** was united under his charismatic leadership; he was God's prophet and the leader of the Muslims. His community in Medina has been idealized ever since; it is the model that Muslim leaders have tried to imitate. But the moment Muhammad died, deep divisions emerged amongst his grief-stricken followers. According to Sunni belief, he had left no instructions for the future; he had no surviving son, and there was no will stipulating a successor. So what was to be done?

The Sunni version of events—the predominant view today—is as follows. Some of Muhammad's closest **Companions** gathered together, including **Abu Bakr**, the father-in-law and faithful friend of Muhammad who had been with him on his *hijra* from Mecca and had taken refuge in a cave with him. When another key figure in the Prophet's inner group, 'Umar (who became the second caliph), stretched out the hand of Abu Bakr and touched it with his own, in what came to be known as the *bay'a* (allegiance) ceremony, other close Companions of Muhammad followed suit and Abu Bakr was declared to be Muhammad's "successor" (*khalifa*—caliph). This event is presented retrospectively by Sunnis as being an appointment approved by the whole Muslim community. With the appointment of Abu Bakr was born the Sunni institution of the caliphate (see Chapter 7, p. 181). It is important to stress that the caliph was never to be considered as a prophet—Muhammad was the last prophet. But the Sunni caliph was the leader of the Muslim community, whose responsibilities were to protect the faith, to uphold Islamic law—based on the Qur'an and the *Sunna* (the model conduct of Muhammad, embodied in the *hadith*, from which the word Sunni derives)[3]—and to defend and expand the borders of the Muslim world.

THE CALIPHATE IN HISTORY

Once the great Muslim world empire had been established, stretching within a century from Spain to northern India and the borders of China, the seat of the caliphate moved away from remote Arabia, first to Kufa in Iraq, then to Damascus, and then to the new city of Baghdad in the second half of the eighth century. There it remained for many centuries. Just as the pope was identified with Rome, so too the name Baghdad evoked the caliph, the supreme leader of the Sunni Muslim community. By the tenth century, the Sunni caliphate in Baghdad had lost a lot of political power, and the religious authority once enjoyed by the caliphs shifted slowly away into the hands of the *'ulama'*, the class of Sunni Muslim religious scholars. The caliph remained until the Mongols sacked Baghdad in 1258, but only as a religious and legal figurehead. Attempts were made thereafter to revive the caliphate, first in Cairo by the **Mamluk** Turkish sultans and then by the **Ottoman** Turks in Istanbul. But it was never the same as it had been in its heyday from the seventh to the ninth centuries. The founder of the Republic of Turkey, **Mustafa Kemal Atatürk** (1881–1938), symbolically abolished the caliphate in 1924 (see also Chapter 7, p. 182).

A century of conquest. Map showing the extent of territories under Muslim control at the end of the Umayyad period, *c.* 750.

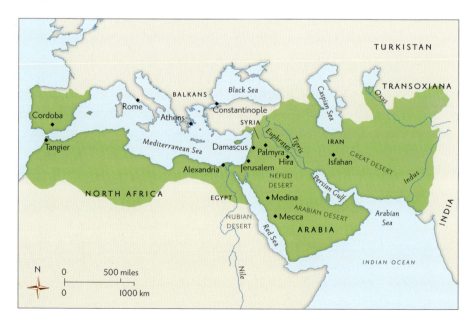

A Shi'ite icon. Image of 'Ali, Istanbul, Turkey. This gigantic poster challenges the cliché that Islamic art avoids religious figures. The fiery background suggests a halo, like the gold of Byzantine icons. Note too the intense gaze and the emphasis on green, the Islamic holy color.

THE EMERGENCE OF SHI'ISM—THE ROLE OF 'ALI

As already mentioned, the core doctrine that differentiates the Shi'ites from other Muslim groupings is imama—charismatic authority vested in the family of the Prophet in a continuous line of Muhammad's descendants, known as Imams. The issue of imama begins for the Shi'ites in Muhammad's lifetime, when, according to their viewpoint, he appointed as his heir **'Ali ibn Abi Talib**, his cousin and son-in-law, the husband of his daughter **Fatima** and the father of his grandsons **Hasan** and Husayn. Whilst 'Ali is admired and revered for his outstanding qualities by all Muslims, not just the Shi'ites, he occupies a very special position in Shi'ite belief and doctrine. Indeed, the terms Shi'ite, Shi'i, and Shi'a all spring from a phrase coined very early in Islamic history: Shi'at 'Ali (the party of 'Ali).[4]

'Ali had to wait for twenty-four years after the death of the Prophet before he became the caliph of the Muslim community. Three other people held the office of caliph before 'Ali was finally appointed in 656. The short period of his caliphate proved to be very turbulent, with two famous battles, in which Muslims fought against Muslims—the Battles of the Camel (in 656) and Siffin (in 657)—and it ended when 'Ali was murdered by a Kharijite in the mosque in Kufa, Iraq, in January 661. But to Shi'ites this narrative does not represent God's true design for Islam. In their view 'Ali should have been the leader of the **umma** from the very beginning. How did 'Ali come to play such a significant role in Shi'ite religious tradition? Why do Shi'ites believe him to be the true legitimate successor of the Prophet and leader of the Muslim community?

The Shi'ite version of events is as follows. The Prophet died in the house of his wife **'A'isha**. This moment was a tragic and devastating blow for the young Muslim community. Muhammad had left no son. Who was to lead the community? That was the burning question.[5] 'Ali's claims to be the best person to succeed Muhammad were most impressive. After Muhammad had been orphaned at a young age, he had been looked after by Abu Talib, 'Ali's father. 'Ali was one of the first followers of Islam. The compiler of the Prophet's biography, **Ibn Hisham**, writes that 'Ali was the first male to accept Islam.[6] When Muhammad made his hijra from Mecca to Medina, 'Ali risked his life by sleeping in Muhammad's bed in Mecca. Once the community had been established in Medina, 'Ali married Fatima, Muhammad's daughter. 'Ali demonstrated legendary military ability and courage; at the Battle of Badr he is said to have killed one third or more of the enemy single-handedly. He defended Muhammad in subsequent fighting at the Battles of Uhud and Hunayn, and at Khaybar he used an iron door as a shield (for these battles, see Chapter 2, pp. 34, 37). He led important missions on behalf of the Prophet, and he served on occasion as his scribe. 'Ali wrote down the terms of the Treaty of Hudaybiyya with the Meccans and in 631 he was asked by Muhammad to recite Chapter 9 of the Qur'an to the pilgrims at Mina and to destroy idols in Mecca.

Over and above 'Ali's important family ties, however, and his pious and courageous actions, which both Sunnis and Shi'ites revere, Shi'ites take their veneration a step further. They speak of an episode that took place on March 16, 632 when the Prophet was returning from his Farewell Pilgrimage to Mecca. He halted at the pool of Ghadir Khumm, where he erected a pulpit with saddles. He took 'Ali by the arm, made him stand next to him, and announced that 'Ali would be his successor and leader of the Muslim community, saying: "O people, know that what Aaron was to **Moses**, 'Ali is to me, except that there shall be no prophet after me, and he ('Ali) is my guardian (*wali*) for you after me. Therefore, for whomever I am their lord (*mawla*), 'Ali is their lord (mawla)."

This tradition lies at the heart of Shi'ite veneration of 'Ali and is the linchpin of the Shi'ite doctrine of the Imamate (imama). The word wali in connection with 'Ali is interpreted by the Shi'ites as meaning that he was the guardian of the community, the sole, explicitly designated successor to Muhammad. According to most Shi'ites, the first three caliphs in the Sunni interpretation of history—Abu Bakr, 'Umar, and 'Uthman—were usurpers. It was 'Ali who inherited the Prophet's knowledge and interpreted it to his fellow Muslims. The sermons, letters, and sayings of 'Ali were collected in the eleventh century by Sharif al-Radi in a massive work entitled *Nahj al-balagha* ("The path of eloquence"). For Shi'ites, 'Ali was the man next best to Muhammad; he was pure, divinely guided, and infallible in matters of faith. He would intercede for those who followed his path on the **Day of Judgment**. Miraculous deeds were attributed to him. He is shown in Muslim calligraphy as the Lion.

Shi'ites show their veneration for 'Ali publicly; as well as the performance of the pilgrimage (*hajj*) to Mecca—which all Muslims should perform, if they are able, once in a lifetime—Shi'ites are recommended to make pious visitations (*ziyara*) to Najaf, an Iraqi city some 100 miles south of Baghdad. For Shi'ites, Najaf is the third holiest city in Islam because it houses the tomb of 'Ali. Despite the recommendation that Muslims should follow the example of

Religious ardor. Shrine of 'Ali, Najaf, Iraq, mainly 17th century onward. Gold domes, often donated by rulers, typify the major Shi'ite shrines, where prayer is held to be more efficacious than elsewhere. Some shrines house museums for displaying their treasures, often acquired over many centuries. Flocks of birds—especially doves, symbols of holiness—congregate there and are fed by the faithful.

the Prophet, who was buried in a simple grave, 'Ali now has a grandiose tomb crowned with a gilded dome. Visits to Najaf are especially recommended on the anniversaries of 'Ali's birth and death, as well as on the Prophet's birthday and other important anniversaries. Shi'ites believe that a true knowledge of Islam comes only from devotion to Ali and his descendants, the Shi'ite Imams; the spirit of Muhammad had, as it were, passed to them. It is important to note that when the call to prayer is made from a Shi'ite mosque, an extra phrase is added at the end of the Sunni version: "and 'Ali is the friend of God (*wali Allah*)." If Muslim visitors find themselves in an unfamiliar city and they hear this phrase in the call to prayer from the minaret of a mosque, they know at once that it is Shi'ite.

THE IMAMATE OF HASAN

The early history of the Muslim community is punctuated with intense social upheavals, and almost from the beginning Shi'ism was associated with struggle, opposition, and persecution. Shi'ites believed that they were the true believers and that the rest were on the wrong path or had strayed from the right path. They rejected the claims to rule of the **Umayyad** dynasty, a family of the Meccan pagan and merchant elite whose members came late to Islam and who ruled over the whole Muslim empire from 661 to 750 from their base in Syria.

After the death of 'Ali, who is regarded by the Shi'ites as their first Imam, he was succeeded in the line of Imams by his elder son, Hasan, who was aged thirty-six or thirty-seven at the time. Threatened militarily by the Umayyad governor of Syria, Mu'awiya, who was seeking to take over power, Hasan publicly renounced his claim to the caliphate in the mosque in Kufa in 661. According to the Shi'ite tradition, he acted in this way because he had a distaste for politics and he wished to prevent bloodshed and to promote peace in the umma. He retired to Medina where he died, possibly poisoned at the instigation of Mu'awiya, in 670 or 678. According to the Shi'ites, he remained the second Imam, the rightful caliph, until his death. Miracles are attributed to him.

It is difficult to reconcile the varying historical accounts of Hasan's abdication. Most mention that a substantial sum of money was paid to Hasan at the time of his abdication, and they point out his many marriages, for which he acquired the nickname al-Mitlaq ("the divorcer").[7]

Shi'ite iconography in shorthand. Cardboard roll with Shi'ite images, Karbala', Iraq, c. 1765. Part souvenir, part meditation aid, it refers to 'Ali (lion and sword); Fatima (hand); Buraq (Muhammad's mount to heaven); sermons (*minbar*); the afterlife (cypresses); the camel with pilgrimage litter (*mahmal*); veneration of the Imams (footprints and buildings); and the *hajj*.

THE IMAMATE OF HUSAYN

In 680 supporters of the family of 'Ali in Kufa persuaded Husayn—'Ali's younger son by Fatima, Muhammad's grandson, and the second major figure in Shi'ite sacred history—to lead them in an uprising against the Umayyad prince Yazid, whose hereditary succession to the caliphate they regarded as illegal. Husayn reluctantly agreed to join them and set out from Arabia with his family and seventy-two men. On the plain of **Karbala'** around twenty-five miles from Kufa, Husayn, hopelessly outnumbered and abandoned by his Kufan supporters, was confronted by an army of four thousand men sent by the Umayyad governor of Kufa, 'Ubaydallah ibn Ziyad. Husayn was brutally murdered, together with all his male relatives (seventy-seven men), except for his son, 'Ali Zayn al-'Abidin, who at the time was either eleven or twelve years old. The Umayyad army looted Husayn's camp, decapitating the corpses of all his companions. Husayn's womenfolk and children were taken captive before eventually being sent back to Medina. The date in the Muslim calendar for this momentous event was AH 10 Muharram 61/October 10, 680 CE.

When the people of Kufa who had allowed this terrible murder to take place saw the severed head of Husayn, the very face that the Prophet himself had kissed, they began to wail and beat their breasts, deeply regretting that they had not come out to help him. These so-called Penitents (*tawwabun*) begged the martyred Husayn to forgive them. From these seminal events have sprung the mourning and atonement rituals of the Shi'ites. For the Shi'ites Husayn became the "prince of martyrs," whose passion (suffering) and death are sometimes compared to the last week in the life of **Jesus**. An eleventh-century historian of the Shi'ites, Shaykh al-Mufid, laments: "He was killed wrongfully, while thirsty, always showing fortitude…His age on that day was 58 years."[8] The great European Enlightenment historian Edward Gibbon echoes this sentiment when he writes that the death of Husayn "will awaken the sympathy of the coldest reader."[9] The shrine of Husayn at Karbala' in Iraq is the most visited holy site for the world's Shi'ites. Many aspire to be buried at Karbala', and go to great lengths to achieve this aim.[10]

DIVISIONS AMONGST THE SHI'ITES

Not all Shi'ites belong to the same groups. Nowadays the term "Shi'ite" is used sweepingly to denote only the **Twelvers**, which is now the most numerous and the most high-profile group (see pp. 155–60). They can be found in sizeable numbers in Iraq and India, and above all in the Islamic Republic of Iran, where the state religion is Twelver Shi'ism (see pp. 165–67). There are at least three major Shi'ite groupings, however: **Zaydis**, **Isma'ilis**, and Twelvers, in order of their historical appearance.

The sacred genealogy of the Shi'ite Imams began as a single line,[11] which continued until the death of the fourth Imam, Husayn's son Zayn al-'Abidin, in 712. Thereafter splits occurred at intervals amongst the Shi'ites, creating different sub-groups, some of which have now disappeared, whilst others have continued to the present day.

ZAYDI SHI'ITES

The first major split amongst the early Shi'ites resulted in the formation of a breakaway group known as the Zaydis,[12] also known as the **Fivers**, because they disputed the succession after the fourth Imam. The group derives its name from **Zayd ibn 'Ali** (695–740), the great-great-grandson of the Prophet, who was killed in a failed rebellion against the Umayyad caliph in Kufa in 740.[13]

After his death his supporters viewed him as the true Imam. After 'Ali's sons Hasan and Husayn, according to the Zaydis, the right to claim the Imamate did not belong to one particular genealogical line from Muhammad—unlike the belief held by other major Shi'ite groups—for the Imamate belonged instead to the whole family of 'Ali. The Zaydis quote a saying of the Prophet announcing that he had left his community two treasures to ensure right guidance: "God's Book and lineage." It is important to stress that the Zaydis do not believe in a hidden Imam, nor is their Imam immaculate or infallible, as the Twelvers believe. Zaydis have their own collections of legal traditions. They view themselves as being the closest to the Sunnis in matters of theology.

In early Islamic times the Zaydis were active militarily. It was their belief that the true Imam is he who actually succeeds in establishing himself by the sword. Indeed, the Imamate should be established through armed rebellion, led by a suitably qualified candidate who possessed religious knowledge amongst his qualifications. After Zayd's death, other abortive rebellions by members of his family followed. The Zaydis then moved to remote areas of the Muslim world to avoid persecution. Two Zaydi states were founded by descendants of the second Imam, Hasan. One was established in 864 in the Caspian area of Iran, where the inaccessibility of the terrain helped their cause to survive. The other was established in the city of Sa'da in the Yemen in 897, where Zaydi Imams ruled until 1962. Since the death of the last Zaydi Imam, Muhammad al-Badr, in the UK in 1996, the Zaydis have had no Imam. There are still around five million Zaydi Shi'ites in the Yemen today.

ISMA'ILI SHI'ITES

A second, more major, split amongst the Shi'ites came in 765 with another breakaway group, the Isma'ilis.[14] They became a dynamic, politically active group during the early medieval period, although from the thirteenth century onward, they have evolved into quiet, unobtrusive Shi'ite Muslim communities. The circumstances around the emergence of the Isma'ilis remain very obscure but involve a disagreement over who should succeed the sixth Imam, Ja'far al-Sadiq, who died in 765. One of his sons, Isma'il, claimed the succession as the seventh Imam. Those who accepted his claims came to be known as **Seveners** or Isma'ilis.

The Isma'ilis came into real prominence in 899 when 'Ubaydallah al-Mahdi, the first Shi'ite ruler of a new dynasty (named Fatimid after Muhammad's daughter), established a rival Isma'ili caliphate in North Africa, claiming that he was a descendant of Muhammad the son of Isma'il and that he,

The mosque as dynastic memorial. Al-Aqmar mosque, Cairo, 1125. Situated beside the eastern Fatimid palace, this is a religious and political manifesto, perhaps serving as a court oratory, teaching institution, and prospective tomb of the Prophet's grandson, al-Husayn. Its decorative motifs successively evoke radiating light; its inscriptions exalt the family of 'Ali and implore God for "victory over all infidels."

'Ubaydallah, was the true Imam. Later, under his successor, the fourth Fatimid caliph al-Mu'izz, the dynasty moved to Egypt, establishing Cairo as their new capital in 969. There then followed the heyday of Fatimid power; under their rule the Isma'ilis were militant and dynamic, intent on taking over the whole Muslim world and imposing on it their own interpretation of Islam. They dominated the Mediterranean politically for nearly two centuries until the great Muslim hero of the Crusades, **Saladin** (see Chapter 9, pp. 233), put an end to their rule in 1171, and restored Egypt and the other lands ruled by the Fatimids to allegiance to the Sunni caliph at Baghdad. But the Fatimids had in any case failed in their more global missionary efforts.

Isma'ili Diversity
Already, quite early on in Fatimid history, a further minor breakaway Isma'ili group had appeared in the reign of the sixth Fatimid caliph, al-Hakim, who was notorious in medieval Christian Europe for destroying the Church of the Holy Sepulchre in Jerusalem in 1009. During his lifetime al-Hakim was deified by certain Isma'ilis through the preaching of a missionary called al-Darazi,

and after this caliph's mysterious disappearance in 1021 his followers formed a new *ghulat* or "extremist" group, the **Druze**,[15] who secluded themselves for safety reasons in the mountains of northern Syria and Lebanon. They are still there today.

A much more famous Isma'ili splinter group, the **Nizaris**, split off from the mainstream Fatimid line in Cairo after 1094, this time in northwest Iran, with its centre at the castle of Alamut. This extreme Shi'ite sect, popularly known by the derogatory title of the **Assassins** (Hashishiyyun) from which our word "assassin" comes, preached a new form of Islam that appealed both to intellectuals who were attracted to its **esoteric** doctrines (those distinguished by hidden meanings and specialized knowledge) and also to the ordinary people, who were promised a more just society. In the space of scarcely thirty years, from 1095 to 1124, the Nizaris, under their charismatic leader Hasan-i Sabbah, carried out a series of around fifty high-profile murders. Their victims were always government ministers or important military or religious figures. The murders were always conducted in the full glare of publicity, often in the courtyard of a mosque on Fridays. After Hasan's death the movement had far less impact and his community turned in on itself. But the formidable reputation of the Assassins lingered on until the thirteenth century, when the Mongols made a special expedition to Alamut to destroy the centre of Nizari operations there definitively. Thereafter the Nizaris went into hiding. They have survived until the present day but they have never again adopted a militant stance, preferring to live out their own interpretation of Islam unobtrusively.

The other Isma'ilis from whom the Nizaris had broken away in Cairo in 1094 became known as the **Bohras**.[16] After 1171 they moved first to the Yemen and then settled in the Indian subcontinent, which has remained their major center of operations ever since, although there are also Bohras living in Pakistan, East Africa, and the West. They form communities that are little known in the outside world, yet they fund many charitable projects, such as hospitals and schools.

Isma'ili Beliefs and Practice

From the beginning Isma'ili beliefs were kept secret. They made a distinction between the external interpretation of the Qur'an, which was accessible to all, and an esoteric inner truth known only to the Imam. Some of the esoteric doctrines of the movement in its medieval heyday were influenced by pre-Islamic belief systems that also emphasized hidden knowledge, such as **Gnosticism** and **Neoplatonism**. In the Isma'ili view, history was cyclical; each cycle of seven thousand years began with a prophet, as well as an "intermediary" and a permanent Imam. Seven is the key symbolic number; Isma'il was the seventh Imam. God is beyond all human understanding, and the world and everything in it flows directly from Him.

The Isma'ilis practiced *taqiyya*, pious dissimulation of their beliefs. This means that in order to preserve their faith in hostile circumstances and avoid persecution they were permitted to pretend to hold other beliefs. On occasion they would claim that they were Twelvers for that very reason. The doctrine of *nass* (designation, investiture) attributed to the sixth Imam, Ja'far al-Sadiq, was crucial to the Isma'ilis; according to this doctrine, the choice of successor in the Imamate depended only on designation by the present Imam, since only he had all-embracing knowledge from God.

Nowadays it is doubtful if the Isma'ili communities care greatly about the obscure philosophical ideas of their medieval predecessors. Even in medieval times, despite the convoluted philosophical doctrines of their intellectual elites, the Isma'ilis shared with other Shi'ite groups many beliefs and rituals. They took part in ceremonies to commemorate the martyrdom of Husayn, either separately or with other Shi'ite groups. Isma'ilis worship on Fridays, not in a mosque but in a special building known as a *jam'atkhana* (house of assembly). That building is also used as a social centre for the community. Theirs is a living faith, with vibrant worship. They leave the interpretation of doctrine to their Imam, who issues regular decrees to his followers. The present leader of the Nizari Isma'ili community is **Karim Aga Khan IV** (b. 1936), who is the forty-ninth Imam. He is the leader of some fifteen million Muslims across the world. He provides guidance on matters of doctrine, which is regarded as infallible, and obedience to him is obligatory. The Aga Khan is an enlightened and tolerant Muslim leader who calls for peace and mutual understanding amongst the world's religions. He supports many educational, cultural, and charitable projects, and is in favor of full participation of women in the community. His followers send him a tithe of their income. His moderate voice is usually overlooked in the Western media.

The Isma'ilis are a much-respected group, well integrated into the disparate societies in which they have settled across the world. They live as religious minorities in more than twenty-five countries in the Middle East, Africa, Asia, Europe, and North America. When newcomers from traditional Isma'ili communities in the East arrive to settle in the West, they are welcomed in the same way as the first Muslims from Mecca were befriended by the Muslims in Medina; for example, in 2001 Afghan Isma'ilis were helped when they first

Charisma. The Aga Khan amidst the faithful. Against the snowy backdrop of the Pamir mountains, the 49th Imam, in direct succession to the Prophet Muhammad, is the focus of the intense gaze of the tightly knit Isma'ili community. He has led it with outstanding success since 1957, while also dedicating his life to educational and cultural projects, the environment, and philanthropy.

arrived to settle in Canada by the local Isma'ilis there, who were called *ansar* (helpers) just as in the Prophet Muhammad's time.

The Isma'ili communities in the Indian subcontinent developed a large collection of poems and songs about the Imams. Known as **ginans**, they were first transmitted orally and later written down in a variety of Indian languages, such as Sindhi, Gujurati, Hindi, and Punjabi; some eight hundred are recorded. The ginans, which are often mystical, tell stories of the Isma'ili past and provide moral instruction to the faithful. Such poems, set to music, form an important part of Isma'ili religious worship not only in India, Pakistan, and East Africa, but also in the West where many Isma'ili communities now live. The ginans must be sung in their original language.[17] When Isma'ilis meet on Fridays, they hear the Qur'an recited in Arabic, as well as instructions from their living Imam and devotional literature read out in their own language.

TWELVER SHI'ITES

Nowadays the Twelvers are by far the biggest Shi'ite group. Unlike the Isma'ilis, the Twelver Shi'ites kept a low profile in the distant past but are very prominent, indeed militant, in today's world, and especially in Iran and Iraq.

History and Doctrine

After the Zaydis and Isma'ilis had branched off and chosen different 'Alid genealogies, the line of the Imams for the remaining Shi'ites (to become known as the Twelvers) continued unbroken until 874. The Sunni authorities had been keeping a close eye on this line of Shi'ite Imams, and the ruling caliph at the time had detained the eleventh Imam, **al-Hasan al-'Askari**, in prison, where he died in that year, apparently with no heir. This presented a major crisis for these Shi'ites. The belief became current, however, that al-Hasan had in fact left a little son named Muhammad. According to the Twelver Shi'ite tradition, at some point Muhammad had been smuggled out of his father's place of imprisonment and declared to be the Twelfth Imam. He was brought up in a secret place, contacting his followers only through four emissaries (*safirs*). This phase in Twelver doctrine is called the **Lesser Occultation** or *ghayba* (absence), a period in which the Twelfth Imam was thought to be hidden, but still somewhere on earth.

When the last of these four emissaries was dying in 941, he announced that Muhammad had not died but that he had cut off all links with the world to retreat into the **Greater Occultation**. He would return at the end of time with the sword in the guise of the **Mahdi**, the Awaited One, the figure expected to usher in an era of justice for the whole earth just before the Day of Judgment and the Resurrection. Cataclysms would precede this event. This remains the belief of the Twelver Shi'ites, who today still await the coming of the Twelfth Imam.

The occultation of the Twelfth Imam presented a problem to his followers, since he was no longer accessible to them to provide them with guidance in this world in all aspects of their lives as Muslims. Like the Isma'ilis, the Twelvers believe that their Imam is immune from error in matters of doctrine. But how could the Twelvers know what the guidance of the Hidden Imam was? Gradually they came to believe that the learned class of scholars, as those best qualified to interpret the counsels of the Hidden Imam, should guide his community in his absence. There would be no more direct political action from or on behalf of living Imams. The doctrine of the Greater Occultation depoliticized Twelver Shi'ism for many centuries, and the Twelvers became quietist, guided in their daily lives by their religious scholars.

According to the Twelvers, therefore, God in His goodness and justice did not leave His community leaderless, and He must have made a decision about the Imamate. Such a leader, the Imam, would be endowed with knowledge to interpret the true meaning of the Qur'an and the conduct of Muhammad.

That knowledge was to be found in 'Ali and the eleven Imams from his line who succeeded him. The Imams, the bearers of "divine light," were the spiritual and political leaders of the community. They were immune from error. Twelver Shi'ites believe in the practice of taqiyya (pious dissimulation; see p. 154), a very pragmatic doctrine for a group who were frequently persecuted and who kept a very low profile for centuries.

Things changed dramatically for the Twelver Shi'ites in Iran at several key historical moments. In 1501 a new dynasty, the **Safavids**, was established. They made Twelver Shi'ism the state religion of Iran. This important development set Iran firmly apart from the other Muslim superpowers of the sixteenth century—the Ottomans in Turkey and the Near East, and the **Mughals** in India, both of whom were staunchly Sunni. In the nineteenth century a small new elite of about ten religious scholars was recognized as being most qualified to guide the Shi'ite faithful in their daily lives: these scholars were given the title of *marja' al-taqlid* (source of imitation). This development helped to create a strong, centralized religious leadership. But the idea that there should be a political state in which Twelver Shi'ite religious scholars actually ruled had to wait until 1979 to come into being (see pp. 165–67).

'Ashura

The tenth century has with some justification been called "the Shi'ite century," a time in which Shi'ite ceremonies were introduced into the heart of the Sunni caliphate in Baghdad. The greatest Shi'ite festival, 'Ashura, was commemorated publicly with great pomp and circumstance from the year 962, and it still is today.[18]

The death of Husayn has long been the emotional mainspring of Shi'ite religious experience. Every year the tenth day (known as 'Ashura) of the first month of the Muslim calendar, Muharram, is the climax of ten days of mourning for his martyrdom. This ritual goes back to Medina in the lifetime of Husayn's only surviving son, 'Ali Zayn al-'Abidin. The 'Ashura cult, involving the narrating of the tragedy of Husayn and the reciting of elegies in his memory, was first developed in the houses of the Imams in Medina. Later the shrines of the Imams—in Najaf and Karbala' in Iraq, and Qumm and Mashhad in Iran—became the focus of pious visitation and pilgrimage where professional storytellers publicly declaimed the martyrdom stories of Husayn.[19] In tenth-century Baghdad, which was under the control of the Buyids, a Shi'ite dynasty, 'Ashura was proclaimed a public day of mourning and shops were draped in black. Later, under the dynamic Safavid dynasty in

Flagellation. Devotees beat themselves with metal barbs on 10th Muharram, in the festival known as 'Ashura, Karbala', Iraq. On this day Shi'ites remember the death of Husayn at the Battle of Karbala' in 680, forsaken by the treacherous men of Kufa; in penitential black (sometimes green) costumes, they process chanting through the streets, wounding themselves as a punishment.

Iran, which came to power in 1501 and made Twelver Shi'ism the state religion, the 'Ashura celebration really came into its own.

Collective lamentation at the martyrdom of Husayn came to include a passion play (*ta'ziya*). In this play, the villains wear red and speak prose, the heroes wear white and green and speak poetry. There are processions in which the participants in the drama beg for water, thus symbolizing the thirst of Husayn and his family during the battle in which he was killed. European and Ottoman travelers to Iran from the seventeenth century onward were fascinated by these rituals and wrote detailed reports about them. One such traveler from the Ottoman Empire described in 1640 the impact of the passion play on the watching crowd in Isfahan. Having seen the re-enactment of the killing of Husayn and his children, he writes: "All spectators weep and wail. Hundreds of Husayn's devotees beat and wound their heads, faces and bodies with swords and knives. For the love of Imam Husayn they make their blood flow. The green grassy field becomes bloodied and looks like a field of poppies."[20]

The story of Husayn is still re-enacted every year in the streets of many cities in Iraq, Iran, and India and a passion play is performed. The audience knows full well what will happen in the play but they are still seized with emotion as they watch and participate. In the first nine days of the month of Muharram groups of men, with their half-naked bodies dyed black or red, go round the streets, pulling out their hair, carrying swords (and sometimes cutting themselves) or dragging chains behind them, a prelude to 'Ashura itself. The death of Husayn is also commemorated at ceremonies known as **rouzeh**s where the participants sing about his life and death. These rituals are at the very heart of Twelver Shi'ite belief and separate them from the Sunnis in a very significant way. They mark a deep gulf that is far more important than differences of dogma.

Is the flagellation real or purely symbolic? Certainly it is sometimes real but there is usually an ambulance standing by. Young men view it as a privilege to do penance on behalf of their whole community and thus bring divine blessing upon it. Chains, swords and daggers are used. White shrouds are worn. Even in the smallest villages the mournful procession can be heard coming from a distance, with the clanging of the chains and men beating their breasts in unison. Women do not take part in the processions but they watch them with rapt attention. In Isfahan in 2004, I saw a performance of the passion play of Husayn. The participants were most welcoming and invited me and my companions to sit and watch the proceedings. The play was performed with all the drama of an open-air theatre and the words were transmitted to the audience through loudspeakers; real horses were used and brightly colored costumes were worn.[21]

Thus through drama and visitation of his shrine, through ritual, myth, and poetry, the memory of Husayn the martyr is kept ever fresh in the hearts of Shi'ite Muslims. The prime emotional focus of Shi'ism is a single event: the death of Husayn at Karbala'. Shi'ites suffer vicariously what he suffered. His death is seen as a voluntary sacrifice on behalf of the whole community, and its commemoration brings spiritual rewards to all who participate in these ceremonies. It is a vivid reminder of how Shi'ites have suffered throughout the ages. In more recent Iranian history 'Ashura and its attendant activities have also served to mobilize the masses against tyrannical governments.

The Sacred Thresholds of the Shi'ites

A number of cities in Iraq—Najaf, Karbala', Kazimayn, and Samarra—house the tombs of six Imams. These cities are called *al-'atabat al-muqaddasa* (the sacred thresholds). Najaf houses the tomb of 'Ali, whilst Karbala' is the burial place of Husayn.[22] (**Ayatollah Ruhollah Mostafavi Musavi Khomeini,**

1902–1989, the first leader of the Republic of Iran, spent his time in exile from 1965 to 1978 at Najaf.) These two cities are the most important centers of Shi'ite visitation. Kazimayn and Samarra house the tombs of the four other ninth-century Imams.

All four sacred thresholds play a significant part in the devotional life of Twelvers, and also of Isma'ilis who live in regions such as Tajikistan, Afghanistan, and northern Pakistan.[23] When they make a pious visitation to one of these cities, Shi'ites circumambulate (walk around) the tombs of the Imams while reading out special words written for such occasions. They stroke the grilles of the tombs and make sacred vows. As Christian pilgrims have done over the ages in Jerusalem, Lourdes, Rome, and Santiago de Compostela, it is customary for Shi'ites to take home from Iraq some small relic with commemorative or medicinal properties. Some soil from Karbala' (*khak–i Karbala'*), mixed with water into a little brick and known as ***ab-i turbat*** (dust water), is believed to help sick and dying people. People who can afford it ask to be buried in one of the sacred thresholds, and especially in Najaf where there is an enormous cemetery called the *wadi al-salam* (the valley of peace) to which Shi'ites aspire to send their dead, even from places as distant as India.

Not surprisingly, these sacred cities have long been centers of Shi'ite intellectual life, where scholars congregate and formulate doctrines and law. Unfortunately, though predictably, the sacred thresholds have often been the site of politically explosive acts to attract maximum publicity. In 1991, in the time of the Iraqi leader **Saddam Husayn**, the golden dome of the Najaf shrine was damaged, and the city has been the scene of the killing of a number of prominent Shi'ite figures in the twenty-first century, while in 2006 the shrine of Samarra was damaged in an explosion.

PERIPHERAL SHI'ITE GROUPS

The word ghulat in Arabic means "extremists"; it was used from an early stage in Islamic history to refer to minority groups who were seen by the majority to be very heterodox in their beliefs. Such groups were often influenced by other religious traditions, including Gnosticism and Christianity, and some attributed divine traits to Muslim holy figures, especially to 'Ali. Some Shi'ite groups were influenced by these trends and were condemned and persecuted as ghulat sects by mainstream Muslims, both Sunni and Shi'ite. Two such groups on the periphery of Shi'ite Islam are the **'Alawis** and the **Alevis** (the Druze of Lebanon have already been discussed; see p. 153).

The 'Alawis

Amongst such ghulat groups are the 'Alawis of western Syria, Lebanon, and southeastern Turkey. Also called **Nusayris**, they belong to a group that split off from the mainstream of Shi'ism in the ninth century. Although at times they have presented themselves as Twelver Shi'ites,[24] their complex and esoteric beliefs and initiation rites clearly contain Gnostic, Isma'ili Shi'ite, and Christian elements. Amongst their heterodox doctrines is the deification of 'Ali.[25]

Hafez al-Assad, the President of Syria until his death in 2000, was an 'Alawi. In 1970 when he was serving as commander of the Syrian air force, he seized supreme power in a coup d'état in Syria. Since then his fellow-'Alawis have enjoyed a monopoly of high-ranking state and army positions (they have a long tradition of military service), although they constitute only a small minority of the Syrian population (some 12 percent). They continue to do so under Hafez al-Assad's son Bashshar.

The Alevis

The Alevis are a very significant minority in present-day Turkey. At the lowest estimate, between seven and eight million Alevis live there.[26] Some 20 percent of them are Kurds; the remainder are Turks. Their beliefs and aspirations need to be better known, not only on account of their presence within Turkey, a key country in the Middle East, but also because many Turks are now working and settling in Germany, and the Alevis are a strong presence among them.

Until recently Alevism has been hard to comprehend because it has been based on oral tradition, and also because Alevis as a religious minority are understandably secretive. Alevism came into contact with many cultures in the course of the long journey of the nomadic Turks from the eleventh century onward, from Central Asia to Anatolia and beyond into the Balkans. Many aspects of Alevi beliefs are clearly based on Shi'ism, but they also reflect the influence of Christianity and **shamanism**. Their rituals have much in common with **Sufi** practice (see Chapter 8). Alevi beliefs have been passed on from one generation to another through the Alevi holy men, who trace their line back to the Sufi saint Hajji Bektash (see Chapter 8, p. 212); his genealogy, in turn, they believe goes back to Muhammad through the sixth Imam, **Ja'far**, and 'Ali. Alevis believe that those who love 'Ali are their friends and those who do not love him are their enemies. Not surprisingly, they see 'Ali as the rightful successor to the Prophet and they curse the first three caliphs in the Sunni tradition, as well as the Umayyad dynasty, one of whom had Husayn killed.

The Alevis fast for twelve days in the month of Muharram to mourn Husayn. They do not forbid alcohol. Alevis do not worship in a mosque. Their major ceremony, the **sema**, takes place in a **cem evi** (house of assembly) and is conducted by their **dede** (prayer leader). Before the ceremony begins, the worshipers remember Karbala' and recite pious verses. The cult of Husayn at Karbala', a story of oppression, injustice, pain, and grief, has become a symbol of Alevi collective consciousness as a minority. In the sema ceremony itself men and women perform a ritual dance accompanied by music, and it also includes the ceremonial eating of food and drinking of wine or raki. Clearly the sema owes much to Sufi ritual and has resonances of the Christian communion service.

Alevis have become more publicly visible of late in Turkey. They now hold their ceremonies in public places and on television, and they wish to have their children taught their faith at school. The increasing number of Alevis in Germany tend to keep themselves to themselves and they have embraced a more secular agenda. [27]

SHI'ITE LAW

When the early Shi'ites separated into various sub-groups, the new "sects"— Twelvers, Isma'ilis, and Zaydis—already had slightly different legal systems, although they shared many common characteristics, such as a body of hadith that went back through their early Imams to 'Ali or to the Prophet himself. Nor did the Shi'ite legal schools—Twelver, Isma'ili, and Zaydi—depart radically from those of the Sunnis in fundamental matters of Islamic law. Nevertheless, it is important to devote some discussion to the special characteristics of Shi'ite law. (For Sunni law, see Chapter 5.)

KEY DIFFERENCES BETWEEN SUNNI AND SHI'ITE LAW

While Sunnis and Shi'ites share the concept of making the Qur'an the key text for establishing certain key legal principles, they diverge in their use of the second foundational source for Islamic law, namely the Sunna (the exemplary conduct) of the Prophet as expounded and clarified by the hadith. Shi'ite hadith are distinctive in the special importance they attach to sayings that concern the Prophet's family (the **ahl al-bayt**). Shi'ite collections of hadith contain much material that is absent from Sunni collections.

A second difference between these two bodies of law is that Shi'ites reject the Sunni concepts of analogy (*qiyas*) and *ijma'* (the consensus of the community). Instead, Shi'ites acknowledge the exclusive authority of their Imam in determining what is and is not legal. For the Twelver Shi'ite group, once the occultation of the Twelfth Imam became official doctrine for them—in other words, there was no longer a living Imam to guide his people—it became necessary in his "absence" to delegate his authority to the religious class to interpret the law. High-ranking legal scholars headed this class. On the other hand, the next most numerous group of Shi'ites, the Isma'ilis, have a line of living Imams who have been given the honorific title of aga khan; their authority in matters of interpreting the law is absolute from one generation to another.

HISTORY OF SHI'ITE LAW

The smallest of the surviving Shi'ite groups, the Zaydis, produced scholars who were interested in formulating Zaydi jurisprudence, based on the sayings of Zayd ibn 'Ali, their founder (see pp. 150–51). Zaydi jurisprudence is quite similar to that of the **Hanafi** Sunnis (see chapter 5, pp. 119–20).[28] The oldest work of Zaydi jurisprudence is called *Al-majmu' al-kabir* (The Great Collection). Consisting of sayings and judgments attributed to Zayd himself, it is thought to have been compiled in the eighth century by Abu Khalid al-Wasiti, who was one of Zayd's closest companions.[29]

One key Isma'ili source should be mentioned. This is the magisterial work of **al-Qadi al-Nu'man** (d. 974), entitled *Da'a'im al-Islam* ("The pillars of Islam"), which codifies Isma'ili law. As with books of Sunni law, this book is divided into two parts, one concerned with the individual Muslim's devotional and religious duties toward God, and the other with his or her dealings with society at large. It has remained the major work on Isma'ili jurisprudence.

The history of Twelver Shi'ite law is extremely well documented. Ja'far al-Sadiq (d. 765), the sixth Imam of the Twelver Shi'ite line, is regarded as the figure whose sayings and judgments form the basis of much of Twelver law. That is why the Twelver legal school is sometimes called **Ja'fari**. However, the definitive elucidation of Twelver Shi'ite law began in the tenth century in the Iranian city of Qumm, where two scholars, **al-Kulayni** (864–941) and **Ibn Babuya** (c. 933–991), assembled and codified thousands of Shi'ite hadith. The work of al-Kulayni called *Kafi*, which contains 16,199 hadith, is the most prestigious collection of Twelver Shi'ite hadith. Important Twelver Shi'ite legal works were also written in Baghdad, where there was a thriving Twelver community under the rule of the Iranian Buyid dynasty (945–1055) whose members were themselves Shi'ites. The Baghdadi scholar **Shaykh al-Mufid** (948–1022) wrote many works that still form the core of the legal curricula in Shi'ite *madrasa*s today.

In the thirteenth and fourteenth centuries, the city of Hilla in central Iraq became a center for the development of Twelver Shi'ite law. Two scholars in particular should be mentioned here, both of whom were called al-Hilli. The first was **Muhaqqiq al-Hilli** (1205–1277), whose writings have always been regarded with great respect. The second al-Hilli, **al-'Allama al-Hilli** (1250–1325) was the first Twelver scholar to be given the title of *ayatollah* (sign of God). Since his time until today a Twelver scholar is accorded the title of aya-tollah not by an examination or certificate, but by an emerging consensus in the scholarly community that he has the status to deserve such a title. The second al-Hilli is especially important, because he validated the principle of personal judgment (*ijtihad*), embedding it in Twelver law and preparing the path that later Shi'ite scholars were to follow. He also specified the particular abilities that a scholar who exercises personal judgment (a *mujtahid*) should possess. He stressed that a mujtahid is not infallible, that he is allowed to change his opinion, and that the fatwas he issues are binding only during his lifetime. Such an approach has kept Twelver legal thought flexible and dynamic.

Twelver Shi'ites who wished to take up a legal career followed the same path as their Sunni counterparts and studied Twelver Shi'ite law at Shi'ite madrasas, such as those in Najaf or Qumm. There they acquired a detailed knowledge of the Qur'an, Shi'ite hadith collections, and the principles of jurisprudence. Alternatively, they could learn about the law and other aspects of their faith in one of the *hawza*s (seminaries) that were lively centers in Najaf and Karbala' in Iraq, and Qumm and Mashhad in Iran, as well as in other areas where Twelver Shi'ism flourished. Twelver Shi'ism became the state religion in Iran in 1501 and in the following centuries the class of religious scholars developed into a formidable body of clergy.

TEMPORARY MARRIAGE

A controversial legal issue that has set the Twelvers apart from Sunnis as well as the other major Shi'ite groups—the Isma'ilis and the Zaydis—is the custom of temporary marriage—*mut'a* (enjoyment). Both Sunnis and Shi'ites agree that initially Muhammad had allowed this ancient pre-Islamic Arab practice to continue when Muslims were on long journeys or military campaigns.[30] Mut'a marriage required a short-term contract between a man and a woman for a definite period of time. During this time the man was permitted to have sexual relations with the woman. At the end of the stated term they parted company, provided the woman had received her dower or the fee due to her. Her tribe did not lose any rights it had previously held over her, and any offspring produced by such a marriage remained with the mother and her family.

Later on, according to the Sunni viewpoint, mut'a marriage was discontinued because this practice did not provide the man with legitimate offspring. The Twelver Shi'ites, on the other hand, assembled many sayings linked to their Imams from the line of the Prophet's family that explicitly approved mut'a marriage and gave rules for how it should be conducted. It should be added that the other two main Shi'ite groups, as well as the Sunnis, reject this practice as "barely concealed prostitution."[31]

THE ISLAMIC REPUBLIC OF IRAN— TWELVER SHI'ISM AS A MODERN STATE IDEOLOGY

The only country in the world today that has Shi'ism as its state ideology is Iran. The Islamic Revolution in Iran in 1979 was not just a change of government. It ushered in a new, dynamic phase in the history of Twelver Shi'ism. When Ayatollah Khomeini returned from his long exile in Najaf and took control of Iran, he ousted a monarchy and replaced it with a **theocracy**. The revolution that he led brought a militant Twelver Shi'ite regime to power, supported by the body of Shi'ite religious scholars in alliance with the *bazaris* (the shopkeeper class).

The new government of Iran under Khomeini was based on a strict interpretation of the Shi'ite Shari'a. The doctrine called *vilayat-i faqih* (the mandate of the religious scholar), which Khomeini had discussed in his most famous book,[32] had proclaimed that Muslim religious scholars held not only religious but also political authority. They must be obeyed at all times as an expression of obedience to God. This doctrine now became the cornerstone of the new government. Its emphasis on the importance of Islamic law is clear. What is less clear is whether Khomeini meant the doctrine to refer to just one scholar (himself) or to the whole body of senior Twelver religious scholars in Iran. But it is indisputable that the strict observance of Twelver Islamic law has been at the heart of the government of Iran since the Revolution. It is, however, significant that Khomeini did not use the phrase *vilayat-i fuqaha'*— "the mandate of the religious scholars"—in the plural. Certainly, the phrase

Clerics in power. Ayatollah Khomeini welcomed in Iran, February 19, 1979. He was the defining president of the newly established Islamic Republic of Iran, the world's most powerful theocracy. He inaugurated the *vilayat-i faqih*, loosely translatable as "the mandate of the religious scholar," as a regency while awaiting the return of the Twelfth Imam, in occultation since 941.

is susceptible to more than one interpretation, but what seems likely is that he saw it as meaning governance by an individual *faqih* (himself) who would ensure Shari'a rule and usher in an Islamic state in which the Twelver clergy as a body would take responsibility for executive, legislative, and judicial matters.

Once in power, Khomeini's Iran imposed a very strict regime, which displayed to the outside world the outward symbol commonly associated with Islamic law, namely the wearing of the *hijab* (headscarf) for women of all ages. Of course, the word fatwa became known all over the world after Ayatollah Khomeini condemned **Salman Rushdie** to death in a fatwa in 1989 because of his book *The Satanic Verses* (see Chapter 2, pp. 50–51). Since then, the Shi'ite clergy in post-1979 Iran, far from being mere reclusive scholars poring over learned books of jurisprudence, have cleverly used the opportunities provided by the Internet to propagate their legal views. Many ayatollahs have their own websites; the holy city of Qumm has been labeled the "IT capital of Iran."

Khomeini showed little interest in the rituals of Shi'ite Islam. He did not personally preside over any 'Ashura celebrations; indeed, he seems to have discouraged public displays of piety and emotion, believing that what really mattered was Islamic law. This emphasis has not changed with the coming to power of his successor, 'Ali Husayni Khamenei (b. 1939). But in Iran today, not just on one day in the year but every day, taxis, cars, and lorries have portraits of 'Ali displayed on their windscreens, and posters and billboards show images of him; the veneration of 'Ali remains very much alive.

SHI'ITES TODAY

The doctrinal labels applied to different Muslim groups need to be applied with care. The Twelvers are the most numerous section of the world's Shi'ites, and nowadays when the term Shi'ite is heard it usually means them. But it is not just Twelvers who are Shi'ites today: Zaydis and Isma'ilis are Shi'ites too, and, as we have seen, there are several still smaller groups. It is one of the least-known of these latter groups—the 'Alawis—that has hit the headlines since 2011 because of the civil war in Syria.

The major split between Sunnis and Shi'ites was originally caused by differing interpretations of who should lead the Muslim community. But Shi'ites—often by a process of splitting off from a larger body of co-religionists—have also evolved their own different salvation history, their own key dates in the calendar, their own rituals of remembrance, their own shrines, their own books of the sayings of Muhammad (hadith), and their own formulation of Islamic law.

When asked about the difference between a Sunni and a Shi'ite, the answers from many non-Muslims are extremely vague and imprecise. This lack of knowledge extends to those in government; an article written by Jeff Stein in *The New York Times* in 2006 displayed the remarkable level of ignorance and nonchalance on this topic in high places in Washington.[33] To cite just one example given by Stein, a Republican who chaired a House intelligence subcommittee responsible for monitoring the CIA's performance in recruiting Muslim spies and analyzing information was asked if she knew the difference between Sunnis and Shi'ites. When asked if she knew which branch **al-Qa'ida's** leaders followed, she replied: "Al Qaeda is the one that's most radical, so I think they're Sunni...I may be wrong, but I think that's right." Such "religious illiteracy" is one of today's major problems, especially when it is found among the major powers.

Shi'ites have traditionally seen themselves as supporting the cause of the downtrodden and underprivileged millions in the world as they struggle against despots and those who exploit the poor. The story of Husayn fits this agenda well; he is a symbol for those who experience suffering and wish to rise up against tyranny. The great emotional intensity of the Shi'ite festivals is enhanced by a consciousness of the periodic persecution that the forebears of the participants have had to endure, and of the ongoing tensions between them and the Sunnis in certain war-torn areas of the world.

Shi'ite Islam today is a global phenomenon. Its diversity is, and no doubt will continue to be, a source of its vitality. Shi'ites are not confined to the Muslim-majority countries of the Middle East, but live in different regions of the world, in communities that have preserved their own special characteristics and practices. Political upheavals and economic problems have caused massive demographic displacement, and so Shi'ite communities have grown up in places as far-flung as Los Angeles, Toronto, and London. Yet thanks to the Internet and the media, there is easy communication between Shi'ites across the world. Links with the original homelands of such immigrants are maintained, notably through recourse to the **maraji'** (the supreme authorities on Shi'ite Islamic law in the Middle East), who provide guidance to their faraway followers on how to live in distant lands that are overwhelmingly non-Muslim.[34]

For many centuries, after the early years of sectarian strife, the Sunnis and Shi'ites lived relatively harmoniously together in the Middle East, but the upheavals in the aftermath of the Arab Spring in the early years of the twenty-first century have stirred up primeval hostilities between the two groups and the possibility of peace and religious harmony often appears tragically remote. Taking the wider view, and looking at the world's Muslims as a whole, however, it is plain that Sunnis and Shi'ites have far more to unite them than to divide them. And that gives solid grounds for hope in the future.

SELECTED READING

Daftary, Farhad, *A Short History of the Isma'ilis*, Edinburgh: Edinburgh University Press, 1998

Halm, Heinz, *Shi'ism*, Edinburgh: Edinburgh University Press, 2004

Madelung, Wilferd, *Arabic Texts Concerning the History of the Zaydi Imams: Tabaristan, Daylaman and Gilan*, Wiesbaden: Franz Steiner, 1987

Shaykh al-Mufid, *Kitab al-irshad* (*The Book of Guidance*), trans. I. K. A. Howard, Horsham: The Muhammadi Trust, 1981

Newman, Andrew, *Twelver Shiism: Unity and Diversity in the Life of Islam, 632 to 1722*, Edinburgh: Edinburgh University Press, 2013

7 THOUGHT

A science which makes it possible to prove the truth of religious doctrines by marshalling arguments and repelling doubts.

THE PERSIAN SCHOLAR AL-IJI PRAISING THE VIRTUES OF ISLAMIC THEOLOGY[1]

There is a class of men who believe in their superiority to others because of their greater intelligence and insight. They have abandoned all the religious duties Islam imposes on its followers.

AL-GHAZALI WRITING ABOUT ISLAMIC PHILOSOPHERS[2]

No book that speaks about **Islamic** society and culture from a historical perspective can afford to overlook the contributions made by **Muslims** in the fields of theology, philosophy, and political thought. Amongst the branches of religious knowledge in Islam it is without doubt Islamic law that has pride of place (see Chapter 5). Nevertheless, both Islamic theology and Islamic philosophy contributed to the evolution of the faith of Islam in a number of significant ways. Medieval Muslim theologians held debates on core theological concepts at the courts of **caliphs** and **sultans** and they wrote theological treatises that helped to shape the key tenets of the faith in a definitive form. In the field of Islamic philosophy, although it tended to be the preserve of an intellectual elite, the contribution of Muslim thinkers was considerable enough for some of their works that had reached the scholarly circles in the Translation House in Toledo in Spain to be translated into Latin and then widely circulated in medieval Christian Europe. Muslim philosophers, such as **Ibn Sina** (980–1037) and **Ibn Rushd** (1126–1198), were given European versions of their names—Avicenna and Averroes. Even those scholars, such as **al-Ghazali** (1058–1111), known as "Gazel" in Europe, and **Ibn Taymiyya** (1263–1328), who regarded Islamic philosophy as a dangerous field of knowledge, had learned how to use the tools of logical philosophical argumentation in order to attack it. As for Islamic political thought, it was elaborated by some of the finest Muslim intellectuals and was, and still is, a crucial area of debate, an area that has had a profound impact on the way in which Muslim societies have been governed. This chapter looks at the development of Islamic theology and Islamic philosophy separately, although during much of the medieval period their preoccupations and concerns overlapped; it then goes on to explore Islamic political thought.

ISLAMIC THEOLOGY

Muslims regard the Prophet **Muhammad** as a prophet who received revelation from God. He was not a systematic thinker who left behind a carefully argued theological framework. The basic message that he conveyed to his followers was that the transcendental One God is all-powerful and that humanity must obey Him. However, as the small community that he left behind developed into a vast empire, conquering countries with different religions and cultures, Muslims needed to have answers to doctrinal questions about Islam, both those posed to them by non-Muslims and other questions that they themselves found they needed to ask.

The term normally used for "theology" in Islam is *kalam*, which literally means "speech." This usage is revealing in that it highlights the fact that discussions on theological matters in the early years of Islam were conducted orally. The term "dialectic"—a way of resolving disagreement through reasoned argument, a method that derived from the Greek philosopher **Aristotle**—adds an extra nuance to the meaning of kalam. Those who took part in such conversations debated, often with fervor, core issues to do with the faith. Especially in the seventh and eighth centuries in Syria, the new faith had to be defended by Muslim scholars in public debate with followers of other religions, particularly the Jews and the Christians. It is important to note that many of the theological issues that exercised the minds of Islamic theologians—for example, the nature of God, the problem of evil, and the question of human free will and predestination—were also the concern of Jewish and Christian thinkers. What was new with the coming of Islam, however, was that Muslims claimed that their revelation superseded what they believed to be the incomplete Jewish and Christian scriptures. Islam was the final monotheistic revelation and Muhammad was the "**Seal of the Prophets**"; there could be no other prophet after him. These were bold claims to make against the followers of long-established monotheistic religions.

Islamic theology seems to have emerged gradually in the second half of the seventh century in **Umayyad** Syria (661–750) and developed more fully after the year 750 in Iraq under **'Abbasid** rule. Contact with the eastern Christians, who were now part of the new Muslim empire, and with scholars of the Iranian religions of **Zoroastrianism** and **Manichaeism**, sharpened Muslim debating and polemical skills. Theological questions, such as the nature of God, and predestination and free will, which had already exercised the minds of Jewish, Christian, Zoroastrian, and Manichaean thinkers, now confronted Muslim scholars. They felt the need to present distinctively Islamic viewpoints on these issues, both to defend the new faith against hostile criticisms from outside and also to formulate clearly what the "correct" Muslim answers to these theological questions should be. Debates in which Muslims and Christians confronted each other to discuss theology were held in the caliphal courts in Damascus and Baghdad. The Christian theologian **John of Damascus** (676–749), who served for a while as a tax official at the Umayyad caliphal court in Damascus, wrote a work entitled *Disputation between a Christian and a Saracen*, setting out arguments that Christians might encounter when talking to Muslims, and suggesting how they might answer them persuasively. The Christian patriarch Timothy is recorded as having participated in one such event in the caliphal court at Baghdad in 781.

Other theological topics, however, were intrinsic to Islam, such as who is entitled to membership of the community. Thus the discipline of Islamic theology took shape in the course of disputes between sectarian groups within the Muslim community as well as with adherents of other religions outside it.

A numinous site. Great Mosque, Damascus, Syria, 715: successively a temple to an Aramean storm god, another to Jupiter, and then a church dedicated to St. John. The three-naved sanctuary, gabled facade, and courtyard are elements long familiar in Christian churches, but now reshuffled most unexpectedly to serve the new Muslim north–south orientation and a different liturgy.

Religious scholars identified key doctrines and passed judgments on what they viewed as either Islamic orthodoxy or heresy. Deeply learned in Muslim law and scripture, they were aware of a *hadith* of the Prophet that said that the Jews were divided into seventy-one or seventy-two sects, as were the Christians. Emphasizing the unconditional and unified nature of his own faith, Muhammad went on to say: "My community will be divided into 73 sects."³ Other hadiths declare that according to the Prophet all but one of these seventy-three sects would be consigned to Hell.

EARLY MUSLIM THEOLOGICAL GROUPS

The **Qadariyya** were a group of thinkers that emerged in Islam in the eighth century. They argued that humankind had free will. God would not, in their view, oblige human beings to behave virtuously if they did not have the power to decide for themselves what they wished to do. In contrast, a second group, known as the **Jabriyya**, argued the exact opposite, namely that human beings have no choice over what they do. Both these groups vanished quite soon, but their appearance had sparked some interest in theological issues, that is those relating to God and humanity's relationship with Him.

A much more significant group, which had been influenced by the Qadariyya, were the **Mu'tazila**. They called themselves "the people of justice and *tawhid* (belief in God's Oneness)." They aimed to create a proper system for Muslim metaphysical doctrines. In particular, they argued that in His justice, God must allow mankind to have free will, otherwise He would be in the position of having to punish human beings for actions that He Himself had pre-ordained them to perform.

The Mu'tazila are famous because of their doctrine of the "created **Qur'an**," whilst the majority of their contemporaries considered the Quran to be co-eternal with God and therefore uncreated. In 827 the intellectual 'Abbasid caliph **al-Ma'mun** (786–833) took the unprecedented step of passing a decree that proclaimed that the Mu'tazilite doctrine of the created Qur'an was henceforth to be the official doctrine of the **Sunni** 'Abbasid empire, and it had to be binding on all Muslims. All Muslim judges (*qadis*) were ordered to accept this doctrine, and told that they would be tested on their views. Those who refused to take this test, or who opposed this doctrine, risked the death penalty. This episode was known as the *mihna* ("test" or "inquisition").

The doctrine of the created Qur'an was opposed by the towering figure of **Ahmad ibn Hanbal** (780–855), a conservative religious scholar who hated theology and believed that truth in Islam lay not in the exercise of reason

The word as icon. Parchment bifolio from the Wetnurse's Qur'an, Tunisia, 1020; five lines, sometimes one word long, per large page (17 ¾ x 11 ⅜ in.). Thick, spatulate forms contrast with razor-thin diagonals, creating a script that rolls, irresistible as a juggernaut, across the page, radiating power. The familiar text is rendered unfamiliar and must be slowly deciphered; this aids meditation.

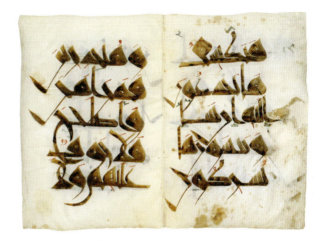

but in following the traditions passed down from the pious ancestors of early Islamic times. (For **Hanbali** law, see Chapter 5, pp. 119–20.) When questioned by the caliph's officials, Ahmad ibn Hanbal refused to comply and he was put in prison several times. The attempt by al-Ma'mun to impose a most unpopular doctrine on his empire was short-lived, and it did the reputation of theologians no favors in the eyes of the Muslim public. A later caliph, al-Mutawakkil, abolished the decree in 850 and declared that the official doctrine was that of the uncreated Qur'an. To simple believers the convoluted byways of Mu'tazilite dialectic must have seemed pointless theological nitpicking. Ahmad ibn Hanbal led the way back to a safer path with his doctrine of *bila kayfa* ("without [asking] how?")—in other words, believers should not question the faith on matters that lie beyond the reach of human understanding. The Mu'tazilites were the first proper school of Islamic theology, but they did not last long. They had alienated ordinary traditionalist Muslim scholars and believers.

AL-ASH'ARI AND HIS SUCCESSORS

The real founder of Islamic theology as an integrated branch of the religious sciences—alongside the Qur'an, hadith, and law—was **al-Ash'ari** (873–935). He had originally been a follower of Mu'tazilite thought, but he seems suddenly to have changed sides and joined the traditionalist Sunni camp. He brought with him, however, the methodology that he had learned from the Mu'tazila. His doctrinal position bears the stamp of what is called mediation theology. On the issue of the two extreme views of free will and predestination, for example, he produces a compromise solution: God pre-ordained human acts, but humans "acquire" responsibility for them before they are performed. Al-Ash'ari and his associates also argued that the anthropomorphic Qur'anic usages that refer to God's face, God's hands, and other similar examples should simply be accepted "without specifying how."[4]

A creed attributed to al-Ash'ari has survived. It aims to present true Sunni Muslim belief and it sums up admirably the dogmatic basis of Sunni Islam in his time, and long thereafter. Like the Apostles' Creed, an early statement of Christian belief which gives the core beliefs of the Christian faith, the long creed of al-Ash'ari lists the tenets that make up the Sunni Islamic faith. It begins:

> A summary of the views of the followers of tradition and *sunna*.
> They profess their belief in God and His angels, His books and His messengers, in that which has come from God and which trustworthy (authorities) have transmitted from the Apostle of God—may God bless him and give him peace—without rejecting any of it. They acknowledge that God the Almighty is one God, unique and eternal, that there is no God but He, that He has neither companion nor children and that Muhammad is His servant and His messenger; that Paradise and the fire of Hell are true and the Hour (the Last Judgment) will come without any doubt and that God will resurrect those who are in their graves.

Belief in God, His angels, His books, and His messengers is stressed at the beginning. Angels are mentioned on many occasions in the Qur'an, for example in the first verse of Chapter 35: "Praise be to God, Creator of the heavens and earth, who made angels messengers with two, three, four [pairs of] wings." Thus we see that angels are created by God. Angels are sometimes given names: some are familiar ones to Jews and Christians, such as **Gabriel** (Jibril) or Michael (Mikhail), whilst others, such as Harut and Marut, two fallen angels who taught mankind magic in Babylon, are not well known.[5] They are mentioned once in the Qur'an (2:102) in a passage condemning Jewish disbelievers who followed the teaching of devils in the time of Solomon. Above all, the Qur'an announces that the angels and messengers of God are on His side: "If anyone is an enemy of God, His angels and His messengers, of Gabriel and Michael, then God is certainly the enemy of such disbelievers" (2:98). The Oneness of God is dramatically emphasized in this lengthy creed, as is the looming certainty of God's judgment. Later in the creed comes the unequivocal statement that "the Qur'an is the Word of God and uncreated."[6]

The trumpet shall sound. The archangel Gabriel, al-Qazwini, *The Wonders of Creation*, Baghdad, Iraq, late 14th century. Muslims particularly venerate Gabriel, "the peacock of the angels"; he brought the first Qur'anic revelation (*sura* 96). The dragon-headed termination of his wing is a borrowing from the ninth zodiacal sign, Sagittarius. His trumpet breaks the margin, thus sounding in our world too.

The successors of al-Ash'ari, especially the eleventh-century al-Juwayni and his much more famous pupil al-Ghazali (see also Chapter 8, pp. 198–99), brought to Islamic theology the tools of logical argument developed by Aristotle, and thus gave it the same rigorous and rational intellectual underpinning that St. Thomas Aquinas brought to Christian theology in the thirteenth century. Indeed, al-Ghazali was sometimes called "the Muslim Aquinas" in medieval Europe. But al-Juwayni and al-Ghazali are better described as legal scholars than as theologians. By this time theology had passed its heyday. Versatility in the various fields of religious studies was natural for al-Ghazali, as it was for other medieval Muslim scholars. The title of his very last book, *The Restraining of the Masses from the Science of Theology*, sends out a very telling message.[7] In it he argues that it would be harmful for most people to indulge in this dangerous subject.

The study of theology lingered on into the later Middle Ages, but the writings produced by such fourteenth-century scholars as al-Iji, al-Taftazani, and others were largely confined to commentaries (or even commentaries on commentaries) on previous works, rather than introducing new approaches to the subject.

KEY ISLAMIC THEOLOGICAL DOCTRINES

Clearly the core doctrine for Muslim theologians was that of absolutely uncompromising monotheism—the Oneness of God (tawhid). God's transcendence excluded any notion of His being either Three in One (the Christian Trinity), or His being one of two basic principles, as in the dualism of God and Satan, Good and Evil, an idea that underpinned the ancient Iranian religions of Zoroastrianism and Manichaeism.

Despite Islam's constant emphasis on the Oneness of God, above all in the Qur'an (Chapter 112), aspects of God are expressed by various terms. An important doctrine is that of "The Beautiful Names of God." Four chapters of the Qur'an mention God's "most beautiful names."[8] Chapter 20:8, for example, declares "God—there is no deity but He. To Him belong the Beautiful Names." A Muslim rosary has ninety-nine beads, and when Muslims pray with a rosary in private they repeat the ninety-nine names of God, although this list does not cover all His names; there are more that remain hidden from humanity.[9] Al-Ghazali wrote a treatise on these names, in which he tries to explain what they mean, whether they are actually found in the Qur'an or implied there. They include "The Compassionate," "The Powerful," "The Noble," and "The Most Holy One."

Another doctrine concerns the title "Seal of the Prophets" given to Muhammad and signifying that he is the last in the succession of prophets sent by God to preach His revelation. Chapter 33 of the Qur'an mentions some of the principal prophets who have preceded Muhammad: "We took a solemn pledge from the prophets—from you (Muhammad), from Noah, from **Abraham**, from **Moses**, from **Jesus**, son of **Mary**—We took a solemn pledge from all of them" (33:7). But Muhammad is more than a prophet in this distinguished line: he is the consummation of them all, as 33:40 announces: "He is God's Messenger and the seal (*khatam*) of the prophets."

I'jaz ("the miraculous character of the Qur'an") is a core Islamic belief, which holds that no human being can ever imitate the incomparable language of the Qur'an. The early medieval Ash'ari theologian al-Baqillani wrote a classic work on the subject of Qur'anic inimitability. In the Qur'an (2:23; 10:38; 11:13) God challenges those who think the revelation sent down to Muhammad could be imitated to produce passages comparable to the Qur'anic verses. They could not do so. Thus 2:23 declares: "And if you are in doubt about what We have sent down upon Our Servant Muhammad, then produce a *sura* the like thereof and call upon your witnesses other than God, if you should be truthful." Chapter 11:13 is even more direct: "Or do they say, 'He invented it'. Say, 'Then bring ten suras like it that have been invented and call upon (for assistance) whomever you can besides God, if you should be truthful.'"

Muhammad's claim to prophethood was a miracle from God, and a reason to silence his opponents.[10] The phrase *al-nabi al-ummi* ("the unlettered prophet"), which is used of Muhammad, acquired for Muslims in the early centuries of Islam the meaning that he could not read or write, thus enhancing the miraculous nature of the revelation.[11]

Themes such as the nature of God, prophethood, and the controversy over whether the Qur'an was created or uncreated, which may seem opaque and even incredible to a modern person, were burning issues with serious political implications at certain moments in Islamic history. In the evolution of early Christianity, when debates over the nature of Jesus raged between various groups, those supporting certain views that were not those of the governing elite were ready at times to die for their beliefs. So too in Islam.

ISLAMIC PHILOSOPHY

The word used in Arabic to denote philosophy is *falsafa*. It is a borrowing from the Greek word *philosophia*; there is no proper Arabic term for it. And this sums up the difficulty that Muslim legal scholars experienced in accepting philosophy as a legitimate and appropriate field of enquiry within the religious sciences.

During the rule of the 'Abbasid caliph al-Ma'mun (ruled 813–33), the House of Wisdom (*Dar al-hikma*) was established in Baghdad. This was a translation center, which triggered a flood of translation activity and brought great fame to Baghdad. Important works of classical Greek science— by Galen, Dioscorides, Euclid, Archimedes, and Ptolemy, among others—as well as some works of **Plato** and Aristotle, the cornerstones of Western philosophy, were translated into Arabic from the original Greek, often through the intermediary of Syriac. Works in Pahlavi, Syriac, and Sanskrit were also translated. Thus Muslim religious scholars came into contact with the ideas developed by classical Greek philosophy. Eventually these Arabic versions were retranslated into Latin in Spain and they made their way into the rest of Europe. In this way key classical Greek writers, in whom most Muslims had little interest, became known to the great Renaissance thinkers of Europe, in one of the seminal moments of Western history.

Global medicine. Man bitten by rabid dog, Arabic translation of *De Materia Medica* by Dioscorides, Iraq or Syria, 1224. This book was the standard pharmaceutical handbook of late antiquity, and was much copied in the Islamic world, enlarged by further material from the Arab and Persian traditions and from still other sources, such as Sanskrit texts describing Indian medicine.

Greek into Arabic. Seminar, al-Mubashshir, *The Best Maxims*, Syria (?), early 13th century. A turbaned Aristotle anachronistically displays an astrolabe, clearly leaving his students floundering. The "House of Wisdom," founded *c.* 830 in Baghdad by the 'Abbasid caliph al-Ma'mun, and staffed by intellectuals of stellar reputation, preserved Greek learning for posterity through Arabic translations, laying the foundations for the European Renaissance.

From 750 onward, Islamic philosophy emerged as a branch of the religious sciences. Scholars—such as al-Kindi in the ninth century, known as "the philosopher of the Arabs," and **al-Farabi** in the tenth, who was called al-Farasius or Avenassar in Europe—saw themselves as students of Aristotle, but within the Muslim world their impact was usually confined to a small circle of others of like mind.

Those scholars who were interested in philosophy were not narrow specialists, however. For example, Ibn Miskawayh, a bureaucrat at the court in Baghdad, Iraq, who wrote a universal history called *The Eclipse of the Abbasid Caliphate*, is also famous for his book on ethics, *The Correction of Ethics (Tadhhib al-akhlaq)*, which is based primarily on the ideas of Plato and Aristotle.

THE INFLUENCE OF NEOPLATONISM

Far more significant for the development of Islamic philosophy was the influence of the **Neoplatonic** school of thought. The major figure in this movement was Plotinus, a third-century philosopher from Egypt. A key text for Muslim philosophers was a work allegedly written by Aristotle called *The Theology of Aristotle*, which actually consisted of a paraphrase of part of Plotinus' most important work, *The Enneads*. Neoplatonism moves away from the idea that God created the universe at a specific moment in time. Instead, it proposes the concept of constant "emanation" by God—the One—who pours out creation in hierarchical layers beneath Him. Emanation unfolds without the One being in any way affected. Beneath the One is the Divine Mind, from which proceeds the World Soul. This in turn produces human souls, and lastly matter itself.

The greatest exponent of Muslim Neoplatonic philosophy was Abu 'Ali al-Husayn Ibn Sina, known in medieval Europe as Avicenna. He was learned in many disciplines, and above all a specialist in medicine; his most famous medical books—*The Book of Healing* and *The Canon of Medicine*—were used for teaching purposes as late as the seventeenth century in Europe. However, it proved very difficult to graft the ideas of Neoplatonic philosophy onto the body of a revealed religion, Islam, which held that God created the world at a given moment in time. And not surprisingly the philosophers came under fierce attack by traditionalist Muslim scholars.

Despite the failure of much Islamic philosophy to become integrated into the religious sciences, it did leave its mark on medieval Muslim scholars, such as the most famous of them all, al-Ghazali, who adopted the tools of Aristotelian logic in order to refute the claims of philosophy itself. Al-Ghazali even wrote a work entitled *The Incoherence of the Philosophers*. Far away in Spain, Abu'l-Walid Ibn Rushd, known in Europe as Averroes, produced a stinging riposte to al-Ghazali in a work punningly called *The Incoherence of the Incoherence*.

It is an irony that the ideas of Muslim theologians had little impact outside the society to which they belonged, whereas those of Muslim philosophers, sidelined or rejected though they were by orthodox Sunni scholars, were much esteemed in medieval Christian Europe. Islamic philosophy within the Muslim world itself fared better within **Shi'ite** circles in the later Middle Ages. Under the title *'irfan*, which can be defined as "philosophical **Sufism**,"[12] philosophy was swept into the mystical tradition in Iran. It was especially important in the cosmological thought of **Mulla Sadra** (1572–1640) in Isfahan. Influenced by the **Illuminationist** Sufi writer **Suhrawardi** (1155–1191; see Chapter 8, pp. 202–3), Mulla Sadra's work is a blend of Shi'ite belief, philosophy, and Sufism. It forms a striking contrast to the stagnating state of philosophy in the same period in countries where Sunni Islam prevailed.

POLITICAL THOUGHT

Other branches of philosophy interested Muslim scholars. Much of what may be regarded as practical ethics was handled in the books of Islamic law (see Chapter 5). In the sphere of political philosophy, al-Farabi (872–950), who was known as the "Second Teacher" (the first being Aristotle), wrote an interesting work on the ideal city, *Epistle on the Views of the People of the Virtuous City*. This work owes much to Plato's great work on the same subject, *The Republic*. In this ideal city there is a social hierarchy. Like the human body in which the limbs and other parts have their specific function, as commanded by the head, which controls the whole body, so too the ideal city operates as a tightly knit entity with every component part in its right place in society. In this way will all citizens achieve happiness. In another of his works, this time on statecraft, al-Farabi argues that just as God rules the world, so the philosopher, as the most perfect kind of man, should rule the state. This is essentially the notion of Plato's "philosopher king." For metaphysical issues, al-Farabi relied on Neoplatonic concepts, developing Arabic terminology from Qur'anic usages. Al-Farabi's philosophical terminology was translated into Latin and used in adapted form by St. Thomas Aquinas.

Another genre of writing on political thought was the ***Mirrors for Princes*** books, which were popular at the courts of caliphs and princes in the medieval Muslim world from an early stage, just as they were in medieval Europe with books such as Niccolò Machiavelli's renowned political treatise, *The Prince*. The Muslim *Mirrors* show a widespread preoccupation with just government and the nature of kingship. They were written by philosophers, government ministers, and lawyers, as well as by rulers themselves to advise their sons and heirs.

THE SUNNI CALIPHATE

Political philosophy shaded over into law on the matter of the crucial and much-discussed institution of the Sunni caliphate. This institution of religious rulers depended on the notion of a successor (**khalifa**), one in a long line that

A language of symbols. Umayyad gold *dinar*, probably Damascus mint, *c.* 694. This coin shows a standing figure, probably the caliph 'Abd al-Malik, frontally depicted and holding his sword across his body—clearly an image of power. Around the rim is the *shahada*, the Muslim creed.

went back all the way to the year 632, when the Prophet died without naming anyone to succeed him (see Chapter 6, pp. 142–43). In the event his friend and father-in-law, **Abu Bakr**, was elected as the first caliph, and Muslims remember with pride his accession speech, recorded by **Ibn Hisham** (d. 833) in his *Life of the Prophet*: "Obey me as long as I obey God and His Prophet. And if I disobey God and His Prophet, you do not owe me obedience."[13]

The term caliph came to be associated with the overarching unity of the community of all believers. The caliph's duties were to enforce the law (*Shari'a*), protect the faith, and defend the frontiers of Muslim lands. The Sunni caliph was the representative of the Shari'a and responsible for applying and defending it. He himself was not above the Shari'a, however; he had to obey it like everyone else.

From the second half of the ninth century, the Sunni caliphs in their capital, Baghdad, lost their political power when they fell into the hands of their own Turkish bodyguards. They were then dominated by Persian military groups and later by nomadic Turkish invaders from Central Asia. However, right up to the time that the Mongols conquered Baghdad in 1258 and put an end to the Sunni 'Abbasid caliphate there by killing the caliph, he remained the ultimate religio-legal authority, despite the dominance of secular rulers and an independent body of religious scholars; the caliph remained a crucial figurehead who symbolized the unity of the Sunni community all over the Muslim world. Military rulers needed their usurpation of power to be legitimized by the caliph, and he would preside over important ceremonies such as the reception of foreign embassies.

Debate on the nature and characteristics of the caliphate began in earnest in the eighth century, in the early 'Abbasid period. Was the caliph the highest, charismatic, law-giving authority in the community, infallible in matters of doctrine and law, as the Shi'ites believed, or was he subject to the consensus of the legal scholars, so that he too had to conform, like everyone else, to the Qur'an and the Sunna of the Prophet? (See Chapter 6, p. 143.) In the event, political reality, tempered by the dynastic principle, dictated who occupied the caliphal office; some 'Abbasid caliphs were even murdered by their own troops, who promptly elevated some other member of the family to the throne. After the fall of Baghdad in 1258, the **Mamluk** sultan Baybars (ruled Egypt 1260–77), clearly reluctant to accept the demise of the venerable office of caliph, established a new centre for a shadow Sunni caliphate in Cairo, effectively under Mamluk control. After the **Ottoman** conquest of Egypt and Syria in 1517, the Turks took over this responsibility and the caliphate was once more relocated, this time to Istanbul. This caliphate, something of a legal fiction, remained in place there until 1924, when the president of the new Turkish republic, **Kemal Atatürk** (1881–1938), definitively abolished the office, thereby bringing to an end an institution that had been in existence since 632 and that for most of that period had been an important part of the Muslim mind-set.

The Syrian Muslim reformer **Muhammad Rashid Rida** (1865–1935) wrote a treatise on the caliphate, called *Al-Khilafa aw al-Imama al-'Uzma* ("The caliphate or the paramount Imamate"), in 1923 just before its abolition by Atatürk. He blamed the corruption of Muslim religious scholars for distorting the caliphate, and he viewed the abolition of this venerable institution as traumatic, because the Muslim world had thereby lost its central representative. He continued to support the idea of the caliphate; a caliph in modern times would, he believed, interpret Islam for all Muslims and guide their governments on how to rule a modern Muslim society.

It was one thing to abolish the caliphate by diktat; it was quite another to expunge the memory of it from Muslim minds. In the twentieth century many Muslim thinkers toyed with the notion of reviving the caliphate in modern dress. Both the Muslim Brotherhood (see p. 185) and one of its offshoots, the group known as Hizb al-Tahrir ("Party of Liberation"), favor the establishment of a new caliphate. This is also the aim of the deputy of **Usama bin Laden** (1957–2011), Ayman al-Zawahiri, who wrote after 9/11 that the attacks of **al-Qa'ida** would be "nothing more than disturbing acts" unless they led to a caliphate in the "heart of the Islamic world."[14] Al-Qa'ida called its regular Internet newscast, which began in September 2005, the "Voice of the Caliphate." Many moderate Muslims, too, have a nostalgic view of the caliphate as a lost symbol of the precious unity of the Muslim community, evoking as it does the archetypally sacred period of the Prophet Muhammad and his successors, the first four Rightly Guided caliphs. Some contemporary

Islamic thinkers stress the need for the revival of the caliphate to reinforce Muslim solidarity and resistance in the face of new forms of adversity, such as Islamophobia and worldwide Western supremacy.

MODERN TRENDS IN ISLAMIC THOUGHT

Muslim thinkers all over the world today share clearly recognizable beliefs and views about their faith, but it is obvious that there is also great diversity and plurality. As with groups belonging to the Christian and Jewish communities, it is untrue to say that one movement or trend in Muslim communities is more "faithful" to Islam than another. Some of these currents of modern Muslim thought will now be examined, taking account of their historical antecedents.

FUNDAMENTALIST THINKERS

So-called "fundamentalism" is a recurring phenomenon in Islam. Movements within Muslim society over the centuries have shared certain core characteristics. Those who propagate fundamentalism do so to express their concern for what they see as decay in that society; they call for a return to the "original," pristine Islam practiced by the Prophet and his closest followers, including the first four caliphs, the Rightly Guided caliphs, who ruled from 632 to 661. Muslim fundamentalists argue that innovations in the way that Muslims practice their faith—unacceptable changes caused internally by Sufism, for example, and externally by other religions such as Christianity (in the Middle East), Hinduism, Buddhism, and **animist** cults (for instance in Indonesia and Africa)—have polluted the true Islam. Muslim fundamentalists condemn practices that have seeped into Muslim ritual from outside—such customs as the visitation of tombs of holy people, prayers of intercession to the "saints" who are buried in these tombs, and indeed the very building of such funerary monuments in the first place. The Prophet was buried without ostentation in a simple unmarked grave, and that, they feel, is therefore the right way for all Muslims to follow.

A significant time in the history of Islamic fundamentalism was the career of the Syrian scholar Ibn Taymiyya. He argued vigorously not against Sufism itself, in which he was actually involved, but against excessive ascetic practices, miracles, and music in religious contexts. He was also extremely hostile to Shi'ism. The word *islah* is of key significance in this context; it

Popular piety. Women at Shahzada shrine, Qazvin, Iran. Visiting shrines answers a widely felt need in Muslim society, especially among Shi'ites, for the expression of personal piety, often with a pronounced emotional tinge. Hence the impassioned invocations of 'Ali and Husayn, and, more generally, the calls for intercession from the Imams and their descendants for those in personal need.

means the reconstructing or restoring of what is viewed as the true Islam. If necessary, the **lesser** *jihad*, armed struggle, must be pursued to achieve this goal (see Chapter 9, p. 220). Those that advocate that there is a single pure Islam are called **Salafis**. Today, their striving (*jihad*) to impose this view on the world is also a protest against what is perceived as the secularism, materialism, oppression, and corruption of the West. The emergence of the **Taliban** in Afghanistan in the later twentieth century fits into a rather extreme model of an islah movement.

The **Wahhabiyya**, a movement of purification of Muslim society begun in Arabia under the leadership of **Muhammad ibn 'Abd al-Wahhab** (1703–1792), argued vigorously against Sufism and Shi'ism and in favor of a return to the exclusive authority of the Qur'an and the way of the Prophet. The founder's major written manifesto, *The Book of Oneness*, sets out in fierce tones the fundamental issues that prevent someone from becoming a member of the Islamic community.[15] At the same time Shah Wali Allah in the Indian subcontinent took up a position like that of Ibn 'Abd al-Wahhab, but expressed it in less forceful language.

The Muslim Brotherhood (*al-ikhwan al-muslimin*) was founded in Egypt in 1928 by Hasan al-Banna'; its message was a return to the principles of the Qur'an and the hadith for the creation of a truly Islamic society. The Muslim Brotherhood now has branches all over the world. An armed group within the Brotherhood assassinated the Egyptian prime minister al-Nuqrashi in 1948, an event soon followed by the assassination of Hasan al-Banna' in 1949. The group was quickly forced to go underground. Since then, the ongoing role of the Muslim Brotherhood in Egypt and elsewhere has continued to be very influential; the events of the so-called Arab Spring—the wave of political protest in many Arab countries that began in 2010—among others, clearly show this.

The Egyptian thinker **Sayyid Qutb** (1906–1966) also advocated a return to pristine Islam, and he argued for the establishment of an Islamic state that alone is the model for society. Qutb was executed in 1966 for his role in opposing the government of the Egyptian president Jamal 'Abd al-Nasser. He had been the chief spokesman for the Muslim Brotherhood. His stance toward Western materialism is elaborated in his famous Qur'anic commentary *In the*

Taliban militiamen and tank, Kabul, Afghanistan, 1995. The absence of religious slogans, and indeed of any kind of uniform, is noteworthy. Facial hair is encouraged, as an external sign of their commitment to the faith. The literal meaning of *taliban* ("students," with the particular gloss of "seminary students") seems strangely inappropriate here; the Taliban in government, however, enforced stringent orthodoxy in Afghanistan, from imposing the veil to forbidding music.

Shade of the Qur'an. It argues that Islam is a perfect system of life, that God's law should be established on this earth, and that it should be the basis for governing God's people. Qutb had lived in the USA for two years and was very hostile to the lifestyle he saw there. For example, he characterized Americans enjoying themselves as a form of "nervous excitement, animal merriment."[16] Qutb made much of the contrast between the Egyptian ruler Pharaoh and Moses. For him Moses was the model Muslim ruler, while Pharaoh epitomized the tyrant who wanted to destroy Islam.

Born in India, **Abu'l-'Ala Mawdudi** (1903–1979) began at an early age to work as a journalist. In 1933, he became editor of a monthly magazine entitled *Tarjuman al-Qur'an* ("Translator of the Qur'an"), published in Hyderabad. He founded the Jama'at-i Islami (the Islamic Party) in 1941. In 1947 he emigrated to the newly founded separate country of Pakistan, where he wished to help in the establishment of a new Islamic state. There he became involved in politics with the Jama'at-i Islami, and spent some time in prison on account of his outspoken views. His biggest work is an Urdu commentary on the Qur'an written for ordinary people in clear, accessible language (see also Chapter 9, pp. 238–39).

A more recent influential figure in the Wahhabi mold is the Saudi scholar **'Abd al-'Aziz ibn 'Abdallah ibn Baz** (1910–1999), who held the position of official *mufti* of Saudi Arabia. He was thus charged with the responsibility for pronouncing on matters of Islamic law and delivering *fatwa*s (legal opinions). Another work of Ibn 'Abd al-Wahhab entitled *Points that Invalidate Islam* now appears in both Arabic and English on the Internet as *Ten Points that Invalidate Islam*; the work is attributed to Ibn Baz.[17] In it he updates the ideas of Ibn 'Abd al-Wahhab and fits them to the challenges of today, taking a tough stance on the issue of those who may legitimately be called Muslims and nonbelievers. The text attacks Jews and Christians, and American and European support for Israel.

MODERNIZING THINKERS

In contrast to the Islamic fundamentalist stance, other Muslims have sought to confront and embrace change and thus to modify and reinterpret aspects of the faith in the context of the modern world. Such an approach evolved in the nineteenth century and featured **Sayyid Ahmad Khan** (1817–1898), **Jamal al-Din Afghani** (1838–1897), and **Muhammad 'Abduh** (1849–1905), among others. The widespread impact of these thinkers dictates a closer though still necessarily brief look at their careers.

Sayyid Ahmad Khan engaged with the issue of how to deal with British rule in India, and where Islam should stand in his colonized homeland. His attitude toward the British in the Indian Mutiny of 1857–58 was supportive; he saw British rule as more beneficial to Islam in India than domination by the Hindu majority. At the theological college that he set up in Aligarh he accepted both Sunni and Shi'ite students as well as Hindus; the curriculum there stressed the importance of science. He hoped that its graduates would one day become the leaders of a separate Muslim state in India. Sayyid Ahmad Khan saw the need to liberate Islamic law to respond to the demands of a modern society.

Jamal al-Din Afghani, who has been called the father of Islamic modernism, was a visionary intellectual who developed the concept of **Pan-Islamism** as a way of uniting and reanimating the Muslim world against the ever-increasing encroachment of the European powers. Born in Asadabad in Afghanistan, he mastered a number of Middle Eastern languages. He sought to modernize Muslim society whilst not losing sight of core Islamic principles. He was strongly anti-British, and more generally anti-imperialist. Whilst in India he became acquainted with the ideas of Sayyid Ahmad Khan. He was sought after as an adviser both by the shah of Iran and by the Ottoman sultan. A controversial figure, and an outspoken public intellectual wherever he went, al-Afghani wanted to build a Muslim society that combined traditional Islamic culture with modern Western science and thought. On the political front, he espoused Pan-Islamism, in an attempt to unite the Muslim world against Western imperialism. He exerted a great influence on Egyptian thinkers, such as Rashid Rida (see p. 182) and Muhammad 'Abduh. And yet he wrote very little. His letter to the French thinker Ernest Renan in response to Renan's lecture in Paris in 1883, in which he accused Islam of being an obstacle to science and philosophy, made it clear that al-Afghani agreed with Renan that all religions display intolerance and hinder the pursuit of science and philosophy. But he went on to argue: "Realizing, however, that the Christian religion preceded the Muslim religion in the world by many centuries, I cannot keep from hoping that Muhammadan society will succeed some day in breaking its bonds and marching resolutely in the path of civilization after the manner of Western society."[18]

Muhammad 'Abduh is widely considered to be the most influential scholar of the modernist approach in nineteenth-century Egypt. He became the chief mufti of Egypt in 1897, and strove to develop the rational principles on which to build a Muslim society in the modern age. His book *Tafsir al-Manar* ("The Manar Commentary"), which refers to a periodical entitled *Al-Manar* edited by his disciple Rashid Rida, aimed to make the Qur'an clear to every Muslim. This was intended to be a commentary uncluttered by the obscurity and pedantry of the past.[19]

More recently, the French-educated Berber Algerian modernist **Mohammed Arkoun** (1928–2010) argued that Muslims should accept science and historical methodology, integrate them into their faith, and reinterpret them. This approach might well lead to symbolic, as opposed to literal, interpretations of religious truths. His views are strongly apolitical and he deplores the way in which, as he sees it, too much Muslim discourse has emphasized what he calls ideologies of domination. Instead of using these, individual Muslims should concentrate on the spiritual power of the Qur'an to transform their lives.[20]

The past 150 years, then, have seen a ferment of intellectual activity, debate, and controversy on the part of Muslim thinkers from the far west of the Islamic world to India—and in all of them there is the same urgent desire to chart a new path for the faith in politically challenging times. These debates are likely not only to continue but also, thanks to the easy availability of electronic communication, to increase in both pace and volume.

SELECTED READING

Adamson, Peter and Taylor, Richard C., *The Cambridge Companion to Arabic Philosophy*, Cambridge: Cambridge University Press, 2005

Crone, Patricia, *Medieval Islamic Political Thought*, Edinburgh: Edinburgh University Press, 2004

Euben, Roxanne L., and Zaman, Muhammad Qasim (eds), *Princeton Readings in Islamist Thought. Texts and Contexts from al-Banna to Bin Laden*, Princeton, NJ: Princeton University Press, 2009

Griffel, Frank, *Al-Ghazali's Philosophical Theology*, New York: Oxford University Press, 2009

Leaman, Oliver and Rizvi, Sajjad, "The Developed Kalam tradition," in Tim Winter (ed.), *The Cambridge Companion to Classical Islamic Theology*, Cambridge: Cambridge University Press, 2008, pp. 77–96

8 SUFISM

And on the earth are signs for those whose faith is sure. And within yourselves. Then will you not see? QUR'AN 51:20–21

Islam has given the world mystics no less than Hinduism or Christianity. GANDHI[1]

Sufism is the inner, mystical dimension of **Islam**. It is always difficult to find a totally satisfactory definition of mysticism. Anyone who tries to do this encounters the insuperable problem presented by the nature of mystical experience itself, which is personal, direct, and indescribable. It is possible to communicate it only in deeply symbolic terms—as the Arabic saying has it: "Metaphor is a bridge to ultimate reality." Mysticism has usually been envisaged in two general ways: externally, as the path or ladder of the human soul as it rises closer toward God, and internally, as the search within the human heart to find God there. Both these symbolic representations are, of course, interconnected, and they express only partly and inadequately the most profound spiritual realities, which cannot be captured in human language.

All the world's major faiths have had famous figures who have experienced direct and close contact with God, the One, the transcendental, or whatever other name can be given to ultimate reality.[2] And the accounts of mystics in the different religions bear certain similarities. Yet there are clear differences too, since mystical experiences are embedded within individual religious traditions that have their own associated rituals, ideals, and ethical systems. Islam, the mystical tradition of which is called *tasawwuf*, is no exception in this matter.

Tasawwuf, usually translated into English as "Sufism," literally means "becoming a Sufi." The word itself appears to have come from the Arabic word *suf* (wool), and it originally referred to the rough woolen garments worn by early **Muslim ascetics** (religious people who abstained from worldly pleasures),[3] but in the course of time, the term tasawwuf came more generally to denote Islamic mysticism. Sufis themselves use the symbol of a path (*tariqa*) to God. The image of a path is well established in Islamic thinking, since the word *Shari'a* is interpreted as being the wide path of the law that provides rules for every aspect of a Muslim's daily life. By contrast, the tariqa is viewed as a narrow path, which believers may tread in order to experience God's ultimate reality.

Mysticism in Islam has existed from the earliest period. At times it has encountered difficulties, hostility, and persecution. On numerous occasions it has been viewed as being outside the main doctrinal evolution of Islam, although many of the greatest Muslim thinkers were indeed Sufis. The most successful missionaries of Islam were the Sufis; they ventured well beyond the Arabic, Persian, and Turkish-speaking lands, spreading the message of Islam from sub-Saharan Africa to Indonesia. Within the Middle East itself, later medieval Muslim dynasties, such as the **Ottomans**, positively favored Sufism, sponsored Sufi leaders at their courts, and traveled with them on military campaigns. Above all, it was the Sufis who served as the major source of personal religious solace for the ordinary people, those unable to understand the legal and theological intricacies of religious debates. Nowadays Sufism is banned in some Muslim countries, but it continues vibrantly in others, as well as gaining many adherents in the non-Muslim West in recent times.

This chapter explores how Sufism emerged, what form it took in various countries, its key concepts and practices, and the writings of Sufi mystics and thinkers.

THE BEGINNINGS OF ASCETICISM AND MYSTICISM IN ISLAM

ASCETICISM

The first contemplative figures in Islam were primarily ascetics who did not find the collective religious observances of the Islamic community sufficient for all their religious needs. They sought more personal certainty of salvation by turning away from the beguiling pleasures of this world in fear of God's imminent **Day of Judgment**. They felt intensely the burden of their own sin, and were in stark terror of the fire of hell. So they practiced fasting, praying, and meditation in seclusion. Amongst such people were famous religious scholars (*'ulama'*), who saw no contradiction between, on the one hand, rigorous personal piety and ascetic practices and, on the other hand, making public pronouncements in the **mosque** or even in the **caliphal** court about the evolving structure of Islamic law.

Several dozen works about asceticism were written between the eighth and tenth centuries. These works focus on the Prophet **Muhammad** as a role model, and also on **Jesus**; they mention too the exemplary lives of Muhammad's **Companions** and the pious eighth-century **Umayyad** caliph 'Umar II. Such ascetics could subject themselves to all kinds of demanding physical tests and extreme mortification of the flesh, but they were still "veiled" from God unless it was His will that they should "see Him."

Amongst the many semi-legendary and historical figures who stand out as models of early Muslim asceticism, **Hasan al-Basri** (642–728) is especially influential. As an ascetic, judge, and preacher, he was a towering personality. Many pious anecdotes about him are recounted in medieval Muslim religious texts. Born in **Medina**, he met people who had known the Prophet himself, and during his long life he practiced meditation, abstinence, and self-control. He examined his conscience every day and he fearlessly warned his fellow Muslims, including the caliph, against the dangers of worldly attitudes and attachment to earthly possessions. As he said, "Beware of this world with all wariness, for it is like a snake, smooth to the touch, but its venom is deadly."[4] Hasan was acutely aware that since this world is transient, we must prepare for the next. He himself may not have been a mystic, but he was adopted as one of them by later Sufis, who quote extensively from his eloquent speeches, sermons, and sayings. In one of his most celebrated sermons he evokes a terrifying picture of the Day of Judgment: "O sons of Adam, glutton, glutton...You will die alone! You will enter the tomb alone! You will be resurrected alone! You will be judged alone!"[5]

In delivering such sermons, Hasan was risking the wrath of the caliphs, as this was an age when Umayyad rule was felt by many to be far removed from the piety of the earliest caliphs.

THE ORIGINS OF SUFISM

Considerable debate exists about the origins of the mystical tradition in Islam, and what is known of the very beginnings of Sufism comes to a large extent from fragmentary evidence preserved in texts of the tenth century and thereafter. It is quite possible that Muslims had mystical experiences from the very beginning of Islam. At some point in the early Islamic period, ascetic exercises came to form the preliminary stage in the longer process of purifying the soul, so that it might know and love God and attain closeness to Him even in this life.

Some Western scholars in earlier generations tended to see Sufism as the result of Christian influence, and especially that of Syrian monasticism.[6] But that view has rightly been superseded by one that argues that the mystical dimension in Islam was there from the beginning;[7] it was an integral part of the Muslim religious experience from the Prophet's spiritual experiences at the Cave of Hira onward. So Sufism was not grafted onto Islam from outside. When after 632 the Muslims took over the predominantly Christian countries that bordered Arabia to the northwest, however, they may have copied

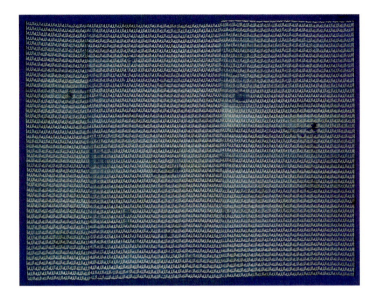

Woven prayer. Textile, West Africa, 19th century. This cloth, perhaps used as a talisman when worn, reflects the common Sufi practice of repeating a single word (for example, as here, "Allah") many times—in this case, 2,397 repetitions—as a devotional aid. Close Christian and Buddhist parallels exist, with the same aim of fostering contemplation.

Christian monks in the Syrian desert in external ways, for example by donning woolen garments and imitating their ascetic exercises.

Just as eastern Christians used the "Jesus prayer," in which they repeated his name constantly over and over again, early Sufis mentioned the name of God in a similarly repetitive crescendo of religious worship and piety. This practice is called *dhikr Allah* (remembrance of God; for the related ceremony called *dhikr* see pp. 208–10). Whilst the **Qur'an** stresses the value of prayer, it declares that remembrance of God is more important.[8] And the idea of a ladder between God and man, with the human soul climbing upward on it, seems to be common to many faiths—including Jacob's ladder in Judaism.[9] It is clearly embedded in Islam too in the Prophet's ascent into heaven (*mi'raj*), which is also a powerful symbol of the human soul's ecstatic movement toward God.

THE IMPORTANCE OF THE QUR'AN

The principal inspiration for Muslims seeking greater personal closeness to God lay firmly within the Qur'an. It seems that soon after the death of the Prophet, pious individuals began to look within the Qur'an for verses that encouraged their personal devotions as they withdrew from this wicked world.

They lived so close to their Holy Book that they were able to view everything in the light of what it said, and used it to follow the example of the Prophet. For Sufis, Muhammad was the first Sufi; all Sufis should model their conduct on his. As the early Sufi **Junayd ibn Muhammad Abu'l-Qasim al-Khazzaz** (830–910), says: "All the mystic paths are barred except to him who follows in the footsteps of the Messenger."[10]

Expounding on Qur'anic verses—the practice known as exegesis—thus formed an essential part of Sufi literature; one early Qur'anic commentator, **Muqatil ibn Sulayman al-Balkhi** (d. 767), developed the concept of the Prophet's light from the mysteriously beautiful Light Verse (24:35). The verse itself describes how God is everywhere, and all-knowing:

> God is the Light of the heavens and of the earth. His light is as if there were a lustrous niche, wherein is a lamp contained in a crystal globe, the globe as bright as a pearly star. The lamp is lit with the oil of a blessed tree, an olive, neither of the east nor of the west. The oil would well-nigh glow forth even though no fire were to touch it. Light upon light! God guides to His light whomsoever He wills. God speaks to mankind in allegories. God knows all things well.

According to this verse, God Himself speaks in the symbolic language of light. His illuminating light is powerful and multi-layered, just like the nature of mystical knowledge. This verse reminds Muqatil of the Prophet in the cave of Hira, when he saw a blinding light on the horizon just before the moment of the first revelation from God. From the very beginning until today, Sufis have contemplated the multiple meanings of this verse.

As early as the eighth century, then, Sufis had formulated a language based on Qur'anic terms in an attempt to put into words their mystical experiences, or those of others who simply could not express what had happened to them. The Qur'an invites believers to leave this wicked world and turn to God. It also tells believers to reflect on the name of God and to mention it unceasingly. Believers are told to trust in God and to love Him. There is ample support within the Qur'an for the practice of fasting as a form of self-discipline, for night prayer, and for the merits of poverty. In the *hadith*, too, there is abundant evidence that the Prophet engaged in ascetic practices, especially when he was still in Mecca, when he withdrew outside the city and fasted and prayed at night.

RABI'A

One of the best loved of all the early Sufis was a woman from Basra, **Rabi'a 'Adawiyya** (c. 715–801). Pious legend has it that, since her father already had three daughters, he called her "the fourth one" (Rabi'a). She is said to have been a slave whom her master, recognizing her saintly qualities, had freed. She became a secluded, celibate mystic, first in the desert and later in Basra, where a group of disciples gathered round her. Her biographer tells how she fasted and served God by day and by night. Being a woman was not a barrier to her prestige and saintly reputation. Indeed, in some of the legends about her, she is shown to get the better of the pious men, even Hasan al-Basri, who came to visit her. When asked by Hasan about her views on marriage she replied that it meant nothing to her since she existed only through God.[11]

The sayings of Rabi'a are quoted by many later celebrated Sufis and scholars. Given the veneration accorded to the Prophet's wife **'A'isha** and his daughter **Fatima**, it is not so surprising that a woman should be ranked as perhaps the most important early Sufi. Rabi'a herself has been compared with the Virgin **Mary**, the mother of **Jesus**.

Rabi'a was doubtless not the first Sufi to realize that the way to God should be sought through love, but generations of later Sufis were especially inspired by her. Rabi'a stripped away all worldly preoccupations that could detract from the exclusive love of God. Pure, disinterested love of Him was achieved in several stages; it involved the exclusion of love of another human being (she is said to have refused many proposals of marriage), love of objects, even of the **Ka'ba**, and love of the Prophet. She also rejected worship of God motivated by thoughts of the Day of Judgment; she said, "O God, if I worship Thee for fear of Hell, burn me in Hell, and if I worship Thee in hope of Paradise, exclude me from Paradise; but if I worship Thee for Thy own sake, grudge me not Thy everlasting beauty."[12] Love for Rabi'a is thus focused exclusively on God. In a moving prayer, she is reported to have said: "O God, my whole occupation and all my desire in this world, of all worldly things, is to remember Thee, and in the world to come, of all the things of the world to come, is to meet Thee."[13]

THE DEVELOPMENT OF MEDIEVAL SUFISM

By around 900 numerous ascetic and mystical practices, beliefs, and concepts had developed across the enormous Muslim empire. Sufi theorists, who were not necessarily those who experienced mystical states themselves, nevertheless

A taste of ecstasy? Tinted drawing, Iran, 17th century. Using techniques recalling marbled paper, this hallucinatory image with its swirling rhythms evokes a mystical journey. It celebrates the unity of being (*wahdat al-wujud*) elaborated by Ibn al-'Arabi. Created forms dissolve into each other and the composition suggests infinity, expanding beyond the frame.

attempted to describe the indescribable. This section details some key figures in the development of Sufism. (For their attempts to use symbolic language and construct a technical vocabulary for Sufism, see pp. 200–204.)

Two broad categories of Sufis began to be distinguished: the so-called "sober" Sufis and the "intoxicated" Sufis. In general, the former group remained acceptable to the religious/legal elite, and they developed concepts of the Sufi path and Sufi love of God that were scrupulously phrased to fit within the norms of Islamic law. The earliest spiritually "intoxicated" Sufis, however, pronounced ecstatic utterances that, as we shall see, appeared abhorrent to the religious establishment. The mystical experiences of both groups may well have been similar, but the "sober" Sufis took more care to be discreet in both their conduct and their writings. Typical of the "sober" Sufi approach was Junayd. He was acutely aware of the dangers of speaking and writing about mystical union with God, and his doctrines are deeply rooted in **Sunni** Islam; he writes that Sufism is to purify the heart, to ascend by means of knowledge of God, and to follow the Prophet in respect of the Shari'a. Thus he argues for the necessity of a harmonious coexistence of the Shari'a and the Sufi path, and he is careful to oppose the extremes to which some Sufis would go when they dared to dispense with Islamic law altogether.[14]

Gradually, the interpretation of concepts such as mystical union with God and mystical love for God caused certain personalities within Sufism to move, or seem to move, outside the mainstream of orthodox Islamic belief with its stress on the One God. Given this core Muslim belief and the dangers of committing the terrible sin of *shirk* (allowing anyone or anything to trespass on the uncompromising, transcendental Oneness of God), Muslims reject the idea that God can dwell within the human body, and so cannot accept the Christian concept of the incarnation of Jesus. Muslims also forbid the notion that God and man can become one entity. So the Sufis tried, when describing their mystical experiences, to use careful terminology such as "arriving" (*wasl*) into the proximity of God or "reaching the full realization of God's oneness" (*tawhid*).

BISTAMI

Two famous figures from the early formative period of Sufism stand out for being "intoxicated" with ecstatic experiential knowledge of God. The first is **Abu Yazid Bayazid Bistami** (804–874 or 877/8) Much of his fame, or notoriety, comes from his ecstatic utterances, in which he expressed his experiences of "losing himself" in the Divine. His teacher was called Abu 'Ali al-Sindi, a title that indicates that he or his family had come from India. Whether this is sufficient evidence to suggest that Bistami was a vehicle through whom Hindu or Buddhist influences came into Sufism is another matter, although there is some similarity between his sayings and the Hindu scriptures. One source says that Bistami taught al-Sindi about Islam whilst al-Sindi taught Bistami about "the truths of religion."

It seems that Bistami himself wrote nothing down, and indeed he could not recall his sayings later, after the ecstasy had gone. But those listening to him passed on stories about him orally, and later Sufi writers collected his sayings and handed them down. Bistami affirmed that those who have mystical knowledge of God are superior to Muslim legal scholars, who are enslaved by chains of knowledge that bind them to previous scholars who have transmitted book learning to them. Addressing scholars directly, he is reported to have said: "You have had your knowledge from a dead man while we have had our knowledge from the Living One who never dies."[15] In moments of ecstasy Bistami is alleged to have spoken as if he were God; he became "filled with God," he no longer existed but only God existed: "I sloughed off my self as a snake sloughs off its skin. Then I looked, and behold, I was He."[16]

Bistami rejected this world as an illusion. Two of his most famous sayings—"Glory be to Me! How great is My majesty!" and "I am He"—in which God appears to be speaking through his own mouth, shocked many people and provoked accusations of blasphemy. He did not seek to preach to the Muslim masses, however. He spent most of his life in his house in Bistam, eastern Iran[17], or in an isolated cell or in the mosque, and was visited only by people wishing to experience his charismatic presence. In this way he avoided personal or legal attack.

HALLAJ

Retrospectively, the career of **Hallaj** (c. 860–922), Sufism's most famous martyr, can be seen as a turning point in the history of Sufism. Born in southern Iran, he went to Baghdad where he got to know the moderate Sufi Junayd and his disciples. Having disagreed with them, he returned to Iran. A most eloquent preacher, he then began to travel around the Muslim world. There he acquired a great public following and allegedly performed miracles. He is reported to have made a number of blasphemous pronouncements, which brought him into conflict with many powerful groups in Baghdad. His recorded ecstatic utterances include his saying that the pilgrimage can be performed in one's heart without going to Mecca. The most famous ecstatic utterance attributed to him—"I am the Truth," thus applying to himself one of the titles of God—has been compared to the saying of Jesus, "I am the Way, the Truth and the Life."[18]

Indeed, some have seen Hallaj as a Jesus figure[19]—and certainly similarities can be drawn between the two. Like Jesus, whose destiny brought him to Jerusalem, Hallaj chose deliberately to expose himself to his opponents in Baghdad, and both suffered the most terrible of deaths by crucifixion. It was not only because of what he had allegedly said whilst in ecstatic states that caused his downfall; Hallaj angered a broad spectrum of opinions. The political establishment, the Sunni caliph, and the religious lawyers all feared the impact of his eloquence on the ordinary people, and also the way in which he tried to popularize Sufism, thus threatening, in their view, the stability of the Muslim community as a whole. Some of his fellow Sufis also opposed him—those who wanted to keep Sufism as an esoteric way only for an elite, and those who accused him of bypassing Islamic law. So he was imprisoned, tortured, and crucified in 922. His followers dispersed to distant places to avoid similar persecution. "Intoxicated" Sufism did not die with Hallaj, but those who adopted the Sufi way thereafter could see the dangers of having too public a profile and of acting, or appearing to act, outside the precepts of the Shari'a.

AL-MUHASIBI AND AL-MAKKI

Two writers from this era should be singled out as being especially influential in the future theoretical development of Sufism: **Harith al-Muhasibi** (781–857) and **Abu Talib al-Makki** (d. 996). Steeped as they were in the traditional religious sciences, they were crucial in the process of Sufism's gradual integration into mainstream medieval Muslim society, and they left written works behind them for later generations to read, absorb, and put into practice. These two authors exerted a great influence on the more famous scholar **al-Ghazali** (c. 1058–1111; see below).

The key to the thought of the Baghdad Sufi al-Muhasibi lies in his name, which means "someone who examines his conscience"; his works reveal a heavy debt to the role model of Hasan al-Basri. Relying for all his ideas on the support of the Qur'an and the hadith, he stresses that believers must be constantly scrupulous in their observance of the faith and scrutinize their inner motives for their actions, and not just observe the outer shell of external rituals. They must always flee this world, "an abode of affliction, a place of care and sorrow,"[20] and keep in mind the terrors of the Day of Judgment and the promises of Paradise to true believers. Only such intense internal spiritual discipline, the contemplation of God, will allow the heart of the believer to be open to receive God's grace.

A century later al-Makki taught that the Muslim faith has two dimensions, external and internal. Both are needed, and both are interdependent and complementary. In his great work, *The Food of Hearts*, he examines the **pillars of Islam** and tries to invest each of them with inner meaning. His work is constructed like a book of conventional Muslim jurisprudence, but it is much more than that. Above all, it is the concept of the "heart," as the title of his work suggests, that is central to his thinking. It is the heart that gives man knowledge of God, which uncovers God's truth. This is faith based on religious certainty rather than on scholastic learning, intellectual reasoning, and tradition.

AL-GHAZALI

A major milestone in the history of Sufism came with the career of al-Ghazali, who is probably the most famous Muslim scholar in classical Islam. Even today, he is much respected not only in the Arab world and in his homeland of Iran, but also in the Indian subcontinent, Malaysia, and Indonesia. His engagement with Sufism is significant not because his ideas were especially new—for they were not—but because he was able to present them in a systematic, structured, and eloquent way. For al-Ghazali, the Sufi path toward true knowledge should not imply a divorce from the Shari‘a, the well-trodden path of the revealed law of Islam. Indeed, a scrupulous observance of outward religious practices is a necessary part of inner piety. He underlines this point in his long master-piece, *The Revival of the Religious Sciences*, where he explains that Sufism is not an alternative to formal Islam, but a completion of it. *The Revival* is directed not just at the majority of Muslims; it is also addressed to the Sufis, some of whom had expressed the opinion that Islamic law could be ignored.

All Muslims, in short, should observe the outward signs of the faith. Yet al-Ghazali is well aware that this is not sufficient without the direct, ecstatic, contemplation of God in the divinely illuminated heart—the inner fire of Sufism. Al-Ghazali believed that faith has its outward and inner aspects, both of which are necessary and interdependent to achieve balance; he calls the inner aspects "the activities of hearts."[21] Faith based on inner certainty, attained through "unveiling," is better than faith based on tradition and reason. So like al-Makki before him, al-Ghazali examines the five pillars of Islam and tries to invest them with inner significance.

Al-Ghazali wrote an autobiography—a rare genre in medieval Islam—called *The Deliverer from Error*.[22] Although a short work, it is a powerful piece of advocacy for the Sufi way. He uses the literary device of his spiritual crisis in 1095, when, at the summit of his career—he was the head of the most important **madrasa** in the **Seljuq** empire, the Nizamiyya in Baghdad, and the friend of the sultan and caliph—he had what we would nowadays call a nervous breakdown. In the middle of lecturing he found he could no longer speak—as he put it, "God put a lock on my tongue."[23] He left Baghdad shortly afterward and wandered round the Muslim world for ten years, dressed as a Sufi, visiting Damascus, Jerusalem, and Mecca, before returning home to eastern Iran. His autobiography was written probably some five years before his death in 1111. It is a moving spiritual self-portrait in which he shows how he has come to realize that all his book knowledge is not able to help him to attain what he most desired—certain knowledge of God. After his crisis he can say confidently to his reader that he knows "with certainty that the Sufis are those who uniquely follow the way to God."[24] Coming from the most famous intellectual of his time, this is powerful support for Sufism. Although there are those who say that al-Ghazali was never a Sufi himself,[25] his passionately positive advocacy for the Sufi way formed the culmination of the work of his predecessors al-Muhasibi and al-Makki, and he helped to integrate a moderate form of Sufism into orthodox Islam.

SOME KEY SUFI CONCEPTS AND SYMBOLS

The Sufis tried to explain in words their striving for union with God through symbols that aimed to give a proper structure to their spiritual experiences. Looking back on their attempts, they may seem now to be obscure, simplistic, or sometimes, perhaps, rather ridiculous, but what matters is that they wrote in a spirit of true piety.

THE SUFI PATH

Sufi theorists tried to chart the mystical journey of the soul as it progresses toward God. Though inconsistent, their treatises agree that there was a distinct sequence of some kind as the traveler treads the Sufi path, and they all speak of hierarchical "stations" (*maqam*), like steps on a spiritual ladder, and "mystical states" (*ahwal*). ʿAbd al-Karim Qushayri, for example, in his concise description of Sufi doctrine in the eleventh century, lists forty-three stations and three states; whilst Abu Nasr al-Sarraj, in a similar work, written in the previous century, mentions only seven stations but ten states. Despite such differences in detail, Sufi theorists gave names, derived from the Qur'an, to the stations, such as "repentance," "striving," "fear," "gratitude," and "patience." It is not clear whether they were intended to be attained by the seeker in an agreed strict sequence. Generally, it was believed that a station could be reached and maintained by a person's own efforts, whereas a mystical state came only from God as a gift of His grace, and during this lifetime at least it would remain only fleetingly within the human heart. As Qushayri puts it: "The states are gifts; the stations are earnings."[26]

Different Sufi mystics and writers emphasize different aspects of the way to God. From the sayings of Rabiʿa, the core Sufi doctrine of mystical love, love of God alone, can be constructed (see p. 194). For al-Ghazali, it is the heart that equips man for knowledge of God (see pp. 198–99). In this context, the heart is not the organ of flesh situated in the chest; it is an organ through which the human being may gaze upon the beauty of the Divine Presence; this is the culmination of his happiness.[27] When speaking about the human heart or soul, Sufi writers frequently used the symbol of the mirror, which in medieval times was often made of metal. The heart is usually dirty, rusty, and soiled with sin and human passions. It must be cleansed of the rust (of this material world) and polished to become the receptacle for knowledge of God.

When Sufis reach the final stage of the path, they become entirely present in God and totally lost to themselves; this is called *fana'* (annihilation of the self in God). This mystical state is permanent only in death, but it may be reached temporarily when Sufis are alive on this earth. When the "sober" Sufi Junayd speaks about this state, his tone is always careful and restrained. He is at pains to suggest that the person who has been blessed with fana' will then "return" to his own human earthly identity to contemplate God anew from afar. Thus the potential dangers of blasphemy, of compromising the unassailable Oneness of God, are averted. As Junayd explains:

> Then, after he (the Sufi) has not been, he is where he has been. He is himself, after he has not really been himself. He is present in himself and in God, after having been present in God and absent in himself. This is because he has left the intoxication of God's overwhelming dominance and come to the clarity of sobriety, and contemplation is once more restored to him, so that he can put everything in its right place and assess it correctly.[28]

Thus Junayd and other "sober" Sufis scrupulously defined fana' in a way that maintained the requisite distinction between God and man, keeping God's uncompromising oneness intact. Another famous "sober" Sufi, **Abu'l-Hasan 'Ali Hujwiri**, writing in the eleventh century, is able to reconcile being a Sunni Muslim with following the Sufi path. He speaks of fana' as "burning by fire, transforming everything to its own quality but leaving its essence unchanged."[29]

Aware of the perceived dangers of mysticism, which would threaten the stability of Muslim society, especially if its secrets were allowed to disrupt the "wide path" of the Shari'a, Sufi writers tried hard to define the conditions of mystical union with God, stressing the inward aspects of true religion without undermining the validity of outward rituals. They argued that the total annihilation of self in God experienced by the Sufi does not mean that he ceases to observe the outward rituals of the faith demanded by the Shari'a.

FINDING THE INNER REALITY: SUFI THEOSOPHY

The dictionary definition of **theosophy** as a philosophy that professes "to attain to a knowledge of God by spiritual ecstasy, direct intuition, or special individual relations" admirably fits Sufism. Sufism involves a search for the inner reality. The Qur'an presents God as both visible and hidden: "He is the external and the internal" (57:3). The believer who treads the path of Sufism moves from the external "shell" to the internal "core," from appearance to essence. And the Qur'an invites the believer to look: "And on the earth are signs for those whose faith is sure. And within yourselves. Then will you not see?" (57:20–21). For Sufis, God has created the world as an image of Himself; behind the world of appearance, of doctrines and law, there lies an inner reality that is its real foundation and that gives it true meaning.

Before al-Ghazali, Sufism lacked theoretical philosophical systemization. The work called *The Niche of Lights*, which may or may not have been written entirely by al-Ghazali, elaborates the mystical nature of light to a fully fledged Sufi theosophy (*'irfan*). This is a very complicated and fluid concept, combining mystical and philosophical elements.[30] The following discussion will concentrate on two major figures of this Sufi theosophical movement, **Suhrawardi** and **Ibn al-'Arabi**.

Suhrawardi

Shihab al-Din Suhrawardi (1155–1191) was given the title al-Maqtul ("the one who was killed") to differentiate him from two other religious scholars of the same name. In his writings, the most important of which was perhaps *The Wisdom of Illumination*, he formulated a theory of **Illuminationism** (*ishraqiyya*), which aroused the wrath even of his pro-Sufi patron, the ruler of Aleppo, al-Malik al-Zahir, who had Suhrawardi accused of heresy and killed in prison. Drawing on a blend of Greek, ancient Iranian, and Islamic elements, Suhrawardi argues that God, the essence of the First Absolute Light, gives constant illumination. Everything in the world is derived from His light, and in reaching this illumination lies salvation for His created beings. The closeness to God of any being is dependent on its degree of illumination or darkness. His theory of **angelology** is particularly intricate and attractive. He teaches that through a hierarchy of innumerable angels God's light radiates downward. Each soul has its own guardian angel. Following a model derived from the Greek philosopher **Plato**, he believes that the soul has had a previous existence in the angelic sphere; when the human being is born, one half of the soul remains in heaven whilst the other descends into the dark prison of the human body where it longs to be reunited with its heavenly counterpart. (For the influence of **Neoplatonism**, see Chapter 7, pp. 179–80.)

For Suhrawardi, existence is light. Absolute light reaches the created world through countless vertical and horizontal rows of angels. It is the duty of the human being to recognize and move closer to the existential light. The more he frees himself from the darkness of the ego and is suffused with light, the nearer he comes to the divine. In one of Suhrawardi's allegorical tales, the human soul finds itself in a dark well in the west and has forgotten its home in the east, the place where the sun rises, the abode of pure light. When it remembers again it sets out homeward, finally reaching Yemen, the land of wisdom where the archangels are to be found. The contrast between the dark, material west and the light-illuminated east is symbolized in his concept of "occidental exile."

Muhyiddin Ibn al-'Arabi

The career of Muhyiddin Ibn al-'Arabi (1165–1240), known as the *Shaykh al-akbar* (the greatest Shaykh), epitomizes that of many medieval Sufis who crisscrossed the vast Muslim world in search of knowledge and enlightenment. Born in Murcia in southeastern Spain, where he studied under two female Sufis, he moved to Egypt, Syria, Iraq, and Anatolia, before settling finally in Damascus. His influence was as widespread as his journeys. He wrote many works, including *The Ring-settings of Wisdom*, which concerns prophets and the wisdom revealed to them. Like al-Ghazali, Ibn al-'Arabi was skilled in writing in a systematic way. He spent several years meditating and receiving visions in Mecca. He writes that when he was forty—an important age in Islamic tradition—he saw in a dream the Ka'ba built of alternately gold and silver bricks and that in one place a gold and a silver one were missing. He goes on to say: "I then saw myself being inserted into the place reserved for the two missing bricks. I myself was the two bricks; with them the wall was complete and the Ka'ba was faultless."[31]

Thereafter, Ibn al-'Arabi claimed that just as Muhammad was the Seal of the Prophets, he, Ibn al-'Arabi, had reached the highest rank that a human being could reach, that of the "Seal of Muhammadan Sainthood," which placed him just below the Prophet in the Muslim spiritual hierarchy. He then composed his *Meccan Revelations*; this massive work of five hundred chapters, which he said were transmitted to him by God through an angel, attempts to present a complete view of God and the world. A key doctrine of his was that of the Perfect Man (*al-insan al-kamil*); this is Muhammad, the prototype of humanity and of the universe. The Perfect Man has achieved total realization of being. He is the means through which God is known and manifested.[32]

Not surprisingly, such concepts as these have appeared to many Muslims to be grandiose and against the teachings of Islam, although Ibn al-'Arabi himself was deeply learned in the Muslim religious sciences. The debate continues. Seyyed Hossein Nasr, an eloquent modern scholar, warns against snap judgments of Ibn al-'Arabi, arguing that he was addressing an audience who took acceptance of the Shari'a for granted and that he was inviting them to penetrate into the inner realities of Islamic law.

The work of Ibn al-'Arabi has profoundly influenced subsequent genera-tions of Sufis. For many Sufis now, Ibn al-'Arabi is the major figure whom they venerate. Indeed, they would go so far as to say that the word Sufism may only be applied to the world view developed by him.

IMAGERY IN SUFI POETRY AND PROSE

The earliest writers on Sufism chose, not surprisingly, to write in Arabic, the language of the Islamic revelation; this choice of Arabic also guaranteed the widest possible audience for their work across the vast Muslim world. However, given the popularity of Sufism in the Persian-speaking lands—Iran, parts of what is now Turkey, Afghanistan, Central Asia, and northern India—it was not long before works on Sufism also appeared in Persian. Sufi authors composed biographical works of celebrated Sufi figures, and they also tried to explain the concepts and rituals of Sufism in practical and popular handbooks for the faithful.

The rhythms and language of poetry lend themselves extremely well to mystical subjects, and such poetic images can give beautiful expression to transcendental realities. The celebrated Arab poet **'Umar Ibn al-Farid** (1181–1235), for example, uses elaborate mystical symbolism in the following lines: "We drank upon the remembrance of the Beloved a wine wherewith we were drunken before ever the vine was created. The full moon was a cup for it."[33] Here wine represents the love of God, the vine is the physical universe, and the moon the shining spirit of Muhammad. Another frequently recurring symbol for the annihilation of the human soul in God is the way that the beloved is depicted as the flame toward which the lover, like a moth, is drawn irresistibly, and within which he is finally consumed.

Al-Ghazali uses a wide repertoire of Sufi images in his works in both Arabic and Persian. He emphasizes that this world is fleeting and impermanent; only God abides for ever. As the Qur'an says (55:26–27), "Everyone who is on the earth passes away. And there survives the face of your Lord with grandeur and glory." Al-Ghazali says this world is to be avoided since it is treacherous and beguiling. Human beauty is defective and deceptive: the world may seem dazzlingly beautiful, like a veiled young woman, but when the veil is lifted, an ugly old crone is revealed.

Rumi

During the period of Mongol conquest and rule in Central Asia and Iran in the thirteenth century, despite the terrible devastation, these lands saw the

Modern America's best-selling poet. Tomb of Rumi, Konya, Turkey, 13th century onward. The conical roof and fluted drum evoke Central Asian yurts or nomads' tents; Rumi wandered from Afghanistan to Anatolia. He is Persia's best-loved lyric poet. His immensely long *Mathnawi*—a treasury of wit, wisdom, anecdote, and profound mystical thought—is a deep ocean of yearning for God.

flowering of the most beautiful Persian poetry. The major writer of Sufi literature, **Jalal al-Din Rumi** (1207–1273), fled from his home in Balkh, Afghanistan, in the wake of the Mongol invasions and settled eventually in Konya, in what is now Turkey. Rumi wrote in Persian; his most celebrated work, the *Mathnawi*, comprising 26,660 rhymed couplets, has been called by many later Sufi writers "the Qur'an in the Persian language."[34] It is full of memorable mystical imagery and yet steeped in a profound knowledge of Islam. In it Rumi longs for union with the Beloved in deeply symbolic language, yet he never loses sight of the importance of the law. A key image of Rumi's poetry is the reed flute (*nay*); it is a nostalgic reminder of our primordial union with God, and its plaintive sounds symbolize the soul yearning to return to its original home with God; as the Qur'an (2:156) expresses it: "We belong to God and to Him we are returning." The *Mathnawi* can be read at a number of different levels of meaning, but Rumi's imagery of reaching God is more memorable than any amount of theorizing: "Then you will have finished with the earth: your home will be heaven. Go beyond the angelic state; go into that ocean so that your drop of water will become one with the sea."[35]

By the fourteenth century miraculous tales were being told about Rumi by the Turkish writer Aflaki, who wanted to teach the faithful how to walk the Sufi path. In subsequent centuries the writing of Sufi poetry in many different languages proved to be a key factor in the spread of core religious concepts right across the Muslim world outside the Middle East. Poets in distant lands began to write mystical verses in Turkic, Urdu, Sindhi, Malay, and other Southeast Asian languages.

THE SUFI BROTHERHOODS (TARIQAS)

The term tariqa means "path" (see p. 189) but it also came to mean a group, order, or brotherhood that walked along the special inner path of Sufism. In the tenth to thirteenth centuries Sufism showed its adaptability by becoming more institutional in form. In periods of great political unrest, notably when the eastern Muslim world underwent the trauma of the Mongol invasions, Muslim society derived much benefit from the growing role of Sufi leaders,[36] to whom the uneducated classes above all would turn for help. These leaders developed regulated forms of Sufi behaviour and practice for their disciples. Hujwiri in the eleventh century mentions twelve different groups of Sufis, of which ten were "orthodox" and two "heretical." But these two categories may well just reflect his own views. What is clear is that particular schools of Sufism developed in important religious centers such as Mecca, Baghdad, and Basra. There were also Sufi circles clustered around individual saintly figures all over the Muslim world. Beginning in the twelfth century such groups then evolved into a large number of Sufi brotherhoods (tariqas) with their own doctrines and ceremonies. There were also some sisterhoods in the thirteenth and fourteenth centuries in Egypt, Syria, and Anatolia.

The Sufi brotherhoods ranged from those actively sponsored by the state to those that were forbidden. Some were firmly embedded within Sunni Islam, others were linked with **Shi'ism**, and yet others incorporated beliefs and practices from folk Islam, Hinduism, Buddhism, Christianity, or from a combination of these. The brotherhoods extended to all classes of society, including the ruler, the army, and the artisans. Many of the large brother-hoods were set up in several different parts of the Muslim world, while smaller new ones were more localized in their impact.

The members of the Sufi brotherhoods were the great missionaries of Islam. Far from forcing conversion at sword point, the Sufis traveled with traders along the Silk Road—the series of trade routes across southern Asia—or by ship to east and west, and spread Islam peacefully to North and sub-Saharan Africa, India, and Central and Southeast Asia. They ministered in pastoral fashion to the needs of the community and converted the local people by living alongside them.

ORGANIZATION AND INITIATION

Each brotherhood was presided over by the successor of its founder. Soon special buildings, or lodges, appeared for Sufi worship and residence; their names differ from country to country.[37] In some ways these buildings could be likened to Christian monasteries, but the Sufi brotherhoods did not generally practice celibacy. Some religious scholars disapproved of Sufi buildings. In the twelfth century, for example, Ibn al-Jawzi roundly condemned *ribat*s and the Sufis who lounged around lazily in them, instead of being with their fellow Muslims in the mosques. But only a few of the Sufis lived in the lodge. The remaining Sufis were lay members of the order who carried out their usual jobs during the week, but attended the rituals in the lodge from time to time. Inside the lodge devotional books were studied, and there were prayers, Qur'anic readings, and recitals of mystical poetry. Alongside the Qur'an, the disciples studied core Sufi commentaries and didactic poetry. They also learned the exact genealogical sequence (the so-called "chain") of the order, which took them right back to the Prophet. Women could also become Sufis. They were usually taught by other women and held their own separate ceremonies.

To be initiated into a brotherhood symbolizes becoming part of the chain. The initiation ceremony may involve hand clasping or the holding out of the *shaykh*'s **rosary** to the novice, who takes the other end whilst he is initiated into the order. The symbolic significance of being attached to the chain is that it allows the initiate to progress further along the spiritual path. Belts are also important in initiation rites. A tying ceremony with a certain number of knots (three, four, seven, or eight) binds the initiate to the tariqa. Much visual impact is made by the clothing in Sufi ceremonies. They had begun by wearing wool, symbolizing their ascetic lifestyle. Later on, they adopted a patched garment (*khirqa*) as a symbol of their attachment to Sufism. Different shapes and colours of hats and turbans characterize membership of particular tariqas. Once the initiation ceremony is over, the new member of the order is given a diploma.

Mobile devotions. The Friday *dhikr* ("remembrance") of the Sammaniyya Sufi brotherhood, Omdurman, Sudan. Shaykh Hasan Qariballah, seated, claps time as his Sufi brethren jump in unison, chanting Qur'anic phrases or the names of God. The form of *dhikr* varies between brotherhoods.

WORSHIP AND PRACTICE

Communal worship for the members of the tariqa takes the form of the ceremony known as dhikr. According to Seyyed Hossein Nasr, a practicing Sufi himself, dhikr is the "primary spiritual technique of Sufism, through which man returns to God"; it is "prayer unified with the rhythm of life itself."[38] As already mentioned (p. 192), dhikr involves remembrance, the constant repetition of the name Allah, accompanied by rhythmic, controlled breathing. Dhikr can be performed silently or aloud, alone or in a group. The sessions in company begin with the reciting of Qur'anic verses and prayers; here it is the shaykh of the order who is the spiritual director controlling the proceedings. If a Sufi is performing dhikr alone, he may use a rosary; but in any case he counts the number of repetitions of God's name, which will probably reach thousands.

After the establishment of the brotherhoods in the twelfth century, the dhikr ceremonies became formalized, and Sufis used various kinds of aids to assist them in their worship, such as prayers of intercession to saints, incense, coffee, and sometimes other stimulants. Coffee drinking spread from Sufi groups in Yemen to other parts of the Muslim world. It was thought to be useful for keeping people awake for night prayers and other spiritual exercises. In Yemen it was believed to encourage mystical experiences. The Sufis there would drink coffee at the same time as reciting the invocation *ya qawi* (O Strong One). Apart from being one of the ninety-nine Beautiful Names of God (see Chapter 7, p. 176), *qawi* also sounds quite similar to *qahwa*, the Arabic word for coffee. The Shadhiliyya Sufi brotherhood is especially famous for coffee drinking. One sixteenth-century saint from this tariqa is reported to have lived his final years on nothing but coffee; as their saying goes: "He who dies with some coffee in his body does not enter hell fire."

Friday worship in the mosque consists of prayers, a sermon, and readings from the Qur'an. This forms a marked contrast with what happens when Sufis come together in the dhikr ceremonies. For them, listening to music (*sama'*) played with instruments or sung with the human voice can help them on their path to ecstatic experiences. The spiritual "hearing" must be carefully controlled to prevent fake results, and participants are prepared morally and spiritually by the shaykh. The ecstatic states aroused by music must be genuinely spontaneous and not forced. Their music is played on the flute, drum,

Paths to God. Sufi gathering, Herat, *c.* 1490, by Bihzad (?). Dancing was held—along with meditation, *dhikr*, music, and stimulants, such as alcohol and narcotics—to liberate the body from quotidian reality, access the deeper self, and attain mystical exaltation. These Sufis meditate, weep, or faint; the raised arms, discarded scarves, jumbled limbs, disheveled clothing, and bare heads suggest abandonment.

and other instruments; solitary playing of the flute is especially loved, since it arouses echoes of man's primordial state and a yearning in the soul for union or reunion with God (see pp. 200–201). In common with some Islamic philosophers, who heard in earthly music the echoes of the music of the spheres (the supposed harmonious relationships between the heavenly bodies), the Sufis see music as spiritual. As one early Sufi, Dhu'l-Nun al-Misri, said, "Listening (to music) is a divine influence which stirs the heart to see God."[39]

In certain of the Sufi groups, the singing is accompanied by dancing, most famously associated with the whirling of the **Mevlevis** (see p. 211). Attempts have been made to explain the significance of the dancing in mystical terms and to link dancing, whirling, and leaping to various stages in the experience of the enraptured Sufi.[40]

FIVE TARIQAS

There have been numerous tariqas in different part of the Muslim world; some have survived until today, while others have long since died out. A short discussion of just five tariqas out of many will reveal their diversity of belief and practice.

The Qadiriyya

The **Qadiriyya**, the first great Sufi order, was established in the twelfth century by **'Abd al-Qadir al-Jilani** (1077–1166), a **Hanbali** lawyer and preacher in Baghdad, who gave mystical sermons both in the mosque and also to groups of Sufis. His religious credentials were impeccable: he had memorized the whole of the Qur'an and he regularly performed ascetic practices until he was fifty. Then, when he was spiritually ready, he preached to the ordinary people in clear and simple language. The brotherhood that bears his name had a great impact on the subsequent development of other brotherhoods. It was firmly rooted in Sunni Islam and spread right across the Muslim world.

The Naqshbandiyya

The **Naqshbandiyya** tariqa was founded by **Baha' al-Din Naqshband Bukhari** (1318–1389). He was born in the Persian-speaking environment of Bukhara in Central Asia. His tomb in Bukhara, a city of which he has become the patron saint, is an important place of visitation. Besides having great importance within Central Asia itself, the order spread widely across the Muslim world. The Sufis in this order perform a silent dhikr, a dhikr of the heart, not of the tongue. Their order too is sober and restrained, loyal to the Shari'a. It was

Cosmic dance. Whirling dervishes, Istanbul, Turkey. The Mevlevi Sufis—named after Mawlana, "Our Master," Rumi's title—display their order's trademark slow rotating rhythm. They seem to move to an unheard music of the spheres, orbiting like satellite planets around an unseen sun, yet all the time approaching inexorably nearer to God: a living metaphor.

popular in the Ottoman empire and is the principal Sufi order in India and Pakistan, as well as being very influential in Indonesia.

The Mevlevis

The Mawlawiyya (more commonly known as the **Mevlevis** or the Dancing or **Whirling Dervishes**) was established after the death of Jalal al-Din Rumi in 1273; one of the founders of the orders was his son Sultan Walad. The Turkish name Mevlevi comes from the Arabic title given to Rumi (Mawlana, meaning Our Master). The Mevlevi center is in Konya, Turkey. They trace their genealogy back to 'Ali. The office of shaykh is hereditary. Their music involves the playing of the flute (*nay*), made from cane or reed.

The Mevlevis are world famous for their whirling, a spiritual dance that symbolizes the movements of the planets round the sun. The ceremony, which follows procedures that are strictly laid down, takes place in a circular room. The dancers, who can include young boys as well as old men, each go and kiss the hand of the shaykh in turn. Dressed in their long skirts, they then turn on the left foot, pushing round with the right; their eyes are closed. Whilst whirling, they say the word "Allah" over and over again. Their joyful dancing is accompanied by the melodious sound of the flute, which, they believe, expresses the harmony of His creation.[41]

The Bektashiyya

The founder of the **Bektashiyya**, Hajji Bektash, came from eastern Iran, but he moved to what is now Turkey in the 1240s, where his message spread quickly amongst the nomadic Turks there. In the sixteenth century the early Ottoman sultans were closely connected with the Bektashis, as were the **Janissary** regiments. Whilst they shared the same beliefs, the same ceremonial chants, the same belief in the divinity of 'Ali, reincarnation, and the symbolic values of the letters of the alphabet, as time went on the urban and educated Bektashis drew away from their illiterate brothers in the countryside. Those in the town became associated with the freemasons, and when the order was officially closed down in 1826 they were forced to become secret societies and to hold their ceremonies at night. These included the lighting of twelve candles to indicate the **Imams** of the **Twelver** Shi'ites. Women are present, unveiled, at the ceremonies. This Sufi order has been very influential in Turkey and the Balkans, including Albania. The Albanian community in Detroit has a Bektashi lodge outside the city.

The Rifa'iyya

As for the **Rifa'iyya** (the Howling Dervishes), this tariqa, now found mainly in Egypt and Syria, is named after Shaykh Ahmad al-Rifa'i, who was born in the marshes of lower Iraq in 1118. Trained as a **Shafi'ite** legal scholar, he is said to have written sermons, prayers, and poems. The tariqa with which his name is associated seems to have developed unorthodox ceremonies that did not come from him. The ceremonial ritual of the Rifa'iyya begins with an elder of the group emitting a number of long pulsating cries to which the rest of the order respond. They then get into a sitting position and rock their heads to and fro. The session ends with wailing. Members of this brotherhood are reported to have performed extraordinary feats whilst in an ecstatic state, such as putting heated iron in their mouths, passing skewers through their cheeks, or eating glass.

REPRESSION AND REVIVAL

For many Muslims some of the beliefs and practices described above are totally unacceptable, and some tariqas have been condemned in the Muslim world. In some countries, and especially in Saudi Arabia, no tariqas are allowed and

Sufism is not discussed in academic circles. The founder of modern Turkey, **Kemal Atatürk** (1881–1938), abolished the tariqas and outlawed many Sufi leaders who resisted his efforts to secularize Turkey. The Mevlevis have now been permitted to make a tentative reappearance in Turkey; they may now perform in public as a folk dance troupe, and in Konya on the anniversary of Rumi's death. The memory of Rumi remains evergreen in modern Turkey, which became his home after he and his family had left Afghanistan. His tomb in Konya, now subsidized as a museum by the Turkish government, has a fluted tile drum and conical vault over it—a visual allusion to reeds growing in a river bed.[42] There was a Turkish 5,000 lira banknote that had the usual image of a serious Atatürk on one side, but the other side depicted Rumi smiling benevolently next to the green dome of his tomb alongside three whirling Mevlevis.[43]

The tariqas have long formed an alternative site for religious observance of a more popular kind that comforts and helps the wider community outside the tariqas themselves. Despite the criticisms of the 'ulama', many seek blessing from the living Sufi shaykh and visit Sufi tombs to pray.

SUFISM OUTSIDE THE MIDDLE EAST

So far the discussion has concentrated mainly on Sufism in the Arab and Persian worlds. It is very important, however, to take account of the huge impact that Sufism has had on other parts of the world. As already mentioned, Sufis traveled far and wide in both East and West, spreading Islam to many different kinds of people, rulers and their subjects alike.

SOUTH ASIA

Islam came to South Asia at the beginning of the eighth century. The first Sufi tariqa there was the **Chishtiyya**.[44] This brotherhood was brought by conquerors from Central Asia and Afghanistan, and became important under the Delhi sultanate (a group of five Muslim dynasties that ruled in India between 1206 and 1526). The Sufi message of love and charity proved very attractive to the under-privileged members of the Hindu caste system. Mu'in al-Din Chishti, after whom the brotherhood is named, introduced the tariqa in Lahore and Ajmer in Rajasthan in the middle of the twelfth century. On the one hand, the Chishtis perform *qawwali*—a blend of devotional poetry and Indian music—in their ceremonies, but at the same time they insist on strict adherence to Islamic law. The father of qawwali music is considered to be the poet and musician Amir Khusrow, who died in 1325. The sixteenth-century **Mughal** emperor Akbar was a great admirer of the Chishtis.[45]

This veneration comes vividly to life in a celebrated Mughal miniature painting datable to the early 1620s. This depicts, in a kind of parallel universe, the ageing emperor Jahangir, resplendent in a gigantic golden halo and attended by a bevy of winged cherubs, seated on an hourglass throne the sands of which are running out. Four men attend him, headed by Shaykh Husayn Chishti, whose thin ascetic face is framed by a huge white beard, obviously intended as a symbol of sanctity. The emperor hands him a book, perhaps chronicling the royal life. Below the shaykh, the Ottoman sultan meekly waits his turn, while still further down the queue is King James I and VI of England and Scotland, whose likeness has been copied with eerily photographic accuracy from a Jacobean miniature. The painter himself is tucked into the bottom left-hand corner. The painting is inscribed, "Though outwardly shahs stand before him, he fixes his gaze on dervishes."

Saints wield power. *The Mughal emperor Jahangir prefers the Sufi Shaykh Husayn to monarchs*, Agra (?), India, *c.* 1620. The emperor's halo conflates sun and moon, reflecting his title "Light of Religion." He is presented as Lord of Time; the cupids have written on his throne "O Shah, may the span of your life be a thousand years." The painter, Bichitr, has humbly signed his name on the royal footstool.

Multi-confessional shrine. The shrine of Nizam al-Din Awliya, Delhi, India, 13th century onward. This wonder-working saint attracts devotees from several faiths, as do many Muslim shrines in India; and there are parallels further afield, for example the shrine of Nabi Musa in Palestine, where Muslims, Jews, and Christians are all equally welcome.

Qawwali Sufi music is still played, and the shrines of Sufi saints are still visited, in the Indian subcontinent and elsewhere. Sufi ceremonies and visitation of saints' shrines flourish in Delhi, Ajmer, and Fatehpur Sikri. In Delhi, for example, the courtyard of the tomb of the Chishti Sufi saint Nizam al-Din Awliya, who died in 1325, is continually visited by devotees of the tariqa and is frequently an arena for Qur'anic recitations, meditation, silent dhikr, and musical sama' ceremonies. There is an especially grand celebration on the anniversary of the saint's death. Although clearly it is the shrine of a famous Sufi, people of other faiths worship there too; indeed, such monuments serve as a force for unity and cohesion across religious divides. There has been much mutual interaction between Islam and Hinduism at a popular level, leading to practices of which Muslim purists would undoubtedly disapprove.

SOUTHEAST ASIA

Islam was brought to Southeast Asia through trading links, especially the sea route from East Africa, Oman, and India. The first evangelists for Islam in Java were Sufis who had come with merchants by land and sea, and it is generally agreed by scholars that Indonesian Islam before the twentieth century was predominantly Sufi.[46] In the sixteenth century, the Sumatran Hamzah Pansuri was composing mystical poetry in Malay, working at the court of the sultan of Aceh.[47] Scholars from Southeast Asia regularly performed the pilgrimage to Mecca; some of them stayed there for many years and acquired a deep knowledge of the Islamic religious sciences. One such figure was 'Abd al-Samad al-Palimbani, who was born in the city of Palembang, South Sumatra, in 1704. His Sufi writings drew on the works of al-Ghazali and Ibn al-'Arabi, and he helped to transmit Islamic learning from Mecca to Southeast Asia. Today Sufi devotional practice in Indonesia is alive and well, both in the countryside and amongst urban intellectuals.[48]

AFRICA

Islam came to Africa very early—to Ethiopia in the time of the Prophet and to Egypt and North Africa soon after his death. In the following centuries Islam spread into the western Sahara, from Morocco across the mountains, and from Egypt along the trans-Saharan caravans that made their way to West Africa in search of gold in the area now known as Mali. It is likely that Sufis accompanied the merchants or were even merchants themselves. The legendary

Guardian of esoteric knowledge.
Sufi, M'Bour, Senegal. In Senegal, 92 percent of Muslims belong to a Sufi brotherhood, chiefly the Tijaniyya (famed for basing its teaching exclusively on the Qur'an and *hadith*). This *marabout* (Arabic *murabit*, Sufi warrior for the faith), with his intense gaze, star-studded robe, rosary (for reciting God's 99 Names), open Qur'an, and apotropaic diagrams, is a deeply spiritual figure.

city of Timbuktu in Mali dates to around the year 1100 and thenceforth became a center of Islamic scholarship and vibrant Sufism; many shrines commemorating Sufi saints were built there. In 2012 hardline Mali Islamists destroyed some of these Sufi tombs in Timbuktu.

Sufi beliefs and practices have proved very attractive in this continent, especially in West and East Africa. Many different Sufi groups are scattered throughout the whole region today. The Tijaniyya is now the largest Sufi brotherhood in West Africa. Named after Ahmad al-Tijani, an Algerian Sufi who died in 1815, this Sufi order aimed to help the poor. There is now a centralized government department in Egypt that deals with the tariqas, and more than sixty orders have acquired formal legal status in this way. In Somalia the Qadiriyya has proved to be very influential. Sufism is still a vibrant force in North Africa, where the Shadhiliyya is the most popular brotherhood, and in sub-Saharan Africa.

Given the enormous size of the continent of Africa, which contains almost one third of the world's Muslims today, it is inevitable that there should be great diversity of Sufi practice there. As in Indonesia, the Balkans, and India, for example, Sufi practices there have been influenced by and integrated with the local religious practices, including **animism**, that existed before the arrival of Islam, a phenomenon frowned upon by those who espouse a stricter form of Islam.

THE WEST

Sufi societies flourish in both Europe and America, many of them still rooted firmly within the Islamic tradition. They use symbols familiar from the classical days of Sufism, and are influenced above all by the poetry of Rumi and the thought of Ibn al-'Arabi. A poem from an edition of the magazine *Sufism*, published in 2003, is a good example: "The Path eventually takes us to a certain still place, to a place of zikr (dhikr), where we resonate with Allah's names, to a place where we no longer need to exist, to a place where we begin the journey back. We came from Allah and to Allah we shall return."[49] The Muhyiddin Ibn 'Arabi Society in Oxford, England, is thriving, as is the 'Alawiyya tariqa in South Africa, the UK, and Spain.

The word Sufi is often used nowadays in a very loose and imprecise way. In the past, Sufis saw themselves as practicing Muslims, but now there is an increasing tendency for people who do not profess Islam at all to be permitted into tariqas in the USA. How, may one ask, can this be called Sufism? As Nasr has pointed out, Islam is like a walnut, of which the shell is the Shari'a, the kernel is the tariqa, and the oil, which is invisible yet present everywhere, is the reality (*haqiqa*).[50] The Shari'a and the tariqa are mutually dependent. There are, therefore, no short cuts to Sufism that bypass formal Islam. Bookshops often place volumes about Sufism on separate shelves from those on Islam, as if the two were not related. But true Sufism is not some new age religion or sect. Sufism cannot exist outside Islam.

Sufism has attracted a number of European intellectuals from the 1930s onward, and several celebrities are drawn to it today. There is, however, a wide gap between intellectual Sufi ideas, eagerly embraced by the devotees of Ibn al-'Arabi, on the one hand, and those Muslims in the Middle East, Indonesia, and many parts of Africa who use recitation, music, and dancing in their worship, and who have recourse to the intercession of saints in their prayers to God. Yet both these facets of Sufism continue to prosper, as it is part of the warp and weft of Islam, and has repeatedly shown itself to be capable of regeneration in new forms.

SELECTED READING

Ernst, Carl, W., *Sufism. An Introduction to the Mystical Tradition of Islam*, Boston, MA: Shambhala Publications, 2011

Karamustafa, Ahmet T., *Sufism, The Formative Period*, Edinburgh: Edinburgh University Press, 2007

Lings, Martin, *What is Sufism?*, Berkeley and Los Angeles, CA: University of California Press, 1975

Renard, John, *Seven Doors to Islam: Spirituality and the Religious Life of Muslims*, Berkeley, CA and London: University of California Press, 1996

Watt, W. Montgomery, *The Faith and Practice of al-Ghazali*, Oxford: Oneworld Publications, 2000

9 | JIHAD

O you who have believed, shall I guide you to a transaction that will save you from a painful punishment? (It is that) you believe in God and His Messenger and strive in the cause of God with your wealth and your lives. QUR'AN 61:10–11

Jihad ("striving") is important to all **Muslims**. Traditionally the concept of jihad has been divided into two dimensions: the **greater *jihad*** (*al-jihad al-akbar*), which is spiritual, and the **lesser *jihad*** (*al-jihad al-asghar*), which is generally interpreted as fighting. By its very title, the greater jihad is considered to be more important than the lesser jihad. The greater jihad is the personal inner striving by Muslims to conquer the ego—removing the baser tendencies and worldly passions within themselves—so that they may lead a righteous life. The lesser jihad, by contrast, denotes a striving to defend the faith—and hence armed struggle. Muslims believe that ideally, given the model of the Prophet **Muhammad**, his pious **Companions**, and other exemplary religious figures in **Islamic** history, both these dimensions—the greater and lesser jihad—should co-exist in the life of one and the same person.[1]

GREATER AND LESSER JIHAD

Given the importance of the concept of jihad—both in the Muslim world and in the West after 9/11—it is more than unfortunate that there is a general misunderstanding in the West about what it means. The spiritual dimension of jihad—the greater jihad—is unknown to most non-Muslims.

THE GREATER JIHAD

It is not surprising that a discussion of the greater jihad is more often to be found in classical **Sufi** treatises than in other kinds of Muslim religious and political works. Indeed, this concept evolved from pious meditation on the **Qur'an** and the *hadith* by the Sufis. For the early Sufi **Harith al-Muhasibi** (781–857), nine-tenths of striving in the path of God occurs within oneself.[2] And in his early Persian treatise on Sufism, **Abu'l-Hasan 'Ali Hujwiri** (*c.* 990–1077) devotes a section to the "mortification of the lower soul"; here he cites certain well-known hadith, such as: "The *mujahid* is he who struggles with all his might against himself for God's sake" and "We have returned from the lesser war (*al-jihad al-asghar*) to the greater war (*al-jihad al-akbar*)." When asked, "What is the greater war?" Muhammad replies, "It is the struggle against one's self." Hujwiri then concludes that the Prophet "adjudged the mortification of the lower soul to be superior to the Holy War against unbelievers."[3] So the greater jihad provides a rich and complex approach to a person's inner spiritual development.

Even though the call to an ever more virtuous life is termed the greater jihad—and justifiably so, since it involves a never-ending battle against the vices and faults that diminish us as human beings and that block the path to proximity to God—it is telling that most discussions on jihad today talk about the lesser jihad. That is as true of Muslim thinkers as of non-Muslim Western scholars. As for the popular press, it leaves the greater jihad completely out of the discussion. The prominent contemporary Egyptian scholar **Yusuf al-Qaradawi** (b. 1926), now living in Qatar, regrets the diminution of the concept of jihad when it is confined to fighting.[3]

The Revival of the Religious Sciences (Ihya' 'ulum al-din) by the scholar **al-Ghazali** (1058–1111) is merely the best known of the many medieval and post-medieval guides to the daily practice of the faith and the ethical challenges that it brings in its train. Al-Ghazali's enormous work covers in precise detail how Muslims should behave toward God and toward their fellow human beings; this work is structured like a book of jurisprudence but it has overarching spiritual dimensions. So the natural context for reflection on the greater jihad is that of the five **pillars of Islam**. They are to be understood as the major signposts for a Muslim's life, and the greater jihad can be seen as a continuous working out of their profound and many-sided practical and spiritual implications.

THE LESSER JIHAD

Even before today there was a perception amongst non-Muslims, and especially Christians, that Islam is a religion of the sword.[4] One Western military historian, for example, states that Islam is "the most martial of the world's religions" because of "its doctrine of holy war (jihad)."[5] Such commentators as this do not have a grounding in the history of Islam and its basic doctrines. In a Gallup poll conducted globally in 2008, for example, only 7 percent of the world's Muslims were in favor of militant extremism.[6]

As Asma Afsaruddin points out on her recent book, Yusuf al-Qaradawi admits that "fighting" has now become "the predominant meaning of jihad."[7] It is therefore important to explain in some detail how this concept was defined in the Islamic canonical sources and how it has evolved in theory and in practice. That is the primary intention of this chapter.

JIHAD IN THE CANONICAL SOURCES

THE QUR'AN

The Qur'an mentions jihad in only twenty-four verses, most of which stress the spiritual aspects of jihad. Chapter 2:218 is a good example: "Indeed, those who have believed and those who have emigrated and striven in the path of God—they may expect the mercy of God." The word used for actual fighting, which leads to killing, is qital; jihad, then, is very different.

Jihad in the Life of the Prophet

In their attempts to understand and explain the meanings and ambiguities of the Holy Book, Qur'anic commentators have traditionally linked certain verses to specific events in the Prophet's life. After all, as well as possessing an eternal message for all people in all times and places, the Qur'an is also a mirror of how Muhammad's life evolved. Revelations from God came to him in times of crisis. When the Prophet's career was based at **Mecca**, the performance of jihad concentrated on the spread of the message of Islam by the Prophet's personal example and by his preaching. This involved difficult spiritual striving (jihad), because the earliest Muslims faced hostility, social ostracism, tribal boycott, harassment, and persecution from the pagan Meccans (see Chapter 2, pp. 31–32). Indeed, Muhammad's very life was in danger. After Muhammad's emigration (*hijra*) to **Medina** in 622, physical fighting became a core issue for the fledgling Muslim community there. Muhammad was building a new **theocratic** social order there, based on the principles of Islam, and he had to struggle against enemies both inside and outside the city. Above all, the Meccans wanted him dead, and they sent armies to attack him; the new faith and the new religion simply had to be defended by force. This was sanctioned by God.

Non-Muslims, and especially Christians familiar with the model of **Jesus**, the Prince of Peace, have had difficulty in accepting the idea of a warrior prophet. Yet the Old Testament, which also forms part of the Christian Bible, contains the famous examples of **Abraham** and especially **Moses**, Jewish prophets who were sent by God to preach the message of the One God to unbelieving peoples and who fought to preserve God's people. Muhammad was well aware of this ancient religious tradition of fighting. But within his own tribal society in Arabia too, tribal raiding and fighting had always been part of life and of the struggle for survival in an extremely harsh physical environment. Muslims, however, believe that the difference between the traditional fighting between warring tribes in Arabia and Muhammad's own military struggle is that his striving had a religious dimension.[8] This was jihad in the path of God.

Converting the Unfaithful

The Qur'an stresses the importance of negotiating in situations of conflict within the community of Muslims as well as against its external enemies; what is crucial is not only to preserve unity and to control rebellion but also to remember the brotherhood of Muslims: "The believers are indeed brothers; so set things right between your two brothers" (49:10).

The Meccan verses of the Qur'an—the revelations received when Muhammad was in Mecca—instruct the believers to endure persecution, and not retaliate; the Medinan verses—when Muhammad was establishing a new community in Medina—advocate fighting back. There are also contradictions within the Medinan verses themselves, some of which allow fighting only when the Muslims have been attacked, whilst others command aggressive action. Clearly political and historical realities determined the policy to some extent. There is no shunning of "this world" in Islam. Muhammad did not advocate disengagement from the politics of this earthly world in the same way as Jesus did in the Christian tradition. Almost from the outset of Islam, its followers were involved in maintaining the survival of their community as well as the beliefs and practices of a new faith. So it is not surprising that in the **polytheistic** milieu of seventh-century Arabia they were soon faced with the need to use force on occasion to defend that fragile little community. If they had not done so, it is doubtful that Islam would have survived at all. Overall, however, the Qur'an does not sanction killing. It emphasizes the voluntary conversion of individuals who are drawn to the message of Islam, described as the natural religion laid down by God for human beings to follow, rather than conversion by force.[9]

THE HADITH

The second canonical source in Islam, the hadith (the recorded sayings and deeds of the Prophet; see Chapter 2, pp. 39–40), has much to say about jihad. Apart from the four canonical **Sunni** collections of hadith, many others were compiled over the centuries by individual scholars and groups—Sunnis, **Shi'ites**, Sufis, and others—and as a result, a wide range of views on jihad can be found there. Many hadiths eloquently praise the merits of jihad: a typical example emphasizes that it is more meritorious to strive one day in the path of God than to fast for a thousand days. One well-known hadith of the Prophet declares: "God knows best who is wounded in His way, but when the Day of Rising comes, blood gushes forth from his wound. It will be the colour of blood, but its scent will be that of musk."[10] The blood of the martyr is especially dear to God because of its scent of musk. Such a pronouncement makes a link between this world and the next: the Qur'an (83:25) promises that the martyr who has fallen in the path of jihad will be rewarded in Paradise with a drink of nectar, perfumed with a fragrance of musk.

Jihad is meritorious, whatever the outcome, successful or otherwise. It must be performed according to certain prescribed conditions. There is meticulous attention to many aspects of jihad in the hadiths, including practical preparations, the observance of rules of engagement, prohibitions on the killing of old people, children, and women, the proper division of booty, and the treatment of prisoners and envoys. Sincere motivation is essential. The sweetness of martydom is promised to those who fall in the path of God. It is often mentioned in the hadith collections that the corpses of those who have fallen as martyrs in the path of God should not be washed or prayed over and that they should be buried, not in a shroud as is customary, but in the garments in which they were slain. The collections of hadith do not lay down systematic rules, but their rudimentary regulations would guide later legal scholars in how to construct proper principles of jihad.

JIHAD IN ISLAMIC LAW

The classical legal theory of jihad evolved from the codification of Sunni jihad that began in the ninth century, when the Muslim empire had attained its greatest size under the **'Abbasid** dynasty.[11] Before that time Muslim scholars and judges had tried to make judgments not only with pragmatism and common sense but also, above all, in a true spirit of piety and with a sincere desire to follow Qur'anic principles and the model conduct of the Prophet. Fighting was not the only way in which the conquests were achieved. Indeed, many cities and territories are recorded in the Muslim sources as having submitted to the conquerors by signing agreements. When the conquest of an area involved fighting, however, the **caliphs** and their commanders saw to it that clear rules were drawn up. Regulations would be needed for proper conduct in battle and in the drawing up of peace treaties. This is the background to the emergence of the classical theory of jihad propounded by Muslim religious scholars in their books of law. These scholars lived some two centuries after the rise of Islam, at a time when the boundaries of the Muslim empire were more or less fixed at where they would remain until the coming of the nomadic Turks in the eleventh century.[12]

THE CLASSICAL THEORY OF JIHAD

The starting point for religious scholars in elaborating the concept of jihad was, as always, the Qur'an, but its sometimes brief or contradictory statements often needed to be amplified and supplemented by reference to the numerous hadiths about jihad. When these two canonical sources—the Qur'an and the hadith collections—did not jointly provide direct solutions to new problems, scholars would draw on two other resources—analogy (*qiyas*) and consensus (*ijma'*). If the problem could not be resolved in this way, then they felt justified on occasion to resort to their own personal judgment (*ijtihad*; see also Chapter 5, p. 119). The chapters on jihad in classical books of jurisprudence (*fiqh*) follow a predictable pattern and their contents, based largely on relevant Qur'anic passages and quotations from the hadiths, are broadly similar, regardless of the author's legal school. Soon whole books were devoted to jihad, one of the earliest to have survived being the *Book of Jihad* written by 'Abdallah ibn Mubarak, who died in 797.[13]

According to medieval Muslim religious scholars, the whole world was divided into two sections: the House of Islam (*Dar al-Islam*) and the House of War (*Dar al-harb*). There are many interpretations of these concepts, but according to one the House of Islam referred to all lands under Muslim control; here Muslims formed the majority and Islamic law prevailed. It also included certain categories of non-Muslims with whom the Muslim overlords had made a covenant. These non-Muslim confessional groups, notably Jews and Christians, were known as the People of the Book. They were allowed to practice their faith within the House of Islam, on payment of a poll tax, and in return they would be protected. Jihad would not be launched against them, but their social status would be inferior to that of Muslims and they were also subjected to certain social and religious restrictions. The regulations for the People of the Book were later applied to those who practiced other faiths not mentioned specifically in this context in the Qur'an, such as **Zoroastrians** and Buddhists.

As for the House of War, this term referred to those territories that were under non-Muslim government, in which Muslims were a minority, and where non-Islamic laws prevailed. Only the leader of the Muslim community, the caliph, could call for and lead the jihad against the House of War, which is the collective duty of the whole community. Elaborate rules were devised for the proper conduct of jihad. Those at whom jihad is directed must always be invited first to embrace Islam. If they do so, hostilities must end then and there. If they refuse to embrace Islam they may submit to Muslim rule and pay the poll tax; otherwise, Muslims must attack them. A distinction was drawn between those who perform jihad and those who engage in other kinds of fighting and violence—the Arabic words used are *harb* (war) or *qital* (fighting). Those who were deemed to be fighting illegally[14] were viewed as enemies of the Islamic community.

MODIFYING THE CLASSICAL THEORY

From the eighth century on, and with the increasing fragmentation of the caliphal empire, Muslim scholars, such as Abu Hanifa, began to widen the scope of jihad so that it incorporated strategies for formalizing peace rather than war. Some scholars began to recognize a third status of territory—the House of Truce (*Dar al-'ahd*) or the House of Peace (*Dar al-sulh*). These terms refer to an intermediate category, that of territories that have entered into a contract with the Muslim community, have paid tribute to the caliph, and have been permitted to keep their own forms of government. This strategy gave legal respectability to the commercial contacts between medieval Muslim and non-Muslim states. For practical reasons too, it became permissible for truces to be made, but these were only temporary and could last for a maximum of ten years. Muslims could reject a truce unilaterally, but they had to inform the enemy of this beforehand.

Over the centuries the theory of jihad became modified in other ways, for example to permit fighting within the Muslim community. In the eleventh century, for instance, al-Mawardi wrote a famous treatise on good government for the ruling Sunni caliph, and included rebels, apostates (those who leave the faith), and Shi'ites as legitimate targets of jihad. A more famous Muslim thinker, **Ibn Khaldun** (d. 1406) proposes four categories of war. The first two, "petty squabbles among rival foes or neighboring tribes" and "war arising from desire for plunder among savage peoples," are illegal. The second two, jihad and wars to suppress internal rebellion, are legitimate.[15] But the classical theory of jihad was neither comprehensive nor clearly defined in every detail.

Thus it left uncertain the proper stance toward non-Muslim countries that housed Muslim minorities—an issue that, with the global spread of Islam, is very relevant to Muslim legal scholars today.

THE TWELVER SHI'ITE VIEW OF JIHAD

Twelver Shi'ite scholars put jihad at the center of their faith (for Twelver Shi'ism see Chapter 6). An early Twelver scholar, Ibn Babawayh, writes that "jihad is a religious duty imposed by God on mankind." Another, Shaykh al-Mufid, declares that "jihad maintains the strength of the foundations of Islam."[16] Several Twelver views on jihad are shared by the Sunnis, for example the definition of jihad as a collective duty; this may become an individual duty when grave danger threatens the Muslim community. Both Twelvers and Sunnis list categories of persons who should be exempt from fighting jihad. For the Twelvers, as for Sunni Islam, the term jihad refers not only to fighting, but can also include other aspects of striving, such as the search for religious knowledge. A hadith attributed to Ja'far al-Sadiq, the sixth **Imam**, declares that on the **Day of Judgment**, "the ink of scholars will outweigh the blood of the martyrs on the scales."[17]

There is a crucial area of difference between the Twelver and Sunni doctrine of jihad, however. Twelvers believe that the leadership of jihad belongs to the only legitimate authority, appointed by God, namely the Hidden Imam (see Chapter 6, p. 156). Hence, after the murders of 'Ali and **Husayn**, they adopted a passive stance toward the dominant Sunni governments, while awaiting the return of the Twelfth Imam.[18] But this view was gradually modified, as Twelver communities needed to ensure their own survival. The first important modification of the classical Twelver theory of jihad was formulated by al-Tusi in 1067; he stressed that a defensive jihad may be fought even when the Imam is absent and that the responsibility for this should devolve onto the religious scholars.

This viewpoint remained thereafter the basis for Twelver jihad theory, although on occasion it was flouted by later rulers. Thus, when the Twelver **Safavid** dynasty took power in Iran in 1501, the first ruler, Shah Isma'il, claimed descent from the Imams and thought it was his right to wage jihad against the Sunni **Ottomans**. The Ottomans retaliated, condemning the Safavids as unbelievers and fighting jihad against them. Under the later dynasty of the **Qajars** (1785–1925), the religious scholars, who had taken over sole responsibility for interpreting Islamic law, played an important role in Twelver jihad, and especially in the wars waged against Russia in 1803–13 and 1826–28. The *fatwas* issued then by religious scholars, and collected in a work called *The Jihad Treatise*, revealed new thinking on the subject. Above all, they established the religious elite as effectively ruling on behalf of the Hidden Imam, and they underscored the centrality of the duty of jihad in Twelver jurisprudence.[19]

AYATOLLAH KHOMEINI

The founder of the Islamic Republic of Iran, **Ayatollah Khomeini** (1902–89; see Chapter 6, pp. 165–67), won widespread popular support for his opposition to the shah of Iran and to the United States, which he termed "The Great Satan." He was also fully behind the Muslim, anti-Zionist jihad to liberate Jerusalem. In the Iran–Iraq war in the 1980s, Iranian soldiers were given maps showing their route through Iraq to Jerusalem. Khomeini made the last Friday of **Ramadan** into Jerusalem Day; a famous Iranian stamp from 1980 commemorating Universal Jerusalem Day bears an inscription "Let us liberate Jerusalem" in Arabic, Persian, and English. Jerusalem Day is now celebrated throughout the Muslim world by postage stamps that depict the quintessential icon of the Holy City, the Dome of the Rock. Some even show **Saladin** (d. 1193) on horseback, returning to recapture Jerusalem (see pp. 233–34).

Khomeini's interpretation of jihad is all-encompassing: "Islam's Holy War is a struggle against idolatry, sexual deviation, plunder, repression, and

Successor to Saladin? Iranian banknote. Khomeini's propaganda linked the desired defeat of Iraq with that of Israel. He inaugurated "Jerusalem Day," celebrated annually on posters, stamps, and coins, thereby reviving the ancient anti-Crusader *jihad* associations of the Dome of the Rock. This message reached all Iranians, since this was the most commonly used banknote of its time.

A lost generation. Woman pays homage to a fallen *jihad* fighter at the Martyrs' Cemetery, Tehran, dedicated to those Iranians who died in the war with Iraq (1980–88). Images of red flags, roses, tulips, and fountains spurting blood underline the theme of martyrdom, which has immemorial and powerful resonances for Iranian Shi'ites, because of the death of Husayn.

cruelty."[20] The terrible conflict of the Iran–Iraq war pitted two countries with Muslim populations against each other, yet Khomeini labeled this war a jihad. The cemetery near his own mausoleum outside Tehran contains the graves of thousands of young men and boys who fell in that war. They had often walked barefoot over minefields, in the belief that they were going toward Paradise. Each grave has a headstone adorned with Qur'anic quotations about jihad in blood-red paint, accompanied by a photo of the fallen mujahid.

JIHAD IN PRACTICE IN PRE-MODERN TIMES

A brief survey of some select examples of how jihad was practiced in pre-modern times illustrates the diversity, versatility, and durability of this concept. Of course, other factors—for example, political and socioeconomic—played a part in these case studies, but what matters here is that Muslim historians, whether writing at the time or a few generations later, viewed them as jihad.

THE ARAB CONQUESTS, SEVENTH TO EIGHTH CENTURY

Ever since the Prophet's death, certain military campaigns were dubbed jihad by medieval Muslim writers. The first such phenomenon was the creation of the Arab Muslim empire in the period 632–711. Some modern scholars have argued that climatic and socioeconomic factors were the most important ones in this period of conquest. Another commonly held view is that many Christians preferred life under Muslim rule to religious persecution from Constantinople. The Muslim promise of religious toleration attracted local Christians and Jews alike, a point worth remembering in the context of today's troubles. Still others believe that the instrument of jihad was used immediately after the death of Muhammad to motivate the Bedouin tribes in the armies and to establish Islam in the newly conquered lands.[21] So what role, if any, did jihad play in this extraordinary phenomenon?

The timing of the conquests is telling. They took off in an enormous surge immediately after the death of Muhammad. Although it is unlikely that the rank and file of the Bedouin troops were already imbued with the spirit of jihad, it is probable that the inner circle of devoted followers of the Prophet were inspired in this way. It seems hard then to deny that the impetus of jihad must have played a key role in the early military successes and that it gave the Arabs an ideological edge over their foes. Islam, as practiced by those who had known Muhammad well, provided the foundation of the embryonic Arab state; it was the jihad of this small elite that fired the early conquests and inspired their troops. As Ibn Khaldun was later to argue, nomad aggression and solidarity are at their most effective when fueled by a powerful religious impulse, namely striving in the path of God.

THE KHARIJITES IN IRAQ, SEVENTH TO NINTH CENTURY

The fragile unity of the young Muslim community was soon threatened by the emergence of various groups who interpreted the concept of jihad in different ways. Within only thirty years of Muhammad's death a marginal group known as the **Kharijites** appeared (see Chapter 6, p. 142).[22] They believed in the theocratic slogan "Rule belongs to God alone." According to their puritanical view of Islam, it was the most virtuous person in the community who should lead it, not necessarily someone from the Prophet's family or a person elected by the whole community. They believed that everyone who did not share their beliefs was not a Muslim and should be killed. The Kharijite murders of leading figures, and above all of 'Ali, have led some scholars to call the Kharijites the first Muslim terrorists. Their military attacks lasted for a century or two before they fled to remote parts of the Muslim world away from the persecution of the Sunni caliphs.

The Kharijites came mainly from Arab tribes with a long oral poetic tradition. Kharijite poets, however, no longer praise tribal virtues; they preach jihad messages. They praise the piety and bravery of their fellow warriors who have fallen in battle striving in the path of God. Those left behind are deeply regretful that they have not also achieved martyrdom. The Kharijite warriors hope to die violently under the point of the lance. Their poets write that by day they fight like lions; by night they pray like weeping women at funerals. For Kharijite fighters death does not bring absolute despair: it is only the entrance to Paradise, where they will meet again their brothers who have preceded them there.

THE SAMANIDS IN CENTRAL ASIA, 819–1005

The frontier areas of Muslim territory—near Byzantium, in Spain, Nubia, and Central Asia—attracted jihad warriors eager to defend and to expand the House of Islam. The easternmost Muslim state in the tenth century was ruled by the ethnically Persian **Samanid** dynasty (819–1005).[23] By virtue of this geographical position, these staunchly Sunni rulers inherited the crucial role of defenders of the eastern frontier against the Turkish nomads of Central and Inner Asia. Two tenth-century Muslim geographers, Ibn Hawqal and **al-Muqaddasi**, have left detailed descriptions of life on this frontier. They speak of thousands of buildings known as *ribat*s. These structures— part military camp protecting the border, part Sufi cloister—were built to house warriors, known as mujahidun or *ghazi*s, who flocked to this area from across the Islamic world to wage jihad against unbelievers, much as in recent years numerous young male Muslims have flocked to Afghanistan and Pakistan to learn to fight alongside the **Taliban** and the followers of **Usama bin Laden** (1957–2011; see pp. 239–41). Whilst it is, of course, difficult to assess how much of this description of the eastern Islamic frontier is retrospective romanticizing of a mythic jihad past, Russian archaeologists have uncovered the remains of many ribats in Central Asia that date from this period.[24]

THE GHAZNAVIDS IN AFGHANISTAN AND NORTHERN INDIA, 977–1186

The campaigns waged by the **Ghaznavids** provide a contrasting example of jihad in some medieval Muslim sources. Founded by a Turkic slave commander, Sebüktegin, this forceful Sunni Muslim state, centered at Ghazna, ruled

The monarch as model *mujahid*. Mahmud of Ghazna (d. 1030) crosses a bridge *en route* to India: Rashid al-Din, *World History*, Tabriz, Iran, 1314. Mahmud, the star of the Ghaznavid dynasty in the Hindu Kush ("Indian-killer"), undertook seventeen *jihadi* raids on northern India. They brought him fabulous wealth and a lasting reputation in later legend and panegyric poetry.

Afghanistan, eastern Iran, and parts of northern India. The Ghaznavid sultans viewed the Hindus of northern India as polytheists. Accordingly, between 999 and 1027 Mahmud of Ghazna, the most famous ruler of the dynasty, felt justified in attacking northern India seventeen times. Retrospectively his court historians defined his raids as jihad campaigns, but their real motive seems to have been booty on an enormous scale from the Hindu princes. Mahmud looted and then destroyed what he considered to be idolatrous works of art, and he gained enormous riches—jewels and other valuable objects—from the Indian princes, as well hundreds of elephants for his army. Despite the panegyric of his Persian-speaking court historians, who praised his actions to the skies, it is doubtful whether Mahmud and his successors invited the non-Muslim rulers in northern India to embrace Islam, as prescribed in Islamic law. Despite this, Mahmud is still viewed as a model jihad warrior (mujahid) in Pakistan today.

THE ALMORAVIDS IN NORTH AFRICA AND SPAIN, 1062–1147

Far away from Central Asia, the **Almoravids**, a Berber tribal confederation, conquered much of North Africa and parts of Muslim Spain.[25] Their jihad ideology is revealed in their very name—in Arabic, *al-Murabitun*, "those who live in ribats." Their founder was a mysterious figure who adopted the name

Ibn Yasin; *ya* and *sin* are two of the so-called mystery letters that come at the beginning of certain chapters in the Qur'an (see Chapter 3, p. 78). Ibn Yasin espoused a strict **Maliki** Sunni form of Islam (see Chapter 5, pp. 119–20) and he preached vigorous, expansionist jihad messages to the veiled Sanhaja Berber warriors in the High Atlas mountains. Ibn Yasin then overran the regions of the Sahara until his death as a martyr (**shahid**) in 1058. His successor, **Yusuf ibn Tashfin** (1061–1107), captured large areas of North Africa, established a new capital in Morocco—Marrakesh—and attacked Muslim Spain. The Almoravids called their campaigns jihad, both those against the pagans of Africa and, perhaps more surprisingly, against the Muslims of North Africa and Spain, whose observance of the faith they considered to be lukewarm and who, they believed, needed "reIslamizing."

As with many a Muslim reformer before and since, Yusuf ibn Tashfin is presented in the medieval Arabic chronicles as the epitome of austerity and piety; it was said that he never drank wine, never listened to a singing girl, and never enjoyed hunting or other such pastimes. At its height his empire extended from near Zaragoza in northern Spain to Ghana. No doubt the jihad spirit of the already militant Almoravid movement was fired up even more by the gradual Christian reconquest of Spain, including the capture of the important Muslim city of Toledo in 1085.

SAYF AL-DAWLA, THE HAMDANID RULER OF SYRIA, 944–67

In the tenth century thousands of mujahidun from Central Asia made the long journey to Syria to join the forces of a celebrated Shi'ite ruler of the **Hamdanid** dynasty, **Sayf al-Dawla**, who led annual jihad campaigns against Byzantium. As in Central Asia, mujahidun on the **Byzantine** border lived in ribats, which were supported by pious donations. Sayf al-Dawla ("the Sword of the State") led his troops into more than forty battles against the Byzantines from his little state at Aleppo. Bedridden from 962, he was carried into battle on a litter, and when he died, he was buried like a true martyr (shahid); a brick made of dust from one of his campaigns was put under his cheek in his mausoleum. Poets and preachers eloquently praised his jihad. The most famous classical Arab poet, **al-Mutanabbi** (d. 965), wrote an ode in praise of the capture by Sayf al-Dawla of a small Byzantine fortress, al-Hadath:

> You were not a king routing an equal,
> But monotheism routing polytheism…
> Through you He (God) cleaves the unbeliever asunder.[26]

At the same time and place, stirring sermons wrapped up in the symbolism of the greater jihad were also addressed to Sayf al-Dawla from a pulpit in 962 by the preacher Ibn Nubata: "Do you imagine that He (God) will desert you, whilst you are steadfast in His path? So put on for the jihad the coat of mail of the faithful and equip yourselves with the armour of those who trust in God."[27] The example of Sayf al-Dawla later inspired the Muslims of Syria and Palestine to fight the **Crusaders**.

JIHAD IN CRUSADER TIMES, 1098–1291

The most famous historical example of medieval jihad was the Muslim response to the threat of the Crusades. This was a threat aimed not at the borders of the Muslim world but at its very heartlands, the Holy City of Jerusalem, the third holiest city in Islam after Mecca and Medina. The warriors of the First Crusade arrived in Syria and Palestine in 1098 at a moment of Muslim weakness and disunity, when Muslims were not ready to wage jihad against them. The Arab geographer al-Muqaddasi (940–991), who, as his name indicates, came from Jerusalem (al-Quds), speaking of the people of Syria, says: "The inhabitants have no enthusiasm for jihad and no energy in the struggle against the enemy."[28] It was therefore easy for the zealous armies of the First Crusade to seize Jerusalem in 1099 after inflicting terrible bloodshed on the population of the city.

However, the behavior of the Crusader newcomers from Europe, with their unfamiliar brand of Western Christian zeal, eventually stirred up the Muslims to remember jihad again and to unite under its banner to remove this unwelcome alien presence from their lands, and above all from Jerusalem. Two generations later, a remarkable wave of jihad, led by an alliance between the Syrian Sunni religious classes and the Turkish warlord **Nur al-Din** (d. 1174), made considerable progress against the Crusaders. In 1187, a Kurdish commander named Saladin, Nur al-Din's successor in leading the jihad, reconquered Jerusalem. The medieval Muslim chronicles portray both Nur al-Din and Saladin as figures in whom personal spiritual jihad and public jihad against the infidel were inextricably combined. Saladin's triumphal entry into Jerusalem, on the anniversary of the Prophet's ascent into heaven from that very city, is portrayed as the crowning moment of his jihad.[29] From 1250 onward the **Mamluk** Turkish sultans—staunch Sunni rulers— and above all Baybars, their most successful leader, were able to continue the jihad, so much so that by 1291 the Mamluks had removed the Crusaders from Muslim territory.

In the Crusading period the Muslim leadership in Syria and Palestine used a wide range of methods to keep the jihad ardor of the faithful at a high level. Nur al-Din sponsored jihad books, jihad sermons, hadith collections, and works praising the Holy City—the Merits of Jerusalem genre. But perhaps the most rousing literary vehicle was the jihad poetry written in praise of Nur al-Din and Saladin, among others; this stresses the spiritual dimensions of their jihad, as well as its military aspects. Saladin's biographer 'Imad al-Din al-Isfahani attributes these words to Nur al-Din: "I have no wish except jihad … Life without the striving of jihad is an (idle) pastime."[30] The Spanish Muslim Ibn Jubayr, passing through the Holy Land in 1183, addresses the following stirring lines to Saladin, using the familiar image of cross-breaking found in other anti-Christian jihad poetry:[31]

> How long have you been hovering among them [i.e. the Crusaders],
> A lion hovering in the thicket?
> You have broken their cross by force
> And what a fine breaker you are!

The blood-red flag. Almohad war banner, Spain, before 1212. This symbol of *jihad* proclaims "In God I find refuge from Satan." Its main inscription (Qur'an 61:10–12) contains promises of Paradise to the faithful who die in holy war. The iconography features a central talismanic star and other celestial motifs, much like contemporary Qur'anic frontispieces.

Soldiers for the faith on parade. Al-Hariri, *Assemblies*, Baghdad, 1237. Banners in various colors, complemented by flags and an enormous standard, all in black, the 'Abbasid dynastic colour, spell out the *shahada*. Pealing trumpets and a drum add the further dimension of music—perhaps a band (*tablkhana*) playing the *nawba* or fanfare, which was a prerequisite of high office.

Other poems play on the need to protect Muslim women from the brutality of the Crusaders. Full of jihad imagery, as well as of yearning for the recapture of the Holy Places in Jerusalem, they depict in glowing terms the rewards that await the mujahid in Paradise.

A TOWERING FIGURE OF JIHAD—IBN TAYMIYYA, 1263–1328

The expulsion of the Crusaders from Muslim territory in 1291 led the Muslim world to focus on other dimensions of jihad. Not only had Islam been attacked from Western Europe for nearly two hundred years, but worse had also come from the East in the thirteenth century through the terrifying onslaught of the pagan Mongol hordes who in 1258 destroyed Baghdad, the seat of the Sunni 'Abbasid caliphate. After 1291 jihad became more introspective and more spiritual; the House of Islam began to close its doors on the rest of the world.

Through the writings of the religious scholar **Ibn Taymiyya**, who had experienced at first hand the devastating impact of the Mongol invasions, jihad was interpreted as a struggle to defend the Muslim world against future external military interference. But Ibn Taymiyya also argued for a more radical change of approach, advocating the greater jihad to purge Muslim society of the spiritual pollution caused by contact with other peoples and faiths, in particular Christians and Mongols.[32] He was also irrevocably hostile to the Shi'ites, whom he accused of collaborating with the Mongols. He condemned many practices and concepts—visiting graves, the veneration of saints, sharing religious festivals with other faiths, theology, philosophy, ostentatious dress, backgammon, chess, and music.

Ibn Taymiyya was no reclusive religious figure. He was fully involved with his own society and its government and was frequently asked for his views by the ruling Mamluk sultan and his entourage. Sometimes his advice pleased the military leaders, though sometimes it did not and he was sent to prison. But his fearless stance and obvious integrity were much admired. Ibn Taymiyya defines the aim of jihad in one of his numerous fatwas, saying that he who strives in the path of God does so "in order that the whole of religion may belong to God." He refers in this fatwa to how the Prophet Muhammad dealt with his enemies and then he moves to the crisis in his own time. He believes the Mamluk state is under attack from many enemies—and above all the Mongols, who have allied with heretics, Armenian Christians, and others.[33] Many religious scholars had been reluctant to wage jihad against the Mongols, for in 1295 they had converted to Islam. In this fatwa on jihad, Ibn Taymiyya establishes conclusively that in the light of the Qur'an and the **Sunna** the Mongols are not Muslims. They do not follow the *Shari'a* exclusively; they still use their own legal code too. In his view, therefore, jihad against them and their allies is a religious obligation.[34]

In his numerous writings Ibn Taymiyya argues that jihad is a community obligation, but that when the enemy initiates aggression, jihad becomes incumbent on every Muslim.[35] Despite the importance of jihad, it should always be preceded, as stated in the Qur'an, by a call to the infidels to embrace Islam and thereby avoid the necessity for military conflict. For Ibn Taymiyya, the overwhelming preoccupation with jihad to regain Jerusalem that had characterized Saladin's time was replaced by jihad in the service of the true religion purged of all deviant beliefs and outside contamination. Small wonder, then, that Ibn Taymiyya has become the model for many modern reformist movements in Islam, such as **Wahhabism** (see Chapter 7, p. 184).

THE OTTOMANS, 1301–1922

After their inexorable conquering sweep across Anatolia (now modern Turkey) from the fourteenth century onward, it became imperative for the Ottoman Turks that Constantinople should no longer remain under the authority of a Christian ruler, let alone the Byzantine emperor himself. The momentous fall of the city to the Ottoman forces on May 29, 1453 represents in many respects the high-water mark of medieval Turkish military achievements, celebrated in many triumphant Muslim writings of the time. A typical example of the way in which the ideology of jihad was used to describe this conflict can be found in *The Crown of Histories*, written by the sixteenth-century court chronicler Sa'd al-Din. The Ottoman sultan Mehmet II, fighting with "heaven-assisted troops," erects the standard of jihad to conquer the city: "He exhorted those furious, blood-lapping lions of the forest of valour…telling them of the universality of the command 'Strive'…and of the purport of the Divine promises in the verses concerning the Holy War."[36]

After seizing Constantinople, the Ottomans ruled vast tracts of traditionally Muslim territory as well as the Balkans, reaching the walls of Vienna, Austria, before being turned back in 1683. As late as 1914, the Ottoman sultan labelled as jihad Turkey's entry into the First World War on the German side.

All the historical examples mentioned here, as well as many others, demonstrate how the lesser jihad was used as the motivating force behind the creation of new political entities and military conquests; these jihad movements were perceived and explained as the defense of existing Muslim territories or the expansion of Islam into new areas. It is clear from these case studies that the memory of the Islamic past could provide ideas and role models that would prove to be usable by modern theorists and proponents of jihad.

JIHAD SINCE THE NINETEENTH CENTURY

From 1798 to 1914 jihad was awakened and interpreted anew in the face of a new external threat, as imperial European powers attempted to colonize Muslim lands. Jihad could be harnessed to the forces of rising Arab nationalism and exploited to the full by those who, following the example of Ibn Taymiyya, wished to purge the Muslim world of all extraneous contamination and to return to a pristine Islam, based exclusively on the teachings of the Qur'an and the hadith. (For the ways in which significant early modern

Muslim thinkers, such as Muhammad ibn 'Abd al-Wahhab, Shah Wali Allah, and Sayyid Qutb, reacted to European colonialism, see Chapter 7, pp. 183–85).

Jihad was invoked sporadically across the Muslim world in this period, from West Africa to Indonesia, including the jihads of the Senussis, who resisted Italian colonization in Libya; the Mahdi, who opposed Turkish and Egyptian control of the Sudan and later fought British occupying forces; and the Wahhabis in Arabia. In Muslim sub-Saharan Africa, religio-political battles were seen as jihads. For example, **Usman dan Fodio** (1754–1817), who lived in the Hausa state of Gobir in what is now northern Nigeria, gathered around him a pious community who formally elected him as their Imam in 1804, and thus established the Sokoto caliphate. Modeling his life closely on that of the Prophet Muhammad, Usman led a successful jihad against the sultan of Gobir from 1804 to 1808, though not himself participating in military campaigns. The rest of Usman's life was spent largely in writing and teaching; he left the administration of the new state to his son and another close disciple.

Just as they had resisted European imperialism, traditionalist Muslim movements opposed the spread of American power after the Second World War (1939–1945). They also campaigned against corrupt rulers in Muslim lands and sought to establish a unified Muslim state on earth, preceded by a radical Islamization of Muslim society at all levels. For example, the leading ideologue of the Muslim Brotherhood, Sayyid Qutb, who was executed for treason in 1966, believed in a centuries-old confrontation of jihad against people he termed "polytheists"—including Christians, Hindus, and Communists. His was a vision of global jihad.

But not all jihad rhetoric had an exclusively religious basis. The secular dictatorship of **Saddam Husayn** (1937–2006) in Iraq fabricated an array of myths to bolster its fragile ideological base and spoke of the necessity for a great battle against what was termed the American–Israeli conspiracy. Despite his obvious lack of religious credentials, Saddam called on occasion for jihad against the West.

ABU'L-'ALA MAWDUDI

Another key opponent of Western encroachment into the Muslim world was the prolific South Asian writer **Abu'l-'Ala Mawdudi** (1903–1979) whose influence has been huge amongst Muslim radicals trained in the religious colleges (*madrasas*) of Pakistan, and notably for the Taliban in Afghanistan (see also Chapter 7, p. 186). The party that he founded, the revivalist Jamaat-i

Islami, envisions a constitutionally based Islamic government promoting Islamic values. The concept of jihad plays a paramount role in Mawdudi's thinking. The fifth edition of his book *Jihad in Islam* has on its front cover the potent image of the word jihad written as a calligraphic blood-red sword. Mawdudi stresses that Islam is a religion for the whole world.

MULLAH 'UMAR

Another case where the claim to exercise religious authority is vigorously contested is that of **Mullah 'Umar** (b. *c.* 1959), who in 1994 founded the Taliban to rid Afghanistan of local warlords, to bring much-needed security after fifteen years of warfare; he also claimed to be restoring the true Shar'ia. Those who joined him were mostly products of madrasas in Pakistan. The views of this group are narrow and exclusive; the only Islam they recognize is their own. In 1996 Mullah 'Umar made himself *amir al-mu'minin*, the title once used only for the caliph, and received the oath of allegiance from his followers. The concept of jihad was expanded so as to fight all those Muslims who refused to accept the authority of the Taliban. Mullah 'Umar took Kabul that same year and imposed the strict form of the Shari'a, powerfully evoked in the novels of Khaled Hosseini.[37] It was Mullah 'Umar who destroyed the ancient rock-carved monumental statues known as the Buddhas of Bamiyan.

USAMA BIN LADEN

In 1997 Usama bin Laden joined Mullah 'Umar, having distinguished himself in the Afghan jihad that sought successively to topple Soviet rule, the local Marxist government, and the Western alliance led by the United States. Although he described himself as issuing fatwas,[38] Usama bin Laden had none of the religious qualifications traditionally expected from someone calling for jihad. He was certainly not a caliph, nor was he the head of a Muslim state, as Islamic law demands. Although he larded his speeches with Qur'anic quotations and references to Muhammad's battles, Usama paid no attention to the legal rules of classical jihad. He quite simply hijacked the concept of jihad and twisted it to suit his own political goals. Usama's aims, in so far as they are clear, seem to have been twofold: his so-called jihad aimed firstly to unseat the Saudi Arabian regime (this is often overlooked), and secondly to undermine American power in the world.

Even before 9/11 Usama bin Laden spoke about fighting a jihad against "Crusaders," thus resorting to an anti-Christian discourse about the medieval Crusades, which he tied into other such anti-Western themes as imperialism and

ABOVE **Symbol of modern extremist *jihad*.** Usama bin Laden, the wealthy dissident Saudi businessman who founded al-Qa'ida with its network of terrorist cells, masterminded the attacks on the Pentagon and Twin Towers in New York on September 11, 2001. After a massive manhunt he was finally tracked down ten years later while hiding in Pakistan, and killed by American forces.

BELOW **The desire of nations.** Aerial view of al-Haram al-Sharif, Jerusalem, mainly 7th century onward. As part of the Umayyad strategy of developing the importance of Islamic Jerusalem, successive caliphs built palaces, gates, and—outdoing local Christian monuments—the Aqsa Mosque (shown in the foreground) and the Dome of the Rock (behind, with golden dome), reviving and Islamizing this storied site of salvation history.

colonialism. In February 1998 he issued a manifesto for an entity that he initially called the International Islamic Front for Jihad against Jews and Crusaders. The fact that European Jews did not play a significant role in the medieval Crusades, and indeed were massacred in large numbers by the Crusaders *en route* to Jerusalem, did not cause him a problem. He described the Americans, who had been allowed to place military bases in Saudi Arabia, the birthplace of Islam, as "Crusader armies, spreading like locusts, eating its riches and wiping out its plantations." Jihad aimed at Jerusalem, and the liberation of the Aqsa Mosque there, was a recurring theme in his public pronouncements.[39]

In his calls for jihad Usama's references were deliberately chosen to validate his own ideological agenda. Besides quoting the Qur'an and hadith, he declaimed Kharijite poetry and trumpeted famous early Muslim military victories, such as those won against the mighty Persians. If the first Muslims could defeat the Persians, he argued, the present struggle against the American superpower could also be won. For Usama the jihad was global—not only in the USA and Europe but also in Pakistan, Afghanistan, Palestine, Iraq, Chechnya, the Philippines, Kashmir, Sudan, and elsewhere.

AL-QA'IDA

Al-Qa'ida is an entity that is difficult to define. The meaning of the word is "rule, principle, model." It does not denote a single organization, and its higher command is riven by squabbles over whether Islamic governments or the USA should be the prime targets.[40] Its influence is especially strong in the puritanical madrasas of Pakistan and in Taliban-dominated areas of Afghanistan. From there the project of al-Qa'ida has inspired and spawned diffuse and constantly changing cells and copycat underground groups elsewhere in the world.[41] The role of these groups does not fit comfortably into that of "freedom fighters," although some have inherited anti-colonialist ideology. Al-Qa'ida-inspired groups share a common ideology that involves jihad against America, the wars in Afghanistan and Iraq, and what they see as the globalization, secularization, and materialism of the West. Their weapons are terror, violence, and the creation of a climate of fear. Their terrorist attacks take place in public places and they are publicized by the media and splashed all over the Internet. Some people thought that Usama's death in 2011 made al-Qa'ida a spent force. But he was not just a global terrorist leader; he was an inspirational model for others to follow. Even without his presence, the elusive body of al-Qa'ida remains a dangerous threat to the world and a force that sullies the reputation of Islam as a world religion.

MODERN JIHAD

What does jihad mean to modern Muslims? Within pious Islamic religious circles its interpretation varies between countries and regimes, between Sunnis and Shi'ites, between modernists and fundamentalists. As for ordinary Muslims, its legal intricacies are not understood by many; for them jihad is often little more than a rhetorical term, a rallying cry in a crisis, in much the same way as non-Muslims in the West use the word crusade. Just as in the West, too, the media in Muslim-majority countries use the word jihad without thinking too deeply about its complex resonances.

Some Muslims say that jihad is an unchanging concept, and certainly it is true that the greater jihad to strive in the path of God, to improve oneself spiritually, is a struggle that has infused Muslim piety ever since the time of the Prophet. Other Muslims argue that the lesser jihad has shown itself to be adaptable to different periods and places. The Qur'anic statements about fighting—both defensive and offensive—have allowed various interpretations of jihad to develop, and even to coexist, in the course of Islamic history. And it is undeniable that some modern interpretations of jihad are rather different from those prevalent in medieval times.[42]

For some contemporary extremist groups a single-minded focus on jihad, as they interpret it, seems to have eclipsed in importance even the five pillars of Islamic faith that underpin the daily lives of Muslims. But is this really jihad? The son of a Muslim jihad fighter against the Russians in Afghanistan in the 1980s condemned the post-2001 terrorist attacks: "We know jihad. It is something very precious and very honourable for a Muslim to do but not in the al-Qa'ida way. My father would have been completely against attacking civilian people living in their own countries…This is not jihad."[43]

Of course, the concept of jihad, laid down in the classical books of fiqh, does not cover twenty-first-century acts of calculated mass murder in airports, planes, trains, stations, and shopping malls. Indeed, the rules of jihad, laid down and elaborated by Muslim lawyers over the centuries, are governed by certain clearly explained protocols. In particular they stipulate that protection should be given to women, the elderly, the sick, and children.[44]

MODERN MUSLIM THINKERS ON JIHAD

The Egyptian cleric **Yusuf al-Qaradawi** (b. 1926) is perhaps the most prominent and authoritative Sunni scholar and preacher. In his monumental work in Arabic, called *The Law of Jihad*, covering more than 1,400 pages, he tries both to defend and—more ambitiously—to rethink Islam for a modern age.[45] He has been attacked by militant Islamists for denouncing the terrorist attacks of 9/11 in the USA and 7/7 in the UK. On the other hand, his support for the cause of the Palestinian suicide bombers has led the USA to ban him from entering that country.

The Syrian scholar **Wahba Zuhayli** (b. 1932), besides confirming the legal precepts outlined above, insists that damage to property is forbidden unless it relates directly to military combat. He also argues that war must never be waged to force non-Muslims to convert to Islam or because of their religion. He rejects the idea that people's religious and cultural identities will be the primary source of conflict in the modern world—the "clash of civilizations" theory—affirming instead that the Qur'an praises the diversity of humanity.[46]

Another Muslim voice speaking against so-called "Islamic" extremists is that of the Kuwaiti-born **Khaled M. Abou El Fadl** (b. 1963). He argues that it is much more appropriate to invoke the words of Ibn Khaldun and his medieval predecessors and to call such extremist groups *hirabi*s or *muharibun*, namely those waging illegal, sinful war (*harb*)—a far cry from jihad.

In his book entitled *Jihad in Islam: How to Understand and Practice it*, the influential Syrian Sunni cleric **Muhammad Sai'd al-Buti** (1929–2013) emphasizes that the essence of jihad has nothing to do with fighting, but is a personal striving against one's lower self. He uses the image of a tree to clarify the distinction between the greater jihad and the lesser jihad: "This fountainhead of jihad may be likened to an unchanging tree-trunk in all conditions and seasons, whereas the kind of jihad which calls for combat is like the shoots (of a tree) which bloom from time to time in accordance with seasons and climates."[47]

The greater jihad, he continues, needs to be nurtured by constant reflection on the Book of God. Al-Buti attacks the many people who, when jihad is mentioned, invoke nothing but armed struggle whilst ignoring the original trunk of the very tree from which they allegedly draw their sustenance. He seems here to be implying that the spiritual dimension is missing in such mujahidin. He draws attention to the great difference between "the everlasting jihad that God ordains and the revolution which has become widespread nowadays, attracting no small number of the younger generation."[48]

SUICIDE AND "MARTYRDOM"

What is martyrdom in a modern context? The distinction between violent methods in pursuit of national liberation, on the one hand, and terrorism on the other, is not always completely clear. In some cases leaders of movements that employed violence are now members of legitimate governments: such is the case in South Africa and Northern Ireland, for example. Minority ethnic groups, such as the Tamil Tigers in Sri Lanka or the Basques in Spain, have used violent means to try to create an autonomous state.[49] The Tamil Tigers carried out hundreds of suicide attacks over the twenty years that spanned the turn of the century, more than all other radical organizations in the world combined.[50] People of many nationalities and faiths have turned to violence in pursuit of their ideals.

Numerous groups around the world that call themselves Muslim have a concept of militant, physical jihad at the heart of their beliefs and violent activities. The members of such groups share a readiness not only to kill innocent people but also to sacrifice themselves as "suicide martyrs" in what they believe to be "jihad in the path of God." The earliest examples of *istishhad* (the seeking or the act of martyrdom) in modern times occurred amongst Shi'ites in Lebanon, Israel, and Iraq. However, the practice has now spread to Sunni extremist groups in Afghanistan and Pakistan as well as in Europe, the USA, and other parts of the world. A seminal event was the death of Muhammad Fahmida, a thirteen-year-old Iranian boy, at the time of the Iran–Iraq War. He strapped grenades to his chest and killed himself in front of an Iraqi tank in November 1980. He was proclaimed a national hero by Ayatollah Khomeini and inspired other young men to behave in the same way. His tomb outside Tehran has become a site of visitation.[51]

Recent attacks made in the name of jihad do not seem to have a nationalist agenda; they are protests against American and British involvement in Iraq and Afghanistan, the plight of the Palestinians, and Western values, which stir up "profound feelings of defeat, frustration and alienation" and fuel a "supremacist Puritanism."[52]

Is Suicide Bombing Islamic?

Although a few Muslims view suicide operations as acts of heroism and resistance, many Sunni and Shi'ite scholars have condemned them. There is a spectrum of opinion on the issue.

The link between jihad and martyrdom is clearly shown in the Qur'an and the hadith. But how is it possible nowadays for suicide bombers to kill themselves "in the path of God," while attacking others, with the sure hope, as they allege, of gaining a martyr's crown and an assured place in Paradise? By what distorted interpretation can they argue that such acts are Islamic? Are there any true foundations in the canonical sources of Islam for such a belief? It would seem not. Hence the adoption by some jihadis of the term istishhad, often in the context of suicide bombing, in preference to "suicide attack"; indeed, some try to justify the practice under Islamic law.

Yet to many Muslims, so-called "martyrdom operations," such as 9/11, reflect a distorted interpretation of Islamic doctrine concerning martyrdom. Just as the deliberate murder of innocent people is not permitted in Christianity, the attacks undertaken on 9/11 do not resemble the model of martyrdom in Islam. Islam has a number of martyrs, above all Husayn, the Prophet's grandson, who is called the "Lord of the martyrs." He was killed at the hands of others (see Chapter 6, pp. 149–50). Islamic suicide bombers, male and female, by contrast, die by their own actions. In the Qur'an martyrdom is achieved in the path of God, by fighting jihad on the battlefield. It is those who die in such fighting, killed by the enemy, who are promised Paradise.

So it would seem that the actions of the 9/11 group and other recent terrorists, who claim to be fighting jihad in the name of Islam, are not heroic deeds of martyrdom conducted in the fast lane leading to Paradise; they are suicides. And the key fact here is that suicide is strictly forbidden in Islam. Although the Qur'an itself contains no clear prohibition of it, the Prophet Muhammad condemned it in a number of his canonical sayings.

OTHER KINDS OF JIHAD

Today jihad is an overused word; but it can serve as a powerful rallying cry against perceived forces of aggression and interference. For some, the call for jihad has a specific political focus, such as Palestine. Other Muslim pressure groups take a strongly ethical stance against America's global economic power as well as political domination; hence the recently instituted "jihad against Coca Cola," an attempt to undermine the product that symbolizes America around the world and to replace it with a substitute drink for millions of Muslims. To this list we can now add cyber jihad waged by hacking into the computers of individual citizens, and indeed government departments and agencies. A recent book entitled i-Muslims reveals how al-Qa'ida uses the Internet with great skill to influence public opinion and advance its aims.[53]

Jihad, then, is a complex and multifaceted topic, as Islamic history shows, and it has provoked major debates among Muslims. They talk about jihad of the pen and jihad of the heart, as well as civilian jihad, non-violent jihad, humanitarian jihad, environmental jihad—all of these are valid and important debates today that are faithful to understanding the actual definition of jihad as struggle. It does not have to be militant or violent any more than the term "crusade," as in a crusade against smoking, need connote violence.

Treatments of jihad ignoring history, anchored only in the present and conceived only in political terms, are simplistic and therefore flawed. Far too much of modern Western discourse in the media is of this type. But the views of the vast majority of Muslims are based on a doctrine of jihad that has been laboriously refined by many generations of scholars, Sunni and Shi'ite, modernist and traditionalist, in a spirit of true piety. That doctrine, incorporating more than a millennium of hard-won wisdom, is not lightly to be brushed aside by upstart warlords, terrorists, or demagogues.

SELECTED READING

Asfaruddin, Asma, *Striving in the Path of God. Jihad and Martyrdom in Islamic Thought*, Oxford: Oxford University Press, 2013

Cook, David, *Understanding Jihad*, Berkeley, CA and London: University of California Press, 2005

Devji, Faisal, *Landscapes of Jihad: Militancy, Morality, Modernity*, Ithaca, NY: Cornell University Press, 2005

Peters, Rudolph, *Jihad in Classical and Modern Islam: A Reader*, Princeton, NJ: Markus Wiener Publishers, 2005

Zaman, Muhammad Qasim, *Modern Islamic Thought in a Radical Age: Religious Authority and Internal Criticism*, Cambridge: Cambridge University Press, 2012

10 WOMEN

Let's face it—the niqab is ridiculous, and the ideology behind it is weird.
JOAN SMITH, BRITISH JOURNALIST[1]

In [Tahrir Square, Cairo] I felt for the first time that women are equal to men.
NAWAL EL SAADAWI, EGYPTIAN FEMINIST WRITER[2]

The position of women in **Islam** has been studied and talked about in recent years from a multiplicity of angles. In this chapter, as is the case throughout the whole book, the aim is to present a historical perspective as well as a contemporary and cultural one. There can be little doubt that for most people in the West the key issue about **Muslim** women today, namely veiling, is one that, when seen from within the culture, is simply not worth the extreme degree of attention it receives in the West. While it is of course necessary to discuss this issue, the subject of Muslim women is much broader and panoramic than a mere discussion of their external appearance in public.

MUSLIM WOMEN AND THE WEST

The subject of women in Islam has long been a sensitive one. Certain entrenched negative Western stereotypes about Islam link it to such abusive practices as forced marriage and honor killings; these images linger in the minds of non-Muslims and they are fueled by the way in which Islam is covered in the Western media.[3] And, by outsiders, Islam is certainly judged today more by its practices regarding gender and sexuality than by its religious beliefs.[4]

Western stereotypes about Muslim women are deeply engrained. It has generally been supposed in the West that women have always occupied a lowly if not servile position in the Islamic social hierarchy and that they were, and are, virtually the property first of their fathers, and then of their husbands. But the situation is much more complex and nuanced than that. Nor should people in the West forget that it was not so long ago in their own culture that women were denied the vote, debarred from tertiary education, excluded from many professions, and forbidden to own property on the same terms as men.

Dress sense. Women strolling along the corniche in Beirut, Lebanon. As in many other countries—including those of the West—clothing is evidently no bar to easy social interaction among women. So an entirely veiled woman may be seen walking hand in hand with a friend wearing a miniskirt. It is they who decide what works for them.

Gender issues to do with Muslim societies are generally represented in Western discourse as clashing with values such as human rights and sexual freedom for women. The West seems to pull in one direction; indeed, the "liberation of Muslim women" was an aim of European colonizing governments in the nineteenth century and is still part of the agenda for Western intervention today in the Middle East. On the other side, this "missionary" stance on the part of the West has provoked a strong response from Islamist groups. It strengthens their resolve to maintain in their own countries, both by legislation and also by brute force on the streets, the long-standing customs that circumscribe the lives of Muslim women and dictate to them what they may do, where they may go, and what they should wear.[5] More recently, a third force is pulling from within Muslim societies in yet another direction; Muslim feminist groups, supported by many Muslim men, are seeking to establish, once and for all, equal rights for Muslim women across the world (see pp. 269–72).

The sheer diversity of Muslim societies forbids glib, global generalizations. Yet certain issues in particular have attracted notoriety in the West—veiling, polygamy, and the punishment for sexual misconduct outside marriage. It is all too easy for people in the West, and especially the Western media, to exaggerate or misrepresent the evidence in these highly sensitive areas. When talking about women in Islam it is important to be precise in mentioning which Muslim country is under discussion, and not to condemn all Muslims everywhere for customs prevalent in certain impoverished areas of the Muslim world. Just as nobody in the Christian-majority countries would dream of representing that faith by means of a remote sect—the Amish in Pennsylvania, for example, who will not use machinery or buttons on clothing because such items are sinful—so too non-Muslims should beware of judging Islam's treatment of women by the grotesque, distorted customs of the **Taliban** in Afghanistan or the barbaric treatment meted out to innocent victims of rape in rural Nigeria or Pakistan.

THE QUR'AN ON WOMEN

As always, it is essential to begin with the **Qur'an**, the fundamental source for all Muslim doctrine. There are two major strands of thought about women in the Qur'an. The first concerns the spiritual sphere, in other words, the personal relationship that human beings have with God, both in this world and the next. Second, the Qur'an also contains many prescriptions covering daily conduct.

SPIRITUAL DIMENSIONS

Spiritually, the Qur'an unambiguously puts men and women on the same level. In terms of their spiritual potential, men and women can both know and serve God and attain Paradise; 33:35 declares:

> Muslim men and Muslim women,
> Believing men and believing women,
> Obedient men and obedient women,
> Truthful men and truthful women,
> Patient men and patient women,
> Humble men and humble women,
> Charitable men and charitable women,
> Fasting men and fasting women,
> Men who guard their chastity and women who guard their chastity,
> Men who remember God often and women who remember God often,
> For them has God prepared forgiveness and a great reward.

These solemn phrases, with their deliberate repetition, memorably underline the spiritual equality of men and women before God in a way that no one could possibly misunderstand. The last phrase—"a great reward"—is used throughout the Qur'an to refer to Paradise. It is important to note that women too are promised Paradise; this verse was revealed to **Muhammad** in response to a request by Muslim women to know what Islam expected specifically of them.

According to the Qur'an, Paradise is not reserved only for men. 2:25 promises Paradise to all those who believe and do good works: "Theirs are Gardens underneath which rivers flow." Other verses speak of green robes of finest silk and gold embroidery, with the believers reclining on thrones. 36:54 mentions those who merit Paradise: "They and their wives are in pleasant shade, on thrones reclining." So we see that in Heaven husbands and wives are together. 43:70 confirms this: "Enter the Garden, you and your wives, to be made glad."

At the same time, however, the Qur'an also promises that believing Muslim men will rewarded in Paradise with the company of "beautiful companions like hidden pearls" (56:22–23), and that they will be wed "to maidens (*houris*) with large, dark eyes" (44:54).

SOCIAL DIMENSIONS

Like the Bible and the sacred books of other world religions, the Qur'an is susceptible to many readings and interpretations, and these are apt to vary from age to age. So it is important to contextualize the Qur'an historically. The Qur'an came to a society that already had long-established norms for the treatment, status, and role of women. Some Qur'anic statements about women are indeed time-bound; they relate to the customs of the society into which Muhammad and the message of Islam came. For example, Qur'an 81:8–9 clearly states that the pre-Islamic practice of female infanticide will be condemned on the **Day of Judgment**.

Marriage and Divorce

Societies described in the Old Testament were long used to polygamy; Solomon, for example, had seven hundred official wives. The society of seventh-century Arabia before Islam practiced a variety of marriage customs and this must be kept in mind when considering how the issue of polygamy is mentioned in the Qur'an. Chapter 4, entitled "Women," is particularly important on this subject. Within a Muslim marriage men are "given charge of women." They should also discipline them (4:34). It is they who choose when to have sexual relations (2:223). The Qur'an points out the qualities desirable in an ideal marriage, such as peace, harmony, and mutual care. The Qur'an allows a man to have up to four wives, but in 4:3 it goes on to stress that this is permissible only if he can treat them all equally: "Marry from among them such as are lawful to you—two, or three, or four. But if you have reason to fear that you might not be able to treat them with equal fairness, then only one."

It is also important to remember the specific circumstances in which 4:3 was revealed; this moment is thought to have come after the defeat of the Muslims by the **Meccans** at the Battle of Uhud in 625, when more than seventy Muslim men were killed. And the Qur'anic permission for a man to have up to four wives came to Muhammad as guidance on how to give the women widowed at Uhud the status of honorable marriage as well as to provide social protection to them and their children. In other words, 4:3 is encouraging men to marry as many as four women in this specific context as a social duty. This recommendation may be viewed both as a worthy solution to a severe social crisis in the tiny Muslim community at a crucial moment in history, as well as being a clear improvement on the motley and only loosely defined marriage customs practiced in Arabia before the coming of Islam.

The second half of 4:3, however, shifts to providing guidance for all men in all ages, since it declares that if a man cannot treat several wives equally, then he should have only one. This clearly implies that monogamy is prefer-able. Indeed, later in the same chapter, in 4:129, with its realistic declaration that it is impossible to achieve fairness in a polygamous marriage, there is an even stronger pointer toward the superiority of monogamy: "And it will not be within your power to treat your wives with equal fairness, however much you may desire it."

According to the Qur'an, divorce is permitted, but only in exceptional cir-cumstances. Every effort should be made to reconcile differences. The Qur'an mentions the procedure to be followed in divorce and a man's responsibilities toward his divorced wife and her children. The husband is required, after a waiting period, to: "either retain them according to acceptable terms or part with them according to acceptable terms. And bring to witness two just men from among you and establish the testimony" (65:2).

Dress

The main Qur'anic commands about what Muslims should wear are found in Chapters 24 and 33. 24:30–33 speaks first to believing men and then to believ-ing women, requiring both sexes "to lower their gaze and to be mindful of

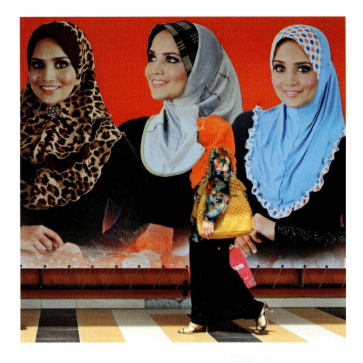

Framing the face. A woman walks past a billboard showcasing fashionable headscarves, Kuala Lumpur, Malaysia. Bright colors and bold patterns are entirely compatible with a head covering that hides the hair. Customs in veiling vary dramatically across the Muslim world, as do the motives of the women who wear the veil in one form or another.

their chastity." In the case of women they are also asked "not to display their charms (in public) beyond what may (decently) be apparent thereof; hence let them draw their head coverings over their bosoms." Medieval Muslim commentators from early on offered very strict interpretations of the key but non-specific words "what may be apparent."[6] But a famous Qur'an translator, Muhammad Asad, argues persuasively that the very vagueness of this phrase allows for time-bound changes to occur and therefore for different interpretations to be possible at different periods in history. This key passage is then followed by a list of those close male relatives in whose company woman are permitted to relax these rules on dress and social behavior—their husbands, fathers, fathers-in-law, and other such close males related to them through blood or marriage ties. Qur'an 33:59 speaks later about Muhammad's wives and addresses him directly: "O Prophet! Tell thy wives and thy daughters as well as all (other) believing women, that they should draw over themselves some of their outer garments (when in public): this will be more conducive to their being recognized (as decent women) and not annoyed."

What is clear from these Qur'anic instructions is that modesty in dress is prescribed for both men and women, although in the latter case these instructions are certainly more specific about what constitutes modesty—a woman's head and bosom should be covered. There is no mention of the face itself.

WOMEN IN ISLAMIC LAW

As Chapter 5 shows, while the Qur'an and the *hadith* are the basis of Islamic faith, the law by which Muslim societies regulate themselves derives from later interpretations and commentaries on all this material. Muslim lawyers drew up rules for the treatment and conduct of women in Islamic society. Predictably enough, the significant areas are those to do with family life. Attention is also paid to the issue of modest dress. (For the controversial punishments sometimes exacted for illicit sexual relations, see Chapter 5, pp. 127–28.)

Until very recently, Muslim religious scholars have generally been men. Thus from the beginning men interpreted the message of the Qur'an about women through the prism of male experiences, male attitudes, and the male psyche. This phenomenon, of course, is not restricted to Muslim societies; it was common in most pre-modern societies, including Christian and Jewish ones, that men interpreted scripture-based law, and that—whether they were fully aware of it or not—they interpreted it to their own advantage. Whilst Muslim scholars did not dispute that the spiritual message of the Qur'an was for all humanity, male and female, they explained and elaborated its pronouncements on the social status of women, and formulated Islamic law accordingly, to the detriment of women and in favor of men.

Apart from the personal opinions of legal scholars, local customs were also crucial. The customary laws in the new territories that the Muslims conquered inevitably influenced the daily lives of Muslims when they settled there and mingled with the indigenous populations. In the Middle East, for example, high-class urban women wore veils and were secluded from the rest of society long before the coming of Islam. These practices were signs of status, revealing that such women did not need to work outside the house. An Assyrian legal text of the thirteenth century BCE refers to the veiling of respectable women, and the custom was known too in Greece and Rome. St. Paul says in the Bible that a woman when prophesying or praying should wear a head covering.[7] When the Muslim Arabs conquered the great **Sasanian** empire of Iran and parts of Byzantium, they saw face-veiling there and it became part of Muslim practice.[8]

MARRIAGE AND DIVORCE

By the twelfth century, works of Islamic jurisprudence were devoted to specific topics; **al-Ghazali** (1058–1111), for example, wrote a *Book of Marriage*, in which he argues that, most importantly, a model wife should be pious and of good character. Marriage between a Muslim man and an unbelieving woman is not allowed,[9] whereas he is allowed to marry a Christian or Jewish wife. Muslim legal scholars generally forbid Muslim women from marrying non-Muslim men.

On the issue of divorce, Islamic law recommends that every effort should be made to reconcile marital differences. Both parties may demand a divorce, but the rulings on divorce and custody of children favor men. A man may divorce his wife by simply making a unilateral declaration three times, uttering the words "I divorce you" before witnesses; he does not need a specific pretext to do so. On the other hand, a woman can divorce only for a prescribed number of reasons agreed by a judge in court. The Qur'an is not very specific about the grounds for divorce. Here, Qur'anic commentators and Muslim lawyers played a significant role. Since the Qur'an does not ask for justification from the husband for divorcing his wife, he is allowed in Islamic law to divorce whenever he wishes. No such privilege is extended to women. Women must wait to see if they are pregnant before remarrying after divorce; men may marry straightaway. The wife retains the right under Islamic law to have custody of young children—boys until the age of seven and girls until they are nine. After that, the father takes care of the children.

INHERITANCE

Following Qur'an 4:11, Islamic law accords a greater degree of equity than in pre-Islamic times to a female family member in the matter of inheritance, allowing her half the share of a male. A woman's testimony in court is also worth half that of a man.[10] Islamic law also ensures that a woman has the right to own and manage her own property, rights denied to women in Christian Europe at the time. She possesses the right to buy and sell, give gifts, and dispense charity. The groom gives a marriage dowry to the bride for her own personal use.

So much, then, for the theoretical position of women in Islamic law, based on the Qur'an and the hadith. As will be demonstrated later, pre-modern Muslim women soon learned strategies to loosen the constraints of their patriarchal societies. Furthermore, it is all too easy to mistake the social engineering of Islam as it has developed over time and place for its true spirit. Islam views men and women as spiritually equal. Whilst it remains true that, in its social injunctions about women, the Qur'an places men in a superior position to women, this disparity can be seen as a reflection of the society into which the Islamic revelation came. Christians who make capital out of this would do well to study, say, some passages in the Epistles of St. Paul.

MARY AND FATIMA—TWO ESPECIALLY VENERATED WOMEN

Many non-Muslims are surprised at the reverence accorded to the Virgin **Mary** by Muslims over the centuries. The Qur'an gives Mary great prominence; indeed, she is mentioned there more frequently than in the whole New Testament (see Chapter 3, pp. 72–74). For the **Sufis**, Mary is not only the mother of **Jesus** but she is also an inspirational figure in her own right. At a popular level too, especially in Egypt, where Coptic Christians and Muslims have on occasion shared festivals and shrines, Mary is a beloved figure. In the course of 1968, the visions of the Virgin of Zaytuna in Egypt, which many Christians and Muslims flocked to see, were reported as headline news in Egypt's most famous newspaper, *al-Ahram*.

The Prophet's daughter **Fatima** also occupies a special place in Muslim piety. Muhammad said of her: "Fatima is a part of me. Whatever pleases her pleases me and whatever angers her angers me."[11] Known as "the Resplendent One," Fatima is portrayed in Islamic tradition as a loving daughter, wife, and mother. She tended Muhammad and her husband ʿAli after the Battle of Uhud, visited the graves of those who had been killed in the conflict, and said prayers for them. She gave the eulogy at her father's funeral. She died in 632, two months after him, and was buried in **Medina**, aged only twenty-nine. As the mother of **Hasan** and **Husayn** she came to be known as the "Mother of the **Imams**" and she has a special place in **Shi'ite** piety.[12] The powerful Fatimid dynasty (909–1171), honored Fatima by taking her name.

Thus we see how Mary and Fatima have shown to Muslim women throughout the ages by their lives and actions how women can make a distinct contribution to Islam; spirituality is not just the preserve of men for men.

MUSLIM WOMEN IN PRE-MODERN TIMES

As in medieval Europe and China, there was inevitably a great gulf in pre-modern times between the lives of royal and upper-class women in Muslim societies and those of the women who came from the poorer echelons, whether in cities, villages, or nomadic encampments.

ROYAL AND UPPER-CLASS WOMEN

From the very beginning, there were powerful Muslim women who served as models for later generations to remember and emulate. Even in Muhammad's lifetime, there was the striking example of his first wife, **Khadija**, a woman of independent mind and income. She asked him to marry her. And 'A'isha, a later wife of his, was a spirited and determined woman, who led the opposition movement against 'Ali. After Muhammad's death, she is mentioned as being present at the famous Battle of the Camel, thus named because she was mounted on a camel.

What did medieval Muslim women actually do, as opposed to what Islamic law and the religious scholars, who were male, prescribed that they should do? Their sphere of non-domestic activities was wide. Among the elite, they acted as regents, held audiences, received petitions, signed edicts, and led armies. They minted coins that bore their titles. Some of these women were of royal pedigree; others had originally been slaves and had risen in power from the **harem**. Royal women are portrayed on occasion as pious and full of charitable works. Such women funded the building of **mosques**, theological colleges, **caravansarys**, fountains, tombs, and shrines, and their names are commemorated on the monuments themselves. They sometimes had their own bodyguards and financial budgets, and they presided over legal proceedings. But rarely did a woman rule a Muslim territory exclusively in her own right,[13] although they often served as regents for their young sons. No woman was ever permitted to become **caliph**. **Viziers** and administrators often resented what they saw as the interference of royal women, especially the queen mother, in state business.

There is evidence from historical sources that some royal and upper-class women could read and write. Some women engaged in religious and cultural pursuits. They were Qur'an and hadith teachers and were licensed to teach Islamic law. They also worked as scribes, calligraphers, and librarians. As Ibn Hazm, a tenth-century intellectual in Cordoba, wrote: "Women taught me the Qur'an, they recited to me much poetry, they trained me in calligraphy." Yet others were gifted scientists, such as the tenth-century astronomer Mariam al-Ijliyya, who was nicknamed al-Asturlabiyya ("the woman who made astro-labes," instruments used to make astronomical measurements). Entries about important women appear in biographical dictionaries. The thirteenth-century Baghdad historian Ibn al-Sa'i wrote biographies of prominent women, such as the wives and concubines of caliphs and sultans. The evidence that he provides indicates persuasively that the court women of the 'Abbasid period were witty, cultivated, and skilled in poetry and music.

POORER WOMEN

Folk tales, travel accounts, poetry, painting, and other kinds of fascinating evidence about the other classes of society, both urban and rural, bring a vibrant world to life, peopled with singing girls, dancers, slaves, musicians and hard-working rural and nomadic women. Popular medieval epics talk of legendary women warriors, such as Princess Dhat al-Himma, the undefeated leader of the Muslim army in its wars against the **Byzantines**.[14] At the other end of the social spectrum, a tale datable to around 1100 is told of a clumsy

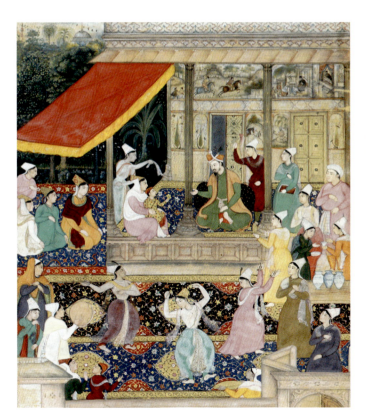

A courtly ethos.
The emperor Humayun at the circumcision celebrations of his young son Akbar in 1545 (detail). Abu'l-Fazl, Akbarnama, Mughal, c. 1604. Female dancers and musicians performed at various festivities (marking, for example, births, marriages, victories, embassies, and receptions) in many pre-modern Muslim courts, especially in Mughal India.

but quick-witted slave girl who, on stumbling and emptying a scalding dish over her master's head, begged him first to restrain his anger, then to forgive her, and finally to do good, quoting at him successive passages from Qur'an 30:128. He promptly freed her. The work called *A Thousand and One Nights*, a rich medley of tales depicting the society of medieval Baghdad and Cairo, is full of memorable women very different from the image of women constructed by the religious lawyers of Islam. Cheeky and smart, they outwit and deceive their husbands. They are bold and resourceful; in a word, they are streetwise. They enjoy considerable freedom and meet men publicly. Such stories give us countless insights into the pulsating daily life of medieval Muslim women. This world is vividly brought to life in thirteenth-century Arab painting, where women not only engage in traditionally female occupations, such as spinning and driving camels, but also argue with preachers, work in taverns, take their husbands to court, flaunt the latest colorful fashions, and haggle in the market.

There were, of course, restrictions. Once the Muslim community became a vast empire, the Muslims, influenced by increasing urbanization, began—like the Byzantines and the Persians before them—to seclude their womenfolk. Urban houses were divided into private apartments (the harem), in which the women resided, and public rooms where business was transacted and male guests were entertained. Nomadic women, on the other hand, enjoyed a greater degree of independence than those in the cities, although—like rural women—they worked hard. In accordance with the traditions of their nomadic heritage, they were unveiled.

It is hard to know how much medieval Muslim women were allowed to travel away from their home town or village. Such journeys were always difficult, unless the woman was accompanied by male relations. Occasional references to royal Turkish princesses setting out independently to perform the pilgrimage to Mecca are greeted in the medieval chronicles with outright disapproval. Wherever possible, the male relations of such a "wayward" woman would be dispatched to take her home again.[15]

MUSLIM WOMEN IN THE EARLY MODERN ERA

The development of European travel to the Middle East in the eighteenth century sparked considerable interest in the **Ottoman** empire, and "Turcomania" in music, literature, and the visual arts gripped Western Europe

Eastern promise for a Western market. Emerging Orientalism: Eugène Delacroix, *Women of Algiers in their apartment*, 1834. The air of relaxed ease and carefree eroticism conjured up by the word "harem" belies the calculated color scheme and the forms borrowed from the 16th-century Italian artist Titian and from Persian painting. The French Romantic artist Delacroix visited Morocco and Algeria with a French embassy and relished the exoticism of local society.

for a while, fed by actual or mental images of Muslim women closeted in **seraglios** or harems and guarded by eunuchs. Such fantasies went even further in the nineteenth century, with the advent of European colonialism in the Middle East and beyond. But the ideas of Europeans about the harem were a figment of their imagination.[16] At one level, Western men were titillated by the image of exotic women in the harem, shut up in a polygamous prison, a multi-ethnic playground. At the same time the harem symbolized all that appeared to be wrong with the despotic Muslim world,[17] evoking as it did a prison of passivity from which incarcerated Muslim women needed to be rescued by masterful European colonial powers.[18]

In fact, the harem never was a single entity; it denoted a "certain arrangement of domestic space" that was applied to a variety of different Muslim societies over the centuries.[19] Generally, the term refers to a part of the house that is forbidden to men who are not close relatives. Far from the voluptuous scenes of "perfect, fair-skinned and beautiful" women being entrusted to the "incomplete, dark and mutilated" figure of black eunuchs, as depicted by such

Orientalist painters as Jean-Léon Gérôme,[20] the harem was a hive of domestic activity and mundane household tasks for the several generations of women who lived there.

Indeed, the dawn of the modern era saw important changes. Muslim women in the nineteenth century in Syria, Egypt, and Lebanon hosted literary salons where intellectuals of both sexes mingled.[21] **Mariyana Marrash** (1848–1919), for example, who lived in Aleppo, Syria, was the first Arab woman to publish an article in a newspaper. When she hosted a salon, she always wore the latest European fashions, and her guests smoked hubble-bubble pipes. Another important figure was the Lebanese-born intellectual and pioneer Arab feminist Zaynab Fawwaz, who moved to Egypt and published numerous essays, as well as a huge biographical dictionary of famous women.

In the same period, a memorable autobiography was written in German by an Arab princess, **Salme Bint Said** (1844–1924), the daughter of Sayyid Said, the ruler of Oman and Zanzibar.[22] Salme's autobiography focuses on her early life in Zanzibar, and especially on the harem (her father had three legal wives and around seventy concubines).[23] At twenty-one she fell in love with a young German, Heinrich Ruete, a minor official in the German consulate in Zanzibar. When she became pregnant, her family, and particularly her brother, who had become sultan by that time, showed great kindness to her—normally the punishment for sexual relations outside marriage would have been death. She escaped to Aden and gave birth in December 1866. She married Ruete in May 1867 and converted to Christianity. They moved to Germany, but three years later Ruete died. Salme spent the rest of her life in Germany. Despite her long and lonely exile in Germany and her change of religious faith, Salme strongly refutes what she calls the "false and preposterous" European views about the position of Arab wives in relation to their husbands. Describing the typical European visitor to the Middle East, she writes that "he throws the reins over the neck of his imagination and gallops away into fable land."[24]

NINETEENTH AND EARLY TWENTIETH CENTURIES

The lives of women in Western countries underwent striking changes in this period, with the demands of war introducing greater employment possibilities for them; they also began to wear more casual clothes. A similar trend occurred in the cities of certain Middle Eastern countries, such as Egypt, Syria, and Jordan, where women removed their veils and started to wear a modest form of Western dress. **Kemal Atatürk** (1881–1938; see Chapter 7, p. 182) in Turkey and **Reza Shah Pahlavi** (1878–1944) of Iran passed laws banning veiling in their respective countries in order to signal their commitment to modernization. To these national leaders, changing their citizens' clothing was a way of changing very much more, notably their own mindsets, and also their national image in the eyes of the progressive European countries they sought to emulate. Reza Shah famously swept through the bazaar in Tabriz, removing the veils from women's faces with his sword, and in 1936 he introduced a law forbidding the wearing of the *hijab* (headscarf; see pp. 266–68). Many Iranian women rebelled by choosing voluntary life imprisonment in their own homes rather than appearing unveiled in public.

PROMINENT MUSLIM WOMEN TODAY

There are many famous Muslim women across the world; they work in diverse fields, and often in several fields at once.

POLITICIANS

Several Muslim women have already been heads of state—Benazir Bhutto in Pakistan, Megawati Sukarnoputri in Indonesia, Tansu Ciller in Turkey, and Khalida Zia and Shaykha Hasina in Bangladesh. These are all Muslim-majority countries. There are also successful Muslim women in politics in North America and Europe. Dalia Mogahed, for example, from Georgetown University, is the first Muslim woman wearing hijab to serve on a presidential advisory panel—President Obama's Advisory Council on Faith-Based and Neighborhood Partnerships. Amongst many Muslim women active in British public life, mention should be made of Baroness Warsi, the first female Muslim to serve as a minister in the British government, and Baroness Afshar, a Shi'ite Muslim scholar of gender studies, who speaks about equality issues in Britain's House of Lords. In January 2009, the Moroccan-born French justice minister Rachida Dati caused an uproar when she left the clinic where she had given birth six days earlier and returned to work. In Germany Ekin Deligöz is one of seven female politicians of Turkish descent who won seats in the federal parliament in 2013.

CELEBRITIES

The Muslim world has its full share of female celebrities. Supreme among them is the Egyptian singer **Umm Kulthum** (1898–1975), also known as the Star of the East. Long after her death, she is still a national treasure, and

Mother of the Nation. Umm Kulthum, legendary Egyptian contralto, moved vast audiences to tears in her epic concerts, with a single love song apt to last up to an hour and a half, depending on her mood. After the Egyptian defeat in the Six-Day War in 1967 her repertoire took on political, soul-searching, and even tragic overtones. French President Charles de Gaulle called her simply "The Lady." She unified the Arabs, old and young, men and women, across the Middle East, as no politician could, to become the cultural icon of the century.

beloved far beyond her homeland by both men and women. She is considered quite simply the greatest Arab singer ever. Her funeral procession was attended in the streets of Cairo by more people than those who witnessed the funeral of President Nasser. More recently, the work of the Iranian photographer and film maker **Shirin Neshat** (b. 1957), exiled from her homeland of Iran for many years, sends out multiple messages to the viewer, in such works as Women of Allah, a series of extraordinary black-and-white photographs depicting female fighters in the 1979 Iranian Islamic Revolution. She has produced images of revolutionary poetry by women, written across women's faces, eyes, hands, and feet, that defy simplistic interpretations. More and more Muslim women have taken part in recent Olympic Games, usually wearing the standard gear for their competitions; Algerian and Moroccan women have won medals. In London in 2012, for the first time ever, Muslim women athletes from Saudi Arabia, Qatar, Brunei, Afghanistan, and Oman were allowed to compete.

PROGRESSIVE AND FEMINIST VOICES

Amina Wadud (b. 1952), a controversial African American Muslim academic, is a very influential figure worldwide; she speaks of a "gender-inclusive" interpretation of Islam.[25] Though a woman, she led on March 18, 2005 the Friday prayer and gave the Friday sermon to a mixed assembly of American Muslim men and women in New York; the call to prayer had also been made by a woman, Suhayla El-Attar. Wadud was well aware of the huge publicity this event would provoke—the entire event took place in the glare of media attention and, moreover, in Manhattan—but she said afterward that during the prayer she was still able to focus on her own personal religious worship.[26] The symbolism of this event was striking. Across the world it challenged stereotypical images of Muslim women as cowed and submissive and pointed the way to the possibility of their assuming roles of religious leadership in Islam. Wadud says that there is nothing in the Qur'an that prohibits women from leading the prayer. She argues that when reading the Qur'an, Muslims have no choice but to select for themselves what to emphasize and what to play down. This is the exercise of personal judgment that is allowed within the framework of the *Shari'a*.

Another landmark move for Muslim women also took place in the USA in 2007 when Laleh Bakhtiar was the first American Muslim woman to translate the Qur'an into English. Far away in Malaysia, Sharifah Khasif is a celebrated woman Qur'an reciter. She was one of the youngest champions of the International Qur'an Reciters' Assembly in 2009 and she is invited all over the world to recite the Qur'an.

Gender equality proclaimed. The African American Amina Wudud leads the Friday prayer for a mixed congregation in a New York mosque, 2005, reflecting the innate capacity of Islam to adapt to change without losing its spiritual integrity. The upper gallery, traditionally reserved for women, is empty. Note the variety of dress codes.

The Moroccan **Fatima Mernissi** (b. 1940) wrote *The Forgotten Queens of Islam* (1993) in response to the claims made in some circles in Pakistan when Benazir Bhutto became prime minister that "no Muslim state has ever been governed by a woman."[27] Here Mernissi passionately denounces what she calls "Muslim misogyny," arguing that this is patently false and providing proof in the form of the biographies of fifteen "queens" who ruled in various Muslim states, in India, Egypt, Iran, the Maldives, Indonesia, and Yemen. Fatima Mernissi has also challenged the male prerogative to determine which hadith are to be considered authoritative guidelines for contemporary society.

The Egyptian writer and feminist activist **Nawal El Saadawi** (b. 1931) is a woman of enormous energy, determination, and courage. She has worked in several spheres, often simultaneously—as a medical doctor, as an indefatigable campaigner, and as an author (she has written forty-two books). In the 1980s she was imprisoned for three months for "crimes against the state" and there she composed a book about life in a female prison, writing with her eyeliner on toilet paper. She continues her career as an activist even though she is now in her eighties, and she was present in Tahrir Square, Cairo, when President Mubarak was toppled from power. She has fought all her life against the hideous practice of female genital mutilation, a procedure to which she herself was subjected aged seven.

It is important to stress in this connection that, contrary to widespread misconceptions, female genital circumcision (FGM) is not an Islamic practice. FGM is a custom that has most unfortunately been associated with Islam and is indeed practiced by Muslim communities across the world. Attested as far back as the second century BCE, and strongly condemned in WHO reports, this brutal practice is still common in sub-Saharan Africa, including countries with substantial Muslim populations, such as Sudan, Eritrea, and Egypt, and it has now appeared in Europe amongst Muslim communities, for example in the UK and the Netherlands. The World Congress of Muslim Women, meeting in early 2002, condemned the practice of FGM as violating Islam.[28] In 2008 the Egyptian government passed a law banning FGM, following the death of a young girl in 2007 during an operation. A *fatwa* against it was pronounced in Mauritania on January 12, 2011, backed up by doctors and religious scholars. Despite the law, El Saadawi believes that about 90 percent of women in Egypt are still circumcised. The first UK prosecutions over female genital mutilation were announced in March 2014. In the past the response there to such medical procedures has been compared unfavorably with France, where there have been more than a hundred successful prosecutions.[29] FGM, once considered primarily a problem of the developing world, is a growing threat to girls and women in the United States, according to a new report, although there are longstanding laws against the practice in that country.[30]

WOMEN IN CONTEMPORARY SOCIETY

This huge and complex topic is subject to ongoing change and wide-ranging regional variations. The discussion that follows will address some topics of particular contemporary interest or controversy.

FAMILY LIFE

Muslims do not forget the Prophet's famous hadith about respect and love for parents, especially mothers.[31] The family remains the key institution of Muslim society. To many non-Muslims, the structure of the modern Muslim family may seem backward. To Muslims, however, Western society seems to undervalue marriage and the family quite disastrously. The traditional Muslim custom of living together in extended families in some Muslim-majority countries tends to devolve authority in the domestic sphere to older women, sometimes known ironically as "the Ministry of the Interior," and especially to the mother and mother-in-law. Such communal living makes for closer bonds between family members but it may at the same time result in reduced levels of privacy for young married couples. So in many Muslim-majority countries now couples are living in their own houses or apartments.

Polygamy is much less common nowadays, although it is making a comeback in the Gulf countries. Monogamy is now the norm for most Muslims, but it is the law only in Tunisia and Turkey. It is clear that in this crucial area of Muslim life, the example of the West and the social stigma of being old-fashioned have influenced traditional Muslim practice. On the other hand, in many parts of the Muslim world arranged marriages are still quite usual; many Muslims feel that it is the parents who know best what is good for their children, and believe that this is why Muslim marriages are stable. As in the West, if a marriage ends in divorce, the people involved will often marry someone else. In many places, however, divorce still leaves a stigma for the woman, and she is usually seen as the person at fault. Remarriage can therefore be difficult, and a divorced woman often has little option beyond returning to her father's house.

DRESS

First, a note about terminology. Today several terms can refer to the head-dress of Muslim women across the world. These names are not used in the same way everywhere, and the items they refer to vary in their appearance too. The hijab is a headscarf that covers the head, loosely or tightly; it can be in a number of colors.[32] The *burqa* covers the whole body, including the face, with a visor for the eyes, whilst the *niqab* is a veil covering only the mouth and nose. The *jilbab*, the *abaya*, and the *chador* are long garments stretching from head to toe. Some women wear headscarves draped in different ways; others are bare-headed.

Many Muslim women rebut the non-Muslim view that they are forbidden to dress as they themselves wish. They argue that this is not their experience at all and that it is they who choose whether or not to wear hijab. Some do and some do not. Some abandon hijab; others adopt it voluntarily. Predictably, then, the reasons why the veil is worn are very diverse. Some women wear the veil because the conservative society in which they live requires them to do so; others to avoid being stared at and molested by men in public places; others for economic reasons, to avoid having to follow the latest fashions in their clothes; and yet others to demonstrate publicly that they have made a positive choice of Islam as their living faith. And, of course, the veil can be worn for a combination of any or all of these reasons.

Moreover, the veil is by no means drab or unpleasing to look at; indeed, for many women it is a fashion accessory, and they possess a number of veils in different colors and designs to suit different public occasions. There are fashion designers who create beautiful—and meaningful—clothing for Muslim women to wear. Earlier this century a German Muslim clothes designer of Turkish descent, Melih Kermen, decided to try to express his beliefs through fashion; among the clothes he designed was a hooded jacket with the words: "hijab, my right, my choice, my life." On the website that he and his wife have set up is the following message: "The headscarf is a symbol for women's liberation from society's constraints." Their business is now booming across the world. Incidentally, an outfit colloquially known as the *burqini* allows Muslim women to swim without displaying any significant amount of flesh.

Dress in Different Countries

Social practice varies greatly from one country to the next, or indeed within certain countries. Veiling conveys a multitude of messages, and not just religious ones. It can tell the viewer which region people come from and to

LEFT **Veiling, Afghan style.** Four women dressed in the fullest head-and-body burqa, Jalalabad, Afghanistan, 2013. The colours are typically Afghan, as is the fabric grille for the face. Elsewhere in the Islamic world, full veiling is usually black.

RIGHT **Muslim catwalk.** A model displays a creation by the Malaysian designer Tuan Hasnah during the Islamic Fashion Festival, Kuala Lumpur, Malaysia. Such outfits attempt to reconcile fashion statements with conservative Muslim custom. Note that indoors, among other women, children, and close male relatives, veiling is customarily discarded.

what level of society they belong. A single country can provide a range of examples of veiling customs—in Oman, for example, some women cover their hair while leaving their face exposed, some veil half or their whole face, and some are covered from head to toe. Different communities live side by side in Oman—**Sunni** Baluchis and **Ibadi** Omanis—and what they wear tells other people which group they belong to. As Dawn Chatty puts it, "face and head covering are only part of a much wider social reality."[33]

In Tunis young women walk along the street holding hands and chatting animatedly; one is wearing a mini-skirt and the other is veiled. In Beirut and Damascus, young Muslim women with and without headscarves smoke hookahs in alfresco cafes with their friends and family. On the other hand, in the Gulf countries, Pakistan, and Afghanistan, women are covered from head to toe, usually in black, with only their eyes showing.[34] In the most zealous period after the Iranian Islamic revolution in 1979, the *pasdaran* (the upholders of Muslim standards) would prowl the streets of Tehran, pouncing on young women who had any strand of hair visible from under their head-scarves. In Iran nowadays, however, those who wish to challenge the severe official enforcers of dress codes tend to experiment with, say, colored head-scarves, or transparent veils, or a style of head covering that allows strands of hair to escape. This issue of showing hair is in continual flux, precisely because women are constantly testing the boundaries.

Women's dress in Indonesia has become a highly controversial issue. New laws have placed restrictions on women's dress in the belief that jilbab-wearing women will create a more moral and stable society. In certain parts of Indonesia, such as Aceh where the Shari'a was imposed in 2001,[35] the police, the army, and other groups of males have compelled women, sometimes by force, to adhere to the dress code. Other areas of the country have followed suit. Since 2001 the Indonesian Islamic University (Univertas Islam Indonesia) has imposed rules requiring all women staff and students—regardless of their religious affiliation—to wear Muslim dress. Iran imposes similar rules on foreign female tourists.

Europe

Muslim women wearing Muslim dress are now visible all across Europe as immigration has rocketed. These Muslims have brought with them their own interpretations of the Qur'anic statements on veiling and their own customs. The response on the part of European governments to this visible statement of "otherness" has been varied, ranging from a ban on wearing the full Muslim veil in public in France to more lenient legislation on it elsewhere. Other European countries, such as Italy, Spain, and Britain, are also trying to tackle this issue, often in an atmosphere of tension caused by Islamophobia and fear about public security. Especially since 9/11 and the grave security issues engendered by that tragic event, many governments have insisted that Muslim women's faces should be identified and checked at airports and at other places of entry and departure, such as national border posts. So, whether they are veiled or unveiled, it seems essential that all women must be willing to submit to the laws of the country in which they reside where issues of public security are involved. (It is worth noting, however, that Western countries used the veil right up to modern times, especially on formal occasions.)

EDUCATION

The level of education, and indeed literacy, for Muslim women across the globe varies enormously.[36] In Pakistan and Yemen women's literacy is shockingly low at 28 percent, and in India 59 percent of Muslim women have never even attended school. On the other hand, in Saudi Arabia and Iran women's literacy rates are 70 percent, and in Jordan and Indonesia they reach 85 percent. The comparable rates of literacy for men in countries with low literacy rates for women are better but still not impressive.

In the Middle East, young women can receive a fine university education and many of them do. Their student experience depends on where they live. In Cairo, Damascus, and Beirut women undergraduates, wearing the hijab or designer jeans, mingle freely with their male counterparts. In Saudi Arabia women receive a totally separate education, often to a very high level: much investment has been made there in women's education, both in state women's universities and private women's colleges, where they are taught by women with PhDs from prestigious Western universities, such as Harvard and Oxford, as well as from Cairo, Beirut, or Amman. A pathbreaking new mixed-gender university, the King Abdullah University of Science and Technology, was established in Saudi Arabia in 2009. There women may mix freely with men and they are not obliged to wear veils in class.

The academic subjects offered in Arab universities are similar to those taught in the West, resulting in better job opportunities for women afterward. In the UK upwardly mobile, well-educated British Muslim women, mostly of South Asian origin, gravitate toward careers as lawyers, doctors, dentists, and pharmacists. And the same is true of many Muslim women in the USA and Canada. A sharp contrast to this is a system of education for Muslim females in some parts of India. For example, in Uttar Pradesh, India's most populated state, young Muslim women are taught in separate *madrasas*. If a man comes into the vicinity he shouts to announce his arrival so that the women there will have time to cover themselves. They are taught a limited range of subjects suitable for their role as good wives and mothers; these subjects include the Qur'an, refined speech, and personal cleanliness, as well as how to perform their domestic responsibilities.[37]

FEMINISM

There are now many Muslim feminist groups. Their members go straight to the Qur'an, to look afresh at its statements about women and to interpret them for Muslim women today. As Yvonne Haddad eloquently puts it, Muslim feminists "do not question the validity of the Qur'anic text as eternally valid guidance for all humanity, but have reservations about the patriarchal interpretations characteristic of traditional societies."[38] Muslim feminists call their own striving for an Islamic way of life a "gender *jihad*." Others call it a "lipstick jihad." Using their own interpretations of the Qur'an and the Prophet's example, they refute patriarchal readings of the Qur'an about women. Alongside this struggle, they are keen to hold on to the basic principles of their religion rather than to accept passively the severe rules that have infiltrated Muslim societies over the centuries. Amongst the numerous Muslim feminist networks facilitated by social media and the Internet are national groups such as Sisters in Islam in Malaysia and BAOBAB for Women's Human Rights in Nigeria (the motto of which is "You can't change the past but you can try to change the future"). The international organization Women Living under Muslim Laws has concentrated on trying to reform the laws of Muslim states to make them accord with the spirit of the Qur'an.

Much of women's activism around the Muslim world is based on the desire for changes to family law, especially on the issues of marriage, divorce, and inheritance. Islam is now a global faith and it is difficult to generalize about how Islamic family law is practiced, if at all, in countries as diverse as, for example, Germany, the Gambia, Pakistan, or Indonesia. Divorce and inheritance have already been mentioned in this chapter. But another key contemporary issue is the global problem of domestic violence, which has long been a taboo subject in Muslim countries, just as it is also often an issue that is concealed by non-Muslim victims of domestic violence out of fear or shame. Much hinges on Qur'an 4:34, a very controversial verse, which feminist Muslim women aim to reinterpret. The latter part of the verse talks about how to deal with a wife who is guilty of recalcitrance (*nushuz*) toward her husband and it is debated whether the verse authorizes him to beat her violently, lightly, or not at all.

The presence of women in the mosque has traditionally presented a special case. Disagreements about the right of women to pray there began after the death of the Prophet. He himself had always permitted women to pray in the mosque; the second caliph 'Umar forbade it, but his successor 'Uthman restored this right. In some regions they were allowed to pray in special sections of the mosque; in others they were told to stay at home. This has become a hot contemporary issue in the USA, and Muslim feminists there have held protests about it. Asra Nomani in West Virginia has argued that, as the Prophet did not seclude women in special sections of the mosque, this practice should not be permitted today.[39] Some mosques in Canada and the United

Segregation in worship. Sufi preaching in a mosque, Mir Kamal al-Din Husayn Gazurgahi, *Majalis al-'Ushshaq* ("Assemblies of Lovers"), Shiraz, 1552. The book comprises biographies of leading Sufis. The men cluster around the *minbar* (pulpit); the women and children are tucked out of sight behind a screen. Sometimes a rope or an upper gallery served the same purpose.

States actually prevent women from entering, resulting in some mosque pray-ins. Some mosques in the USA have already led the way in allowing women into the main prayer halls and giving them positions on mosque committees.

A US study of 2007 shows that Muslim women are seeking the same rights as men, they wish to vote without family pressure, to work in any job for which they are qualified, and even to attain high government positions. This same study also points out that Muslim women in general cherish great loyalty to their religion, which they believe guarantees them clearly defined rights and security. They wish to achieve these aims, therefore, within the framework of their faith.[40]

Despite substantial progress in recent years, there is still a long way to go with respect to women's rights and social position in certain parts of the Muslim world. A UN report entitled *Arab Human Development Report 2005: Towards the Rise of Women in the Arab World*—and written, it should be emphasized, by Arab researchers—criticized Middle Eastern governments for neglecting the talents and potential contribution of half of their population, namely the women, and the report advocated greater empowerment of women.[41] Through the global social media links now available, Muslim feminist thinkers in the USA and elsewhere are encouraging and empowering their fellow activists in the Middle East, Indonesia, and Africa. It now looks as if there will be no turning back.

CONVERSION TO ISLAM

Conversions are occurring right across the Western world. For example, there is a steady stream of women converting to Islam in Britain. The conversion of Lauren Booth, the sister-in-law of the former prime minister Tony Blair, was greeted in the media with derision and contempt. She responded vigorously, criticizing herself for her own previous condescending attitude to Muslim women, whom she presumed would be "little more than black-robed blobs." She added that the reality of life in the Middle East revealed "a lot of women of all ages, in all manner of head coverings, who also held positions of power."[42]

A report from 2013 about British converts to Islam indicates that there are more females than males in this increasingly large group. Why do women today convert to Islam? Some say that they are seeking a new kind of spiritual life. Others experience feelings of increased self-confidence and empowerment as a result of wearing hijab. This is the very opposite of the usual way in which such a practice is perceived.[43]

MUSLIM WOMEN IN THE ARAB SPRING

Women have already played a huge part in the epoch-making events of the **Arab Spring**—the democratic protests that have spread across the Middle East since 2011—and they continue to do so, bringing great changes to the lives of people in the region. Their participation is obvious to the rest of the world by their presence in pictures of demonstrations and protests that are sent across the world on television and on the Internet. Whether they are in Tunisia, Egypt, Algeria, or elsewhere in the Arab world, women are visible, often in the front row, waving flags and shouting slogans. They protest, they blog, they go on hunger strikes, they speak publicly. In Tunisia, for example, the voice of the sister of Mohamed Bouazizi, whose suicide sparked off the Tunisian uprising, is still heard in the media demanding political rights for all. Such militant women have sometimes paid a heavy price for their militancy—rape,

Women on the march. Demonstration against the government of President Mubarak in Tahrir Square, Cairo, February 5, 2011. A passionate unity of political purpose makes differences in dress code irrelevant. Women from all sectors of society—the middle-aged as well as the young—took to the streets and played a key role in toppling the Mubarak regime.

harassment, arrests, and death at the hands of men, including the police. Muslim women will undoubtedly figure largely in the future path their countries will take. They will aim to become full members of their societies. They have already opened the door, and, at last, a brighter future beckons.

SELECTED READING

Ahmed, Leila, *Women and Gender in Islam: Historical Roots of a Modern Debate*, New Haven, CT: Yale University Press, 1999

Haddad, Yvonne, Jane I. Smith and Kathleen Moore, *Muslim Women in America: Gender, Islam, and Society*, New York: Oxford University Press, 2006

Booth, Marilyn (ed.), *Harem Histories: Envisioning Places and Living Spaces*, Durham, NC: Duke University Press, 2010

Keddie, Nikki R. and Beth Baron, *Women in Middle Eastern History: Shifting Boundaries in Sex and Gender*, New Haven, CT: Yale University Press, 1992

Wadud, Amina, *Qur'an and Woman: Rereading the Sacred Text from a Woman's Perspective*, New York and Oxford: Oxford University Press, 1999

▌▌TOMORROW

Muslims and Christians together make up well over half of the world's population. Without peace and justice between these two religious communities, there can be no meaningful peace in the world. The future of the world depends on peace between Muslims and Christians.

THE ROYAL AAL AL-BAYT INSTITUTE FOR ISLAMIC THOUGHT, JORDAN, 2007[1]

Prophecies of the future are apt to look foolish or inane in the harsh light of hindsight. So this chapter will try to avoid prophecy, and also polemic. Instead, it will focus on the kinds of problems that face **Muslims** at present. Clearly the future of our world will be affected by how these problems are met, so it will occasionally speculate about that future. These problems include the need for women to play a more important role in society; the lack of visibility of widely respected Muslim spokespeople in the media; terrorism in the name of **Islam**; the volatile mix of politics and religion in Muslim-majority countries; the impact of changes in society, such as social media and the ambitions and ideals of young people; the need for good governments that enjoy a wide measure of popular support manifested through free elections; and the changes that the faith is likely to undergo in the foreseeable future.

The preceding chapters of this book have explored the origins and practice of key aspects of Muslim beliefs and the ways in which Muslims have adapted their faith to historical changes and developments over the last fourteen centuries since the death of the Prophet **Muhammad**. I have tried to highlight the essential beliefs, doctrines, and rituals of Islam—God's revelation to His prophet manifested in the **Qur'an**, the solid foundation provided by the five **pillars of the faith** that unite the world's Muslims, and especially the annually repeated symbol of that unity, the pilgrimage, and the reassuring knowledge that they belong to a worldwide community of believers. The **mosque** serves as an easily recognizable symbol of Islamic religious worship. Islam also has a distinguished tradition of religious tolerance for other faiths.

While there are many constants in Muslim beliefs, it is hardly surprising that interpretations of certain aspects of the faith in our twenty-first-century globalized world should differ from those of seventh-century Arabia. We can trace with reasonable certainty the ways in which the faith has changed, but it is much more difficult to see clearly what the future holds for Islam and its role in all our lives, both Muslims and non-Muslims.

In considering how Muslim society stands at present and wrestles with contemporary issues, this chapter will also attempt to pinpoint some of the misunderstandings and prejudices about Islam, whether as a religion, a culture, or a society, or indeed as a combination of all three, that are widely current today amongst non-Muslims, particularly in the West. It is important to do this, for several reasons. The future of our world will be affected by how we regard each other. In addition, we can probe the nature of a complex topic by tackling popular miscomprehension and misconceptions held about it. It is disturbing to take stock of the misunderstandings about Islam. They fall into familiar patterns, and many readers of this book will have encountered some if not all of them. An obvious example is the knee-jerk reaction that associates Muslims with terrorism. A second is the uncritical assumption that Muslims form a single united community. Another is the proposition that Islam suppresses and oppresses women, more than other societies or faiths. Still others exhibit a visceral dislike of *Shari'a* law, believing that Muslim-majority societies routinely hand down such reprehensible punishments as amputation for theft and stoning for adultery. And far too often, Islam is equated with the Arab world, and in particular with the few oil-rich states, when in fact Arabs account for no more than one-fifth of the world's Muslims.

THE MANY FACES OF ISLAM

There is no single united Muslim community. This is not to deny that Muslims *en masse* share many beliefs and practices: the centrality of the Qur'an, the belief in One God, the veneration of the Prophet Muhammad, the practice of the five pillars of the faith. But a faith that stretches from Morocco to Indonesia, from northern Europe to sub-Saharan Africa, is bound to find the most varied expression. The impact of local cultures and customs affects the practice of Islam in numberless ways.[2] It is crucial to avoid mistaking the dictates of custom for those of doctrine—and many of those who purport to speak for Islam are in fact speaking only for their particular community or group within the faith. In effect, they are misrepresenting the very faith for which they claim to speak. For example, it is custom, not doctrine based on the Qur'an and on the sayings and example of the Prophet, that underlies and perpetuates such practices as the overall veil for women, let alone honor killings, female genital mutilation, or stoning. We always hear in the media about Islam, what Islam is, what Muslims do, but it is hard to exaggerate the negative impact of sweeping generalizations of this kind. The idea of there being a monolithic, united body of Muslims is also nurtured, of course, by hard-liners within Islam who wish to convey this impression to the world at large for their own political reasons. But given that there are now more than one-and-a-half billion Muslims in every part of the globe, in the Middle and Far East, South and Southeast Asia, Africa, Europe, and the Americas, it is scarcely surprising that there are many faces of Islam; and there always have been. There are conservatives and radicals, literalists and intellectuals, those who have a vision of a worldwide faith and those whose vision will not reach beyond their own familiar community.

The linguistic and ethnic nature of the major Muslim communities in Europe is very diverse. Britain's Muslims are mainly of South Asian extraction, France's Muslims have overwhelmingly come from North Africa, while Germany's Muslims are largely Turkish in origin, those of the Netherlands are of Indonesian ancestry, and there is a strong Somali presence in Sweden. And Muslim immigration to the USA over the past couple of generations also has a very varied demographic. In Europe, the emphasis is steadily shifting toward an ideal of the civic assimilation of Muslim immigrants, and such countries as Greece, Italy, and Spain are trying hard to curb fresh waves of illegal migration from Muslim lands. Early in 2011 the German chancellor, Angela Merkel, declared in a speech that multiculturalism had failed. Her words are in tune with a widely held belief that the Muslim presence challenges the liberal secular state, and indeed several European leaders have implied that the Christian tradition in Europe needs to be defended against the influence of these Muslim immigrants. The former president of France, Giscard d'Estaing, said that he never went to church but that he nevertheless believed Europe was a Christian continent. Meanwhile, secular and anti-religious thinkers argue that religious beliefs and discourse should be excluded from public life and politics and from state-funded activities. So there is a wide spectrum of opinion in Europe on the many issues associated with Muslim immigration, all this at a time of heightened security awareness after terrorist strikes in Madrid in 2004 and in London the following year.

It is, therefore, unhelpful and misleading to make generalizations about ethnic communities as diverse as this. There is another implication of this diversity: who, in this welter of traditions, ethnicities, and approaches, speaks for Islam? Non-Muslims do not know who to turn to for an authoritative statement about the Muslim attitude to the burning issues of our time. The Muslim world lacks religious leaders who are empowered to speak for more than a limited constituency of believers. The authority of an Iranian *ayatollah* does not extend beyond the **Twelver Shi'ite** community, just as the **Aga Khan** speaks only for the **Isma'ilis**. The grand mufti of Jerusalem, despite his resounding title, wields an authority that is limited to Palestine. Even the Shaykh al-Azhar in Cairo, who is the major figure at al-Azhar, the oldest university in the Muslim world, although he is widely recognized as a distinguished expert in theological issues, has no brief to be the spokesman of the world's **Sunni** Muslims at large. Spiritual leadership in the next few decades may well be found in new places, drawing probably on Muslim communities in Europe and America. The Sunni tradition follows the Prophet's well-known saying that "my community cannot err." But that community is hard to define. In Muhammad's time, things were simpler—he took the Arabian egalitarian principle into Islam. In a world of superpowers and nation states, that formula does not apply.

Observers who are not Muslims may ask, and perhaps rightly so, why Muslim leaders do not speak up more vociferously in condemnation of acts of terrorism committed in the name of Islam. And this perceived reluctance to speak out against terrorism is liable to be interpreted, especially by the media, as tacit approval of it. A major contemporary problem, then, is precisely the absence of a clearly identified figure, comparable to the pope in Christianity, who can pronounce on behalf of Muslims globally. The **caliph**—whether in **Medina**, Damascus, Baghdad, Cairo, or Istanbul—used to do just that. But the caliphate is long since dead. So who speaks for Islam today? And when figures of authority do just that, who listens? Having said that, it is easy to be critical of such diversity and of the lack of a central authority. Nobody expects the Christian communities scattered over the face of the globe to speak with one voice, whether it be that of Catholic pope, Orthodox patriarch, or Anglican archbishop. Southern Baptists or Presbyterians, Roman Catholic or Greek Orthodox believers, and the millions of Arab Christians in the Middle East, all thrive under the wide umbrella of Christianity.

The diverse nature of Islam has another important aspect to which it is worth drawing attention: about half of the world's Muslims now live in South and Southeast Asia. There is a growing recognition of the increasing global significance of the Indian subcontinent, of Southeast Asia, and especially of Indonesia, which claims to represent a quarter of a billion Muslims, making it in population terms the largest Muslim country in the world. As one of the most populous countries in the world in its own right, Indonesia has the ambition to join other upcoming global powers, such as Brazil and Russia.

This has also raised awareness of Indonesia's position within the Muslim world, leading to a greater appreciation for the role of Islam in Indonesian culture, society, and politics.

Islam cannot, then, be equated with the Arab world, as it so often is in the West. The problem is compounded in the West's eyes by the enormous wealth of a few oil-rich states, including some areas where oil is cheaper than fresh water, which excites widespread jealousy and censure in a world increasingly preoccupied with climate change, pollution, and diminishing resources. These reactions are liable to affect public attitudes to other and very different Muslim countries. The blooming of the desert in lands where that blooming is plainly unnatural offends some modern notions of sustainable growth and the need to plan for a bleak future. Should the desert be made to sprout golf courses? It is true enough that extremely ostentatious lifestyles can be observed in a few areas of the Muslim world. But the West has long been, and still is, no stranger to the flaunting of wealth. Moreover, it is precisely some of these oil-rich countries that are putting significant resources into long-term plans for exploiting solar, wind, or wave energy, as well as into developing desalination plants and fostering technology from which the planet at large will eventually benefit.

RELIGION AND POLITICS

What possibilities present themselves today from the likely interplay between religion and politics in Muslim societies in the next few generations? Much of what is traditionally viewed as the Muslim world, that is the Middle East, is undergoing a period of rapid and radical change both politically and socially, and this is bound to have its repercussions in the religious sphere too. A major area of change is demography: a runaway population explosion is in full swing all over the Middle East, where half the people in some Muslim-majority countries are under twenty-five years old. Indeed, the Egyptian census of 2006 revealed that half the population was under fifteen. The consequent unemployment problems facing the young are nothing short of dire. Disaffected, jobless young people with time on their hands and instant means of communication at their disposal can, as recent events in Egypt and elsewhere demonstrate, become flashpoints of protest, and even of rebellion and insurrection. A proportion of them have chosen radical paths in matters of religion. Poverty and a runaway boom in population make for a dangerous combination.

There is no agreement on what to call the revolutionary movements that have been happening, and still are happening, in the Arab world since 2010. People in Europe and America are calling the phenomenon the **Arab Spring**. The Arabs themselves call them the Arab revolutions. Whatever the title used, however, it is clear that something extraordinary is going on—that we are witnessing historic milestones in the countries involved. It is unlikely, too, that there will be any definitive turning back, despite the uncertainties of the situation in Syria at the time of writing, for the rejection of despotic regimes in the Arab world has moved in a steady stream across the region. Will it become a tidal wave eventually engulfing the whole of the Middle East? Whatever the future holds, it is already clear that the Arab Spring takes different forms from one country to the next, as seen, for example, in the contrasting extent of the role of the military in the changes in Egypt and Tunisia.

The role played by religion in the countries involved in the Arab Spring is unclear. It has long been the case in the Middle East that political and social agendas are couched in religious terms. Whether the new political entities that eventually emerge in Egypt, Tunisia, Libya, Syria, Yemen, Iraq, and other countries at present in turmoil will opt for so-called Islamic governments remains to be seen. Such an outcome would not be viewed as a positive one in the rest of today's secular world, where religion and state have long been separated. If justice and freedom from despotic rule for the peoples of the Arab world can be achieved, and if freedom of speech and their own forms of indigenous democracy (however that term is interpreted) can be put in place, systems like the one operating in France, in which a secular government rules society, and religion of all kinds becomes a matter of choice for individual citizens within that state, can flourish. Perhaps a pointer to the future is President Erdoğan of Turkey, whose vision is of a secular state that allows freedom of conscience and religion to its citizens. In such a situation, the Christian Copts of Egypt would be given rights of citizenship surpassing those that, as a protected minority, they generally had received under Muslim rule ever since the coming of Islam. Liberal American Muslim academics have expressed strong views on these issues. In the USA Abdullahi an-Na'im, for example, insists that Islam is radically democratic. The problem, in his view, is simply that sociologically the world of Islam is conservative. He is trying in his writings to break that mold. He insists that heresy should be celebrated: "To keep the religion honest, it is very important that somebody should take the risk of being denounced as heretical."[3] He argues that his liberal reading of Islam is closer to the roots of the faith than are the interpretations of the **theocrats**.

TERRORISM AND VIOLENCE

The horrific events of September 11, 2001, known globally as 9/11 and regarded as the worst crime in American history, will not be forgotten for many generations to come. The bombers who perpetrated those awful acts have done considerable harm to the reputation of Islam around the world. Although **Usama bin Laden** (1957–2011) is dead, he casts his shadow from the grave. The movement known as **al-Qa'ida**, and other spin-off groups that are modeled on it, continue to pose a serious threat in many countries, from Morocco, Algeria, and Mali to the Philippines. 9/11 triggered an immense backlash of fury directed by the West at the Muslim world at large. This fury was compounded by ignorance and incomprehension, and its ramifications have been incalculable. Security checks and precautions, imposed in places of work and leisure, from offices to museums to airports, have invaded and impoverished the lives of ordinary citizens around the world to a degree that would have been hard to imagine a generation ago. Muslims everywhere have suffered as a result. Too often, much public opinion in the West has tended to tar all Muslims with the same brush, and to equate terrorism not with a tiny minority of highly radicalized people but with the entire Islamic community. The only escape from such widespread and unjust stereotyping is by way of better knowledge, although this knowledge—to which this book is intended as a modest contribution—is slow to percolate into the public consciousness. In Britain, for example, the prominent Muslim academic Tim Winter—also known as 'Abd al-Hakim Murad—has spoken out, distancing Islam from terrorist activity. He asks how the 9/11 bombers could possibly be viewed as Muslims. He stresses that neither bin Laden nor his associate, Ayman al-Zawahiri, possessed proper Muslim religious credentials and that they were not qualified to deliver *fatwa*s and to call for *jihad*. In his view, "the West must drain the swamp of rage by securing a fair resolution of the Palestinian tragedy. But it is the responsibility of the Islamic world to defeat the terrorist aberration theologically."[4]

According to a poll conducted in 2007 by Georgetown University in Washington, D.C., 93 percent of the world's Muslims denounced religiously inspired violence. Further details are available in several more Gallup and Pew polls. These Muslims are seen as the silent majority, perhaps because they genuinely do not have a voice. But it is often the case that their voice is not picked up in the Western media, because it is heard in languages other than English and if it is understood, it is not deemed to be newsworthy. Negative news is more "interesting" than positive news. So it is the radicalized, fundamentalist 7 percent, those who regard the 9/11 attacks as justified, who grab the headlines and who incessantly claim to speak for Islam.[5] And if the statistic just quoted is accurate, there are some 100 million of them. Yet America's Muslims, when asked what they admire least about Muslim societies today, put extremism and terrorism at the top of the list. And we should note that the victims of most Muslim terrorism are not the people of the West, as the media would frequently encourage us to believe, but fellow Muslims.

So what makes the 100 million radicalized Muslims believe what they believe and do what they do? What exactly is radical or fundamentalist Islam? This is, of course, a very difficult subject, all the more so as we are right in the middle of the problem. In fifty years' time many things may be clearer than they are now. No figures are available for what the vast majority of Muslims think about these issues, but it is a reasonable assumption that most of them also denounce violence. Thus a few terrorists wearing the mask of religion have trumped the hundreds of millions of faithful, undemonstrative believers. If public opinion in the West is to change, this situation has to be rectified. The voice of moderation and tolerance has to be heard, especially in view of the sharp increase in the persecution of religious minorities in several Muslim countries in the last couple of decades, which is a stain on a long and distinguished tradition of religious tolerance in the Muslim world. It is the responsibility of the worldwide Muslim community to make sure that the voice of the majority expresses itself, loudly, clearly, and quickly. That community must help itself. A good beginning might be if the leaders of the world's most populous Muslim countries—Indonesia, India, Pakistan, Bangladesh, Nigeria—started to speak out. This would help to rectify the low profile of these under-valued areas of the Muslim world.

SOCIAL CHANGE

Events in the last few decades have underlined the crucial role played in regime change by new methods of communication. This has been especially important in countries where the flow of information was controlled by the state. Thus in Iran in 1979, cassette tapes of speeches by **Ayatollah Khomeini** (1902–1989) circulated in secret and proved a key agent of change in the revolution that toppled the shah. Similarly, in 1989–90, when the Communist Party in the Soviet Union was in its death throes and free communication with the outside world was largely blocked, the fax machine became the indispensable means of sharing information, and thus contributed to the collapse of communism and Boris Yeltsin's ascent to power. So too social media—the cell phone, Facebook, YouTube, and Twitter—have been of crucial importance in mobilizing public opinion and decisive action in the countries that have so far experienced the Arab Spring. More countries will follow, and the same means will be employed to hasten regime change. A new generation of cyber-savvy and media-savvy Muslims is growing up—whether in Tunisia, Tahrir Square in Cairo, Libya, or Yemen—and the revolutions in which they have participated have often had a strong Islamist element. The social media they employed to such great effect are no respecters of ideology. They lend themselves with equal ease to the spread of fundamentalist Islam, nationalism, and the radical left. Indeed, the Internet has seen much polemical discussion between **Salafis** and Twelver Shi'ites; so while it can foster a community spirit, it can also exacerbate discord.

If events in the years of the Arab Spring so far indicate anything, it is that many Muslims living in the Middle East are not looking for a militantly Islamic route to realize their ambitions. They want jobs, they want a better lifestyle, they want a fairer division of resources, they want an end to corruption, and they yearn for stability and, above all, social justice. And as the population explosion gathers yet further momentum, these aspirations will become more intense. What seems clear already is that change will come, but it will take time. When it does come, it will come from the grass roots up, not imposed from the top down. And it will come from within and not from outside the Muslim world.

The treatment of women and the workings of the law in Muslim societies have been discussed in the relevant chapters in this book. In both of these areas of social life, too, the trajectory of change is unmistakable. Naturally the pace of that change differs from one country to the next. Indonesia, Pakistan, Bangladesh, and Turkey have all had female heads of state (contrast the USA, where even a female vice-president has yet to be elected), while in Saudi Arabia women are only now poised to get the vote. In many Muslim countries female politicians now hold ministerial office; universities are no longer the province of men (indeed, there are many female-only universities of high calibre in Saudi Arabia, as well as the first mixed-gender university there); and the number of women holding high office in business and commerce is expanding all the time. In rural areas, the pace of change is much slower, but even here the impact of education is steadily making itself felt. None of this is to deny that there are many areas, and not only in the countryside, where the plight of women is still lamentable. But it will become increasingly hard to isolate such women from the knowledge of what is going on elsewhere in the Muslim world. Similarly, it is certain that women will increasingly make their presence felt in matters of faith, even to the extent of leading the Friday prayer, paralleling later twentieth-century developments in the leadership roles of women in Judaism and Christianity, such as the ordination of women priests.

As for the practice of law, here too the cumulative evidence of many Muslim societies makes it abundantly clear that, while the legal system comprises a mixture of secular and Shariʻa elements, the secular code is the dominant one, and this trend is set to continue. This secular code, moreover, far from being devised from scratch, owes much to Western models. In the minority of countries where the authority of Shariʻa law is much stronger, lawmakers are confronted with an ever-increasing number of problematic issues—stem-cell research, genetically enhanced crops, copyright provisions, in vitro fertilization—which cannot be tackled using well-rehearsed Islamic legal techniques, such as analogy. These have in any case long since been shown to be of limited use in determining the legality of drinking coffee, smoking tobacco, or taking recreational drugs—some of the challenges to the legal system that emerged in the early modern period. The foundations of Shariʻa law have traditionally been the Qurʼan, together with the words and the practice of the Prophet Muhammad, and these cannot easily be adapted to deal with the minutiae of modern life, from parking regulations to corporation tax. This is not to deny the possibility of distinctively Islamic responses to problems facing the rest of the world, but such responses are formulated piecemeal and may well differ from one part of the Muslim world to another. Thus the question of how the role of the Qurʼan should be defined in any problem that is of the twenty-first century, rather than for all time, remains contested.

Moreover, while there are indeed areas in the Muslim world in which severe penalties, such as flogging and even amputation, are known, they are very much the exception, so that the much-simplified popular image of Muslim societies fossilized in medieval legal systems is very far from the truth. Nor should recent examples of the persecution of Christians, as in Egypt and Iraq, airbrush out the powerful tradition of religious tolerance—a much prouder tradition than Christianity can point to—enshrined in Islamic law but also manifested in standard Muslim practice over the centuries, for instance in Yemen, Iran, and Central Asia.

MUSLIMS AND NON-MUSLIMS

What is the future of the relations between Muslims and non-Muslims? This is a perennially vexed question. The former colonial powers, especially Britain and France, have left an ambiguous legacy across all of North Africa and much of the Middle East, as well as in South and Southeast Asia. Italian adventures in Africa, and the Dutch presence in Indonesia, are also remembered. Western countries have recently waged war in Iraq and Afghanistan, although they have also intervened to halt the genocide of Muslims in the Balkans, albeit a little late in the day. The West armed **Saddam Husayn** (1937–2006), and helped the **Taliban** and al-Qa'ida to fight the Soviet takeover of Afghanistan; yet both those countries were eventually invaded by Western troops. The relationship between America and Iran has been in a state of simmering tension for more than three decades, and Iran's march to nuclear power foreshadows further crises. But by far the most serious issue is the sustained American involvement in the Israeli–Palestinian conflict, still unresolved after more than sixty years. Whatever the ups and downs of diplomacy and power-plays between the Arab countries, their populations are solidly on the Palestinian side, and this basic groundswell of popular support, accompanied by a corresponding furious resentment against the United States, needs to be taken into account by American foreign policy makers. Palestine is an issue that simply will not go away. These, then, remain matters that disturb even many moderate Muslims and that have the potential to stir up violent reactions in extremist Muslim circles.

Finally, the dynamic nature of the faith needs to be stressed. Islam is currently the fastest-growing major faith in the world. In sub-Saharan Africa, for example, it challenges Christianity almost everywhere. And not just in Africa, for many of its converts are, unexpectedly, highly educated and articulate Westerners who have confounded the expectations of their friends and families to make a solid commitment to Islam. These citizens of a secular, postmodern Europe are attracted to this vibrant, confident religion, which is making such rapid strides in gaining new adherents. As a London newspaper article describes them: "They're People Like Us, only they're not. They're Muslims. They pray five times a day, fast during Ramadan and hope to go to Mecca before they die. They answer their mobiles with 'salaam alaikum'."[6] Such European Muslims will be well placed to work toward defining an Islam compatible with democracy and gender equality.

One symptom is symbolic of this ever-changing picture: the new importance allotted to the English language. We now live in an increasingly borderless world where the international language of choice is English. Fatwas are now written as much in English as in Arabic. The role of the Internet is crucial here, for it fosters the use of English to access key texts of the faith, such as Qur'an translations, *hadith* collections, and the precepts of the Shari'a, all previously available only in Arabic and in major libraries. This hugely increased access to the texts that are foundational for the faith will generate a flood of informed discussion, with Google and Wikipedia providing instant answers to frequently asked questions to do with Muslim behavior, doctrine, and belief. Attitudes to the faith will therefore not stand still. Perhaps Islam will be affected in a similar way to that in which textual scholarship on the Bible from the 1860s onward by German theologians—who, led by their intellects, challenged long-established "truths"—decisively changed the way Christianity was understood. This book is being published in the early fifteenth century of the Islamic calendar; it is worth remembering that Christianity in its own fifteenth century wore a very different face from the one it wears today. And that was before the sixteenth- and seventeenth-century wars of religion had degraded Europe and defaced Christianity. Even more recently—only a couple of generations away from living memory—the issue of slavery convulsed the United States in a catastrophic civil war. Although this conflict is not obviously equivalent to any situation in the present-day Muslim world, it too generated ferocious religious controversy. The current tribulations of the Muslim world, then, have some striking parallels in the Christian West. Who knows where they will end? In any event, given the long perspective of history, it is not for the West to sit in judgment over such crises.

So what course will Islam chart in the future? The options are bewilderingly diverse. Some Muslims believe that religion should be a personal spiritual matter. Others believe with equal fervor that Islam should govern life in all its variety, in the public and personal spheres and in the workplace. In the last few decades it has become plain that we live in a world that, in the matter of religion, has become increasingly pluralistic. That calls for a broad-minded attitude to other faiths on the part of all, believers and non-believers alike, and an end to exclusivism. Will Islam be reduced to a personal belief system largely bereft of its political, social, and legal institutions and subservient to secular, pluralist, societies? Or will the Muslim masses finally be aroused and turn again to military conflict? Or will some modernist yet Islamic solution be found in which Islam, as a political and social force, adapts to the modern world? Only time will tell.

NOTES

1 INTRODUCTION pp. 17–22

[1] M. K. Gandhi (ed. Anand A. T. Hingorani), *All Religions Are True* (Bombay: Bharatiya Vidya Bhavan), 1962, p. 2.

2 MUHAMMAD pp. 23–57

[1] In the same way, in the Old Testament (Joshua 6:3) God commands the Children of Israel to march round the city of Jericho seven times a day for seven days.

[2] The old name for Ethiopia.

[3] The exact date of this event is not known; all that is known is the Muslim year in which it took place. The Muslim year is lunar and has only 360 days, thus it often straddles two Christian years. It is the convention to give both Christian years in which this event could have taken place.

[4] Al-Azraqi, *Akhbar Makkah* (Beirut, n. d.), p. 165.

[5] Richard Bell, *The Qur'an Translated with a Critical Re-Arrangement of the Surahs*, 2 vols. (Edinburgh: T. & T. Clark), 1937.

[6] See Robert Hoyland, *Seeing Islam as Others Saw It: A Survey and Evaluation of Christian, Jewish and Zoroastrian Writings on Islam* (Princeton, NJ: The Darwin Press, Inc.), 1997, pp. 124–31.

[7] Hoyland, *Seeing Islam*, p. 129.

[8] Ibid., p. 413.

[9] See Daniel J. Sahas, *John of Damascus on Islam: the "Heresy of the Ishmaelites"* (Leiden: Brill), 1972, pp. 142–49; also see Hoyland, *Seeing Islam*, pp. 485–86.

[10] Michael Cook, *Muhammad* (Oxford and New York: Oxford University Press), 1983, p. 74.

[11] The grave belongs to a person named 'Abd al-Rahman b. Khayr (Museum of Islamic Art, Cairo, object no. 1508/20).

[12] Quoted in Andrew Rippin, *Muslims: Their Religious Beliefs and Practices, Volume 1: The Formative Period* (London: Routledge), 1990, p. 43.

[13] See, for example, the balanced comments of Paul Brians, "Notes on Salman Rushdie, *The Satanic Verses* (1988)," *Home Page of Paul Brians* (n. d.), http://public.wsu.edu/~brians/anglophone/satanic_verses/

[14] Ian Richard Netton, *Text and Trauma: An East–West Primer* (London: Routledge), 1996, p. 22.

[15] Shahab Ahmed, "Satanic Verses," in Jane Dammen McAuliffe (ed.), *Encyclopedia of the Qur'an* (Leiden: Brill), 2002, vol. 4, p. 531.

[16] John L. Esposito and Dalia Mogahed, *Who Speaks For Islam? What A Billion Muslims Really Think* (New York: Gallup Press), 2008, p. 97.

[17] The Times, February 2006.

[18] See Sahas, *John of Damascus on Islam*, p. 73.

[19] Dante Alighieri, *Inferno*, Canto 28, verses 30–31.

3 QUR'AN pp. 58–88

[1] All quotations are from the Qur'an unless otherwise specified.

[2] Sahar El-Nadi, *Sandcastles and Snowmen: A Personal Search for Spirituality* (San Clemente, CA: FB Publishing), 2013, p. 54.

[3] Pope Pius XII, "*Divino Afflante Spiritu*," (Given on September 30, 1943) *The Holy See* (n. d.), http://www.vatican.va/holy_father/pius_xii/encyclicals/documents/hf_p-xii_enc_30091943_divino-afflante-spiritu_en.html

[4] The Pew Research Center reports 1.6 billion: Drew DeSilver, "World's Muslim population more widespread than you might think," *Pew Research Center* (June 7, 2013), http://www.pewresearch.org/fact-tank/2013/06/07/worlds-muslim-population-more-widespread-than-you-might-think/

[5] Carl W. Ernst, *How to Read the Qur'an: A New Guide, with Select Translations* (Edinburgh: Edinburgh University Press), 2011, p. 38. Ernst also explains that the Christian Letter of St. Paul and the Jewish Mishnah are arranged in the same way.

[6] The translation of this line is based on the wording of Marmaduke Pickthall in *The Meaning of the Glorious Koran: An Explanatory Translation* (London: Allen & Unwin), 1957, p. 659.

[7] Pickthall, *The Meaning of the Glorious Koran*, p. 119.

[8] A. J. Arberry, *The Koran Interpreted* (London: Oxford University Press), 1964, x.

[9] See also Qur'an 81:1–14.

[10] This refrain occurs thirty-one times in the chapter.

[11] John L. Esposito, *What Everyone Needs to Know about Islam* (Oxford and New York: Oxford University Press), 2011, p. 35.

[12] The Qur'an uses the words *nabi* (prophet) and *rasul* (messenger or apostle) without explaining any difference in meaning between them. Whilst these words can be used interchangeably, or may even be used to refer to the same person, classical Muslim Qur'anic commentators have argued that *rasul* stands for a prophet who brings a scripture to his people (for example: Abraham, Moses, and Jesus), whilst *nabi* refers to prophets in general.

[13] Some Western scholars of Islamic studies view the concept of the pre-Islamic *hanif* as a retrospective projection; others find it more credible: see Urin Rabin, "*hanif*," in McAuliffe (ed.), *Encyclopedia of the Qur'an*, vol. 4, pp. 402–3.

[14] Qur'an 12:28.

[15] See Brannon Wheeler, *Moses in the Qur'an and Islamic Exegesis* (London: Bloomsbury Academic), 2002.

[16] See also Jesus's words in John 2:31: "Our fathers did eat manna in the desert; as it is written, He gave them bread from heaven to eat."

17 Mary is discussed in this section for simplicity's sake, although she was not, of course, a prophet.

18 In the Qur'an Jesus is referred to simply as Mary's son; he has no earthly father. Arab patrilineal custom, however, emphasizes the name of the child's father (for example, Ahmad b. 'Ali means Ahmad son of 'Ali).

19 In Chapter 3 of the Qur'an it is the angels who come to Mary (3:42–45).

20 Standing up to give birth was a very common practice in the Middle East.

21 Al-Masih (the "Anointed One") is used eleven times to denote Jesus. Rippin concludes that this word in connection with Jesus is understood as a proper name or a title of honor: Andrew Rippin, "Anointing," in McAuliffe (ed.), *Encyclopedia of the Qur'an*, vol. 1, pp. 102–3.

22 See the Apocryphal Gospel of Thomas for a similar story.

23 M. A. S. Abdel Haleem, *The Qur'an, A New Translation by M. A. S. Abdel Haleem* (Oxford: Oxford University Press), 2004, p. 37, note b, citing the medieval Muslim scholar al-Razi.

24 See St John's Gospel (1:1) and Revelation (19:13): "His name is called the Word of God."

25 This viewpoint was shared by the followers of Docetism, an early Christian sect.

26 See the excellent analysis entitled "A Sketch of the Qur'anic Jesus," in Tarif Khalidi, *The Muslim Jesus* (Cambridge, MA: Harvard University Press), 2001, pp. 9–17.

27 Imam al-Nawawi, "*Riyad as-Salihin* (The Book of Virtues) Book 9, Hadith 16," *Sunnah.com* (n. d.), http://sunnah.com/riyadussaliheen/9

28 M. H. A. Mukhtar, "Teaching the Qur'an in Prison," in *Saudi Government Concern for the Qur'an and Qur'anic Sciences* (Riyadh), 2000, pp. 34–39.

29 Iqra Satellite TV channel, Dubai, "Horizons on the Air," October 19, 2003; *Journal of Qur'anic Studies*, 5/2, 2003, pp. 159–60.

30 Thomas Carlyle, *Heroes and Hero Worship*, part 2, *FullBooks.com* (n. d.), http://www.fullbooks.com/Heroes-and-Hero-Worship2.html

31 Al-Bukhari, *Fada'il al-Qur'an*, Bab 3.

32 AH (*anno Hegirae*, i.e. "in the year of the *hijra*") relates to the lunar Muslim calendar; AH 1 corresponds to AD 622, the year of Muhammad's *hijra* from Mecca to Medina.

33 Gerhard Böwering, "Chronology and the Qur'an," in McAuliffe (ed.), *Encyclopedia of the Qur'an*, vol. 1, p. 331.

34 John Wansbrough, *Qur'anic Studies: Sources and Methods of Scriptural Interpretation* (Oxford: Oxford University Press), 1977; John Wansbrough, *The Sectarian Milieu: Content and Composition of Islamic Salvation History* (Oxford and New York: Oxford University Press), 1978.

35 For an extended discussion of Nasr Hamid Abu Zayd, see Michael Cook, *The Koran: A Very Short Introduction* (Oxford: Oxford University Press), 2000, pp. 45–47.

36 Arberry, *The Koran Interpreted*, IX.

37 Pickthall, *The Meaning of the Glorious Koran*, VII.

38 Ibid., VII.

39 For a detailed scholarly discussion of Qur'anic translations, see Hartmut Bobzin, "Translations of the Qur'an," in McAuliffe (ed.), *Encyclopedia of the Qur'an*, vol. 5, pp. 340–58.

40 Arberry, *The Koran Interpreted*, VII.

41 George Sale, *The Koran Commonly Called the Alkoran of Mohammed* (London and New York: Frederick Warne and Co.), 1892, v. Sale's translation was first published in 1734, but the first actual translation of the Qur'an into English predated his version. It was the work of Alexander Ross, and is dated 1649. Ross knew no Arabic; he translated a French translation of the Qur'an produced in 1647 by Sieur du Ryer.

42 Frithhof Schuon, *Understanding Islam* (London: Allen & Unwin), 1963, p. 61.

43 Pickthall, *The Meaning of the Glorious Koran*, VII.

4 FAITH pp. 89–113

1 Giles Whittell, "Allah came knocking at my heart," *The Times*, January 7, 2000.

2 At certain times in the history of Islam some Muslim scholars have included *jihad* (see Chapter 9) among the pillars of the faith, calling it the "sixth pillar." This key tenet of the faith has not, however, become fixed in Muslim consciousness as a pillar.

3 Al-Ghazali (trans. Muhtar Holland), *Inner Dimensions of Islamic Worship* (Leicester: The Islamic Foundation), 1983, p. 82. This book translates a part of the *Revival of the Sciences of Religion* by al-Ghazali.

4 In much the same concise way, Jesus, recalling Deuteronomy 6:5 and Leviticus 19:18, presents the essentials of faith in the following words: "'Love the Lord your God with all your heart and with all your soul and with all your mind.' This is the first and greatest commandment. And the second is similar: 'Love your neighbor as yourself'" (Matthew 22:37–39).

5 As quoted in W. Montgomery Watt, *Islamic Creeds* (Edinburgh: Edinburgh University Press), 1994, p. 73.

6 Watt, *Creeds*, p. 77.

7 Ibid., p. 95.

8 Ibid., p. 90.

9 Other unclean bodily functions are ejaculation without intercourse; bloodletting; and contact with a corpse.

10 See Leviticus 15:19–33.

11 This last requirement is reminiscent of the Christian ceremony of the churching of women, which also takes place forty days after giving birth. At this ceremony—which was common within living memory (and still exists in some places) in both Western and Eastern Christianity—thanks are given to God for the mother's recovery from childbirth. This ritual was probably inherited from the Jewish practice, mentioned in the Bible in Leviticus 12:2–8, that stipulates that women should be purified forty days after giving birth.

12 Qur'an 4:43 and 5:6.

13 W. M. Watt, *The Faith and Practice of al-Ghazali* (London, Allen & Unwin), 1953, p. 97. See also al-Ghazali, *Inner Dimensions*.

14 This is a grey area in Islamic law, as the opinion of the various legal schools varies. According to the Shafi'i legal school, for example, older women are tolerated at the Friday noon prayer but younger women are not. In cases where men and women pray together, adult males are stationed in front of pre-adult males, and women behind the latter.

15 The number of men required for a quorum at the Friday prayer in the mosque varies according to individual legal schools, ranging from forty to only three.

16 See, for example, al Bukhari, *Al-Sahih*, Book 24, no. 486: "Allah's Apostle said, 'Whoever is made wealthy by Allah and does not pay the zakat of his wealth, then on the Day of Resurrection his wealth will be made like a bald-headed poisonous male snake with two black spots over the eyes. The snake will encircle his neck and bite his cheeks and say, "I am your wealth, I am your treasure.""

17 Heinz Halm (trans. Janet Watson and Marion Hill), *Shi'ism* (Edinburgh: Edinburgh University Press), 2004, pp. 100–101, 115.

18 Al-Azhar Al-Sharif (trans. N. Saad), "Fatwa on Fasting in North Pole Regions," *Mission Al Noor* (November 21, 2010), http://mission-alnoor.org/ Admin/asp/Mailed_details.asp?M_ID=821

19 A different version of the appearance of the water is given in Genesis 21:19: "And God opened her (Hagar's) eyes, and she saw a well of water; and she went, and filled the bottle with water, and gave the lad drink."

20 Al-Ghazali, *Inner Dimensions*, p. 109.

21 H. A. R. Gibb, *The Travels of Ibn Battuta A.D. 1325–1354* (New Delhi: Munshiram Manoharlal Publishers, Pvt Ltd.), 1999, vol. 1, p. 8.

22 Nahid Hiermandi quoted in S. Akhter, "Word on the Street: 'How was your experience with Hajj/ Umrah like?'," *Muslim Voice* (n. d.), http://www. azmuslimvoice.info/index.php?option=com_ content&view=article&id=691:word-on-the-streethow-was-your-experience-with-hajjumrah-like&catid=27:community&Itemid=29

5 LAW pp. 114–137

1 Quoted in Michael Gryboski, "Kansas Anti-Sharia Bill Awaits Governor's Signature," *Christian Post* (May 17, 2012), http://www.christianpost.com/ news/kansas-anti-sharia-bill-awaits-governors-signature-75136/

2 Seyyed Hossein Nasr, *Ideals and Realities of Islam* (Boston, MA: George Allen & Unwin), revised edition, 1975, p. 93.

3 For example, Acts 9:2.

4 Matthew 22:21.

5 See Wael B. Hallaq, "Law and the Qur'an," in McAuliffe (ed.), *Encyclopedia of the Qur'an*, vol. 3, pp. 149–50.

6 Quoted in J. A. Williams, *Themes of Islamic Civilization* (Berkeley and Los Angeles, CA: University of California Press), 1971, p. 31.

7 Four other *hadith* collections are also important: those of Abu Da'ud (817–889), al-Tirmidhi (824–892), al-Nasa'i (c. 829–915), and Ibn Majah (824–887).

8 Rippin, *Muslims*, p. 75.

9 Nizam al-Mulk (trans. Hubert Darke), *The Book of Government or Rules for Kings* (Boston, MA and London: Kegan Paul and Routledge), 1960, p. 13.

10 Edward William Lane, *An Arabic-English Lexicon*, part 1 (Beirut: Librairie du Liban), 1980, p. 2429.

11 A. Kevin Reinhart, "Islamic Law as Islamic Ethics," *The Journal of Religious Ethics*, vol. 11, no. 2, Fall, 1983, pp. 186–87.

12 See Marshall G. S. Hodgson, *The Venture of Islam: Conscience and History in a World Civilization, Vol. 1: The Classical Age of Islam* (Chicago, IL: The University of Chicago Press), 1974, p. 252: Lane, *Lexicon*, part 1, p. 1438.

13 Ibn Khaldun (trans. Franz Rosenthal), *The Muqaddimah* (Princeton, NJ: Princeton University Press), 1980, vol. 2, pp. 436–38.

14 Majid Khadduri (trans. Majid Khadduri), *Al-Imam Muhammad Ibn Idris al-Shafi'i's al-Risala fi usul al-fiqh. Treatise on the Foundations of Islamic Jurisprudence* (Cambridge: The Islamic Texts Society), 1997, pp. 35–37.

15 Views differed on the definition of consensus. For some it meant the consensus of the whole Muslim community, whilst for others it was the consensus of religious scholars. For example, the doctrine of al-Shafi'i developed in his writings; it began as the consensus of a few scholars in a given locality and became a concept that comprised the whole community: see J. Schacht, *Origins of Muhammadan Jurisprudence* (Oxford: Oxford University Press), 1950, p. 88; Khadduri, *Risala*, p. 37.

16 For example, Qur'an 5:90.

17 For a more detailed analysis of all these terms, see Reinhart, "Islamic Law as Islamic Ethics," p. 195.

18 See Wael B. Hallaq, "Was the Gate of Ijtihad

Closed?," *International Journal of Middle East Studies* 16/1, March 1984, pp. 3–41; Wael B. Hallaq, *The Origins and Evolution of Islamic Law* (Cambridge: Cambridge University Press), 2005, pp. 146–47.

19 Hallaq, *Origins*, pp. 202–3.

20 Wael B. Hallaq, *Shari'a. Theory, Practice, Transformations* (Cambridge: Cambridge University Press), 2009, p. 273.

21 Colin Imber, *Ebu's-Su'ud. The Islamic Legal Tradition* (Stanford: Stanford University Press), 1997, p. 38.

22 Carole Hillenbrand, "al-Mustansir," in P. Bearman et al (eds.), *Encyclopaedia of Islam, Brill Online* (2012), http://referenceworks.brillonline.com/entries/encyclopaedia-of-islam-2/al-mustansir-SIM_5627?s.num=682&s.rows=100&s.start=600

23 Thomas Raff, *An Anti-Mongol Fatwa of Ibn Taimiya* (Leiden: Brill), 1973.

24 Ralph S. Hattox, *Coffee and Coffeehouses: The Origins of a Social Beverage in the Medieval Near East* (Seattle, WA: University of Washington Press), 2000.

25 J. B. Hava, *Al-fara'id Arabic-English Dictionary* (Beirut: Dar al-mashriq), 1987, p. 113.

26 For example, Leviticus 20:10–14, 27.

27 R Peters, "*zina* or *zina*'," in P. Bearman et al (eds.), *Encyclopaedia of Islam, Brill Online* (2012), http://referenceworks.brillonline.com/entries/encyclopaedia-of-islam-2/zina-or-zina-SIM_8168?s.num=8&s.f.s2_parent=s.f.cluster.Encyclopaedia+of+Islam&s.q=stoning+

28 For example, al-Bukhari, Book 56, hadith 829; Book 60, hadith 79; Book 78, hadith 629; Book 82, hadith 809; Malik, *Muwatta', Kitab al-hudud*, p. 349: www.searchtruth.com/searchHadith.php/

29 Joseph Schacht, "*zina*'," in M. Th. Houtsma et al (eds.), *Encyclopedia of Islam*, first edition (1913–36) and online at *Encyclopedia of Islam, Brill Online* (2012), http://referenceworks.brillonline.com/entries/encyclopaedia-of-islam-1/zina-SIM_6097?s.num=2

30 n. a., "Current Issues: Stoning," *WISE Muslim Women* (n. d.), http://www.wisemuslimwomen.org/currentissues/stoning/

31 According to Ziba Mir-Hosseini, a specialist on Iranian family law, "it is no accident that stoning has increased in Iran in the midst of political unrest." Quoted in n. a., "Current Issues: Stoning," *WISE Muslim Women* (n. d.), http://www.wisemuslimwomen.org/currentissues/stoning/

32 Imber, *Ebu's-Su'ud*, 1997, p. 272.

33 Ebrahim Moosa, "Colonialism and Islamic Law," in Muhammad Khalid Masud, Armando Salvatore, and Martin Bruinessen (eds.), *Islam and Modernity. Key Issues and Debates* (Edinburgh: Edinburgh University Press), 2009, p. 158.

34 Ebrahim Moosa, "Colonialism and Islamic Law," p. 166; Jörg Fisch, *Cheap Lives and Dear Limbs: the British Transformation of the Bengal Criminal Law, 1769–1817* (Wiesbaden: Franz Steiner), 1983, p. 53.

35 Malcolm H. Kerr, "Muhammad 'Abduh," in *Encyclopaedia Britannica Online* (2014), http://www.britannica.com/EBchecked/topic/892/Muhammad-Abduh

36 Albert Hourani, *A History of the Arab Peoples* (Cambridge, MA: Harvard University Press), 1991, pp. 345–46.

37 John L. Esposito and John J. Donohue (eds.), *Islam in Transition: Muslim Perspectives* (New York: Oxford University Press), 1982, pp. 181–82.

38 Sobhi Mahmassani, "Muslims: Decadence and Renaissance: Adaptation of Islamic Jurisprudence to Modern Social Needs," *The Muslim World* 44, 1954, p. 201.

39 Esposito and Donohue, *Islam in Transition*, p. 182.

40 A. A. A. Fyzee, *A Modern Approach to Islam* (Oxford and New York: Oxford University Press), 1963, p. 112.

41 L. Ali Khan and Hisham M. Ramadan, *Contemporary Ijtihad: Limits and Controversies* (Edinburgh: Edinburgh University Press), 2011, pp. 65–67.

42 Maleiha Malik, *Minority Legal Orders in the UK* (London: British Academy), 2012, p. 10; Shaykh Muhammad Taqi Usmani, "Islamic Investments: Shari'ah Principles Behind Them," *Islamic Mortgages* (n. d.), http://www.islamicmortgages.co.uk/index.php?id=276

43 Timur Kuran, *Islam and Mammon: The Economic Predicaments of Islamism* (Princeton, NJ: Princeton University Press), 2005, pp. 596–97.

44 Andrew Marr, *A History of Modern Britain* (London: Macmillan), 2007, p. 601.

45 Center for Security Policy, *Shariah Law and American Courts: An Assessment of State Appellate Court Cases*, The Occasional Papers Series, Washington D. C., May 20, 2011, p. 8.

46 Ibid., pp. 12–13.

47 Ibid., p. 16.

48 Ibid., p. 17; see also: Ketron, *Senate Bill* 1028 (2011), www.capitol.tn.gov/Bills/107/Bill/SB1028.pdf

49 Rowan Williams, quoted in n. a., "Sharia law in UK is 'unavoidable'," *BBC News* (February 7, 2008), http://news.bbc.co.uk/go/pr/fr/-/1/hi/uk/7232661.stm

50 Nick Tarry, "Religious courts already in use," *BBC News* (February 7, 2008), http://news.bbc.co.uk/go/pr/fr/-/1/hi/uk/7233040.stm

51 Malik, *Minority Legal Orders*, 2012.

52 Fazlur Rahman, *Islam* (London: Weidenfeld & Nicolson), 1966, p. 256.

53 Mohammed H. Kamali, "Shari'ah and the Challenge of Modernity," *Islamic University*

[54] For example: *The Kite Runner* (London: Bloomsbury Publishing), 2006; and *A Thousand Splendid Suns* (London: Bloomsbury Publishing), 2007.

[55] Najib Mahfuz, "Debate on the Application of the Shari'a in Egypt," *Al-Ahram*, May 17, 1977, translated in Esposito and Donohue (eds.), *Islam in Transition*, pp. 239–40.

[56] Kamali, "Shari'ah and the Challenge of Modernity," p. 25.

[57] Malik, *Minority Legal Orders*, pp. 4–10.

[58] Malik, *Minority Legal Orders*, p. 51.

[59] Khaled M. Abou El Fadl, "Dogs in the Islamic Tradition and Nature," in Bron Taylor (ed.), *Encyclopedia of Religion and Nature* (New York: Continuum International), 2004, also online at *Scholar of the House* (n. d.), http://www.scholarofthehouse.org/dinistrandna.html

[60] Malik, *Minority Legal Orders*, pp. 15–16.

6 DIVERSITY pp. 138–168

[1] The exact percentage of Sunni and Shi'ites is disputed. Shi'ites prefer to say that they constitute 15 percent of the world's Muslims.

[2] There are also significant numbers of Shi'ites in Lebanon, India, Pakistan, Tanzania, Yemen, and Bahrayn.

[3] Andrew Rippin, *Muslims: Their Religious Beliefs and Practices, Volume 1: The Formative Period* (London: Routledge), 1990, p. 89.

[4] It is correct to speak of the Shi'a as a group. But it is incorrect, though it is common usage nowadays in the West, to speak of the Shi'as. The correct term for them is Shi'ites or Shi'is.

[5] H. M. Balyuzi, *Muhammad and the Course of Islam* (Oxford: George Ronald), 1976, pp. 165–68; I. K. Poonawala and E. Kohlberg "Ali b. Abi Taleb," *Encyclopedia Iranica* (1982), http://www.iranicaonline.org/articles/ali-b-abi-taleb

[6] Alfred Guillaume, *The Life of Muhammad* (Karachi, Pakistan: Oxford University Press), 1980, p. 114.

[7] Halm, *Shi'ism*, pp. 12–13.

[8] Shaykh al-Mufid (trans. I. K. A. Howard), *Kitab al-irshad (The Book of Guidance)* (Horsham: The Muhammadi Trust), 1981, p. 370.

[9] Edward Gibbon, *The Decline and Fall of the Roman Empire* (Edinburgh: T. Nelson and P. Brown), 1832, vol. 5, pp. 391–92.

[10] Meir Litvak, "Karbala," *Encyclopaedia Iranica* (December 15, 2010), http://www.iranicaonline.org/articles/karbala

[11] The beginning of the line of Shi'ite Imams, accepted by all three major Shi'ite groups, is as follows: 1. 'Ali (d. 661); 2. Hasan (d. 680); 3. Husayn (d. 680); 4. Zayn al-'Abidin (d. 712).

[12] Halm, *Shi'ism*, pp. 202–5.

[13] Halm, *Shi'ism*, pp. 202–7.

[14] See Farhad Daftary, *A Short History of the Isma'ilis* (Edinburgh: Edinburgh University Press), 1998; Halm, *Shi'ism*, pp. 160–201.

[15] The name Druze comes from al-Darazi. For the history and beliefs of this group, see Sonia and Fuad I. Khuri, *Being a Druze* (London: Druze Heritage Foundation), 2004; Nissim Dana, *The Druse: A Religious Community in Transition* (Jerusalem: Turtledove Publishing), 1980.

[16] They are also called Musta'lians. The name Bohras means "tradesmen"; see Halm, *Shi'ism*, p. 192.

[17] See A. S. Asani, *Ecstasy and Enlightenment: The Ismaili Devotional Literature of South Asia* (London and New York: I. B. Tauris), 2002.

[18] As far as is known, the first 10 Muharram procession was held in 962.

[19] See E. G. Browne, *A Literary History of Persia* (Cambridge: Cambridge University Press), 1924, vol. 4, pp. 172–77.

[20] Quoted by Elaine Sciolino, *Persian Mirrors: The Elusive Face of Iran* (New York: The Free Press), 2000, p. 174.

[21] See also Peter J. Chelkowski (ed.), *Ta'ziyeh: Rituals and Drama* (New York: New York University Press), 1979, pp. 88–94.

[22] The tombs of Husayn's half-brother 'Abbas and his son 'Ali Akbar are also in Najaf.

[23] Personal communication from Dr Shainool Jiwa.

[24] In 1974, Musa Sadr, a senior Lebanese Twelver Shi'ite, issued a fatwa stating that the 'Alawis were a community of Twelver Shi'ite Muslims.

[25] See Yaron Friedman, *The Nusayri-'Alawis: An Introduction to the Religion, History and Identity of the Leading Minority in Syria* (Leiden: Brill), 2009; see also Halm, *Shi'ism*, pp. 156–58.

[26] Estimates of the number of Alevis in Turkey in 2013 vary between 10 percent and 30 percent, out of a total population of around 76 million. Despite the similarity in the meaning of the names of their two groups, the Alevis of Turkey are definitely not the same as the 'Alawis.

[27] David Shankland, *The Alevis in Modern Turkey: the Emergence of a Secular Islamic Tradition* (Abingdon, Oxford: Routledge), 2003.

[28] See Wilferd Madelung, *Arabic Texts Concerning the History of the Zaydi Imams: Tabaristan, Daylaman and Gilan* (Wiesbaden: Franz Steiner), 1987.

[29] See A. K. Kazi, "Notes on the Development of Zaidi Law," *Abr Nahrain* 2, 1960–61, pp. 36–40.

[30] See Qur'an 4:24. See also Nayer Honarvar, "Behind the Veil: Women's Rights in Islamic Societies," *Journal of Law and Religion*, 6, 1988, pp. 365–66; "Mutah: A Comprehensive Guide," *Answering Ansar*, No. 2, 2008.

31 Halm, *Shi'ism*, p. 136.

32 Ruhollah Khomeini, *Hukumat-i Islami* (Najaf) 1971, trans. H. Algar as *Islamic Government: Governance of the Jurist* (Tehran: Alhoda UK), 2002.

33 Jeff Stein, "Can You Tell a Sunni from a Shiite?," *The New York Times*, 17 October 2006.

34 See, for example, L. N. Takim, *Shi'ism in America* (New York: New York University Press), 2009.

7 THOUGHT pp. 169–188

1 Al-Ijli, *Al-mawaqif fi 'ilm al-kalam (Stations in the Knowledge of Kalam)*, (Cairo: Dar al-'ulum), 1938. Cited by Abdel Wahab El-Affendi in "Islamic Theology," *Muslim Philosophy* (1998), http://www.muslimphilosophy.com/ip/rep/H009.htm

2 Muhammed al-Ghazali (trans. Sabih Ahmad Kamali), "*Tahafut Al-Falasifah* (Incoherence of the Philosophers)," *Intellectual Takeout* (n. d.), http://www.intellectualtakeout.org/library/primary-sources/al-ghazalis-tahafut-al-falasifah-incoherence-philosophers

3 Sheikh Salman al-Qadah, "73 sects," *Islam Today* (May 30, 2006), http://en.islamtoday.net/artshow-438-3468.htm

4 See, for example, Qur'an 32:4, where God mounts a throne.

5 For a detailed study of the naming of angels in Islam, see S. R. Burge, *Angels in Islam. Jalal al-Din al-Suyuti's al-Haba'ik fi akhbar al-mala'ik* (London and New York: Routledge), 2012, pp. 31–51.

6 Al-Ash'ari (ed. Hellmut Ritter), *Maqalat al-Islamiyyin* (Istanbul: Matba'at al-Dawla), 1929, pp. 290–93.

7 Al-Ghazali (ed. Muhammad al-Baghdadi), *Iljam al-'awamm 'an 'ilm al-kalam* (Beirut: Dar al-kitab al-'arabi), 1985.

8 20:8; 17:110; 7:180; and 59:24.

9 Al-Ghazali (trans. R. C. Stade), *al-Maqsad al-asna* (Ibadan, Nigeria: Daystar), 1970.

10 W. Montgomery Watt, *Islamic Philosophy and Theology* (Edinburgh: Edinburgh University Press), 1985, p. 78.

11 Isaiah Goldfeld, "The Illiterate Prophet," *Der Islam* 57, 1980, pp. 58–67.

12 The greatest exponent of philosophical Sufism, Ibn al-'Arabi, was called the "son of Plato" (Ibn Aflatun).

13 Bernard Lewis, *Islam from the Prophet Muhammad to the Capture of Constantinople* (Oxford: Oxford University Press), 1974, vol. 1, p. 5.

14 Daniel Pipes, "The Caliphate," *Daniel Pipes Middle East Forum* (December 12, 2005), www.danielpipes.org/blog/2005/12/the-caliphate

15 For a biography and context for Ibn 'Abd-al-Wahhab, see John Obert Voll, "Foundations for Renewal and Reform. Islamic Movements in the Eighteenth and Nineteenth Centuries," in John

L. Esposito (ed.), *The Oxford Dictionary of Islam* (New York: Oxford University Press), 2004, pp. 516–19.

16 Yvonne Haddad, *Contemporary Islam and the Challenge of History* (Albany, NY: State University of New York Press), 1982, p. 90.

17 Shaykh Ibn Baaz, "Ten things which nullify one's Islaam," *Fatwa Online* (n. d.), http://www.fatwa-online.com/FATAAWA/CREED/SHIRK/9991120_1.HTM

18 Al-Afghani, "Answer of Jamal al-Din to Renan, *Journal des Débats*, 18 May 1883," in N. R. Keddie, *An Islamic Response to Imperialism. Political and Religious Writings of Sayyid Jamal ad-Din al-Afghani*. (Berkeley, CA: University of California Press), 1972.

19 Elma Harder, "Muhammad 'Abduh," *Center for Islamic Studies* (n. d.), http://www.cis-ca.org/voices/a/abduh.htm

20 Mohammed Arkoun, *Rethinking Islam: Common Questions, Uncommon Answers* (Boulder, CO: Westview Press), 1994.

8 SUFISM pp. 189–218

1 Anand T. Hingorani and Ganga Anand Hingorani (eds.), *The Encyclopaedia of Gandhian Thoughts*, (New Delhi: All India Congress Committee), 1985, p. 182.

2 See R. S. Elwood Jr., *Mysticism and Religion* (Englewood Cliff, NJ: Prentice Hall), 1980.

3 There are other proposed etymologies for the word "Sufi"; one suggests that it comes from the Arabic *safa* (meaning to "to be pure") and another possible theory argues that the word comes from *sophia* (the Greek word for "wisdom").

4 Quoted in A. J. Arberry, *Sufism: An Account of the Mystics of Islam* (London: Unwin), 1950, p. 33.

5 H. Ritter, "Studien zur Geschichte der islamischen Frömmigkeit," *Islamica*, xiv (1925), p. 21.

6 Notably Margaret Smith, *Studies in Early Mysticism in the Near and Middle East* (Oxford: One World), republished 1995.

7 See, for example, the eminent French Catholic historian of Islam, Louis Massignon, *Essay on the Origins of the Technical Language of Islam* (Notre Dame, IN: University of Notre Dame Press), 1997.

8 Qur'an 29:45 and 13:28.

9 See also the Ladder of Divine Ascent in early Christianity, as depicted in a twelfth-century icon found in Saint Catherine's Monastery on Mount Sinai in Egypt, in which monks, guided by John Climacus, climb up the spiritual ladder toward Jesus.

10 Martin Lings, *What is Sufism?* (Berkeley and Los Angeles, CA: University of California Press), 1975, p. 101.

11 Farid al-Din Attar, *Muslim Saints and Mystics: Episodes from the Tadhkirat al-Auliya' (Memorial of the Saints) by Farid al-Din Attar*, trans. A. J. Arberry (London, Boston, MA, and Henley: Persian Heritage Series No. 1), 1966, p. 46. It is historically impossible that this meeting ever took place, however, because Hasan died in 728 when Rabi'a was only a young girl.

12 Attar, p. 51.

13 Ibid., p. 51; for the biography of Rabi'a, see Ibn Khallikan, *Wafayat al-a'yan*, trans. W. M. de Slane as *Ibn Khallikan's Biographical Dictionary* (Paris), 1843–71, vol. 3, p. 215; Farid al-Din al-Attar (ed. R. Nicholson), *Tadhkirat al-awliya' [Memorial of the Saints]*, (London: Luzac & Company Ltd), 1907, p. 59.

14 For a thorough study of Junayd, see Ali Hassan Abdel-Kader, *The Life, Personality and Writings of al-Junayd* (London: Gibb Memorial Trust), 1976.

15 One of the 99 Beautiful Names of God.

16 Julian Baldick, *Mystical Islam: An Introduction to Sufism* (London: I. B. Tauris), 1989, p. 36.

17 The shrine complex that has developed around his tomb is still visited today.

18 John 14:6.

19 Notably, Louis Massignon (trans. H. Mason), *The Passion of Al-Hallaj: Mystic and Martyr of Islam* (Princeton, NJ: Princeton University Press), 1994.

20 Margaret Smith, *An Early Mystic of Baghdad: A Study of the Life and Teaching of Harith b. Asad al-Muhasibi*, (London: Sheldon Press), 1935, pp. 156–57.

21 Al-Ghazali, *Alchemy of Happiness (Kimiya al-sa'adat)*, trans. Jay R. Crook (Chicago, IL: Great Books of the Islamic World, Inc.), 2005.

22 This was not an autobiography in a modern sense. It was a spiritual autobiography, charting his search for religious certainty. In this way this work of al-Ghazali can be likened to the aims of the most famous Christian spiritual autobiography, that of St. Augustine (AD 354–430).

23 Richard J. McCarthy, *Freedom and Fulfillment: An Annotated Translation of Al-Ghazali's al-Munqidh min al-dalal and Other Relevant Works* (Boston, MA: Twayne Publishers), 1980.

24 McCarthy, *Freedom*, p. 94.

25 For example, Baldick, *Mystical Islam*, p. 99.

26 Phyllis G. Jestice (ed.), *Holy People of the World: A Cross-cultural Encyclopedia* (Santa Barbara, CA: ABC-CLIO Inc.), 2004, vol. 1, p. 713.

27 Al-Ghazali, *Al-Munqidh min al-dalal (The Deliverer from Error)*, trans. Richard McCarthy (Boston, MA: Twayne Publishers), 1980, p. 101.

28 Ali Hassan Abdel-Kader, *The Life, Personality and Writings of Al-Junayd* (London: Luzac), 1976, p. 90.

29 Ali b. 'Uthman al-Jullabi al-Hujwiri, *The Kashf Al-Mahjub: The Oldest Persian Treatise on Sufism*, trans. Reynald A. Nicholson (London: Luzac), 1976, preface, p. xiii.

30 G. Böwering, "*erfan*," *Encyclopedia Iranica* (December 15, 1998), http://www.iranicaonline.org/articles/erfan-1

31 Claude Addas (trans. Peter Kingsley), *Quest for the Red Sulphur: The Life of Ibn 'Arabi* (Cambridge: Islamic Texts Society), 1993, p. 213.

32 Anne-Marie Schimmel, *Mystical Dimensions of Islam* (Chapel Hill, NC: The University of North Carolina Press), 1975, p. 272.

33 A. J. Arberry, *Arabic Poetry: A Primer for Students* (Cambridge: Cambridge University Press), 1965, p. 126.

34 This famous saying is quoted in many books: see, for example, Jawid Mojaddedi, *Beyond Dogma: Rumi's Teachings on Friendship with God and Early Sufi Theories* (Oxford: Oxford University Press), 2012, p. 63.

35 Quoted in Cyril Glassé, "Jalal ad-Din ar-Rumi," in *The New Encyclopedia of Islam* (Walnut Creek, CA: Altamira Press), 2003, p. 235.

36 Variously called *shaykhs*, *pirs*, or *babas*, depending whether Arabic, Persian, or Turkish was spoken.

37 Including *ribat* and *zawiya* (in Arabic-speaking lands), *khanqah* (especially in Egypt, Iran, and Central Asia), and *tekke* (in Turkey and the Balkans).

38 Seyyed Hossein Nasr, *Ideals and Realities of Islam* (Boston, MA: Beacon Press), 1966, p. 142.

39 Dhu'l-Nun al-Misri, quoted in Hujwiri, *Kashf*, p. 204.

40 For a discussion of this controversial topic, see Annemarie Schimmel, "*raks*," in P. Bearman et al (eds), *Encyclopaedia of Islam*, Brill Online (2012), http://www.referenceworks.brillonline.com/entries/encyclopaedia-of-islam-2/raks-SIM_6205?s.num=0&s.f.s2_parent=s.f.book.encyclopaedia-of-islam-2&s.q=raks

41 For further analysis of the significance of the whirling Sufis, see Franklin Lewis, *Rumi: Past and Present, East and West. The Life, Teaching and Poetry of Jalal al-din Rumi* (Oxford: Oneworld), 2000, pp. 309–13, 461–63.

42 John Renard, *Seven Doors to Islam: Spirituality and the Religious Life of Muslims* (Berkeley, CA and London: University of California Press), 1996, p. 67.

43 Renard, *Seven Doors*, p. 180.

44 Muneera Haeri, *The Chishtis: A Living Light* (Oxford: Oxford University Press), 2000; Carl W. Ernst and Bruce B. Lawrence, *Sufi Martyrs of Love: The Chishti Order in South Asia and Beyond* (New York: Palgrave Macmillan), 2002.

45 The other significant tariqas in South Asia have been the Qadiriyya, the Suhrawardiyya, and the Naqshhandiyya.

46 Martin van Bruinessen, "Studies of Sufism and the Sufi Orders in Indonesia," *Die Welt des Islams*, 38, 2, July 1998, p. 204.

47 G. W. J. Drewes and L. F. Brakel (eds. and trans.), *The Poems of Hamzah Fansuri* (Dordrecht, Holland and Cinnaminson, NJ: Fortis), 1986; Anthony Johns, "Sufism in Southeast Asia: Reflections and Reconsiderations," *Journal of Asian Studies*, 19, April 1975, p. 45.

48 Julia Day Howell, "Sufism and the Indonesian Islamic Revival," *The Journal of Asian Studies*, 60, 3, August 2001, 702.

49 Musa Muhaiyaddeen, "Recite," *Sufism*, 11, 1, 2003, p. 7.

50 Seyyed Hossein Nasr, *Ideals and Realities of Islam* (Boston, MA: George Allen & Unwin), revised edition, 1975, p. 124.

9 JIHAD pp. 219–246

1 For a pathbreaking new study on *jihad*, see Asma Afsaruddin, *Striving in the Path of God: Jihad and Martyrdom in Islamic Thought* (Oxford: Oxford University Press), 2013.

2 Smith, *An Early Mystic*, p. 76.

3 Hujwiri (trans. Reynald A. Nicholson), *Kashf al-Mahjub of Al Hujwiri: The Oldest Persian Treatise in Sufism* (London: Luzac & Company Ltd), 1976, p. 200.

4 Afsaruddin, *Striving in the Path of God*, p. 225.

5 D. A. Rustow, in V. J. Parry and M. E. Yapp (eds.), *War, Technology and Society in the Middle East* (London: Oxford University Press), 1975, p. 386.

6 Esposito and Mogahed, *Who Speaks For Islam?* 2008.

7 Afsaruddin, *Striving in the Path of God*, p. 225.

8 Mustansir Mir, "Jihad in Islam," in Hadia Dajani-Shakeel and Ronald Messier (eds.), *The Jihad and Its Times* (Ann Arbor, MI: University of Michigan Press), 1991, p. 114.

9 See also Qur'an 30:30.

10 Al-Bukhari (trans. M. Muhsin Khan), "Book 67: Hunting, Slaughtering," *Islamicity* (n. d.), http://www.islamicity.com/mosque/sunnah/bukhari/067.sbt.html#007.067.44:17/67/441

11 Wael B. Hallaq, *An Introduction to Islamic Law* (Cambridge: Cambridge University Press), 2009.

12 For an excellent analysis of the Muslim conquests, see H. Kennedy, *The Great Arab Conquests* (Philadelphia, PA: Da Capo Press), 2007.

13 Ibn Mubarak, "'Abdallah," in N. Hammad (ed.), *Kitab al-jihad* (Beirut: Al-maktaba al-mu'asiriyya), 1971.

14 Rudolph Peters, *Jihad in Medieval and Modern Islam* (Leiden: Brill), 1977, pp. 9–25.

15 Ibn Khaldun, *Muqaddimah*, 1967, p. 224.

16 Etan Kohlberg, "The Development of the Imami Shi'i Doctrine of Jihad," *Zeitschrift der Deutschen Morgenländischen Gesellshaft* 126, 1976, pp. 64–86.

17 Kohlberg, "The Development of the Imami Shi'i Doctrine of Jihad," p. 66.

18 Robert Gleave, "Recent Research into the History of Early Shi'ism," *History Compass*, 7/6, 2009, pp. 1593–1605.

19 Kohlberg, "The Development of the Imami Shi'i Doctrine of Jihad," 1976.

20 Amir Taheri, *Holy Terror: The Inside Story of Islamic Terrorism* (London, Sphere Books), 1987, p. 241.

21 Majid Khadduri, *The Law of War and Peace in Islam* (London: Luzac & Company Ltd), 1940, p. 19.

22 Wilferd Madelung, "Kharijism: the 'Ajarida and the Ibadiyya," in *Religious Trends in Early Islamic Iran* (Albany, NY: Bibliotheca Persica), 1988, pp. 54–55; Paul L. Heck, "Eschatological Scripturalism and the End of Community: The Case of Early Kharijism," *Archiv für Religionsgeschichte* 7, 2005, pp. 137–52.

23 Luke Treadwell, "The Account of the Samanid Dynasty in Ibn Zafir al-Azdi's Akhbar al-duwal al-munqati'a," *Iran*, 43, 2005, pp. 135–71.

24 Narshakhi (trans. Richard N. Frye), *The History of Bukhara* (Cambridge, MA: The Medieval Academy of America), 1954, p. 18; Sergei P. Tolstow (trans. O. Mehlitz), *Auf den Spuren der altchoresmischen Kultur* (Berlin), 1953, p. 267.

25 Ronald A. Messier, *Almoravids and the Meanings of Jihad* (Santa Barbara, CA: Praeger), 2010; Dierk Lange, "The Almoravid Expansion and the Downfall of Ghana," *Der Islam* 73, 1996, pp. 122–59.

26 Andras Hamori, *The Composition of Mutanabbi's Panegyrics to Sayf al-Dawla* (Leiden: Brill), 1992; Carole Hillenbrand, "Jihad Poetry in the Age of the Crusades," in Thomas Madden, James L. Naus, and Vincent Ryan (eds.), *Crusades: Medieval Worlds in Conflict. Proceedings of the Crusades conference held at the University of Saint Louis, 2007* (Aldershot: Ashgate), 2010, pp. 10–12.

27 Carole Hillenbrand, *The Crusades: Islamic Perspectives* (Edinburgh: Edinburgh University Press), 1999, p. 102; see also Ephesians 6:10–17.

28 Hillenbrand, *Crusades*, p. 103.

29 Malcolm Cameron Lyons and D. E. P. Jackson, *Saladin: The Politics of the Holy War* (Cambridge: Cambridge University Press), 1982, p. 189.

30 Hillenbrand, *Crusades*, p. 166.

31 Ibn Jubayr (ed. W. Wright), *Rihla* (Leiden: Brill), 1907, pp. 28–31.

32 A. Morabia, "Ibn Taymiyya, dernier grand théoricien du jihad médiéval," *Bulletin d'études orientales* 30/2, 1978, pp. 85–99.

33 Denise Aigle, "The Mongol Invasions of Bilad al-Sham by Ghazan Khan and Ibn Taymiyah's Three 'Anti-Mongol' Fatwas," *Mamluk Studies Review* XI/2, 2007, pp. 89–120.

34 Aigle, "Mongol Invasions," 2007; Qamaruddin Khan, *The Political Thought of Ibn Taymiyah* (Islamabad), 1973, p. 20, n. 2.

35 Khan, *Ibn Taymiyyah*, p. 155.

36 Carole Hillenbrand, *Turkish Myth and Muslim Symbol: The Battle of Manzikert* (Edinburgh: Edinburgh University Press), 2007.

37 *The Kite Runner* and *A Thousand Splendid Suns*.

38 Transcript of "Usamah Bin-Ladin, the Destruction of the Base" (interview aired June 10, 1999), *The Terrorist Research Center* (n. d.), http://web.archive.org/web/20021113111503/http://www.terrorism.com/terrorism/BinLadinTranscript.shtml

39 Usama bin Laden, "World Islamic Front statement," *Federation of American Scientists* (February 23, 1998), http://www.fas.org/irp/world/para/docs/980223-fatwa.htm

40 Natana DeLong-Bas, "al-Qaeda," *Oxford Bibliographies Online* (December 14, 2009), http://www.oxfordbibliographies.com/view/document/obo-9780195390155/obo-9780195390155-0065.xml?rskey=N3ltW7&result=121

41 Faisal Devji, *Landscapes of Jihad: Militancy, Morality, Modernity* (Ithaca, NY: Cornell University Press), 2005.

42 Mir, "Jihad in Islam," p. 113.

43 Alison Pargeter, *The New Frontiers of Jihad: Radical Islam In Europe* (London: I. B. Tauris), 2008.

44 Peters, *Jihad in Medieval and Modern Islam,* 1977.

45 Muhammad Qasim Zaman, *Modern Islamic Thought in a Radical Age: Religious Authority and Internal Criticism* (Cambridge: Cambridge University Press), 2012, pp. 71–72, 273–81, 304–8.

46 Wahba Zuhayli, "Islam and International Law," *International Review of the Red Cross*, vol. 87, number 858, June 2005, pp. 269–83.

47 Al-Buti, Muhammad Sa'id (trans. Munzer Adel Absi), *Jihad in Islam: How to Understand and Practice It* (Damascus: Dar al-Fikr Publishing House), 1995.

48 Ibid.

49 R. A. Pape, *Dying to Win: the Strategic Logic of Suicide Terrorism* (New York: Random House), 2006.

50 Niromi de Soyza, "Sisters in arms," *Telegraph Magazine*, May 9, 2009, p. 35.

51 R. Baer, *The Sunday Times*, September 3, 2006.

52 Khaled M. Abou El Fadl, "Islam and the Theology of Power," *Middle East Report* 221, Winter 2001, p. 31.

53 Gary Bunt, *iMuslims: Rewiring the House of Islam* (Chapel Hill, NC: University of North Carolina Press), 2009.

10 WOMEN pp. 247–273

1 Joan Smith, *The Independent*, September 22, 2013.

2 Nawal El Saadawi, quoted in Robert Marquand, "Arab women: this time, the revolution won't leave us behind," *The Christian Science Monitor* (March 8, 2011), http://www.csmonitor.com

3 Kate Zebiri, "The Redeployment of Orientalist Themes in Contemporary Islamophobia," *Studies in Contemporary Islam* 10, 2008, p. 5.

4 Zebiri, "Redeployment," p. 36.

5 Ibid., p. 9.

6 Muhammad Asad, *The Message of the Qur'an* (London: The Book Foundation), 2003, p. 600, n. 37.

7 1 Cor. 11:16.

8 Nikki R. Keddie and Beth Baron, *Women in Middle Eastern History: Shifting Boundaries in Sex and Gender* (New Haven, CT: Yale University Press), 1992.

9 Qur'an 2:221.

10 John L. Esposito with Natana J. DeLong-Bas, *Women in Muslim Family Law* (Syracuse, NY: Syracuse University Press), 2001.

11 n. a, "Fatima bint Muhammad," *Guide to Salvation* (n. d.), http://www.guidetosalvation.com/Website/fatima_bint_muhammad.htm

12 Jean Calmard, "Fateema," *Encyclopedia Iranica* (December 15, 1999), http://www.iranicaonline.org/articles/fatema

13 The only known examples are the twelfth-century Sulayhid queens of Yemen, and a thirteenth-century Turkish sultana who ruled for a few months only in Mamluk Egypt.

14 Remke Kruk, *The Warrior Women of Islam: Female Empowerment in Arabic Popular Culture* (London: I.B. Tauris), 2013.

15 Carole Hillenbrand, "Women in the Seljuq Period," in G. Nashat and L. Beck (eds.), *Women in Iran from the Rise of Islam to 1800* (Urbana, IL: University of Illinois Press), 2003, pp. 103–20; Gavin Hambly, *Women in the Medieval Islamic World: Power, Patronage, and Piety* (Basingstoke: Macmillian), 1998.

16 Leslie Pierce, *The Imperial Harem: Women and Sovereignty in the Ottoman Empire* (Oxford: Oxford University Press), 1993.

17 Leila Ahmed, *Women and Gender in Islam: Historical Roots of a Modern Debate* (Newhaven, CT: Yale University Press), 1999, p. 75; Sumbul Ali-Karamali, *The Muslim Next Door: The Qur'an, the Media, and That Veil Thing* (Ashland, OR: White Cloud Press), 2008, p. 153.

18 Marilyn Booth, "Introduction," in Marilyn Booth (ed.), *Harem Histories: Envisioning Places and Living Spaces* (Durham, NC: Duke University Press), 2010, p. 18.

19 Booth, "Introduction," in *Harem Histories*, p. 13.

20 Jateen Lad, "Panoptic Bodies: Black Eunuchs as Guardians of the Topkapi Harem," in *Harem Histories*, pp. 136–76.

21 Heghnar Zeitlin Watenpaugh, "The Harem as Biography: Domestic Architecture, Gender and Nostalgia in Modern Syria," in *Harem Histories*, p. 227.

22 Emily Said-Ruete (ed. G. S. P. Freeman-Grenville), *Memoirs of an Arabian Princess* (London and the Hague: East-West), 1994.

23 Said-Ruete, *Memoirs*, viii.

24 Said-Ruete, *Memoirs*, pp. 97–98.

25 Amina Wadud, *Qur'an and Woman: Rereading the Sacred Text from a Woman's Perspective* (New York and Oxford: Oxford University Press), 1999; BBC News, October 27, 2008.

26 Amina Wadud, *Inside the Gender Jihad: Women's Reform in Islam* (Oxford: Oneworld Publications), 2006.

27 Fatima Mernissi, *The Forgotten Queens of Islam* (Boston, MA and Cambridge: Polity Press), 1994.

28 *Islamic Horizons* 1423/2002, p. 16, cited in Ali-Karamali, *The Muslim Next Door*, p. 135.

29 n. a., "FGM: UK's first female genital mutilation prosecutions announced," *BBC News* (March 21, 2014), http://www.bbc.co.uk/news/uk-26681364

30 n. a., "On International Women's Day, Sanctuary calls for an end to FGM and Vacation Cutting," *Sanctuary for Families* (May 8, 2013), http://www.sanctuaryforfamilies.org/index.php?option=content&task=view&id=618

31 n. a., "Sayings of the Prophet: On Parents," *The Islamic Bulletin* issue 16 (August/September 1998), http://www.islamicbulletin.org/newsletters/issue_16/prophet.aspx

32 Sara Silvestri, *Unveiled issues. Europe's Muslim Women's Potential, Problems and Aspirations* (Brussels: King Badouin Foundation), 2009.

33 Dawn Chatty, "Veiling in Oman," *The Middle East in London*, 8/1, October–November 2011, p. 11.

34 During the five daily prayers and pilgrimage (when men and women perform the rituals together), it is imperative that women have their faces and hands uncovered.

35 Islamic Sharia-base Law no. 18/2001.

36 John Esposito, "Muslim women reclaiming their rights," *Institute for Social Policy and Understanding* (July 22, 2009), http://www.ispu.org/content/Muslim_Women_Reclaiming_Their_Rights

37 Patricia Jeffery, *Frogs in a Well: Indian Women in Purdah* (London: Lawrence Hill & Co.), 1979.

38 Yvonne Haddad, Jane I. Smith, and Kathleen Moore, *Muslim Women in America: Gender, Islam, and Society* (New York: Oxford University Press), 2006.

39 Islamic Social Services Associations and Women In Islam, Inc., "Women Friendly Mosques and Community Centers: Working Together to Reclaim Our Heritage," *Islamic Awareness* (n. d.), http://www.islamawareness.net/Mosque/WomenAndMosquesBooklet.pdf

40 Esposito and Mogahed, *Who Speaks for Islam?*, 2007.

41 United Nations Development Programme, "Towards the Rise of Women in the Arab World," *Arab Human Development Report* (2005), http://www.arab-hdr.org/publications/contents/2005/execsummary-e.pdf

42 Booth, *Harem Histories*, 2010.

43 Yasir Suleiman, *Narratives of Conversion to Islam. Female Perspectives* (Cambridge and Markfield: Prince Alwaleed Bin Talal Centre of Islamic Studies, University of Cambridge, in association with the New Muslims Project), 2013.

II TOMORROW pp. 274–285

1 n. a., "The ACW Letter," *A Common Word* (2007), http://www.acommonword.com/the-acw-document/

2 See Chapter 6.

3 "From harsh terrain," *The Economist*, August 6, 2009.

4 Tim Winter, "Bin Laden's violence is a heresy," *The Daily Telegraph* (October 15, 2001), http://beta.radicalmiddleway.co.uk/articles.php?id=6&art=11

5 Esposito and Mogahed, *Who Speaks for Islam*, p. 69.

6 Giles Whittell, *The Times*, January 7, 2000.

GLOSSARY

This glossary comprises, firstly, key and most commonly used terms; secondly, the names of significant people in the history and development of Islam. The list of names can be found on pp. 302–5.

TERMINOLOGY

abaya A long dress worn by Muslim women.

'Abbasids The second dynasty of the Islamic empire (750–1258 CE).

ab-i turbat Dust water: water mixed with soil from Karbala', believed to have healing powers.

Abrahamic Belonging to Abraham: a term used for the shared heritage of the three religions of Abraham: Judaism, Christianity, and Islam.

adhan The Islamic call to prayer.

ahl al-bayt Literally, "the People of the House." The descendants of the Prophet Muhammad through his daughter Fatima and her husband 'Ali ibn Abi Talib, Muhammad's cousin.

ahwal Mystical states; achieved by Sufis on the journey of the soul toward God.

'Alawis Also called Nusayris. Esoteric minority Shi'ites, found mainly in Syria and Lebanon. The ruling family of Syria today belong to this group.

Alevis A significant minority group in present-day Turkey. Their beliefs are based on Shi'ism and influenced by Sufism, Christianity, and Shamanism.

Allah "The One God."

Almoravids (*al-Murabitun*) A Berber dynasty that ruled in North Africa and then Spain (1056–1147 CE).

angel A messenger from God, a spiritual being that mediates between God and humanity.

angelology Knowledge about angels.

animist A person who believes that certain objects—trees, plants, stones, and animals—have within them an individual spirit that governs their existence.

Arab Spring The name given since 2011 to ongoing uprisings in the Arab world; the Arabs call this phenomenon "the Arab awakening."

arkan al-din "The supports of religion." The five pillars of Islam: devotional duties required of all Muslims. Performing the five pillars enhances their worship of God and fosters communal identity.

ascetics Holy men and women, in many religions, who practice in solitude extremely rigorous self-discipline, meditation, prayer, fasting, and self-denial.

'Ashura The most important Shi'ite festival, which takes place every year on the tenth day ('*Ashura* is Arabic for "tenth") of the first month of the Muslim calendar, Muharram. '*Ashura* is the climax of ten days of mourning for the martyrdom of Husayn.

Assassins (*Hashishiyyun*) A popular but derogatory title given by medieval Sunni Muslims and then later by the Crusaders to the Nizaris, a breakaway Isma'ili Shi'ite group. "Assassin" comes from the word hashish, but it is very unlikely that the group actually used the drug. (See also **Nizaris**.)

al-'atabat al-muqaddasa "The sacred thresholds." The Shi'ite holy shrines in Iraq: Karbala', Najaf, Kazimayn, and Samarra.

ayatollah "Sign of God." A title given to a Twelver Shi'ite scholar, not after passing an examination, but by an emerging consensus in the scholarly community that he has the knowledge and status to deserve such a title.

bay'a "Oath of allegiance," sworn to the Sunni caliph on his accession to the caliphate by military leaders, religious scholars, and administrators.

bazaris The shopkeeper class; their role in the Islamic Revolution of 1979 helped bring a militant Twelver Shi'ite regime to power.

Bektashiyya A Sufi brotherhood named after its founder, Hajji Bektash (d. 1270).

bila kayfa "Without [asking] how," in other words, "without seeking to understand how." An approach advocated by Ahmad b. Hanbal (d. 855), who preached that believers should not question the faith on matters that lie beyond the reach of human understanding.

Bohras Isma'ili Shi'ite group that moved first to Yemen in 1171 and then settled in India.

burqa Long, loose-fitting garment worn by a Muslim woman, covering the whole body and leaving only a small space for the eyes.

Byzantine empire (*c.* 330–1453 CE) The successor to the Roman empire in the eastern Mediterranean. The Byzantines were Greek Orthodox Christians.

caliph (*khalifa*) "Successor" of Muhammad; later, the religious and legal leader of the Sunni community of believers.

caravansaray Also known as *khan*. A building where travelers and caravans stay overnight with their animals and merchandise.

cem evi "House of Assembly." A place where the principal ceremony of the Alevis, the *sema*, takes place, conducted by their *dede* (prayer leader).

chador Garment worn by women, especially in Iran, that covers the whole body except for the top half of the face.

Chishtiyya Sufi order named after its founder, Mu'in al-Din Chishti (d. 1236). It became popular in India.

Companions (*sahaba*) The people most closely associated with Muhammad.

Constitution of Medina (sometimes called the Medina Charter) A foundational document, dating from the second or third year of the Medinan period, which mentions a community of believers—the *umma*—from Mecca and Medina, but also allows for the inclusion of Jews, Christians, and pagans.

Crusaders Western European Christians who set out to reconquer the Holy Land from the Muslims. Their presence in the Middle East lasted from 1099 to 1291 CE.

Dar al-'ahd "The House of Truce." See *Dar al-sulh*.

Dar al-harb "The House of War." Territories that are not yet under Islamic rule and that have made a peace treaty with Muslims.

Dar al-hikma "The House of Wisdom." The translation center, set up in 830 CE by the caliph al-Ma'mun, in which works of foreign scholarship were translated into Arabic.

Dar al-Islam "The House of Islam." The entire Islamic community: the region of Muslim sovereignty where Islamic law prevails.

Dar al-sulh "The House of Peace." Non-Muslim territory that has concluded a treaty with a Muslim government to protect Muslims there. Often includes an agreement to pay (or receive) tribute.

Day of Judgment (**Last Day**) Also called the Day of Reckoning or the Day of Resurrection. The end of the world, when all people will be judged by God.

dede Alevi leader of the *sema* ceremony.

dhikr Literally "mention." Sufi ceremony that involves remembrance and the constant repetition of the name of God. It can be performed alone or in a group.

dhikr Allah "Remembrance of God." A prayer in which Sufis mention the name of God in a repetitive crescendo.

du'a' Prayers in addition to the five daily ritual prayers.

Druze Breakaway group of Isma'ili Shi'ites that deified the sixth Fatimid caliph al-Hakim after his mysterious disappearance in 1021 CE. The Druze now live mainly in Lebanon with some in Israel.

Emigrants (*Muhajirun*) The companions of Muhammad, who left their homes and followed him when he made his *hijra* (emigration) from Mecca to Medina in 622 CE; there they became a key part of his new community of Muslims.

esoteric Secret, hidden, and understood by only a select group of people who have special knowledge.

fana' "Annihilation of the self in God." Achieved when a Sufi reaches the final stage of the mystical path, becomes entirely present in God and completely lost to himself.

faqih A scholar knowledgeable in Islamic jurisprudence (*fiqh*).

fard Human actions that are classified by the *Shari'a* as obligatory.

Fatiha "The Opening." Chapter 1 of the Qur'an.

fatwa A legal opinion or pronouncement made by a *mufti* (a Muslim scholar) on whether an action is permitted or forbidden by the *Shari'a*.

fiqh "Understanding." Classical Sunni Muslim jurisprudence.

Fivers See **Zaydis**.

fuqaha' Legal scholars, specialists in Islamic jurisprudence (*fiqh*).

Gabriel (Jibril) The Angel of Revelation.

ghayba (occultation) Literally "absence." A core Twelver Shi'ite doctrine, referring first to the Lesser Occultation, a period in which the Twelfth Imam, who had disappeared in 874, was thought to be hidden, but still somewhere on earth. From 941 (see also *safir*) this doctrine was changed to that of the Greater Occultation: it was believed that the Twelfth Imam had cut off all links with the world until his return at the end of time. Twelver Shi'ites today still await the coming of the Twelfth Imam.

Ghaznavids A Turkish dynasty (961–1186 CE) that ruled first in eastern Iran and Afghanistan, and later in northern India.

ghulat Extremist Shi'ites who deify 'Ali.

ghusl The "greater ablution." The complete washing of the body to ensure ritual purity, an action necessary before prayer.

ginan An Isma'ili Shi'ite poem or song about the Imams, first transmitted orally and later written down in Indian languages, such as Sindhi, Gujurati, Hindi, and Punjabi; some 800 are recorded. A *ginan* can be mystical or it can tell stories to provide moral instruction to the faithful.

Gnosticism A dualistic religious and philosophical movement of the late Hellenistic (Greek) and early Christian eras. The numerous gnostic sects all promised salvation through an occult knowledge that they asserted was revealed to them alone.

greater *jihad* see *jihad*.

Greater Occultation See *ghayba*.

hadith A report of something that the Prophet Muhammad said or did. The reports comprise a vast corpus of recorded sayings and deeds of the Prophet, believed to have been transmitted by the Companions.

hafiz A person who has learned the whole Qur'an by heart.

hajj The annual ritual pilgrimage: the fifth pillar of Islam. The journey to Mecca, which should be undertaken in the month of Dhu'l Hijja once in a lifetime by all those Muslims who are physically and financially able.

halakha Literally "path." Jewish law.

halal "Permitted." A term used particularly for meat that has been slaughtered according to the rules of the *Shari'a*.

Hamdanids A Shi'ite Arab dynasty in northern Syria that ruled 906–1004 CE.

Hanafi Follower of the legal school (*madhhab*) of Abu Hanifa.

Hanbali Follower of the legal school (*madhhab*) of Ahmad ibn Hanbal.

hanif A word used in the Qur'an to denote a true believer in the One God before the coming of

Islam; the term is used particularly in reference to Abraham.

haram Human actions that are classified by the *Shari'a* as forbidden.

harem The women's quarters in a Muslim household.

hawza A Twelver Shi'ite seminary, where students are taught Shi'ite law.

hijab A general term for women's clothing that covers the whole body except the hands and face; it can also mean the head covering that conceals the hair.

hijra The emigration of Muhammad and the first Muslims from Mecca to Medina in 622 CE. This year is the first year of the Islamic calendar.

hiyal Legal strategies used by Muslim lawyers to circumvent difficult problems.

hudud Fixed *Shari'a* penalties, which can be broadly defined as "bounds set by God on human freedom."

hukm A legal judgment.

'ibadat Devotional duties laid down for Muslims; actions associated with the worship of God.

Ibadis The modern descendants of the Kharijites. The vast majority today live in Oman; smaller groups are in Zanzibar and parts of Algeria. They worship separately from Sunnis and Shi'ites, but live in harmony with other Muslims.

'id al-adha "The Day of Sacrifice": 10 Dhu'l–Hijja. A great day of celebration throughout the Muslim world, during the month of the *hajj*.

'id al-fitr "The feast of breaking the fast." The joyful festival at the end of the fasting month of Ramadan. At this time, Muslims wear their best clothes, exchange gifts, visit the mosque, and eat special meals with their family and friends.

ihram The consecrated state into which a pilgrim enters in order to perform the *hajj* or the *'umra*.

i'jaz A doctrine that states that the Qur'an cannot be imitated.

ijma' "Consensus." In Sunni Islam a unanimous agreement by religious scholars at a particular time on a point of law; one of the four core elements upon which religious scholars relied for systematizing the *Shari'a*.

ijtihad "Effort." The exercise of a religious lawyer's independent reasoning in coming to a decision.

Illuminationist See *ishraqiyya*.

imam/Imam "Model." Prayer leader at the Friday prayers in the mosque (*imam*). For the Shi'ites, a descendant of the Prophet chosen by God to lead them (Imam). For the Twelvers and the Isma'ilis the Imam is infallible in matters of doctrine; for Sunnis the title *imam* is sometimes used interchangeably with the title caliph, or to honor a great scholar, such as al-Ghazali.

imama The core concept or doctrine focused on the role of the Imam in Shi'ism, and on that of the caliph in Sunni Islam.

al-insan al-kamil "The Perfect Man." This theosophical doctrine, elaborated by the great Sufi Ibn al-'Arabi, refers to Muhammad, the prototype of humanity. He is the means through which God is known and manifested to the world.

'irfan Philosophical Sufism.

ishraqiyya (Illuminationism) A doctrine elaborated by Suhrawardi, blending Greek, ancient Iranian, and Islamic elements. He argues that God, the essence of the First Absolute Light, gives constant illumination. Everything in the world is derived from His light, and in reaching this illumination lies salvation for His created beings. The closeness to God of any being is dependent on its degree of illumination.

islah The reconstructing or restoring of what is viewed as the true Islam.

Islam Surrender to God in accordance with the message of the Qur'an.

Isma'ilis Also known as "Seveners," named after their seventh Imam, Isma'il. The Isma'ilis believe in a living Imam, who is a descendant of Muhammad. The Fatimids established an Isma'ili caliphate in Egypt in 969 CE and dominated the Mediterranean for nearly two centuries. Thereafter, one wing of the movement (see **Nizaris**) broke away in 1094 CE. Today the Nizaris are a much-respected group, well integrated into the disparate societies in which they have settled across the world. They view their leader, the Aga Khan, as infallible in matters of doctrine. The other line of Isma'ilis, the Bohras, who are mostly in India, are less well known and are not politically active.

Isra'iliyyat "Israelite stories." Narratives known across the Middle East that came from Jewish and Christian traditions as well as ancient Middle Eastern folklore.

istishhad The seeking of, or act of, martyrdom.

Jabriyya An early Muslim theological group that lasted a short time in the eighth century. It argued that human beings have no choice over what they do.

Ja'fari A name sometimes given to the Twelver Shi'ite legal school, because the sayings and judgments of Ja'far al-Sadiq (d. 765)—the sixth Imam of the Twelver line—form the basis of much Twelver law.

jam'atkhana "house of assembly." A special building in which Isma'ilis worship on Fridays.

Janissaries Elite military regiments in the service of the Ottoman Turkish empire.

jihad "Striving" in the path of God. Two dimensions of *jihad* are identified by Muslim religious scholars: the greater *jihad* denotes a person's striving to purify his or her baser instincts and impure tendencies, while the lesser *jihad* means fighting either to defend or to expand the lands of Islam.

jilbab A long garment worn by Muslim women that covers the whole body, except for the hands, face, and head. The head is then covered with a scarf. In Indonesia *jilbab* refers to a headscarf.

298

Ka'ba A square building, in Mecca, containing the sacred Black Stone toward which prayer is directed; pilgrims performing the *hajj* or *'umra* walk around it. Muslims believe it was built by Ibrahim (Abraham) and his son Isma'il (Ishmael).

kafir An unbeliever, one who refuses to submit to God.

kalam Literally, "speech." Theology.

Karbala' The place in Iraq where Husayn was martyred; one of the sacred shrines in Iraq visited by Shi'ites today.

khak-i Karbala' "The soil of Karbala'." Mixed with water into a little brick and known as *ab-i turbat* (dust water), it is believed to help sick and dying people.

khalifa See **caliph**.

Kharijites An early group within Islam that believed that the most virtuous person in the community should lead it, and that person would not necessarily be from the Prophet's family or someone elected by the whole community. Anyone who did not agree with this was, in the Kharijites' view, not a Muslim at all and should be killed.

khums A tax consisting of a fifth part of the income of Twelver Shi'ite Muslims.

khutba A sermon delivered in the mosque by the imam (prayer leader) on Fridays and on the two major Islamic festival days.

Last Day See **Day of Judgment**.

laylat al-qadr "Night of Power." The holiest night of the Muslim calendar, celebrated on 26–27 Ramadan, when it is believed that the Qur'an descended in full into the soul of Muhammad.

lesser jihad See *jihad*.

Lesser Occultation See *ghayba*.

madhhab "Way of going." A school of law. The Sunnis have four *madhhab*s, all recognized as equally valid. The Shi'ites also have their own *madhhab*s.

madrasa A building in which students learn about the law of the particular *madhhab* to which they belong. The curriculum also covers other subjects, such as Arabic grammar and the Islamic religious sciences.

maghazi **books** Books that record the military campaigns (*maghazi*) of Muhammad.

Mahdi "The Rightly Guided One." A figure chosen by God to usher in an era of justice for the whole earth just before the Day of Judgment and the Resurrection; for the Twelver Shi'ites the *Mahdi* is the Twelfth Imam on his return to earth.

makruh Human actions that are classified by the *Shari'a* as reprehensible.

Maliki Belonging to the Maliki legal school (*madhhab*), named after Malik ibn Anas (d. 795).

Mamluks A Turkish dynasty that ruled a large empire from its base in Egypt (1250–1517 CE).

mandub Human actions that are classified by the *Shari'a* as recommended.

Manichaeism A dualistic religion founded by Mani (216–274 CE), in which the two principles of good and evil—God and Satan—are co-eternal.

maqam A named "station" on the Sufi path, similar to one of the steps on a spiritual ladder.

maraji' The supreme authorities on Twelver Shi'ite Islamic law in the Middle East, who provide guidance today to faraway followers on how to live in distant lands that are majority non-Muslim.

marja' al-taqlid "Source of imitation." A title given in the nineteenth century to the members of a new elite of about ten religious scholars, who were recognized as being most qualified to guide the Twelver Shi'ite faithful in their daily lives.

al-masjid al-haram The sacred mosque in Mecca.

maslaha Making a legal decision in the public interest.

mawla A term with a wide range of meanings, including master, lord, or protector.

mazalim Grievance courts held by rulers.

Mecca The city in Arabia in which the Prophet Muhammad was born and the place where he began his preaching. The destination of the *hajj*, a pilgrimage undertaken at least once in a lifetime by all Muslims who are fit and able.

Medina An abbreviated name for *madinat-al-nabi* (the city of the Prophet). Its old name was Yathrib. In 622 CE Muhammad made his *hijra* to Medina and established the *umma* (the Islamic community).

Medina Charter See **Constitution of Medina**.

Mevlevis (Mawlawiyya) Also known as the Whirling Dervishes. A Sufi order founded in Konya in Turkey by Jalal al-Din Rumi (d. 1273).

mihna "Trial," "test," "inquisition." The attempt—mainly by the 'Abbasid caliph al-Ma'mun in 827 CE—to force the religious scholars and government officials to accept the Mu'tazilite doctrine of the created Qur'an as the official doctrine of the Sunni 'Abbasid empire. It was opposed by the towering figure of Ahmad b. Hanbal (d. 855), a conservative religious scholar who hated theology.

mihrab A flat or concave arch or niche in the inner wall of the mosque, which indicates the *qibla* (the direction of Mecca).

minaret Tower attached to a mosque, from which the call to prayer is made.

mi'raj Muhammad's Night Journey (around the sixth year of the *hijra*) from Mecca to Jerusalem, and his ascent from there into heaven, where he met the prophets of old and gazed upon God.

Mirrors for Princes Books written to advise rulers on good government.

monotheist A believer in the One and only God.

mosque (*masjid*) Literally, a "place of prostration." An ordinary mosque in which ritual prayer is performed. The Friday mosque—*jami'*—is the building in which the solemn Friday prayer takes place and where the Friday sermon (*khutba*) is given from the pulpit (*minbar*).

mu'amalat As defined in books of jurisprudence, actions that have to do with humans' relationship with one another.

mubah Human actions that are classified by the *Shari'a* as allowed.

muezzin The person who makes the call to prayer from the minaret of the mosque.

mufti A Muslim scholar qualified to give a legal opinion (*fatwa*).

Mughals The dynasty that ruled India 1526–1858 CE.

Muhajirun See Emigrants.

mujahid A person who strives in the path of God, a *jihad* warrior.

mujtahid A religious lawyer who makes personal legal judgments (see *ijtihad*).

Muslim "A person who has surrendered to God."

The Muslim Brotherhood (*al-ikhwan al-muslimin*) Founded in Egypt in 1928 by Hasan al-Banna'; its message was a return to the principles of the Qur'an and the *hadith*, for the creation of a truly Islamic society.

mut'a Temporary marriage permitted in Shi'ism.

Mu'tazila A Muslim theological group, also called "the people of justice and *tawhid* (belief in God's Oneness)"; it was known especially for its adoption of the doctrine of the "created Qur'an."

nabi A prophet, a person chosen by God to deliver a message to humankind.

al-nabi al-ummi "The unlettered prophet." A title given to Muhammad, through whom the Qur'an was revealed. To emphasize the miraculous nature of the Islamic revelation, Muslim scholars came to believe that he was unable to read and write.

Naqshbandiyya Sufi order founded by Muhammad ibn Muhammad Naqshband (d. 1389).

nass Designation of authority passed on to a new Shi'ite Imam at the time of his succession.

Neoplatonism The last school of Classical Greek philosophy, shaped definitively by Plotinus (205–270 CE), a philosopher from Egypt, in his most important work, *The Enneads*. Neoplatonism moves away from the idea that God created the universe at a specific moment in time, proposing instead the concept of constant "emanation" by God, who pours out creation in hierarchical layers beneath Him.

Night Journey See *mi'raj*.

Night of Power See *laylat al-qadr*.

niqab A veil worn by Muslim women, which covers only the mouth and nose.

nisab The minimum amount of wealth that one must have before *zakat* becomes payable.

Nizaris A famous Isma'ili splinter group that broke away from the mainstream Fatimid line in Cairo after 1094, and made its center in north-west Iran, at the castle of Alamut. See also Isma'ilis.

Nusayris See 'Alawis.

Ottomans A Sunni Muslim Turkish dynasty that ruled a vast empire comprising the Middle East, North Africa, and the Balkans, from 1342 to 1924 CE.

Pan-Islamism A political movement that aims to create a single, overarching Islamic state in the world; often linked to the idea—from the 1920s onward—of reviving the universal caliphate.

pillars of Islam See *arkan-al-din*.

polytheism Belief in more than one god.

Qadariyya A group of Islamic theologians in the eighth century that argued that humanity had free will. They believed that God would not oblige human beings to behave virtuously if they did not have the power to decide for themselves what they wished to do.

qadi A *Shari'a* judge.

al-Qa'ida (Al Qaeda) Literally, "base." Global extremist groups that carry out in the name of Islam terrorist campaigns and suicide bombings, including the tragic attack on the Twin Towers in New York City on September 11, 2001.

Qajars A dynasty of Turcoman origin that ruled in Iran from 1779 to 1925 CE.

qanun Secular law.

qawwali A blend of devotional poetry and Indian music performed in India by the Chishti Sufis.

qibla The Islamic direction of prayer, indicated by the *mihrab* in the mosque.

qiyas Analogical reasoning: a principle in Islamic law whereby an established law is applied to a new situation.

Quraysh Muhammad's tribe in Arabia. Sunni caliphs originated from this tribe.

Qur'an "Recitation." The whole revelation transmitted in Arabic to Muhammad through the Angel Gabriel and recorded by his Companions. It is the Holy Book of Islam; in its written form it is called the *mushaf*.

rak'a A sequence of movements—including recitation, bowing, and prostration—that constitute one cycle of prayer.

Ramadan The Muslim month of fasting; the ninth month of the lunar Islamic calendar.

rasul Allah The Prophet of God, a title given to Muhammad.

ribats Frontier buildings that housed *jihad* warriors fighting on the borders of the Islamic world. The warriors fought to defend Islamic borders and to conduct missionary activities in such areas as Central Asia in an attempt to convert the pagan Turks.

Rifa'iyya Also known as the "Howling Dervishes." A heterodox Sufi order named after al-Rifa'i (d. 1182) and now found mainly in Egypt and Syria.

rosary Prayer beads, made up of ninety-nine beads that represent the number of Beautiful Names of God.

rouzehs Shi'ite ceremonies commemorating the life and death of Husayn.

sadaqa Voluntary almsgiving.

Safavids An initially Turkish-speaking dynasty that ruled Iran 1501–1722 CE. The Safavids established Twelver Shi'ism as the state religion of Iran.

safir (emissary) A Twelver Shi'ite term used for four representatives to whom the Hidden Twelver Imam transmitted his message during his Lesser Occultation (see *ghayba*).

Salafis Those who revere the first three generations of Muslims, known as the pious ancestors (*salaf*). Some modern Salafis advocate a return to the single pure Islam of the period 632–661 CE, when the first four caliphs of Islam, known as the "Rightly Guided caliphs," had charge of the Muslim community.

salat Canonical or ritual prayer to be performed five times a day: the second pillar of Islam.

salat al-tawarih A voluntary prayer consisting of twenty, thirty-two, or forty *rak'as* recited only in Ramadan, after the evening prayer and at the end of the night before the canonical morning prayer.

sama' (listening) The use of music by Sufis to aid contemplation. See also *sema*.

Samanids A Persian dynasty that ruled in eastern Iran and Central Asia from 819 to 1005 CE and supported a strong Sunni orthodoxy.

Sasanians A pre-Islamic Persian dynasty that ruled a vast empire from 224 to 651 CE comprising Iraq, Iran, and parts of Central Asia. Their state religion was Zoroastrianism.

sawm Fasting: the fourth pillar of Islam.

Seal of the Prophets A title given to the Prophet Muhammad, who is believed by Muslims to be the last prophet before the Day of Judgment. The revelation made to him by God was the final one.

Seljuqs A Turkish dynasty that conquered Iran and Iraq and parts of Syria, Palestine, Anatolia (now called Turkey), and central Asia. They ruled from 1040 to 1194 CE, during which time they encouraged the building of many Sunni mosques and *madrasas*.

sema Turkish form of the Arabic and Persian term *sama'*.

Semitic A term derived from Shem, one of the three sons of Noah. The Semitic peoples include Jews, Arabs, and Ethiopians. Amongst Semitic languages are Akkadian, Phoenician, Amharic, Aramaic (the language spoken by Jesus), Syriac, Hebrew, and Arabic.

seraglio The private living quarters of the wives and concubines in an Ottoman palace.

Seveners See **Isma'ilis**.

Shafi'i Belonging to the legal school named after Muhammad ibn Idris al-Shafi'i (767–820 CE).

shahada The Muslim profession of faith: the first pillar of Islam.

shahid Literally "witness." One who has died in the "path of God," a martyr.

Shamanism A set of beliefs and practices, found in tribal societies, which focus on a shaman who is believed to have the power to achieve communion with the spirit world.

Shari'a Literally "a path to water." Islamic religious law.

shaykh A word with a variety of uses, including: a venerable old man, a tribal leader, and a Sufi master.

Shi'ites The major Muslim minority groups that believe that government and interpretation of doctrine in the Islamic community should be vested in the charismatic line of the descendants of the Prophet Muhammad.

shirk To claim that any entity or person can share in the Oneness of God; the worst transgression in Islam.

sira Literally "a way of behaving." This term was used in the title of the canonical biography of Muhammad, written by Ibn Ishaq (d. 770) and revised by Ibn Hisham (d. 833).

Sufi A Muslim mystic.

sultan Literally "authority." A title given by the Sunni caliph to a military leader to legitimize his temporal powers. The title is used by many Muslim rulers.

sunna Custom.

Sunna The model conduct of the Prophet Muhammad, as recorded in his canonical sayings (*hadith*).

Sunnis The mainstream body of the Muslim community, as opposed to the Shi'ites and other groups, such as the Ibadis.

sura A chapter of the Qur'an.

tahara Ritual purity.

tajwid "Adornment." The science that establishes a full, smooth, and balanced pronunciation of each letter and syllable of Qur'anic words.

takbir The recitation of the phrase "*Allahu akbar*" (God is greatest).

talbiyya The words "At your service, O God, at your service," recited by Muslim pilgrims at 'Arafat on 9 Dhu'l –Hijja.

Taliban Literally "students." Extremist Muslim organization founded by Mullah Omar in 1994 and linked to al-Qa'ida. They governed Afghanistan from 1996 to 2001.

taqiyya Pious dissimulation, practiced especially by Shi'ites, who pretended to other beliefs in order to avoid being persecuted for their minority opinions.

tariqa Spiritual path in Sufism; a Sufi order.

tasawwuf (**Sufism**) The mystical dimension of Islam.

tawhid The Oneness of God: the central doctrine of Islam.

tawwabun "Penitents." The people of Kufa who allowed the terrible murder of Husayn to take place at Karbala' in Iraq in 680. When they saw his severed head, they began to wail and beat their breasts, deeply regretting that they had not come out to help him. From this seminal event sprang the mourning and atonement rituals of the Shi'ites.

ta'ziya A poem of religious mourning, often performed dramatically during the Shi'ite *'Ashura* festival, commemorating the murder of Husayn.

theocracy A form of government in which God is recognized as its ruler.

theosophy Literally "God's wisdom." Esoteric philosophical investigation seeking to understand God and His mysteries; an approach adopted by Sufi thinkers in Iran, such as Mulla Sadra (d. 1640); a philosophy that professes to attain a knowledge of God by spiritual ecstasy, direct intuition, or special individual relations.

Twelvers Those who follow the Twelver Shi'ite form of Islam. It is now the most numerous and the most high-profile Shi'ite group in the world.

'ulama' Religious scholars.

Umayyads Rulers of the Muslim empire (661–750 CE). After 750 an Umayyad dynasty was also founded in Spain; it lasted until 1031.

umma The community of Muslims established by Muhammad; the worldwide Islamic community.

'umra The lesser pilgrimage. A shortened version of the *hajj*.

'urf Customary law.

vilayat-i faqih "The mandate of the religious scholar." A doctrine discussed by Ayatollah Khomeini according to which Muslim jurists held not only religious but also political authority. The jurists must be obeyed at all times as an expression of obedience to God. This doctrine became the cornerstone of the Islamic Republic of Iran.

vizier See *wazir*.

Wahhabiyya/Wahhabis A politico-religious Muslim group named after its founder, Muhammad ibn 'Abd al-Wahhab (d. 1792). The movement, derived from a strict Hanbali interpretation of Islamic law, became closely allied with the Al Sa'ud family, who took power in Saudi Arabia in 1744.

wali A term with several meanings, including: guardian, saint, friend.

wasl "Arriving." Used by Sufis to describe with caution their mystical state of coming near to God.

wazir (vizier) Chief minister in pre-modern Muslim governments.

Whirling Dervishes See **Mevlevis**.

wudu' The lesser ablution, necessary to be in the correct state to perform the canonical prayer.

zakat Literally "purification." Obligatory almsgiving: the third pillar of Islam.

Zamzam The name of a well near the Ka'ba in Mecca. Drinking its water is a ritual of the pilgrimage.

Zaydis Also known as "Fivers." The oldest surviving Shi'ite group, named after Husayn's grandson Zayd ibn 'Ali (d. 740). In early Islamic times the Zaydis believed that the true Imam is a descendant of Muhammad who succeeds in establishing

himself by the sword. He must also be endowed with religious knowledge, but unlike the Twelvers or the Isma'ilis the Zaydi Imam is not infallible in matters of doctrine. A Zaydi state lasted until 1962 in Yemen.

ziyara A visit to Muhammad's tomb and other sacred sites of Medina. The term *ziyara* is also used for visitation to the tombs of Shi'ite Imams and to Sufi shrines.

Zoroastrianism The major ancient pre-Islamic religion of Iran. It still survives there in isolated areas, and it continues to flourish amongst the Parsee community in India. Zoroastrians believe in one God, called Ahura Mazda; beneath Him a cosmic struggle is waged between two opposing forces, good and evil.

Zoroastrians (Also known as *majus*, hence the word magi). The followers of the religion founded by the philosopher Zoroaster (died *c*. 550s CE). It became the state religion of the Sasanian empire (see **Sasanians**).

PEOPLE

'Abduh, Muhammad (1849–1905) An Egyptian modernist reformer who had a great influence throughout the Islamic world.

Abraham (**Ibrahim**) A Biblical and Qur'anic figure. He is known in the Qur'an as *khalil Allah* (the "friend of God"). He is seen by Muslims as the founder of monotheism and the builder of the Ka'ba shrine at Mecca, who established the rituals of the *hajj*.

Abu Bakr, 'Abd Allah (*c*. 570–634) Muhammad's father-in-law; the first caliph of the Islamic community from 632–34.

Abu Hanifa, al-Nu'man ibn Thabit (700–767) An early scholar of religious law, considered to be the founder of the Hanafi legal school.

al-Afghani, Sayyid Jamal al-Din (1838–1897) A modernist reformer and controversial political activist.

Aga Khan IV, Karim (b. 1936) The forty-ninth Imam and present spiritual leader of the Nizari Isma'ili Shi'ites.

'A'isha (613–678) Generally viewed as the favorite wife of the Prophet Muhammad; the daughter of Abu Bakr, the first caliph.

'Ali ibn Abi Talib (*c*. 600–661) The cousin and son-in-law of Muhammad, and the fourth caliph of Islam. He was assassinated in 661.

Aristotle (384–322 BCE) Prolific Greek philosopher and scientist, whose work has had an enormous impact on later scholars for many centuries.

Arkoun, Mohammed (1928–2010) Algerian Muslim modernist thinker.

al-Ash'ari, Abu'l-Hasan (874–936) A Sunni theologian

who sought to prove the truths of traditional beliefs by rational means.

al-'Askari, al-Hasan (*c.* 846–874) The eleventh Imam of the Twelver Shi'ites, buried in Samarra in Iraq.

Atatürk, Mustafa Kemal (1881–1938) The founder of the Turkish Republic in 1923.

al-Basri, Hasan (642–728) An early Muslim ascetic, judge, and preacher.

Bistami, Bayazid Abu Yazid (804–874) A controversial Iranian Sufi famous for his mystical experiences.

al-Bukhari, Muhammad ibn Isma'il (810–870) The compiler of one of the two most authoritative collections of *hadith* (the *Sahih al-Bukhari*).

al-Busiri (1211–1294) An Egyptian Sufi poet who wrote the most beloved Arabic religious poem, *Qasidat al-Burda* (the *Ode of the Cloak*), which praises the birth, ascent into heaven, and *jihad* of the Prophet Muhammad. It is believed to possess special powers and is read at funerals and other religious ceremonies.

al-Buti, Muhammad Sa'id Ramadan (1929–2013) A Syrian Sunni cleric who emphasized the "greater *jihad*" in his writings. He was killed in a suicide bombing that struck a Damascus mosque.

Ebadi, Shirin (b. 1947) An Iranian lawyer and human rights activist, often in conflict with the Iranian government. She won the Nobel Peace Prize in 2003.

Ebu's-Su'ud (*c.* 1490–1574) An Ottoman Hanafi legal scholar.

al-Farabi, Abu Nasr (*c.* 870–950) An early Muslim philosopher.

Fatima (d. 633) The daughter of Muhammad, the wife of 'Ali, and the mother of Hasan and Husayn. She is given the honorific title *al-Zahra'* ("the shining one.")

Fyzee, Asaf 'Ali Asghar (1899–1981) An Indian Muslim Isma'ili Bohra legal scholar. His most famous work, *Outlines of Muhammadan Law*, shows his radical, modernizing approach to the *Shari'a*.

al-Ghazali, Abu Hamid Muhammad (1058–1111) The prolific Iranian Muslim scholar, known in medieval Europe as Gazel.

Hagar A Biblical and Qur'anic figure. The slave girl of Abraham and the mother of Ishmael.

al-Hallaj, Mansur Abu'l-Mughith (857–922) An Iranian Sufi and Sufism's most famous martyr, crucified in Baghdad in 922. He had made Sufism accessible to the ordinary people and was considered by the Sunni scholarly elite to be a threat to the stability of the faith.

Hasan (625–670) The grandson of Muhammad, the elder son of Fatima and 'Ali, and the second Imam of the Shi'ites.

al-Hilli, al-Muhaqqiq Ja'far ibn al-Hasan (1205–1277) A Twelver Shi'ite scholar from the city of Hilla in central Iraq. He wrote a manual of Twelver law that is still in use today.

al-Hilli, al-Hasan ibn Yusuf al-'Allama (1250–1325) The first Twelver Shi'ite scholar to be given the title of *ayatollah* ("sign of God"). He validated the principle of personal judgment (*ijtihad*), embedding it in Twelver law.

Hujwiri, Abu'l-Hasan 'Ali (*c.* 990–1077) Persian author of one of the earliest and most famous treatises on Sufism.

Husayn (620–680) The grandson of Muhammad, the younger son of Fatima and 'Ali, and the third Imam of the Shi'ites, martyred at Karbala' in Iraq by an Umayyad army sent by the caliph Yazid. The memory of Husayn's murder is the focus of the Muharram rituals performed by the Shi'ites.

Ibn 'Abd al-Wahhab, Muhammad (1703–1787) The leader of the Wahhabiyya, a movement that began in Arabia and aimed to purify Islam. He was hostile to Sufism and Shi'ism, and in favor of a return to the exclusive authority of the Qur'an and the way of the Prophet.

Ibn al-'Arabi, Muhyi al-Din (Muhyiddin) (1165–1240) The most celebrated Sufi theosopher, known especially for his controversial doctrine *wahdat al-wujud* ("the unity of existence").

Ibn Battuta (d. 1368 or 1377) The most famous medieval Muslim traveler. His diary describes his journeys from Morocco to the Far East.

Ibn al-Farid, 'Umar (118–1235) An Egyptian Sufi poet.

Ibn Baz, 'Abd al-'Aziz ibn 'Abdallah (1910–1999) A Saudi Wahhabi scholar, who was the official *mufti* of Saudi Arabia.

Ibn Hanbal, Ahmad ibn Muhammad (780–855) Considered to be the founder of the Hanbali legal school (*madhhab*). He refused to accept the Mu'tazili doctrine of the created Qur'an, which the 'Abbasid caliph al-Ma'mun had tried to impose on the Islamic world in the *mihna* of 833; he was imprisoned and then later released.

Ibn Hisham, Abu Muhammad (d. 834) The compiler of the canonical biography of the Prophet Muhammad, known as the *sira*, based on the earlier work of Ibn Ishaq.

Ibn Ishaq, Muhammad ibn Yasar (704–767) Author of the canonical biography (*sira*) of Muhammad, which has survived in the revised form compiled by Ibn Hisham.

Ibn Khaldun, 'Abd al-Rahman (1332–1406) Often called the "father of sociology," born in Tunisia, a much-traveled legal scholar who worked in many places across the Muslim world. He is famous for his path-breaking essay, the *Muqaddima* (Introduction), which looks at the laws and patterns underlying history.

Ibn Rushd, Abu'l-Walid Muhammad ibn Ahmad (called Averroes in medieval Europe) (1126–1198) A Muslim Arab philosopher from Spain, famous for his book *The Incoherence of the Incoherence*.

Ibn Sina, Abu 'Ali (called Avicenna in medieval Europe) (980–1037) A very well-known Muslim philosopher, scientist, and medical doctor.

Ibn Taymiyya (1263–1328) A Syrian Hanbali scholar and prolific writer, much admired by the Wahhabis.

Ishmael (Isma'il) A Biblical figure also mentioned in the Qur'an as the son of Abraham and Hagar. He helped his father to build the Ka'ba, and, according to most commentators, he was the son who was almost sacrificed by Abraham. Isma'il is regarded as the father of the Arabs.

Ja'far al-Sadiq (699–765) The sixth Imam of the Isma'ilis and of the Twelvers; he was an important transmitter of *hadith*.

Jesus (known in the Qur'an as 'Isa ibn Maryam (Jesus son of Mary)) Believed by Muslims to be a very important prophet of God. His miraculous conception is recorded in the Qur'an.

al-Jilani, 'Abd al-Qadir (1077–1166) A famous Sufi of Persian origin, the founder of the Qadiriyya Sufi order.

John of Damascus (676–749) A Christian monk and theologian who served for a while as a tax official at the Umayyad caliphal court in Damascus; his work *Disputation between a Christian and a Saracen* set out the arguments that Christians might encounter when talking about religion with Muslims.

Junayd ibn Muhammad Abu'l-Qasim al-Khazzaz (830–910) An early Sufi who taught in Baghdad, advocating a careful approach to Sufism that was well integrated into Sunni orthodoxy.

Khadija (554–619) The first wife of Muhammad, and, while she lived, his only wife.

Khaled M. Abou El-Fadl (b.1963 in Kuwait) A leading authority on Islamic law and a prominent US academic in the field of human rights.

Khan, Sayyid Ahmad (1817–1898) An Indian Muslim modernist who engaged with the issues of how to deal with British rule in India and where Islam should stand in his colonized homeland. He wished to liberate Islamic law to respond to the demands of a modern society.

Khomeini, Ayatollah Sayyid Ruhollah (1902–1989) The leader of the Iranian Revolution and the founder of the Islamic Republic of Iran in 1979.

al-Kulayni, Muhamad ibn Ya'qub (864–940) An Iranian Shi'ite theologian and author of a very large work in which he collected and arranged systematically 16,000 *hadith*, including those special to the Shi'ite tradition.

Mahmassani, Sobhi (1909–1986) A Lebanese scholar who advocated change, arguing that Islamic law should be adapted to the conditions of modern society.

al-Makki, Abu Talib (d. 996) A Shafi'i legal scholar and Sufi, whose writings were a valuable source for al-Ghazali.

Malik ibn Anas, Abu 'Abdallah (716–795) The founder of the Malik legal school (*madhhab*).

al-Ma'mun, Abu'l-'Abbas 'Abdallah (786–833) An 'Abbasid caliph with wide intellectual and theological interests who founded the famous translation house known as the "House of Wisdom."

Marrash, Mariyana (1848–1919) The first Arab woman to publish an article in a newspaper. She hosted a salon in Aleppo in Syria, where she always wore the latest European fashions.

Mary (c. 18–41) The mother of Jesus. The Chapter of Mary in the Qur'an mentions the Annunciation and the Nativity of Jesus.

Mawdudi, Sayyid Abu'l-'Ala (1903–1979) An Indian journalist who founded the political party *Jama'at-i Islami* in 1941. In 1947 he emigrated to the newly founded separate country of Pakistan, where he continued to expound his Islamist views.

Mernissi, Fatima (b. 1940) A well-known Moroccan sociologist and feminist writer.

Moses A Jewish religious leader who took the Israelites out of Egypt across the Red Sea. At Mount Sinai he received the Ten Commandments. After forty years in the desert, he died within sight of the Promised Land. Moses is also an important prophet in Islam.

al-Mufid, Shaykh Abu 'Abd Allah Muhammad (948–1022) A Twelver Shi'ite scholar whose books still form the core of the legal curricula in Twelver *madrasa*s today.

al-Muhasibi, Abu 'Abdallah al-Harith (781–857) A Baghdad Sufi whose writings placed Sufism within the framework of orthodox Sunni Islam.

Muhammad (c. 570–632) The Prophet of Islam, to whom the Qur'an was revealed; Muslims view him as the final monotheistic prophet, the "Seal of the Prophets."

Muqatil ibn Sulayman al-Balkhi (d. 767) An early Qur'anic commentator.

al-Muqaddasi, Muhammad ibn Ahmad Shams al-Din (c. 945/46–991) Arab Muslim traveler who wrote a comprehensive geographical work on all the countries of the Muslim world.

Muslim, Abu'l-Husayn (816–873) The compiler of one of the two *hadith* collections regarded as the most authentic.

al-Mustansir, Abu Ja'far (1192–1242) An 'Abbasid caliph who built the Mustansiriyya *madrasa* in Baghdad in 1232 to house all four Sunni legal schools (*madhhab*s).

al-Mutanabbi, Abu'l-Tayyib Ahmad (915–965) One of the best-loved classical Arab poets.

Naqshband Bukhari, Baha' al-Din (1318–1389) The founder of the Sufi Naqshbandiyya order.

Neshat, Shirin (b. 1957) An Iranian photographer and filmmaker, exiled from Iran for more than thirty years.

Nizam al-Mulk, Abu 'Ali Hasan al-Tusi (1018–1092)
The famous, long-serving Persian vizier of two
Seljuq Turkish sultans, Alp Arslan and Malikshah.

**al-Nu'man, al-Qadi al-Nu'man ibn Muhammad
al-Tamimi** (d. 974) The legal scholar who
expounded Isma'ili law in his monumental
compendium, "*The Pillars of Islam.*"

Nur al-Din, Mahmud, ibn 'Imad al-Din Zengi (1118–
1174) Turkish military leader who ruled Syria and
Palestine and was a major Counter-Crusade fighter,
paving the way for Saladin.

al-Palimbani, 'Abd al-Samad (*c.* 1704–*c.* 1790) A Sufi
writer from South Sumatra, influenced by the works
of al-Ghazali and Ibn al-'Arabi.

Plato (*c.* 428/427 or 424/423–348/347 BCE) World-
famous Greek philosopher and scientist, who helped
to lay the foundations of Western philosophy.

al-Qaradawi, Yusuf (b. 1926) An Egyptian scholar,
perhaps today's most authoritative Sunni voice
across the world. His program on al-Jazeera is very
well known.

Qutb, Sayyid (1906–1966) Often described as "the
father of modern Islamic fundamentalism" and
the chief spokesman for the radical Islamist Muslim
Brotherhood. He was executed in 1966 for his
role in opposing the government of the Egyptian
president Jamal 'Abd al-Nasser.

Rabi'a 'Adawiyya (*c.* 715–801) A saintly female Sufi
in Iraq and a secluded, celibate mystic, first in the
desert and later in Basra, where a group of disciples
gathered round her.

Reza Shah Pahlavi (1878–1944) The ruler of Iran
from 1925 until his forced abdication in 1941.

Rida, Muhammad Rashid (1865–1935) A Syrian
Muslim reformer who wrote a treatise on the
caliphate just before its abolition by Atatürk.

Rumi, Jalal al-Din (1207–1273) The major Persian
Sufi poet who came from Balkh in Afghanistan
and settled in Konya (in what is now Turkey).

Rushdie, Salman (b. 1947) The Indian British
author of essays and books. Ayatollah Khomeini
pronounced a *fatwa* against him because of his
book *The Satanic Verses*, published in 1988.

El-Saadawi, Nawal (b. 1931) A prolific Egyptian
writer and feminist activist.

Saddam Husayn, 'Abd al-Majid al-Tikriti (1937–2006)
The fifth President of Iraq, 1979–2006.

Sadra, Mulla (1572–1640) A Persian Sufi theosopher.

Saladin, known in the Muslim world as **Salah al-Din
Yusuf ibn Ayyub** (1138–1193) The Kurdish Muslim
hero of the Crusades, who reconquered Jerusalem
in 1187 and was famous in Europe for his chivalry
and generosity.

Salme, Bint Said (1844–1924) An Arab princess, the
daughter of Sayyid Said, the ruler of Oman and
Zanzibar. She married a young German, Heinrich
Ruete, and fled to Europe, where she wrote her
autobiography.

al-Sanhuri, 'Abd al-Razzaq (1895–1971) A key figure
in the Arab world, who introduced a new Egyptian
civil code, which drew on French models and
existing legislation in Egypt as well as on elements
of the *Shari'a*.

Sayf al-Dawla, 'Ali ibn Abu'l-Hayja 'Abdallah
(916–967) The Hamdanid Arab Twelver Shi'ite
prince of a small border state in northern Syria,
where he ruled from 944–67 and led annual *jihad*
campaigns against Byzantium.

al-Shafi'i, Muhammad ibn Idris (768–820) The
founder of the Shafi'i legal school (*madhhab*).

Suhrawardi, Shihab al-Din Yahya (1154–1191)
An Illuminationist Sufi writer. He is often given
the title "al-Maqtul" ("the one who was killed")
because he was accused of heresy and executed
in prison in Aleppo.

'Umar, Mullah Muhammad (b. 1959) The spiritual
leader of the Taliban in Afghanistan.

Umm Kulthum (1898–1975) The Egyptian woman
(also known as "the Star of the East") who is
considered the greatest ever Arab singer.

Usama bin Laden (1957–2011) The founder of
al-Qa'ida, the militant Islamist organization that
claimed responsibility for the 9/11 attacks on the
US in 2001. He was killed in Pakistan in 2011.

Usman dan Fodio (1754–1817) A religious teacher
and reformer who lived in the Hausa state of
Gobir in what is now northern Nigeria; in 1804
he established the Sokoto caliphate.

Wadud, Amina (b. 1952) A high-profile African
American Muslim academic who advocates a
"gender-inclusive" interpretation of Islam. In
2005 she led the Friday prayer and gave the Friday
sermon in New York.

Yusuf ibn Tashfin (1061–1107) The second leader
of the Almoravid Berber dynasty, who captured
large areas of North Africa, established a new
capital in Morocco—Marrakesh—and attacked
Muslim Spain.

Zayd ibn 'Ali (695–740) The great-great grandson of
the Prophet Muhammad, who was killed in a failed
rebellion against the Umayyad caliph in Kufa in 740.
He is the fifth Imam of the Zaydi Shi'ites, otherwise
known as the Fivers.

Zuhayli, Wahba (b. 1932) A Syrian legal scholar
and interpreter of *jihad*, who argues that war
should never be waged to force non-Muslims to
convert to Islam.

FURTHER READING

For more key titles see also the Selected Reading sections at the end of chapters 2–10.

Andaya, B. W. and L. Y. Andaya, *A History of Malaysia*, Honolulu, HI: University of Hawaii Press, 2001

Arberry, A. J., *Sufism: An Account of the Mystics of Islam*, New York: Harper & Row, 1970

Asad, Muhammad, *The Message of the Qur'an*, London: The Book Foundation, 2003

Aslan, R., *No God But God: The Origins, Evolution, and Future of Islam*, New York: Random House, 2006

Attar, Farid al-Din, *Muslim Saints and Mystics*, trans. A. J. Arberry, London: Routledge and Kegan Paul, 1979

Ayoob, Mohammed, *The Many Faces of Political Islam: Religion and Politics in the Muslim World*, Ann Arbor, MI: University of Michigan Press, 2007

Bearman P., R. Peters and F. E. Vogel (eds.), *The Islamic School of Law: Evolution, Devolution, and Progress*, Cambridge, MA: Harvard University Press, 2006

Black, Anthony, *The History of Islamic Political Thought from the Prophet to the Present*, Edinburgh: Edinburgh University Press, 2001

Bloom, Jonathan and Sheila Blair, *Islam: A Thousand Years of Faith and Power*, New Haven, CT: Yale University Press, 2002

Boland, B. J., *The Struggle of Islam in Modern Indonesia*, The Hague, Netherlands: Nijhoff, 1971

Bonner, Michael, *Jihad in Islamic History: Doctrines and Practices*, Princeton, NJ: Princeton University Press, 2006

Bukhari-al, *Sahih al-Bukhari*, trans. M. Muhsin Khan, Chicago, IL: Kazi Publications, 1979

Bunt, Gary, *Islam in the Digital Age: E-Jihad, Online Fatwas and Cyber Islamic Environments*, London: Pluto Press, 2003

Burke, Jason, *Al-Qaeda: Casting a Shadow of Terror*, London: I. B. Tauris, 2003

Calmard, Jean, "Fatema," in *Encyclopedia Iranica*: http://www.iranicaonline.org/articles/fatema

Cole, J., *Sacred Space and Holy War: The Politics, Culture and History of Shi'ite Islam*, London: I. B. Tauris, 2002

Cook, David, *Martyrdom in Islam*, Cambridge: Cambridge University Press, 2007

Cooke, Miriam and Bruce B. Lawrence (eds.), *Muslim Networks from Hajj to Hiphop*, Chapel Hill, NC: University of North Carolina Press, 2005

Cortese, D. and S. Calderini, *Women and the Fatimids in the World of Islam*, Edinburgh: Edinburgh University Press, 2006

Denny, Fred, *An Introduction to Islam*, New York: Macmillan, 2006

Doorn-Harder, P. van, *Women Shaping Islam: Indonesian Women Reading the Qur'an*, Urbana, IL: University of Illinois Press, 2006

Elias, Jamal J., *Islam*, Abingdon, Oxford: Taylor & Francis, 2003

Ernst, Carl, *Following Muhammad: Rethinking Islam in the Contemporary World*, Edinburgh: Edinburgh University Press, 2004

Esposito, John L. and Dalia Mogahed, *Who Speaks for Islam? What a Billion Muslims Really Think*, New York: Gallup Press, 2008

Esposito, John L. (ed.), *The Oxford History of Islam*, New York: Oxford University Press, 1999

Esposito, John L., *Women in Muslim Family Law*, Syracuse, NY: Syracuse University Press, 2001

Ess, J. van, *The Flowering of Muslim Theology*, trans. J. M. Todd, Cambridge, MA: Harvard University Press, 2006

Ewing, Katherine P. (ed.), *Being and Belonging: Muslims in the United States Since 9/11*, New York: Russell Sage, 2008

Firestone, Reuven, *Jihad: The Origins of Holy War in Islam*, New York: Oxford University Press, 1999

Fletcher, J., *Studies on Chinese and Islamic Inner Asia*, ed. B. F. Manz, Aldershot: Variorum, 1995

Ghaneabassiri, Kamran, *A History of Islam in America*, New York: Cambridge University Press, 2010

Goodman, L. E., *Avicenna*, London: Routledge, 1992

Goody, J., *Islam in Europe*, Cambridge: Cambridge University Press, 2004

Haeri, Shaykh Fadhlalla (ed. and trans.), *The Sayings and Wisdom of Imam Ali*, London: Muhammadi Trust of Great Britain and Northern Ireland, 1999

Hambly, Gavin, *Women in the Medieval Islamic World: Power, Patronage, and Piety*, Basingstoke: Macmillan, 1998

Hodgson, Marshall G. S., *The Venture of Islam: Conscience and History in a World Civilization*, 3 vols., Chicago, IL: University of Chicago Press, 1974

Hoyland, Robert, *Seeing Islam as Others Saw It: A Survey and Evaluation of Christian, Jewish, and Zoroastrian Writings on Islam*, Princeton, NJ: The Darwin Press, 1997

Huda, Qamarul, *The Diversity of Muslims in the United States: Views as Americans*, Washington, DC: United States Institute of Peace, 2006

Ibn Ishaq, *The Life of Muhammad (Sirat Rasul Allah)*, trans. A. Guillaume, London: Oxford University Press, 1955

Ibn Khaldun, *The Muqaddimah: An Introduction to History*, trans. F. Rosenthal, abridged N. J. Dawood, Princeton, NJ: Princeton University Press, 1969

Jeffrey, Patricia, *Frogs in a Well: Indian Women in Purdah*, London: Zed Press, 1979.

Joseph, Suad (ed.), *Encyclopedia of Women and Islamic Cultures*, Leiden: Brill, 2003

Kepel, Gilles and Jean-Pierre Milleli (eds.), Al-Qaeda in its Own Words, Cambridge, MA and London: Belknap Press, 2008

Khomeini, R. M., Islam and Revolution, Writings and Declarations of Imam Khomeini, trans. H. Algar, Berkeley, CA: Mizan Press, 1981

Kruk, Remke, The Warrior Women of Islam: Female Empowerment in Arabic Popular Culture, London: I. B. Tauris, 2013

Lawrence, Bruce (ed.), Messages to the World: the Statements of Osama Bin Laden, trans. James Howarth, London: Verso, 2005

Lewis, Franklin, Rumi: Past and Present, East and West: The Life, Teachings and Poetry of Jalal al-Din Rumi, Oxford: Oneworld, 2000

Lewis, P., Islamic Britain: Religion, Politics, and Identity Among British Muslims, London: Palgrave, 2002

Long, David E., The Hajj Today, Albany, NY: State University of New York Press, 1979

Makdisi, George, The Rise of Colleges: Institutions of Learning in Islam and the West, Edinburgh: Edinburgh University Press, 1981

Martin, R. C., M. R. Woodward and D. S. Atmaja, Defenders of Reason in Islam: Mut'azilism from Medieval School to Modern Symbol, Oxford: Oneworld, 1997

McAuliffe, Jane Dammen (ed.), Encyclopedia of the Quran, Leiden: Brill, 2001–2006

Melchert, C., The Formation of the Sunni Schools of Law, 9th–10th Centuries C. E., Leiden: Brill, 2002

Mernissi, Fatima, The Forgotten Queens of Islam, London: Polity Press, 1993.

Mottahedeh, Roy, The Mantle of the Prophet, Harmondsworth: Penguin Books, 1987

Motzki, H. (ed.), The Biography of Muhammad: The Issue of the Sources, Leiden: Brill, 2000

Nashat, G. and L. Beck (eds.), Women in Iran from the Rise of Islam to 1800, Urbana, IL: University of Illinois Press, 2003

Nasr, Seyyed Hossein, Islam: Religion, History and Civilization, San Francisco, CA: HarperOne, 2002

Netton, Ian Richard, Text and Trauma: An East-West Primer, London: Routledge, 1996

Nielsen, Jorgen, Muslims in Western Europe, Edinburgh: Edinburgh University Press, 1992

Pierce, Leslie, The Imperial Harem: Women and Sovereignty in the Ottoman Empire, Oxford: Oxford University Press, 1993

Qaradawi, Yusuf, The Lawful and the Prohibited in Islam, Indianapolis, IN: American Trust Publications, n. d.

Rahman, Fazlur, Major Themes of the Qur'an, Minneapolis, MN: Bibliotheca Islamica, 1980

Renard, John, Seven Doors to Islam: Spirituality and the Religious Life of Muslims, Berkeley, CA and London: University of California Press, 1996

Rippin, Andrew (ed.), The Blackwell Companion to the Qur'an, Malden, MA: Blackwell, 2006

Rippin, Andrew, The Qur'an and Its Interpretative Tradition, Aldershot: Ashgate, 2001

Rizvi, S. H., "Mysticism and Philosophy: Ibn 'Arabi and Mulla Sadra," in eds. R. Taylor and P. Adamson, The Cambridge Companion to Arabic Philosophy, Cambridge: Cambridge University Press, 2005, pp. 224–46

Robinson, Francis (ed.), The Cambridge Illustrated History of the Islamic World, Cambridge: Cambridge University Press, 1996

Safi, Omid (ed.), Progressive Muslims: On Gender, Justice and Pluralism, Oxford: Oneworld, 2003

Sahas, Daniel J., John of Damascus on Islam: The "Heresy of the Ishmaelites", Leiden: Brill, 1972

Said-Ruete, Emily, Memoirs of an Arabian Princess, ed. G. S. P. Freeman-Grenville, London and The Hague, Netherlands: East-West, 1994

Sajoo, Amyn, Muslim Ethics: Emerging Vistas, London: I. B. Tauris, 2004

Shepard, William, Introducing Islam, Abingdon, Oxford: Routledge, 2009

Silvestri, Sara, Unveiled Issues: Europe's Muslim Women: Potential, Aspirations and Challenges, Brussels: King Badouin Foundation, 2009

Smith, Jane I., Islam in America, New York: Columbia University Press, 1999

Smith, Margaret, Readings From the Mystics of Islam, London: Luzac, 1972

Suleiman, Yasir, Narratives of Conversion to Islam: Female Perspectives, Cambridge: Prince Alwaleed Bin Talal Centre of Islamic Studies, University of Cambridge, in association with the New Muslims Project: Markfield, 2013.

Taji-Farouki, Suha (ed.), Modern Muslim Intellectuals and the Qur'an, London: Oxford University Press, 2004

The Koran Interpreted, trans. A. J. Arberry, London: Allen & Unwin, 1980

Trimingham, J. S., The Sufi Orders in Islam, Oxford: Clarendon Press, 1971

Tucker, Judith, Women, Family, and Gender in Islamic Law, Cambridge: Cambridge University Press, 2008

Turner, Colin, Islam: The Basics, London: Routledge, 2005

Turner, Richard Brent, Islam in the African-American Experience, Bloomington, IN: Indiana University Press, 2003

Wadud, Amina, Inside the Gender Jihad: Women's Reform in Islam, Oxford: Oneworld, 2006

Woodward, Mark R. (ed.), Toward a New Paradigm: Recent Developments in Indonesian Islamic Thought, Tempe, AZ: Arizona State University Program for Southeast Asian Studies, 1996

Zubaida, Sami, Law and Power in the Islamic World, London and New York: I. B. Tauris, 2003

SOURCES OF ILLUSTRATIONS

INDEX